Revolution and State
in Modern Mexico

PRAISE FOR THE BOOK

"Drawing on classics of Marxist social theory, Adam Morton skillfully interweaves theory and history to reveal the dynamic of state intervention from above and mass mobilization from below that shaped the modern state and capitalist social relations in postrevolution Mexico. He provides fresh insight into how the process of revolutionary rupture and conservative restoration was initiated and reproduced in the absence of bourgeois hegemony, which took distinct forms in the immediate aftermath of the Mexican revolution and subsequently. Morton also provides a provocative analysis of the literary and political work of Carlos Fuentes, a discussion of the specificity of Mexico's political transition to a form of bourgeois democracy congruent with capitalist social relations, and an assessment of the rise and endurance of the EZLN that has provided a catalyst for resistance to neoliberalism in Mexico as well as other parts of the world. In sum, Morton has produced a very important and impressive study which advances both theoretical analysis and our understanding of the economic, cultural, political and social dynamics of contemporary Mexico."
—**Nora Hamilton**, author of *Mexico: Political, Social and Economic Evolution*

"Adam Morton has produced an exceptional work in radical historicism on postrevolutionary Mexico and a virtuoso's exposition of Antonio Gramsci's theory of hegemony, passive revolution, and uneven development. His ambitious and successful undertaking delivers a highly nuanced understanding of postrevolutionary Mexican history intertwined with an analysis of the passive revolution of capital on a world scale. Weaving theory and history throughout, Morton engages a wide range of scholarly debates about the state, postcolonialism, democratization, and resistance. This book will be a must-read in the fields of Mexican and Latin American studies and provides a provocative and contrasting interpretation to mainstream 'transition studies' in political science. It converses with and provides a welcome contribution to the most prominent strands in historical sociology, the sociology of power, international political economy, and geography."
—**Gerardo Otero**, author of *Farewell to the Peasantry*

"This is a work of remarkable erudition in which Adam Morton brings fresh perspectives to our understanding of the Mexican Revolution and its aftermath, employing Antonio Gramsci's concept of 'passive revolution' to explain how and why dependent capitalist development and neoliberalism took the form they did in Mexico. In a sweeping interdisciplinary survey, Morton draws on interviews with economic elites, politicians, state functionaries, and public intellectuals. Above all, he engages with theorists who consider not only state formation but also the roles of popular culture, literature, and spatial relations as expressed in architecture, city planning, and public art. As telling examples, Morton provides a study of the 'social function' of the novelist Carlos Fuentes as a 'mixture of critical opposition and accommodation' to passive revolution and of the Zapatistas as a counter-space of resistance—however imperfect—to passive revolution. Along with much else in this audacious book, these two studies give readers stimulating material with which to agree and disagree."
—**Judith Adler Hellman**, author of *The World of Mexican Migrants*

Revolution and State in Modern Mexico

The Political Economy of Uneven Development

Adam David Morton

ROWMAN & LITTLEFIELD PUBLISHERS, INC.
Lanham • Boulder • New York • Toronto • Plymouth, UK

Published by Rowman & Littlefield Publishers, Inc.
A wholly owned subsidiary of The Rowman & Littlefield Publishing Group, Inc.
4501 Forbes Boulevard, Suite 200, Lanham, Maryland 20706
http://www.rowmanlittlefield.com

Estover Road, Plymouth PL6 7PY, United Kingdom

British Library Cataloguing in Publication Information Available

Library of Congress Cataloging-in-Publication Data

Morton, Adam David, 1971–
   Revolution and state in modern Mexico : the political economy of uneven development / Adam David Morton.
      p. cm. — (Critical currents in Latin American perspective)
      Summary: "This groundbreaking study develops a new approach to understanding the formation of the postrevolutionary state in Mexico. Adam Morton links the rise and demise of the modern Mexican state to ongoing forms of class struggle that have shaped and restructured state and civil society. He thus sheds valuable interdisciplinary light on debates on state formation by recovering radical tools of analysis, such as uneven development and class struggle, for the wider study of past and present politics in Mexico and, more broadly, Latin America." —Provided by publisher.
      Includes bibliographical references and index.
      ISBN 978-0-7425-5489-4 (hardback) — ISBN 978-1-4422-1351-7 (electronic)
      1. Mexico—Economic conditions—1918– —Regional disparities. I. Title.
   HC135.M74 2011
   338.972—dc23

                                                                                    2011030239

♾™ The paper used in this publication meets the minimum requirements of American National Standard for Information Sciences—Permanence of Paper for Printed Library Materials, ANSI/NISO Z39.48-1992.

Printed in the United States of America

For "the girls"—Julie and Amie

¡Que chasco, amigo mío, si los que venimos a ofrecer todo nuestro entusiasmo, nuestra misma vida por derribar a un miserable asesino, resultásemos los obreros de un enorme pedestal donde pudieran levantarse cien o doscientos mil monstruos de la misma especie! . . . ¡Pueblo sin ideales, pueblo de tiranos! . . . ¡Lástima de sangre!

What a failure, my friend, if we, who offer our enthusiasm and our lives to overthrow a miserable assassin, turn out to be the architects of a pedestal enormous enough to hold one or two hundred thousand monsters of the same species! . . . People without ideals! People of tyrants! . . . Vain bloodshed!

—Mariano Azuela, *The Underdogs* [1915]

Contents

Illustrations

FIGURES

MAP

TABLES

Acknowledgments

Perhaps only the vainglorious would assert the individual "I" over the collective "we" in the course of writing a book. Without doubt, an enormous debt is owed to a community of friends, colleagues, and scholars that supported me throughout this book's completion. For their advice and encouragement a great deal of thanks are due. Of course, despite all their advice and assistance, full and final responsibility for any remaining errors or omissions in this book is my own.

Several institutions contributed materially to the completion of the book. The financial support of the Economic and Social Research Council (ESRC), for both a Ph.D. studentship (reference: R0042963410) and a postdoctoral fellowship (reference: T026271041), is acknowledged. Similarly, the encouragement of Graciela Platero and Kevin Middlebrook to visit the Center for U.S.-Mexican Studies (San Diego, California) as a guest scholar in 1999, is greatly appreciated as is the help and friendship of Hilda Wynans who saved me from the possibility of "one hundred days of solitude" during my stay. More recently, the book would not have been completed without the unstinting faith and support of Ron Chilcote in hosting me as the inaugural Latin American Perspectives Visiting Fellow in 2008 at the University of Riverside and backing my proposal from the start during our meeting in Laguna Beach, California, in 2006. Without his extremely open-minded comradeship this book would not have come to fruition. Special thanks are also due to Fran Chilcote for her warmth and hospitality during my stay in Riverside and Rhonda Neugebauer who was truly outstanding in providing information on the general library holdings and the special collections at Riverside. My work on the historical sociology of state formation in Mexico was also supported by the University of Nottingham's Research Innovation Services study leave fund, during 2007–2008. In times of austerity this is surely a testament to the fact that university-funded study leave is a sine qua non for the completion of large projects. Equally important has been the solidarity from fellows within the Centre for the Study of Social and Global Justice (CSSGJ) at the University of Nottingham, the largest and most successful center of its kind within the School of Politics and International Relations at my host institution, the University of Nottingham.

A number of people over recent years have given their time and effort to comment and converse on the project. At risk of oversight this has included Pinar Bilgin, Derek Boothman, Tony Burns, Alex Callinicos, Paul Cammack, Robert Cox, Nikki Craske, Neil Davidson, Matt Davies, Bill Dunne, Enrique Dussel Peters, Ertan Erol, Catherine Gegout, Randall Germain, Stephen Gill, Adolfo Gilly, Marcus Green, Tom Hansen, Judith Adler Hellman, Steve Hobden, Peter Ives, Bob Jessop, Alan Knight, Marie-Josée Massicotte, Nicola Miller, Sara Motta, Ronaldo Munck, Alf Nilsen, Gerardo Otero, Philip Oxhorn, Bill Robinson, Justin Rosenberg, David Ruccio, Mark Rupert, Jan Rus, Anne Showstack Sassoon, Stuart Shields, Nicola Short, David Slater, Graham Smith, Susanne Soederberg, Marcus Taylor, Benno Teschke, and Peter Thomas.

As the book took final form, three particular comrades took the time to read and critique one or more drafts of the entire manuscript. I especially wish to thank, therefore, Andreas Bieler, Ian Bruff, and Chris Hesketh for their insightful comments and criticisms. Without their support, the research and writing process would have been a solitary endeavor indeed.

Publishers' permission to draw material from the following articles was gratefully received: "The Social Function of Carlos Fuentes: A Critical Intellectual or in the 'Shadow of the State'?," *Bulletin of Latin American Research* 22:1 (2003): 27–51; "Structural Change and Neoliberalism in Mexico: 'Passive Revolution' in the Global Political Economy," *Third World Quarterly* 24:4 (2003): 631–53; "Change within Continuity: The Political Economy of Democratic Transition in Mexico," *New Political Economy* 10:2 (2005): 181–202; "Global Capitalism and the Peasantry in Latin America: The Recomposition of Class Struggle," *Journal of Peasant Studies* 34:3–4 (2007): 441–73; "Reflections on Uneven Development: Mexican Revolution, Primitive Accumulation, Passive Revolution," *Latin American Perspectives* 37:1 (2010): 7–34. The content herein, though, has been substantially revised and new advances have been developed throughout the book to produce a coherent, original, and fresh argument.

I wish to thank Susan McEachern, vice president and editorial director for International Studies at Rowman & Littlefield Publishers for her patient assistance in bringing a long book manuscript to completion. Her expertise in recommending a "final" deadline was immensely effective in precipitating greater focus and productivity on my behalf. I thank her for her experienced and tactful cajoling and advice, as well as for supporting the book through to its final stages. Thanks are also due to Jesús Álvarez Amaya, in Mexico City, a progeny of the Taller de Gráfica Popular (TGP), for permission to reprint Jesús Escobedo's *Como combatir el fascismo* [1939] in the book. A painter, printmaker, and muralist in his own right, Jesús Álvarez Amaya sadly died at the age of eighty-five on 21 June 2010, just as this book was drawing to completion (see *La Jornada*, 22 June 2010: 16). Additionally, Kristen Wenger at the British Museum Images, in London, was also essential in tracking down the TGP images. Finally, a word or two on the photograph that appears on the front cover, taken by the author in 2008. Capturing El Ángel de la Independencia in Mexico City, completed in 1910, alongside the contemporary forces of transnational capital, this image directly speaks to the typology sketched by Néstor García Canclini on urban monuments. In this instance, it teases out the ironic implications of a historical symbol through its relationship with the new urban context; see Néstor García Canclini, "Monuments, Billboards and Graffiti," in Helen Escobedo (ed.) *Mexican Monuments: Strange Encounters*, 1989. One can add, of course, that it also visually expresses and captures the very contradictions of uneven development assessed throughout the book linked to the making of the modern state in Mexico.

This book is dedicated to the two most important people in my life: my wife, Julie Morton, and our daughter, Amie Morton. They have both brought much fun, love, and games into my world beyond levels possibly imagined. Now that this book is finished, it will be exciting to contemplate much more of the same in the future.

Acronyms

ABM	Asociación de Banqueros Mexicanos / Mexican Bankers' Association
ACILS	American Center for International Labor Solidarity
AFL-CIO	American Federation of Labor-Congress of Industrial Organizations
APPO	Asamblea Popular de los Pueblos de Oaxaca / Popular Assembly of the Peoples of Oaxaca
CANACINTRA	Cámara Nacional de la Industria de Transformación / National Chamber of Manufacturing Industries
CCE	Consejo Coordinador Empresarial / Private Sector Coordinating Council
CELMRAZ	Centro de Lenguas Tsotsil y Español / Tzotzil and Spanish Languages Center
CEPAL	Comisión Económica para América Latina y el Caribe / Economic Commission for Latin America and the Caribbean
CFE	Comisión Federal de Electricidad / Federal Electricity Commission
CGOCM	Confederación General de Obreros y Campesinos de México / General Confederation of Mexican Workers and Peasants
CGT	Confederación General de Trabajadores / General Confederation of Labor
CIPE	Center for International Private Enterprise
CMHN	Consejo Mexicano de Hombres de Negocios / Mexican Council of Businessmen

CNC	Confederación Nacional Campesina / National Peasants' Confederation
CND	Convención Nacional Democrática / National Democratic Convention
CNI	Congreso Nacional Indígena / National Indigenous Congress
CNOP	Confederación Nacional de Organizaciones Populares / National Confederation of Popular Organizations
CNTE	Coordinadora Nacional de Trabajadores de la Educación / National Coordinating Committee of Education Workers
COCOPA	Comisión de Concordia y Pacificación / Commission on Concordance and Pacification
CONAI	Comisión Nacional de Intermediación / National Intermediation Commission
CONASUPO	Compañia Nacional de Subsistencias Populares / National Basic Foods Company
CONCAMIN	Confederación de Cámaras Industriales / National Confederation of Chambers of Industry
CONCANACO	Confederación de Cámaras Nacionales de Comercio / Confederation of National Chambers of Commerce
COPARMEX	Confederación Patronal de la República Mexicana / Mexican Employers' Confederation
CROM	Confederación Regional Obrera Mexicana / Mexican Regional Labor Confederation
CSUM	Confederación Sindical Unitaria de México / Unitary Mexican Union Confederation
CTM	Confederación de Trabajadores de México / Confederation of Mexican Workers
DINA	Diesel Nacional / National Diesel
EAP	Economically active population
EPRAZ	Escuela Primaria Rebelde Autónoma Zapatista / Zapatista Rebel Autonomous Primary School
ESF	European Social Forum
ESRAZ	Escuela Secundaria Rebelde Autónoma Zapatista Primero de Enero / Zapatista Rebel Autonomous Secondary School
EU	European Union
EZLN	Ejército Zapatista de Liberación Nacional / Zapatista Army of National Liberation
FAT	Frente Auténtico del Trabajo / Authentic Labor Front
FDI	Foreign direct investment

FDN	Frente Democrático Nacional / National Democratic Front
FESEBES	Federación de Sindicatos de Empresas de Bienes y Servicios / Federation of Unions of Goods and Services Enterprises
FPFVI	Frente Popular Francisco Villa-Independiente / Independent Popular Front of Francisco Villa
FSM	Frente Sindical Mexicano / Mexican Union Front
FSTSE	Federación Sindicatos de Trabajadores al Servicio del Estado / Federation of Public Service Workers' Unions
FTAA	Free Trade Areas of the Americas
FTUI	Free Trade Union Institute
FZLN	Frente Zapatista de Liberación Nacional / Zapatista Front of National Liberation
GATT	General Agreement on Tariffs and Trade
GDP	Gross domestic product
HSIR	Historical sociology of international relations
IAF	Inter-American Foundation
IBRD	International Bank for Reconstruction and Development (World Bank)
ICRC	International Committee for the Red Cross
IFE	Instituto Federal Electoral / Federal Electoral Institute
IMF	International Monetary Fund
IMSS	Instituto Mexicano del Seguro Social / Mexican Social Security Institute
INMECAFÉ	Instituto Mexicano del Café
ISI	Import substitution industrialization
ISSSTE	Instituto de Seguridad y Servicios Sociales de los Trabajadores del Estado / Social Security Institute for State Workers
LEAR	Liga de Escritores y Artistas Revolucionarios / League of Revolutionary Writers and Artists
LFOPEE	Ley Federal de Organizaciones Políticas y Procesos Electorales / Federal Law on Political Organizations and Electoral Processes
LyFC	Compañía Luz y Fuerza del Centro / Central Light & Power Company
MSN	Mexico Solidarity Network
MST	Movimento dos Trabalhadores Rurais Sem Terra / Landless Workers' Movement
NAFINSA	Nacional Financiera, S.A.

NAFTA	North American Free Trade Agreement
NDI	National Democratic Institute for International Affairs
NED	National Endowment for Democracy
NEP	New Economic Policy
NGOs	Nongovernmental organizations
NRI	National Republican Institute for International Affairs
NTAEs	Nontraditional agricultural exports
OECD	Organisation for Economic Co-operation and Development
PAN	Partido Acción Nacional / National Action Party
PCM	Partido Comunista Mexicano / Mexican Communist Party
PEMEX	Petróleos Mexicanos / Mexican Petroleum Company
PIDER	Programa Integral para el Desarrollo Rural / Integral Program for Rural Development
PNA	Partido Nacional Agrarista / National Agrarian Party
PNR	Partido Nacional Revolucionario / Revolutionary National Party
PRD	Partido de la Revolución Democrática / Party of the Democratic Revolution
PRI	Partido Revolucionario Institucional / Institutional Revolutionary Party
PRM	Partido de la Revolución Mexicana / Party of the Mexican Revolution
PROCAMPO	Programa Nacional de Apoyos Directos al Campo / Direct-Support Program for the Farm Sector
PROGRESA	Programa de Educación, Salud y Alimentación / Program for Education, Health and Nutrition
PRONASOL	Programa Nacional de Solidaridad / National Solidarity Program
PSE	Pacto de Solidaridad Económica / Economic Solidarity Pact
PSUM	Partido Socialista Unificado de México / Mexican Unified Socialist Party
PVEM	Partido Verde Ecologista de México / Mexican Ecological Green Party
SAM	Sistema Alimentario Mexicano / Mexican Food System
SECOFI	Secretaría de Comercio y Fomento Industrial / Ministry of Commerce and Industrial Development
SEDESOL	Secretaría de Desarrollo Social / Ministry of Social Development

SEP	Secretaría de Educación Pública / Ministry of Public Education
SHCP	Secretaría de Hacienda y Crédito Público / Ministry of Finance and Public Credit
SME	Sindicato Mexicano de Electricistas / Mexican Electricians' Union
SNTE	Sindicato Nacional de Trabajadores de la Educación / National Education Workers' Union
SNTMMSRM	Sindicato Nacional de Trabajadores Mineros, Metalúrgicos y Similares de la República Mexicana / Mexican Mining and Metalworkers' Union
SOEs	State-owned enterprises
SPP	Secretaría de Programación y Presupuesto / Ministry of Programming and Budget
STFRM	Sindicato de Trabajadores Ferrocarrileros de la República Mexicana / Mexican Railroad Workers' Union
STPRM	Sindicato Trabajadores de Petroleros de la República Mexicana / Mexican Petroleum Workers' Union
STPS	Secretaría del Trabajo y Previsión Social / Ministry of Labor and Social Welfare
STRM	Sindicato de Telefonistas de la República Mexicana / Mexican Telephone Workers' Union
SUTERM	Sindicato Unico de Trabajadores Electricistas de la República Mexicana / General Union of Mexican Electrical Workers
SUTGDF	Sindicato Único de Trabajadores del Gobierno del Distrito Federal / Federal District Government Workers' Union
TELMEX	Teléfonos de México / Mexican Telephone Company
TGP	Taller de Gráfica Popular / Peoples' Graphic Workshop
TNC	Transnational corporation
TRIFE	Tribunal Federal Electoral / Federal Electoral Tribunal
UNDP	United Nations Development Program
UNOPII	Unidad Nacional de Organizaciones Populares de Izquierda Independientes / National Unity of Independent-Left Popular Organizations
UNT	Unión Nacional de Trabajadores / National Union of Workers
USAID	United States Agency for International Development

Chapter One

Coordinates of Revolution, State, and Uneven Development in Modern Mexico

In 1939 the Mexican artist Jesús Escobedo produced a work simply entitled *Las clases* that captured in a single composition the history and imagery of the outcome of the Mexican Revolution. This socially committed artwork contained four figures standing equally side-by-side and arm-in-arm: the bourgeois, the soldier, the proletarian, and the campesino. The ordering in terms of importance and priority is, perhaps, significant. Equally, the inclusion of neither a female character, nor an indigenous member, in the group is revealing in terms of assessing *Las clases* as a representative image of Mexico's postrevolutionary state and society.[1] The significance of this artwork, however, as a window on the historical sociology of modern state formation in Mexico should not be underestimated. In responding to Comintern resolutions calling for the formation of popular organizations in the fight against fascism, artists Leopoldo Méndez, Pablo O'Higgins, and Luis Arenal, as well as writer Juan de la Cabada, founded the Liga de Escritores y Artistas Revolucionarios (LEAR) in 1934. The LEAR comprised all spheres including music, theater, photography, architecture, and graphic art and was closely linked to the Partido Comunista Mexicano (PCM). Its main publication, *Frente a Frente* (with a print run from two thousand to ten thousand copies at its peak) pursued open class confrontation with the Lázaro Cárdenas administration (1934–1940) and maintained that "the basic social function of a revolutionary intellectual is to be an active militant, a skillful guide capable of pointing out dangers that culture confronts."[2] Yet, by 1937, the LEAR's membership had already fractured and declined with artists regrouping in the more cohesive Taller de Gráfica Popular (TGP), which became the most important producer of antifascist visuals in Mexico at the time and would lay claim to an international presence and membership, including the African American artist Elizabeth Catlett. Specializing in linocuts, woodcuts, and lithoprints, the

1

TGP was officially formed in 1938 stating in its Declaration of Principles that "art must reflect the social reality of the times and have unity of content and form." Indicating its insertion within the politics of the masses during Cárdenas's administration (see Córdova 1974), it also stated that "the TGP will cooperate professionally with other cultural workshops and institutions, workers' organizations and progressive movements and institutions in general" (TGP 1937/1989: Articles 3 and 4). At the same time, the Liga Pro-Cultura Alemana, formed in 1938, was also engaged in incorporating the emerging geopolitical conflict of the period into a local context, aiming to combat the spread of fascism in Mexico and facilitate the dissemination of anti-Nazi propaganda. With a membership that would include Hannes Meyer—the former director of the Bauhaus and then director of the Instituto del Urbanismo y Planificación (1942–1949)—the Liga, as early as 1938, organized a series of conferences in Mexico City as the basis of a propaganda strategy against fascism. Hosted at the Palacio de Bellas Artes and attracting audiences of one thousand to five thousand people, these conferences were advertised with anti-fascist posters produced by TGP artists. And so it came to pass that Jesús Escobedo's *Las clases* was incorporated into the poster *Como combatir el fascismo*, advertising Lombardo Toledano as a guest speaker at one of the conferences, with the aim of projecting to the public the unity of the various factions of the Mexican Revolution in the 1930s against reactionary threats (see figure 1.1).[3] In commenting on the intelligibility of this composition and its appeal to egalitarianism, even to a largely illiterate public, it has been stated that "the power of these revolutionary icons would not have been lost on any Mexican viewer or, for that matter, on anyone familiar with the history and iconology of the Mexican Revolution" (Bardach 2008: 191).

Yet the TGP itself would become embedded within a propaganda mosaic whose foundations were laid not only in the import substitution industrialization (ISI) policies to come in Mexico but also the rhetoric of production and patriotism conjoined within the ideology of national unity forged by the postrevolutionary state (see Rankin 2009). In addition to its commitment to Cardenismo, the TGP would subsequently come to accept government commissions alongside occasional support for significant miners' strikes, such as in Cloete and Nueva Rosita in 1950 and 1952. However, following its disinclination to respond to the violent suppression of the Sindicato Nacional de Trabajadores de la Educación (SNTE) in 1956, the TGP by the 1960s had disintegrated as a cohesive social movement. "The 1960s thus became a decade of marginalisation and growing obscurity for the TGP," writes Alison McClean (2009: 42), "indeed, the final exodus of its remaining senior members, Luis Arenal, Ángel Bracho and Adolfo Quinteros, coincided with the massacre of students by government forces in Mexico City in 1968," at

Figure 1.1.   Jesús Escobedo, *Como combatir el fascismo* [How to combat fascism], Liga Pro-Cultura Alemana poster, 1939, lithograph in black and red. Photograph courtesy of the Taller de Gráfica Popular (TGP), México, and the British Museum, London.

Tlatelolco. In microcosm, then, Jesús Escobedo's depiction of the postrevolutionary state captures what has been called the paradox of revolution: "the paradox of social revolution is that popular mobilisation and socioeconomic transformation most commonly eventuate in a new form of authoritarian rule" (Middlebrook 1995: 1). But is this process as paradoxical as claimed, especially for postcolonial state forms that emerge within a global division of labor, shaped by geopolitical pressures through the expansion of capitalism, and the uneven and combined tendencies of development? For states in Latin America, commonly confronted with an impasse between contending class forces, or a lack of any established bourgeois hegemony, how are the social relations of capitalist development commonly set in motion?

This book addresses these and other issues by placing them within a framework of analysis that emphasizes a historical sociological approach to understanding modern state formation and the political economy of uneven development in Mexico. It does so by drawing insights both from Leon Trotsky's writings on the world historical process of uneven and combined development, indicating the insertion and adaptation of states to different stages of development, and Antonio Gramsci's theorizing on modern capitalist state formation. It therefore teases out something substantive from Michael

Burawoy's (1989: 793) rather illusive statement that "where Trotsky's horizons stop, Gramsci's begin." It is argued here that drawing from Trotsky's theory of uneven and combined development (as a conditioning situation) and Gramsci's theory of passive revolution (as a set of class strategies) offers a fruitful approach to illuminating the historical sociology of modern state formation. More precisely, this study argues that the struggle-driven course of uneven and combined development and modern state formation in Mexico can be best understood as a set of constructed and contested class practices characteristic of a passive revolution, that is, a condition in which capitalist development is either instituted and/or expanded, resulting in both a "revolutionary" rupture and a "restoration" of social relations. Definitionally, passive revolution is therefore a mode of class rule associated with both ruptural conditions of state development, ushering in the world of capitalist production, and class strategies linked to the continual furtherance of capitalism as a response to its crisis conditions of accumulation: more of which shortly. A central proposition of the book is that the historical sociology of modern Mexican state formation in the twentieth century be understood as a condition of passive revolution. The key argument is that this unfolding history of passive revolution has been shaped by the ruptural conditions of the Mexican Revolution as well as a series of subsequent transformations in state and civil society marked by ongoing forms of capitalist restructuring. Both the initial ruptural conditions in *constructing* state identity through the Mexican Revolution and subsequent capitalist reorganization and *contestation* are to be understood as forms of passive revolution shaping the history of modern Mexico. Although it has been stated that Gramsci's work "was readily appropriated into historical sociology because of the interest in definitions of historically specific institutional regimes . . . and his concern for historical variations in class struggle" (Calhoun 2003: 389), this is the first book-length study to assert a focus on passive revolution as relevant to state formation processes in Latin America.[4] Rather than a seemingly absurd or contradictory outcome of social revolution (as a putative "paradox" of revolution), the underlying argument of this book—drawing from the Mexican experience—is that both repression and national-popular influence commonly undergird the road to modern state formation in postcolonial states. The chapters that follow will therefore trace the construction and contestation of the modern state in twentieth-century Mexico that "initiated capitalist development as a passive revolution within an authoritarian framework under state leadership for lack of any established bourgeois hegemony" (Cox 1987: 218).

The remainder of this introductory chapter will outline, in the first section to follow, how this volume goes beyond previous work on Mexico by fleshing out its contribution to recent and ongoing debates on Mexican historiography and cultural history. The second section explores some of the coordinates of state formation and uneven development regarded as significant in shaping modern capitalism in Mexico. A third section will then offer a little more conceptual detail on the relevance of passive revolution, rather than the more common recourse to hegemony, in understanding state formation processes in Mexico. It should be clear, however, that this is not an attempt to provide a "theory" chapter separate from the study of the construction and contestation of the modern state in Mexico pursued in the rest of the book. Instead, cascading throughout each following chapter, conceptual and theoretical contributions on the "abstract" dimensions of uneven development and passive revolution and its embeddedness in the "concrete" will be present. There is no separation of "theory" and "case study" framing the argument in this volume. Rather, the aim is to tease out the ever further refinement of the condition of passive revolution present throughout the various step changes in Mexican history. This will be completed by introducing novel contributions on issues of state formation; state theory; political economy; literary criticism; democratization; or resistance, which respectively infuse all the chapters to follow. An overview of the plan of the book will then close the present chapter and provide an outlook on the key themes addressed in its focus on the construction and contestation of revolution and state in modern Mexico.

FROM HEGEMONIC PROCESSES
TO UNEVEN DEVELOPMENT

From 1850 onward most countries in Latin America experienced heightened conditions of dependent development resting on an ever-increasing integration within the world economy. Initially this was based on "outward-oriented" growth linked to direct foreign investment. Yet, following the Great Depression of the 1930s, severe restraints on imports were experienced by Latin American states. Thereafter active state intervention would characterize a form of developmentalism (*desarrollismo*) through ISI policies marked by a social division of labor involving the production of nondurable goods (processed foods, beverages, tobacco products, cotton textiles) and some capital goods undertaken by domestic capital and the production of durable goods (household appliances and automobile assembly) produced by transnational corporations (TNCs). Between 1945 and 1973, Latin America's gross domestic product (GDP) grew at 5.3 percent per annum with rapid industrializers including Argentina, Chile, Uruguay, Brazil, and Mexico (Munck 2003: 48). Between 1940 and 1960, in Mexico, the economic strategy of ISI ensured a per capita GDP growth rate of 3.3 percent per annum; while in the late 1970s manufacturing as a result of this "Mexican Miracle" had come to represent nearly 40 percent of national output (Cornelius, Gentleman, and Smith 1989: 4). Masked by these factors, though, was the worsening condition of income distribution under ISI in Mexico, in which poorer families in 1950 received only 19 percent of national income, with that share dropping in 1975 to just 13 percent of the total (Aguilar Camín and Meyer 1993: 164). Nevertheless, the *desarrollista* state in Latin America and its nation-building strategies and populist policies came to be explained through the notion of state corporatism. This section outlines the debate that revolved around the analysis of state corporatism and its limits in accounting for state-civil society relations in Mexico. This is an important backdrop prior to considering more recent developments in Latin American and Mexican studies, which also lay claim to a focus on hegemonic processes of state formation and the cultural practices shaping state power.

State corporatism was a widely popular approach across European and Latin American contexts in the 1970s purporting to understand the system of interest representation linking the organized interests of civil society with the decisional structures of the state. In Latin America it claimed to encapsulate a system of interest representation by referring to competing factions (trade unions, peasant organizations, business councils), sometimes organized and licensed by a single party. In exchange, such factions were granted a representational role within the state at the expense of having limitations imposed on their demands and actions. Philippe Schmitter developed the canonical essay in this regard to distinguish between *societal corporatism*, that was autonomous and penetrative, characteristic of competitive electoral political systems, and *state corporatism*, that was dependent and penetrated, associated with the prevalence of centralized bureaucratic power within a dominant party system.

> State corporatism tends to be associated with political systems in which territorial sub-units are tightly subordinated to central bureaucratic power; elections are nonexistent or plebiscitary; party systems are dominated or monopolised by a weak single party; executive authorities are ideologically exclusive and more narrowly recruited and are such that political subcultures based on class, ethnicity, language or regionalism are repressed. (Schmitter 1979: 22)

Allied with a focus on specific types of authoritarianism in Latin America, writings on state corporatism were taken as a point of departure to examine patterns of historical change set within the context of ISI dependent capitalism (see O'Donnell 1973). This involved highlighting

1. high governmental positions occupied by state managers who have risen through bureaucratic organizations (the armed forces, public bureaucracy, large firms);

2. closed channels of political access to the popular sector, leading to the neutralization, repression, or imposition of controls by the state on civil society;
3. economic exclusion and depoliticization in attempts to reduce the aspirations of the popular sector; and
4. the deepening of capital accumulation during conditions of dependent capitalism through extensive industrialization.

In sum, the form of state corporatism and its bureaucratic authoritarian character came to be defined as "a system of exclusion of the popular sector, based on the reaction of dominant sectors and classes to the political and economic crises to which populism and its developmentalist successors led" (O'Donnell 1978: 13). Across Latin America, bureaucratic authoritarian regimes were "characterised by strong and relatively autonomous governmental structures that seek to impose on the society a system of interest representation based on enforced limited pluralism" (Malloy 1977: 4).

Although it has been claimed that this theorization of the state provides "an account on which one can build with effect" (Jessop 1990: 113), at least two reasons can be provided for seeking alternative state theoretical resources. First, rather than conceptually redeeming the state, there was a swing in this literature toward privileging "the state" held as a public sphere interacting separately with "civil society." This is evident in the focus on state capabilities existing in a mélange of civil society organizations resulting in the state-in-society approach (Migdal 1988). The duality of the state is therefore taken to refer to a focus on how state and civil society are in a recursive relationship of mutual engagement, constitution, and transformation. Hence, "state leaders need a set of strong state agencies to be able to make their own strategy of survival acceptable to the peasants and labourers of the Third World" (Migdal 2001: 68). Primarily, "the state" itself is regarded as a discrete institutional category, a reified thing, held in a relationship of exteriority to "civil society." State and civil society are thus taken as two separate, albeit mutually interacting, entities resulting in their juxtaposition and obscuring their complex character. Yet civil society is not simply a mere appendage of the state. In Mexican studies, though, one consequence of this separate and then additive approach to "the state" and "civil society" has been the conflation of hegemonic processes with domination, coercion, or just straight brute state control (see Meyer 1977; Reyna 1977). The constitutive role of the state, as a strategic field in which the relations of production are bound up with political and ideological relations that consecrate and legitimize them, is thereby lost (Poulantzas 1978: 36). The inner connection of the political economy of state–civil society relations is rent asunder in such state corporatist approaches, meaning that the apparent separation of the economic and the

political cannot be problematized or, most crucially, related to an understanding of capitalism (Wood 1995: 31–36). In sum, there is a failure to conceive
the state as a form of capitalist social relations, as an aspect of the social
relations of production, predicated upon the reproduction of antagonisms and
class-driven struggle.

Second, the corporatist assessment of the state commonly relies on a Weberian ideal-type definition meaning "the Weberian tradition [that] sees the
state as a set of institutions that claims control over territories and people
based on a monopoly of organised forces and that performs administra-
tive, legal, coercive and extractive functions" (Huber 1995: 165). However,
common to similar strands of argument on social revolutions in historical
sociology about "bringing the state back in," this is again a restrictive form
of state-centrism, which tends to obscure class relations (e.g., Skocpol 1979;
Evans, Rueschemeyer, and Skocpol 1985). The result is often a form of state-
centrism, or "statolatry," which tends to obscure class relations in favor of
more anodyne cognates like social actors that, while related to the state, are
still held in a relationship of exteriority to it.[5] Historical sociology in this vein
does not explain the state as such but explains it away (Abrams 1977/1988:
67). After all, in concurrence with Herbert Marcuse, although Max Weber
analyzed processes of industrialization these were not rooted in the structure
of capitalism itself, so that his analysis became the formal analysis of domination (Marcuse 1965/1968: 210, 215). As a result, works across state corporatism and historical sociology succumb to counterpoising the state and civil
society as polar opposites, held in a relationship of exteriority, to deny the
presence of classes and class struggle (Cammack 1989). What is missing is
a more relational approach to state power that can recognize the internal link
between modern state formation and capitalism, meaning that "the structural
specificity of state sovereignty lies in its 'abstraction' from civil society—an
abstraction which is constitutive of the private sphere of the market, and
hence inseparable from capitalist relations of production" (Rosenberg 1994:
123–24). The binary line drawn between state and civil society within state
corporatist studies of Latin American politics cannot therefore reveal the
core locus of class-driven power relations in production (Collier 1995: 145;
Oxhorn 1998: 204).

These criticisms can be added to more recent moves in Mexican studies
that have called for the abandonment of state corporatist views on the state in
Latin America (Rubin 1990: 258). Asserted, instead, by more recent literature
is the need for a concentration on the uneven shape of state power in light of
regional and cultural practices involving the multiple dynamics of ethnicity,
language, gender, class, and religion. A compelling case is therefore made
for a decentered conception of politics by examining the interconnectedness

and permeability of state and civil society in order to appreciate the multiple sites of resistance contesting state hegemonic processes (Rubin 1997). Parallel to this decentered focus on localized contestations of state power, a stress on popular culture and hegemonic processes has come to the fore within studies on "everyday" forms of state formation in Latin America (e.g., Latin American Subaltern Studies Group 1993; Joseph and Nugent 1994; Mallon 1995; Nugent 1998; Joseph, Rubenstein, and Zolov 2001). Brought to center stage here is a focus on state formation, popular culture, and hegemonic processes in order to grapple with power relations at the local level. The result is a break with the Pax Priísta: an overriding narrative of modernization inflected through the "Golden Age" of the Mexican Miracle, which asserted the uninterrupted rise of the state Leviathan and the hegemony of the Partido Revolucionario Institucional (PRI). "As scholars began to fully consider both the PRI's repressive measures and the social consequences of its economic policies," states Tanalís Padilla (2008: 12), "a different view of Mexico and the revolution that spawned its modern state came into focus."

Various broadsides against this literature on the "new cultural history" have followed, as well as defenses of its theoretical grounding and empirical accomplishments (see inter alia Haber 1999; Mallon 1999; Vaughan 1999). Stepping aside from the "historiographical hectoring" evident in this ongoing debate (Knight 2002c: 143), three observations relevant to the schema of this book can be made. First, although it has been asserted that "we cannot simply take it for granted that state elites *have* a 'hegemonic project' at all" (Scott 1994: xi, original emphasis), the common recourse is nevertheless to focus on hegemonic processes. Evident in Mexican studies more generally, there has been a tendency to invoke reference to the concept of hegemony while revealing a reluctance to explicate any meaning of the term, for example, by referring to the "end" of PRI hegemony or perennial transitions in the hegemony of the once-ruling party (see e.g., Fox 1994; Serrano 1994). Any sojourn through the literature on Mexican studies thus reveals a repeated conflation of hegemony and authoritarianism, the use of hegemony as a synonym for dominance, or conceptually vague references to "contending hegemonic forces" and descriptions of the PRI as losing its monopoly on power but still holding to some form of imprecise hegemony (e.g., Collier 1992; Whitehead 1994; Cornelius 1996; Dresser 1996a; Rodríguez and Ward 1996). Across the board, then, there seems something valid in the claim that there is indeterminacy in the way hegemony is understood, which reduces the term to a conceptual catchall and prevents clear theoretical and practical understanding (Haber 1997). More attentiveness to Alan Knight's (1994c: 42) counsel that the notion of hegemony "should be used cautiously and sparingly, certainly not as some kind of blanket explanation analogous to those

mindless *passe-partouts*, 'national character' or 'human nature,'" seems
well-founded. Second, calls for a wholesale retreat from the logic of hegemony and the move towards a posthegemonic politics should be resisted. A
posthegemonic condition refers here to the presumption that ideology critique
is now superfluous in an age where affective relations or bodily dispositions
are regnant (Beasley-Murray 2003; Arditi 2007). Posthegemony debates are
unpersuasive because they invoke the same rhetoric, noted above, of bringing the study of the state back into Latin American cultural and subaltern
studies. Hence a repetition of tired frames of reference on "the state" and
"culture," posited in exterior relation, and then attempts to study both in
terms of how they interrelate, as mixtures, coalescing lines, assemblages,
or processes of incorporation (Beasley-Murray and Moreiras 1999: 17–18).
What is always-already separated and then combined will persistently fail to
grasp relations that are internal to each other. Equally problematic is the associated argument that "at its limit, the logic of hegemony simply identifies
with the state, by taking it for granted," so instead, one should come to accept
the ubiquity of power within posthegemonic times and the constituent power
of the multitude as the subject of society (Beasley-Murray 2010: x, xv). This
extremist take on hegemony theory and its attempt to decenter analysis from
the strategic field of the state, however, merely collapses into a "pluralism of
micropowers," conceiving ever more microcosms of meaning within a world
of individuated actors (Poulantzas 1978: 44). One consequence is that the
posthegemony argument grants scant attention to its own historical conditions
of emergence. This means the need to accord attention to the material and
discursive context of knowledge production in order to "grasp the struggle for
hegemony on the part of the posthegemony proponents" within and beyond
the academic field of power (Binford 2004). Third, wider cultural approaches
to state formation breaking with the Pax Priísta have contributed enormously
to understanding the regional context of state formation processes and forms
of local consciousness, the spatial dimensions of regional culture, and politics at the subnational level (Lomnitz 1992; Cornelius 1999). However, this
capacity to trace the scalar organization of state power to local configurations
of regional space may come at the price of appreciating transformations in
the production of space under capitalism at the national scale (Clarke 1996).
Most representative is Benjamin Smith's (2009: 9) declaration, embedded in
his critique of broad studies on hegemonic processes, that there needs to be a
"move away from these overarching models of state formation and towards
an analysis of distinct, contained moments of interaction between regional
elites, popular groups and the state." What positions such as this neglect,
though, is a focus on spaces of hegemony, meaning the complex dialectic
of statist productions of culture and differentiated regional contexts in the

organization of culture. A spatial perspective on regional and national logics needs to capture the dynamics of both differentiation and homogenization marking national space. In this regard, as Claudio Lomnitz attests, even in analyzing the social production of cultural relations at the regional level, the state is paramount in producing an ordered space for capital. "Hegemony is achieved, first and foremost, at the level of the state; as capitalism develops, the hegemonic systems of different states, insofar as they are capitalist states, should tend to develop certain similarities" (Lomnitz 1992: 40). Without neglect for differentiated cultural production in regional social spaces, then, the key is to highlight the mediating social relations and processes that constitute state power as a spatial order. After all, as Jorge Luis Borges reminds us in "On Exactitude in Science," cartographers embarking on an attempt to capture space on the same scale as a fictional empire run the risk of overdetailing geographical place and space (Borges 1960/2000: 325). In concurrence, therefore, with Néstor García Canclini (1988: 491), "by thus shrinking the scale of observation and by abstracting it from any macrosocial paradigm, studies of the everyday in local cultures limit themselves to a description of elementary forms of sociability and tend to privilege that which is common to distinct strata." Methodologically, it is therefore important to enable a focus on the distinctive geographical scales shaping state territorial organization and the contradictory class forces associated with capitalist spatiality. My argument in this book is that a twin focus on the production of spatial scale within conditions of uneven and combined development through the class practices of passive revolution shaping state formation processes offers such potential. As Henri Lefebvre states:

> The violence of the state must not be viewed in isolation: it cannot be separated either from the accumulation of capital or from the rational and political principle of *unification*, which subordinates and totalises the various aspects of social practice—legislation, culture, knowledge, education—within a determinate space; namely the space of the ruling class's hegemony over its people and over the nationhood that it has arrogated. (Lefebvre 1991: 280–81, original emphasis)

Yet, rather than showing how hegemony operates through sociospatial practices of territoriality (see Bobrow-Strain 2007), this volume goes beyond previous work on Mexico by fleshing out the relevance of the specific practices of passive revolution to understanding state formation processes. As William Roseberry puts it, "Gramsci draws our attention to *spatial* differentiation, to the uneven and unequal development of social powers in regional spaces." But often forgotten is his succeeding comment that Gramsci's "consideration of the failures of state formation and hegemony in the Italian peninsula begins with the difficulties imposed by regionally distinct fields of force" (Roseberry 1994: 359–60, original emphasis). It is to the process of passive revolution, therefore, and its relevance to understanding the historical construction and contestation of the state in Mexico that attention is cast in this book. Before elaborating more on that front, the next section outlines some of the basic coordinates of uneven development shaping the past and present historical sociology of state formation in Mexico. These features of uneven development are then developed in more detail in the various chapters to follow throughout the book.

FROM UNEVEN DEVELOPMENT TO PASSIVE REVOLUTION

In Mexico "the uneven and combined development of modern capitalist forms of production" was reflected "with harsh, dictatorial social and political forms of control over the populace" (Cockcroft 1974: 249). As Leon Trotsky outlines, uneven and combined development is a historic process that compels, "under the whip of external necessity," states in the capitalist periphery to engage in developmental catch-up with their more advanced counterparts (Trotsky 1936/1980: 28). Hence, "national peculiarity is nothing else but the most general product of the unevenness of historical development, its summary result" (Trotsky 1929/2004: 24). This cue has been adopted by Adolfo Gilly (1971/2007: 60–62) to insert the combination of the nationally specific development of capitalism in Mexico within its uneven mode of insertion into the world market. A discussion of these circumstances of uneven development is best left for the chapter to follow, where a detailed analysis of the specificities of class struggle, capitalist accumulation, and state formation in Mexico is taken up. For the present outline, one assessment of the condition of uneven development in modern Mexico concluded that the regional inequalities present at the end of the Porfiriato (1876–1911) were still manifest in similar ways up to, at least, the 1960s. Those states, led by the primacy of the Federal District in Mexico City, which experienced earlier spurts of economic and social development had remained dominant, while disparities accelerated between the foremost regional poles (the State of Mexico, Baja California Norte, Nuevo León) and the slower growth centers in the southern states (Guerrero, Oaxaca, Chiapas) (Appendini et al. 1972: 9, 21). More recently, this north–south divide has drawn increased attention, not least by highlighting the disparities in "Mexico's mezzogiorno," the nine states of the south and southeast of the country (Chiapas, Campeche, Yucatán, Quintana Roo, Tabasco, Oaxaca, Guerrero, Veracruz, Puebla), which account for almost a quarter of Mexico's total area and population and are still more rural, indigenous, and poorer than the rest of the country. According to this view, presented in a recent country survey from the *Economist*, almost 45 percent of the population in these southern states live in settlements of less than twenty-five hundred people (compared with 20 percent elsewhere across the country), twice as many people lack electricity, and half as many can read and write. These circumstances of uneven development are in stark contrast to the presence of urban growth in regional clusters in the northern border states (Baja California Norte, Sonora, Chihuahua, Coahuila, Nuevo León, Tamaulipas). As the survey concludes:

> In Ciudad Juárez, across the border from El Paso, industrial parks, shopping malls and brand-new housing estates in faux-colonial style stretch out endlessly into the Chihuahua desert. Monterrey, the industrial hub of north-east Mexico, has become a handsome North American city of swirling freeways and glass office blocks, just the place to hold international conferences. . . . It is time for the government to sweep away the remnants of crony capitalism, set the economy free and liberate the south from backwardness.[6]

This is a view shared somewhat by Agustín Carstens, as the secretary of finance (from 2006 to 2009), who pronounced at a similar time that Mexico was on track to become a "fully developed" state within twenty years.[7] Yet these sanguine visions are made problematic not simply by Mexico's recent economic downturn, nor even the *Economist*'s own admission (despite its earlier view, noted above) that the current violence swirling around drug trafficking in Monterrey means that "hotels are less than half full: almost every week a business conference or international sporting event is cancelled."[8] Rather, although continuities between past and present disparities of uneven development are evident, a much more variegated set of conditions marks the circumstances of uneven development in Mexico today. It is therefore pertinent to provide some basic coordinates of uneven development in Mexico, which are addressed in more detail in the chapters to follow. Despite the dominant pattern of a divide between north and south holding purchase on the uneven development of Mexico, there is *una geografía revuelta* (a "scrambled geography") denoting the spatial organization of state power and its socially produced configuration through local, regional, national, and global scales.[9] Just as "core" and "periphery" should be regarded as relational, rather than as immutable geographical positions, then so too should the points of reference of uneven development (see Cox 1987: 318–28). (See map 1.1.)

Whereas the urban system in 1960 was concentrated around three dominant cities (Mexico City, Guadalajara, Monterrey), a change in the urban hierarchy has proceeded since, entailing a shift from the dominance of one metropolis (Mexico City) to the consolidation of a polycentric concentration

Map 1.1.   Mexico. Courtesy of Eureka Cartography.

across various city forms (Monterrey, Torreón, Chihuahua, Tampico, Tijuana, Ciudad Juárez), alongside further conglomeration in the Mexico City megalopolis with various urban centers (Puebla, Toluca, Querétaro). In terms of continuity and dominance, the Federal District and the State of Mexico together accounted for 15.7 percent of national GDP in 1900, which increased to 33 percent of national GDP by 1999. Continuous regional clusters of growth could also be witnessed, with the Centre East (Federal District, Hidalgo, State of Mexico, Morelos, Puebla, Querétaro, Tlaxcala) as a whole maintaining its share of national GDP from 43 percent in 1970 to 41.7 percent in 1999. Meanwhile the share of national GDP in the six northern border states, mentioned above, was sustained from 21.1 percent in 1970 to 23.3 percent in 1999. The three southern states of Chiapas, Guerrero, and Oaxaca also retained their own similar patterns of national GDP: Chiapas increased from 1.6 percent in 1970 to 1.7 percent in 1999, in Guerrero the same share of national GDP in 1970 at 1.7 percent was present in 1999, and in Oaxaca again the same share of national GDP in 1970 at 1.5 percent was evident in

1999 (Garza 2003: 489–91). By the 1990s, although continuities existed, there was a change from the 1960s in that the urban system in Mexico moved to a polycentric concentration across five metropolitan areas; there was the consolidation of the megapolitan cluster of Mexico City that by the mid-twenty-first century is likely to annex Cuernavaca, Puebla, Cuautla, Pachuca, and Querétaro; and polycentric regional forms had also emerged in the Valley of Mexico anchored in the megalopolis of Mexico City; in the west with its center in Guadalajara; and in the northeast with Monterrey as its hub (Garza 1999: 155–56). Elsewhere, this new economic geography has been described as the emergence of three Mexicos revolving around the border and central regions shaped by maquila export-led production; the metropole of Mexico City; and the southern states of Oaxaca, Chiapas, and Guerrero (see Dávila Flores 2008). Overall, it has therefore been argued that "Mexico today is essentially an urban nation, and it is in the urban world that spatial disparities are increasingly apparent" (Garza 2003: 488). Indeed, the noteworthy growth in Mexico's urban population, as indicated in table 1.1, has entailed an increase in urban population from 23,828,000 (in 1970) to 64,673,000 (in 2000) and an increase in urban areas as a percentage of the total population from 49.4 percent (in 1970) to 66.3 percent (in 2000). Yet this is only one aspect of the reconfiguring of uneven development and the spatial form of the state in Mexico.

An additional feature of any depiction of the conditions of uneven development is the set of transformations wrought in the countryside and the impact on rural forms of production in Mexico. In addition to migratory flows to the United States, out-migration from the countryside to the city in Mexico includes peasant producers moving to midsize cities, other rural localities, as well as major urban conurbations. In terms of population dynamics and uneven development, according to the 1995 population census, in relation to the combined agricultural, livestock sector, and agroindustrial sector (food, beverages, and tobacco), the proportion of GDP derived from primary economic activities was 37.7 percent of the total (6.4 percent contributed by the agricultural and livestock sector and 31.3 percent by the agroindustrial sector). The latter therefore has a highly skewed impact on local wage

Table 1.1.   Distribution of Mexico's Urban Population, 1960–2000

	1960	*1970*	*1980*	*1990*	*2000*
Population (000s)	14,382	23,828	37,584	49,604	64,673
Number of Cities[a]	119	166	229	309	362
Urban Areas as a Percentage of Total Population	41.2	49.4	56.2	60.8	66.3

Source: Interpolation and extrapolation of data from Garza (1999: 150–56) and Garza (2003: 502–53).
[a]Referring to localities with 15,000 or more inhabitants.

labor and polarizes patterns of uneven development in the countryside between dominant agroindustries, producing nontraditional agricultural export
(NTAE) commodities, and struggling commercial producers of grains, meat,
and milk for the domestic market (C. de Grammont 2003: 373). As a result,
the population engaged in agriculture and livestock raising has declined
from 6,144,930 (in 1960), or 54.2 percent of agricultural employment as a
percentage of the total economically active population (EAP), to 5,300,114
(in 1990), or 22.6 percent of the total EAP. Yet, from 1990, the population
engaged in agriculture and livestock raising expanded from this figure of just
over 5 million to 8,208,709 (in 1999), or 21.0 percent of the EAP. Masked
by these trends, however, is the shift from peasants producing for their own
means of subsistence to becoming compelled to sell their labor power through
the purely "economic" mechanisms of the market, as agricultural day laborers
and wage workers, female workers, and child labor. This proletarianization
has particularly been a feature of the NTAE fruit-producing and horticultural
regions of Mexico's northwest (horticulture, grapes, and citrus in Baja California, Baja California Sur, Sinaloa, and Sonora), in the northeast (citrus in
northern Veracruz and horticulture in Tamaulipas), and in the north (fruit in
Chihuahua, fruit and citrus in Montemorelos, Nuevo León) (C. de Grammont
2003: 365–76). In states such as Oaxaca, temporary labor migration can range
from 25 percent of the population rising up to 90 percent to the extent that
"one outcome is the appearance of 'ghost towns' and villages that remain
empty for several months of the year, stripped of their entire economically
active population" (C. de Grammont 2003: 369). Between 2000 and 2005, out
of 2,435 municipalities in Mexico, 1,243 experienced a negative population
growth rate adding to the impression of a landscape of depopulated ghost
towns (see Cypher and Delgado Wise 2010: 146, 149; and Hellman 2008:
208, 212). How are these basic coordinates and contradictions of uneven
development to be assessed in more detail in this study on the historical and
contemporary construction and contestation of the modern state in Mexico?
Moreover, how is the conditioning situation of uneven development linked
to the mode of class rule of passive revolution and its association both with
the ruptural conditions of state formation and the furtherance of capitalism
through crisis periods?

   The social relations of uneven development are articulated in this book in
a spatially sensitive account of the inherited territorial state form, linked to
the Porfirio Díaz period, to explain transformations in this landscape in modern Mexico and thus how space has been produced in the twentieth century
through the class strategies of passive revolution. After all, modern capitalism
has absorbed, realized, and integrated the history transmitted to it from precapitalist relations of production and the territorial inscribing of uneven de-

velopment within the spatial fix of the state is one crucial component of that inheritance (Lefebvre 1976: 37). A nodal analysis of the spatial scale of state power is therefore adopted in this book, meaning that the state is regarded as "the cohesive factor in a determinate social formation and the nodal point of its transformations" (Poulantzas 1973: 93). Beyond the key role of state space in the territorialization of capital, this nodal approach also recognizes the importance of alternative geographical scales. Hence, analysis will ensue not only of the scalar fix of the state in organizing capital accumulation but also how the urban form plays a role in the historical constitution and transformation of capitalist organization. After all, Mexico City has been heralded as the "Paris of the Latin American Revolution," something that receives much more detailed attention later in the book.

> During the 20th century Mexico City spread the ideas of the Mexican Revolution far and wide, just as Paris had radiated the principles of the French Revolution during the 19th century. What Paris and the French Revolution were to Karl Marx in 1844–45 and again in 1848, Mexico City and the Mexican Revolution were to the Peruvian revolutionary Víctor Raúl Haya de la Torre in 1923–24 and again in 1927–28, to Leon Trotsky from 1938–1940 and, to a lesser extent, to Che Guevara and Fidel Castro during 1955 and 1956. (Hodges and Gandy 1983: 130–1)

In the twentieth century of modern Mexico, the role of both the state and the urban form in the production of scalar fixes for capital accumulation will therefore receive paramount attention, notably in the first half of the book (see Brenner 1998). This account of the production of space in Mexico through the conditions of uneven development and the subsequent class strategies of passive revolution does not, of course, exhaust the options for analysis of the contradictions of space at other scales, namely, local, national, regional, or transnational. No argument is presented here that the conditions of uneven development and the strategies of passive revolution can only be assessed at the scalar fixes of the city or state form. Nor is there any intention, in the present argument, to deny the possibility of analyzing spatial developments of passive revolution, for example, at the regional scale (see Hesketh 2010a, for a significant endeavor in this regard, focusing on Chiapas and Oaxaca). Hence the account to follow of the uneven development of capitalism and state formation in Mexico will also address, at key stages, the regional and global scales in tension with the organization of capital at the scale of the state (see Smith 1984/2008). As a result, the issues covered in this book on the production of spatial relations through uneven and combined development and the form of emergence of passive revolutionary strategies of class rule offers an important window through which to analyze the historical sociology of modern state formation and the organization of capitalism in Mexico. It is to the relevancy of passive revolution in contributing to an understanding of the construction and contestation of the modern history of Mexican state formation that we shall now turn.

THE CONTINUUM OF PASSIVE REVOLUTION[10]

The passive revolution syntagma captures the attempt to establish the political rule of capital and how processes of state formation are embedded in the circumstances of uneven and combined development (see Morton 2007a: 63–73; Morton 2007c). "Capitalism is a world historical phenomenon and its uneven development," Gramsci (1977: 69) stated, "means that individual nations cannot be at the same level of economic development at the same time." Greater detail on the affinal relation of uneven and combined development and passive revolution is provided in the next chapter. For the present discussion, as noted above, the concept of passive revolution refers to instances in which aspects of the social relations of capitalist development are either instituted and/or expanded, resulting in both "revolutionary" rupture and a "restoration" of social relations. It emphasizes progressive aspects of historical change during revolutionary upheaval that become undermined resulting in the reconstitution of social relations but within *new forms* of capitalist order. This aspect of the Mexican Revolution is captured well in Arnaldo Córdova's (1973: 24) assessment that its social dimension revolved around agrarian reform and the rights of workers, "but without endangering the existence of capital that was not only necessary but indispensable to the nation." According to Gramsci, after the French Revolution (1789), the emergent bourgeoisie there "was able to present itself as an integral 'state,' with all the intellectual and moral forces that were necessary and adequate to the task of organising a complete and perfect society" (Gramsci 2007: 9, Q6§10). In contrast to this instance of state formation, other European countries went through a passive revolution in which the old feudal classes were not destroyed but maintained a political role through state power.

[The] birth of the modern European states [proceeded] by successive waves of reform rather than by revolutionary explosions like the original French one. The "successive waves" were made up of a combination of social struggles, interventions from above of the enlightened monarchy type, and national wars . . . restoration becomes the first policy whereby social struggles find sufficiently elastic frameworks to allow the bourgeoisie to gain power without dramatic upheavals, without the French machinery of terror. . . . The old feudal classes are demoted from their dominant position to a "governing" one, but are not eliminated, nor is there any attempt to liquidate them as an organic whole. (Gramsci 1971: 115 Q10II§61)

There is therefore a dialectic of revolution and restoration that becomes blocked in a situation of passive revolution as neither the old nor new class forces become hegemonic (Buci-Glucksmann 1980: 315). "The problem," Gramsci (1971: 219, Q13§27) stated, "is to see whether in the dialectic of 'revolution/restoration' it is revolution or restoration which predominates." It is important to retain this emphasis on the struggle-driven contradictions of both revolution and restoration in instances of passive revolution. To be clear, a passive revolution does not refer to an inert, literally passive, course of action. The process of a passive revolution can be violent and brutal, the outcome neither predetermined nor inevitable.

The term *passive revolution* itself is a derivative and modified borrowing, and was developed to directly refer to the Risorgimento movement culminating in the unification of Italy in 1860–1861 (see Macciocchi 1975: 112–14; Thomas 2009: 133–57).[11] Yet Gramsci also extended the term through a historical methodology to refer to nineteenth-century liberal-constitutionalist movements as a whole; to the post-Napoleonic restoration (1815–1848); as well as to the restorations following the social upheaval of World War I culminating in the rise of fascism (see Morton 2007b). Passive revolution therefore generally refers to the epoch of "bourgeois revolution"—involving social upheaval or overthrow of an existing political order—leading to the creation of state power as well as the reorganization of capitalism. "All history from 1815 onwards," wrote Gramsci (1971: 132, Q13§1), "shows the efforts of the traditional classes to prevent the formation of a collective will . . . and to maintain 'economic-corporate' power in an international system of passive equilibrium."

The epoch of passive revolution is therefore a reflection of modern state formation set within inherited territorial and geopolitical conditions. It is also linked to wider deliberations on state and civil society evident in the *Prison Notebooks* and the expansion of the structures of state organization, the complexes of associations in civil society, the role of trade union and party organizational forms, and the extension of parliamentarism that are all noted as indicative of "the modern world" (Gramsci 1971: 220, Q13§27). "In the period after 1870, with the colonial expansion of Europe, all these elements change," wrote Gramsci, "the internal and international organisational relations of the state become more complex and massive" (Gramsci 1971: 243: Q13§7). Hence Gramsci's notion of the extended state—referred to as the "integral state"—is a more fruitful approach to grasping the class dynamics of capital accumulation than, for example, the "statolatry" of alternative approaches in historical sociology or state corporatism (Gramsci 1971: 239, Q6§155). As outlined in one of his prison letters:

> My study . . . leads to certain definitions of the concept of the state that is usually understood as a political society (or dictatorship, or coercive apparatus meant to mould the popular mass in accordance with the type of production and economy at a given moment) and not as a balance between the political society and the civil society (or the hegemony of a social group over the entire national society, exercised through the so-called private organizations, such as the church, the unions, the schools, etc.). (Gramsci 1994b: 67)

The state was not conceived as a thing in itself, or as a rational absolute, that was extraneous to individuals in a reified or fetishistic sense (Gramsci 1992: 229, Q1§150). The latter refers to the tendency to view the state as a thing-like entity so that people believe that "in actual fact there exists above them a phantom entity, the abstraction of the collective organism, a species of autonomous divinity that thinks, not with the head of a specific being, yet nevertheless thinks, that moves, not with the real legs of a person, yet still moves" (Gramsci 1995: 15, Q15§13). Instead, a relational approach to state power was envisaged within which the ensemble of "private" organisms in civil society is internally related to the state or "political" society (Gramsci 1971: 158–67, Q13§18). The notion of the "integral state" was therefore developed in order to counter the separation of powers embedded in liberal conceptions of politics. A critique was particularly developed of the notion that the state simply referred to the representative apparatus of government, which did not intervene in the economy except as a "nightwatchman" safeguarding public order (Gramsci 1971: 245–46, Q6§81; 262–63, Q6§88). By equating power simply with the state apparatus the significance of class struggle outside the parameters of the state, in the narrow sense, was diminished leading to the formula: "Everything within the state, nothing outside the state, nothing against the state" (Gramsci 1971: 261, Q8§190). Rather, it was acknowledged that the state plays a role in the economy as a substitute for so-called private enterprise by "manufacturing the manufacturers" through protectionism and privileges (Gramsci 1995: 243–44, Q15§1; 248–53, Q19§7). Hence the state is not agnostic and the ensemble of classes that constitute it have a formative activity in the economy and society to the extent that "one cannot speak of the power of the state but only of the camouflaging of power" (Gramsci 1985: 191, Q27§1; Gramsci 1995: 217–18, Q6§75; 237–39, Q19§6). Therefore *"laissez-faire* too is a form of state 'regulation,' introduced and maintained by legislative and coercive means" (Gramsci 1971: 160, Q13§18).

An organic relation between state and civil society, through the development of active consensus alongside a variable mix of force, is emblematic of the relational articulation of hegemony (see Morton 2007a: 87–94). Instead, in a situation of passive revolution, "the important thing is to analyse more profoundly . . . the fact that a state replaces the local social groups in leading a struggle of renewal" (Gramsci 1971: 105–6, Q15§59). Here there is a "statisation" of civil society (Portelli 1973: 33), a situation when the ruling class is unable to fully integrate the people through conditions of hegemony, or when "they were aiming at the creation of a modern state . . . [but] in fact produced a bastard" (Gramsci 1971: 90, Q19§28; Gramsci 2007: 378, Q8§236). The condition of passive revolution can therefore be regarded as a counterpart to a situation of hegemony, perhaps with the two concepts marking points on a continuum (Cox 1983: 167; Gill 2008: 58). However, to be a little more analytically particular, it is important to recognize that, for Gramsci, hegemonic processes were carefully distinguished from, albeit related to, conditions of passive revolution. To concur with Hugues Portelli's (1973: 30) adroit synopsis: "There is no social system where consensus serves as the sole basis of hegemony, nor a state where the same social group can maintain durably its domination on the basis of pure coercion." The shifting sands of hegemonic situations therefore always need to be located in the dynamics of historical development. At least three intersecting gradations can therefore be distinguished (Femia 1981: 35–50):

1. *integral hegemony* based on an organic relationship between rulers and ruled: referring to how "the 'normal' exercise of hegemony on the now classical terrain of the parliamentary regime is characterized by the combination of force and consent, which balance each other reciprocally, without force predominating excessively over consent" (Gramsci 1971: 80n.49, Q19§24);
2. *decadent hegemony* indicating the ideological decay of a ruling power bloc with fragile cultural and political integration: "between coercion and force stands corruption/fraud (which is characteristic of certain situations when it is hard to exercise the hegemonic function and when the use of force is too risky" (Gramsci 1971: 80n.4, Q19§24); and
3. *minimal hegemony* based on "hegemonic activity" but where state power "became merely an aspect of the function of domination," indicative of the condition of passive revolution: the state-coercion element superintends the hegemonic activity (Gramsci 1971: 59, Q19§24; Gramsci 2007: 75, Q6§88).

For postcolonial states confronted with the impasse of uneven development, or a blocked dialectic of revolution-restoration, the more common route to the modern world is therefore passive revolution (see Riley and Desai 2007).

When it comes to understanding the historical sociology of modern state formation in Mexico, then, my major claim is that in order to break fully with the Pax Priísta theory of history (at local, regional, or national scales), and to grapple with the repression that undergirded the PRI's rule, greater attention needs to be cast toward the condition of passive revolution. For sure, "the analysis of hegemonic processes is a conceptual thicket in which more than one clever social scientist has been lost" (Scott 1994: xi). Yet, rather than assuming the articulation of hegemonic processes, it is more apposite to remain sensitive to the coercive circumstances constituting modern state formation, to how the construction and contestation of the modern state is never settled or completed, and to focus on the changing ideological devices and class practices by which state power is legitimated. Passive revolution is a more accurate pathway to take in attempting to trace the postrevolutionary processes of state formation in the making of modern Mexico. As Gramsci (1971: 115, Q10§61) states, "Can this 'model' for the creation of the modern states [passive revolution] be repeated in other conditions?"

In Latin America, various passive revolutions (or "semirevolutions from above") have been recognized as drivers of the developmental catch-up process through planned action, the mobilization of the social base, and populist-style national development, for example, in Mexico under Lázaro Cárdenas (1934–1940), in Brazil under Getúlio Vargas establishing the *Estado Nôvo* (1937–1945), or in Argentina under Juan Perón (1944–1955) (see Löwy 1981: 162–66; Munck 1979; van der Pijl 2006a: 17–21, 177–80).[12] Hence, in commenting on trends shaping the southern cone political economies of Latin America, Ronaldo Munck (1989: 31) states that "the theme of 'passive revolution,' as elaborated by Gramsci, does provide certain clues to understanding the unity within diversity of Latin American history from 1930 to the mid-1960s." While in Latin America the potential instance of a passive revolution will, clearly, be different in terms of the blocked dialectic of revolution and restoration, or process and outcome, "in every historical case movements 'from above' and 'from below' interacted with each other, sometimes as a conflictual balance of forces, at other times as a succession of phases" (Löwy 1981: 164). There is thus a need, as Carlos Nelson Coutinho states, to "embrace the Gramsci . . . who researched the 'nonclassical' forms of the transition to capitalist modernity (the problematic of the 'passive revolution')" in Latin America (as cited in Burgos 2002: 13–14). Most recently, social class forces seeking to normalize a "passive revolutionary" path to neoliberalism in Latin America have been assessed in relation to the Augusto Pinochet era in Chile and then through the Partido Socialista de Chile (Motta 2008); in relation to the rise of neoliberalism as an accumulation strategy in Mexico to highlight the survival and reorganization of capitalism through periods of state crisis (Soederberg 2001); and with reference to the peace process in Guatemala that enacted development programs to modernize the state and capital through institutional processes (Short 2007). Passive revolution is therefore a mode of class rule associated both with ruptural conditions of modern state development, ushering in the world of capitalist production, and class strategies linked to the continual furtherance of capitalism as a response to its crisis conditions of accumulation (see Morton 2010b).

In this approach, there is a significant departure from alternative literature on the historical sociology of Mexico in that the focus is on the emergence of specific relations of production constructing modern state formation processes. At the hub of the argument, developed in far more detail in the next chapter, is therefore the condition that "can spring into life, only when the owner of the means of production and subsistence meets in the market with the free labourer selling his [*sic*] labour power." This is the age of capital referring to the emergence and consolidation of capitalism as a mode of production within a social formation, which is the "one historical condition" that "comprises a world history" (Marx 1887/1996: 180). It is therefore the *passive revolution of capital* marking state formation processes and the modern state in Mexico that is the subject of this study.[13] This contrasts noticeably with Enrique Semo's brief excursus on the relevance of passive revolution to Mexican historiography in his essay "Revoluciones pasivas en México." According to Semo, three periods mark the history of passive revolution in Mexico: (1) the eighteenth-century era of Bourbon reforms; (2) the fin de siècle dictatorship of Porfirio Díaz; and (3) the era of neoliberalism since the 1980s (see Semo 1997/2003: 171). What is common to all "three" passive revolutions, following the argument, is a form of modernization from above linked to the expansion of the world market and relations of mercantile capitalism (see also Semo 1978: 299–315; Semo 1979). Yet, if one heeds Eric Wolf's (1997: 79) opinion that "there is no such thing as mercantile or merchant capitalism" and that "capitalism, to be capitalism, must be capitalism-in-production," as noted above, then quite simply there is a serious problem with the transhistorical extension of passive revolution beyond modern capitalist relations of production. Equally, those seeking to ground the modern Mexican state in transformations of governmentality, from the colonial system in the Americas; to transformations in colonial government under the Bourbon administration and the creation of a liberal republic in 1810; to the Mexican Revolution and its institutionalization under the PRI; to processes of neoliberal governmentality, give no sense of how variable these moments of modernity are in relation to historically specific social property relations (Higgins 2004). Rather than as some transhistorical affirmation, the continuum of passive revolution and its relevance for the study of state formation in Mexico is therefore asserted in this book in a historically specific sense encompassing the twentieth-century transition to and transformation of modern capitalist political space.

Finally, this book makes an important contribution to historical sociology of international relations (HSIR) debates that have attempted to understand the origins of capitalism in terms of feudal crisis, agrarian class structures, and economic development in Europe (see e.g., Anderson 1974; Brenner 1985a; Brenner 1985b; Comninel 1987; Wood 1991; Rosenberg 1994; Teschke 2003; Lacher 2006). This work has been distinctive in highlighting long-term patterns of social property relations central to shaping late medieval and early modern Europe, variegated patterns of serfdom within feudalism, class conflicts intrinsic to the emergence of agrarian capitalism, and thus capitalist "transition" through different paths of development. One charge leveled at such analyses is that of "Eurocentric diffusionism"—the interpretation of the spread of capitalism in terms of a wave of diffusion unfolding outward from Western Europe to the non-European periphery without examining conditions of class struggle in the latter (Blaut 1993; Blaut 1999: 130–32).[14] Furthermore, the unfulfilled promise of HSIR theorizations on uneven and combined development is to combine an appreciation of the generality of capitalism with a historical sociology of transformations within specific state forms (Kiely 2005: 33). Along with the predominant stress on distinctively European experiences of state formation and the rise of modern capitalism, then, there is equally a macrosociological preoccupation that has evaded fine-grained analysis of contemporary history (Bruff 2010). The appeal of this book is therefore also based in its engagement with these HSIR debates by delivering, for the first time, an exclusive focus on the historical sociology of modern Mexican state formation in the twentieth century understood as a condition of passive revolution, which has relevance to discussions across political economy, historical sociology, international relations, development studies, and postcolonial theory.

PLAN OF THE BOOK

As this book hopes to intervene in debates on Mexican studies and historical sociology, part I organizes the first three substantive chapters by analyzing key factors in the construction of the modern state. Chapter 2 sets the stage by examining the outcome of the Mexican Revolution (1910–1920) and the emergence of capitalism and modern state formation. Set within the conditioning situation of uneven and combined development, it is argued that the Mexican Revolution resulted in a passive revolution whereby both state intervention and mass mobilization were conjoined to ensure processes of primitive accumulation and the creation of modern capitalism. The class strategies in the reorganization and consolidation of the postrevolutionary state under import substitution industrialization (ISI) are the subject of chapter 3. This chapter analyzes the rise of the state in capitalist society, the development and role of dominant fractions within the capitalist class shaping the form of state, and attendant cultural, political, and economic processes in furthering the passive revolution of capital in Mexico. Amid the class confrontations challenging the course of modern state formation, attention is accorded here to the centralization of fixed capital in the drive for surplus value, not least through pivotal agents such as Nacional Financiera, S.A. (NAFINSA), alongside the state financing of agricultural production and transformations of the agrarian landscape. The spatial practices of passive revolution also receive consideration in this chapter not only in terms of how the modern state binds itself to space but also how Mexico City became a crucial scalar fix for the territorialization of capital. While, in the period of the 1950s, the *historiografía capitalina* may have been best captured in the avant-garde photographs of Nacho López, documenting both worker and bourgeois worlds in magazines such as *Siempre* and *Mañana*,[15] or in Luis Buñuel's cinematographic stroke of genius in *Los Olvidados* [1950], to name just two sources, the focus here is more on the literal "architecture" of passive revolution as part of a particular production of space linked to the formation of the modern state. As the Mexican art historian Rita Eder (1989: 70) once put it in relation to this period of monumentalism in Mexico: "Monuments were in a sense like the picture of Dorian Gray, where the state was eager to protect an image of national prosperity and social justice, although the end result would in fact enrich the then incipient bourgeoisie." How this class became consolidated through the move to a capitalist type of state and the emergence of neoliberalism is then the subject of chapter 4. Set against arguments on the dynamics of global capitalism, this chapter addresses Mexico's shift from the *desarrollo estabilizador* (stabilized development) model of ISI toward the creation of an alternative spatiotemporal fix for capital accumulation. The analysis of passive revolution is therefore linked here to the rise of a neoliberal strategy of capitalist accumulation and the projection of class power, albeit in a different context of state formation and restructuring.[16] These changing dynamics in the spatial orbit of capital are, perhaps, neatly captured in the artwork that closes the first part of the book, Oswaldo Sagástegui's *Orbitas* [1983], which reveals Mexico's newfound place in the global political economy of the 1980s. Part II of the book provides three studies—on intellectuals and the state, democratization, and struggles of resistance—that lay claim to contesting the construction of the revolution and the modern state in Mexico. Chapter 5 traces the contradictory social function of intellectuals in the shadow of Mexican state formation processes in, perhaps, contesting the historical conditions of passive revolution. Given that the literature on the "new cultural history" of Mexico has highlighted Carlos Fuentes as pivotal in producing the definitive statement of revisionist historical narrative, combined with his ambiguous ties to the "hegemonic activity of the state" (see Joseph, Rubenstein, Zolov 2001: 5), the specific literary and political activity of this figure receives detailed examination. Passive revolution finds its expression not only in the spatial dimension of architecture and state power but also in its literature characteristic of modern Mexico. In light of this chapter and arguments elsewhere throughout the book it should be evident that there is a clear break with the supposed traits of "monochromatic Marxism," deemed so dissatisfying in Latin American historiography (Knight 2006: 353n33). Chapter 6 explores the much heralded "transition" to democracy in Mexico as a central element of the passive revolution of capital and the reorganization of the capitalist type of state and class power that it has entrained. Here, democratization is understood as a specific strategy in which the class relations of capitalism are reorganized on a new basis within the uneven developmental conditions inscribing state space. As a restorative strategy, democratic "transition" is therefore a quintessential aspect of passive revolution. While the struggle-driven and crisis-torn course of uneven development appears throughout the book, chapter 7 examines the origins and advance of spaces of resistance shaping the agrarian landscape in Mexico, in the case of the Ejército Zapatista de Liberación Nacional (EZLN). After all, as Henri Lefebvre (1978/2009: 235) reminds us, "revolt can and must start from the presentation of counter-projects, of counter-spaces, leading to sometimes violent protests, and culminating in a radical revolt that calls into question the entirety of interchangeable, spectacular space." Relating back to the general concerns of passive revolution and modern state formation, the Zapatista experience is regarded as pivotal in reconsidering the construction and contestation of Mexico's faltered entrance into modernity and in commanding space by formulating what are recognized as "antipassive revolution" strategies of resistance. Cutting across the focus in this book on the historical sociology of modern state formation in Mexico and the constructed and contested class practices characteristic of a passive revolution, three features merit some detailed deliberation in the conclusion. Therefore, chapter 8 analyzes, first, the continuum of passive revolution, meaning its relatively "permanent" character within historically specific circumstances, as a hallmark of postcolonial state formation in the throes of uneven and combined development. This then provides, second, an opportunity to reflect on the possible temporal and spatial occurrence of passive revolutions in world history, demanding some pointers on how best to methodologically relate instances of passive revolution in a comparative manner. Finally, the book closes with a reflection on the trends of contemporary capitalism and the current adaptive capacity of neoliberalism in order to critique the emerging configuration of postneoliberalism, shaping the contemporary Mexican state and the present political economy of Latin America.

NOTES

1. Jesús Escobedo's original artwork *Las clases* [1939] was displayed as part of the exhibition, *México y la estampa moderna: Una revolución en las artes gráficas, 1920–1950*, at the Museo Nacional de Arte, Mexico City (2 April–8 June 2008), which the author attended.

2. LEAR, "Notas y actividades de la LEAR," *Frente a Frente* [August 1936]: 23 as cited in Azuela (1993): 86.

3. In an overlapping but also distinct event to that held in Mexico City, Jesús Escobedo's *Como combatir el fascismo* [1939] was displayed as part of the exhibition, *Revolution on Paper: Mexican Prints, 1910–1960*, at the British Museum, London (22 October 2009–5 April 2010), again which the author attended.

4. Elsewhere, a noteworthy focus on historical state formation in Turkey can be noted (see Tuğal 2009), which traces the integration of both secularism and capitalism as a condition of passive revolution. However, Erol (2010: 539) has argued that "Tuğal's failure to grasp the historical materialist dimensions of concepts such as hegemony and passive revolution in the context of Turkey emanate from his lack of engagement with Gramsci's own leitmotiv or rhythm of thought."

5. Further critiques of "statolatry" in historical sociology and Mexican studies, its teleological account of history, and its overemphasis on state breakdown can be found in Knight (1985: 10–11); Knight (1986b: 3); Knight (1990a); and Tutino (1986: 20–21, 367–68). The pejorative term *statolatry* was coined by Gramsci to refer to a sole concentration on features of political leadership associated with state functionaries, entailing a view of the state as a perpetual entity limited to actors within political society, see Gramsci (1971: 178, Q13§17); Gramsci (2007: 310–11, Q8§130). A specific convention associated with citing the *Prison Notebooks* is adopted throughout this book. In addition to giving the reference to the selected anthologies, the notebook number (Q) and section (§) accompanies all citations, to enable the reader to trace their specific collocation. The concordance table used is that compiled by Marcus Green and is available at the website of the International Gramsci Society, http://www.internationalgramscisociety.org/.

6. *The Economist* [London], "Time to Wake Up: A Survey of Mexico" (18 November 2006): 7–9. Subsequently, the same newspaper captured differentiated geographical space in Mexico thus: "Monterrey, Mexico's northern industrial capital, is starting to resemble Texas. Many parts of the south still look like a northern extension of Guatemala," see *The Economist* [London], "A Tale of Two Mexicos" (26 April 2008): 53–54.

7. *Financial Times* [London], "Minister Sees Fully Developed Mexico in 20 years" (15 February 2007): 6. Of course, Carstens was previously deputy managing director of the International Monetary Fund (IMF) from 2003 to 2006.

8. *The Economist* [London], "A One-Two Punch" (29 May 2010): 54.

9. As a depiction and contestation of spatial configurations, Subcomandante Marcos has articulated the notion of *una geografía revuelta* as an apposite account of the condition of uneven development in Mexico, see El Kilombo Intergaláctico (2007: 22–29) and the EZLN's essay "7 piezas sueltas del rompecabezas mundial" [The seven loose pieces of the global jigsaw puzzle], June 1997 (EZLN 2003, vol. 4: 47–72).

10. This section draws, in part, from the discussion present in Morton (2007a) and Morton (2010b), which the reader may find useful in presenting a more detailed overview of passive revolution.

11. The term *passive revolution* can be linked to Vincenzo Cuoco (1770–1823) and his account of the 1799 revolution, or Parthenopian Republic, in Naples as well as the coupling "revolution-restoration" coined by the French historian Edgar Quinet (1803–1875). There is also a rather differently rendered precursor to the term evident in Thomas Paine's *Rights of Man* where it is stated: "In contemplating revolutions, it is easy to perceive that they may arise from two distinct causes: the one, to avoid or get rid of some great calamity; the other, to obtain some great and positive good: *and the two may be distinguished by the names of active and passive revolutions.* In those which proceed from the former cause, the temper becomes soured; and the redress, obtained by danger, is too often sullied by revenge. But in those which proceed from the latter . . . reason and discussion, persuasion and conviction, become the weapons in the contest, and it is only when those are attempted to be suppressed that recourse is had to violence" (Paine 1791/1985: 269).

12. A reflection on the historical experience of failed revolution in Argentina, in Nicolás Casullo's *Las cuestiones*, is also relevant here with its resonances across other Latin American countries, see Casullo (2007, 2009).

13. See Chatterjee (1986: 46–47) on the appreciation of the passive revolution of capital in relation to modern state formation.

14. Knight (2002a: 197–99) also notes the "strongly Anglo-centric lens" of this literature to state "but what works for England (if, indeed, it does) may not work for the rest of Europe, still less for the rest of the world." At the same time, dismissing grand theorists simply on the basis of their European origins would be distinctly parochial for, to some degree, "it is not the provenance, but the utility, of theories that matters" (Knight 2001: 204).

15. See the excellent feature on Nacho López in the journal of photography and culture, *Luna Córnea*, número 31, ed. Patricia Gola (México, DF: Consejo Nacional para la Cultura y las Artes, 2007), which carries the now famous series of photographs of his girlfriend strolling down Avenida Juárez, with the Monument to the Revolution in the background, in full bourgeois regalia set amid the skyscrapers of modernizing Mexico City. The chauvinist and stereotypical dimensions of this photo-essay are pursued in various contributions to the issue.

16. The irony of NAFINSA's own transformation over the years, marked most recently by the appointment during Felipe Calderón's administration of Héctor Rangel Domene, as director general, in January 2009, has not been lost in Mexico. Previously, Héctor Rangel Domene had been president of the Consejo Coordinador Empresarial (CCE) [2002–2004] and president of the Centro de Estudios Económicos del Sector Privado (CEESP) [2007–2008], leading fractions of transnational capital in Mexico. At the time of writing, he is also director general of the Banco Nacional de Comercio Exterior (BANCOMEXT), aimed at fostering the "entrepreneurial" feature of small and medium-sized businesses, see *La Jornada*, "Calderón entrega NAFIN y BANCOMEXT a sus amigos," 1 December 2008.

Part I

CONSTRUCTING REVOLUTION
AND STATE IN MODERN MEXICO

Chapter Two

Mexican Revolution, Primitive Accumulation, Passive Revolution

This study aims to make a substantive contribution to the debate on the emergence of capitalism and modern state formation in Mexico by offering a focus on transformations in social property relations that unfolded as a result of the Mexican Revolution (1910–1920). As mentioned in the previous chapter, my focus relates to discussions across Mexican studies and the historical sociology of international relations (HSIR) on the rise of capitalism and state formation, while asserting how the history of passive revolution contributes to understanding the constitutive class struggles involved in constructing the modern Mexican state. A key argument, underlying the theme of the book as a whole, is that the social origins of the transition to capitalist modernity in the making of modern Mexico can be understood as a passive revolution. This means that within the conditioning situation of uneven and combined development the Mexican Revolution resulted in a passive revolution whereby state intervention and mass mobilization from below shaped capital accumulation and political modernization resulting in a form of capitalism consistent with both authoritarian and national-popular appeal. To cite Eric Hobsbawm (1987: 286), "the Mexican Revolution is significant, because it was directly born of the contradictions within the world empire, and because it was the first of the great revolutions in the colonial and dependent world in which the labouring masses played a major part."

This chapter details the theorizing of political modernity offered by Antonio Gramsci and his contribution to understanding the international history of state formation and processes intrinsic to the rise of the modern capitalist states-system (see Morton 2005; Morton 2007a; Morton 2007b; Morton 2007c). It is argued that the case of the Mexican Revolution offers a fruitful opportunity in which to provide an account of the passive revolution of capital and thus the class strategy of state formation processes in the making of a modern state. The notion of passive revolution refers to processes of state formation that arise within a framework consonant with capitalist social property relations. As outlined in chapter 1, a passive revolution is linked to the process of modern state formation as the necessary precondition for the establishment of capitalism (Gramsci 1971: 106–7, Q15§17). It is perhaps for this reason that the historian John Womack (1978: 97–98) has asserted that if any of the conditions of European history can be compared with the Mexican experience it would not be the French or Russian Revolution, but the Italian Risorgimento.[1] Recalling the discussion in the preceding chapter, this was itself understood as a case of passive revolution and mode of capitalist "transition" where bourgeois hegemony is not accomplished but the creation of a modern state becomes the requirement for social development. In order to propel the argument, this chapter is structured into five sections.

The first section extends the discussion on the notion of passive revolution by highlighting its relevance to understanding the unevenness of development and thus how social formations combine, at different stages, precapitalist and capitalist relations. "It is false," writes Leon Trotsky (1929/2004: 23), "that world economy is simply a sum of national parts of one and the same type. . . . In reality, the national peculiarities represent an original combination of the basic features of the world process." This section analyzes in more detail the affinal relation of uneven and combined development and passive revolution in accounting for such national peculiarities in Mexico set against the background of geopolitical capitalist pressures. Hence the significance of situating the theory of passive revolution alongside cognate considerations of uneven and combined development, or the "whip of external necessity" (Trotsky 1936/1980: 28), in order to develop an account of processes of primitive accumulation and capitalist expansion relevant to the rise of the modern state in Mexico. My argument in this chapter breaks new ground by drawing together the relevancy of theorizations on passive revolution and uneven and combined development to the case history of the Mexican Revolution and its specificities and peculiarities in terms of class struggle, capitalist accumulation, and patterns of state formation.

The second section widens the relevance of the themes of primitive accumulation, uneven and combined development, and passive revolution to land tenure arrangements in Latin America and the arrangement of property relations confronting Mexico prior to the Mexican Revolution. The third section then details how the understanding of state formation as the passive revolution of capital within conditions of uneven and combined development proves advantageous in relation to interpretations of the Mexican Revolution as a "bourgeois revolution." Two following sections then address specific moments in the struggle between social class forces in Mexico between 1920 and 1940, which eventually resulted in conditions of passive revolution. A series of continuities *and* changes in the arrangement of social property relations in Mexico during the period 1920–1940 are highlighted in the fourth section, which adds further strength to understanding it as an era of passive revolution. As the administration of Lázaro Cárdenas (1934–1940) is widely regarded as the period when the state consolidated a social basis of support, a fifth section then analyzes to what extent Cardenismo went beyond the politics of passive revolution to secure a minimal form of hegemony under the auspices of the evolving state-party of the Partido Revolucionario Institucional (PRI). The circumstances in which the state was formed—including the nature of social class forces on which it was based—gave Mexican capitalism a particular form. Yet, it will be argued, this should not be seen as part of an inexorable drive toward state formation and state-building. Throughout the period, political developments were part of an open-ended struggle between contesting social class forces. This was the case during the initial phase of passive revolution in Mexico as much as it was during subsequent periods in the country's reordering of capitalism. As argued in the chapter's conclusion, theorizing the history of Mexico as the history of passive revolution assists most directly in addressing the form of class strategy that has had a persistent bearing on social development and state transformation within the world market conditions of expanding capitalism up to the present day. Subsequent chapters will then elaborate the ongoing presence of the contradictions of passive revolution throughout the history of modern Mexico, commencing in chapter 3 with the consolidation of the modern state under import substitution industrialization (ISI).

APPROACHING PASSIVE REVOLUTION: GIVING THE OLD REGIMES A POWERFUL SHOVE

Distinct processes of state formation and associated forms of sovereignty evident in the postcolonial world emerged historically within a global division of labor that was also shaped by the expansion of capitalism and the unevenness of development characterized by a combination of capitalist, precapitalist, and semicapitalist social relations (see also Massey 1995). Put differently, the *combined* geopolitical circumstances of the modern states-system are embedded within the context of the socially *uneven* worldwide spread of capitalism. The foremost theoretician of this expression of the world historical process of uneven and combined development and its impact on states' adaptation to the world economy is, of course, Leon Trotsky. "Unevenness," in his regard, "is the most general law of the historic process [that] reveals itself most sharply and complexly in the destiny of the backward countries" (Trotsky 1936/1980: 28). Due to the unevenness of the developmental process, features appropriate to different historical periods become combined within the character of a social formation. Therefore a "peculiar mixture of backward elements with the most modern factors" arises within a social formation confronted with insertion into, and catch-up with, the expanding system of capitalism (Trotsky 1936/1980: 31–32, 36, 72). In the case of Russia, "the law of uneven development brought it about that the contradiction between the technique and property relations of capitalism shattered the weakest link in the world chain" (Trotsky 1937/1972: 299).

While it has been argued that the theory of uneven and combined development is a "rather fragmentary and undeveloped conception" (Romagnolo 1975: 8n.2),[2] it can be countered that such a historical sociological generalization provides a useful guide to the investigation and analysis of the fusion of precapitalist and capitalist relations within postcolonial states and is "indispensable for understanding the development of Latin America over the past four centuries" (Novack 1976: 103; Novack 1972: 189). This is because, following Ernest Mandel (1975: 46–61, 85–103), the process of uneven and combined development has contributed greatly to shaping state sovereignty and economic development in postcolonial states. The uneven tendencies of capitalist development have thus unfolded within the framework of an already existing world market and international states-system (see Teschke 2003: 152; Lacher 2006: 79–83; Rosenberg 2006: 308–13). This also means that the international growth and spread of capitalism in postcolonial states occurs through ongoing processes of primitive accumulation. The latter classically entails both the dispossession of the peasantry of their land through appropriation and concentration and the displacement of "politically" constituted property by "economic" power involving a "historical process of divorcing the producer from the means of production" generating propertyless individuals compelled to sell their labor (Marx 1887/1996: 705–6). Yet, due to the presence of a territorialized framework, processes of primitive accumulation become heavily reliant on the state as the locus of capital accumulation. The momentum of primitive accumulation thus employs "the power of the state, the concentrated and organised force of society, *to hasten, hothouse fashion*, the process of transformation of the feudal mode of production into the capitalist mode" (Marx 1887/1996: 739, emphasis added). As Marx (1887/1996: 752) also indicated, where economic conditions are less developed, the process of primitive accumulation proceeds alongside antiquated property relations that may "continue to exist side by side with it in gradual decay." The result is a "statified" form of development through which the reproduction of capitalist property relations become extended via a process of *permanent primitive accumulation*, rather than as a momentary historical epoch, in which the peasantry constantly faces its own demise (see Marx 1894/1998: 246; Trotsky 1938/1979: 790; Amin 1974: 3; Bartra 1982: 46; Bartra 1993: 29, 75–78). "Much has therefore depended on how the state has been constituted and by whom, and what the state was and is able or prepared to do in support of or in opposition to processes of capital accumulation" (Harvey 2003a: 91).[3] Following Marx's reflections on state force within the colonial system *as itself* an economic power, Mandel then pointedly notes that in these instances the state comes to act as the "midwife of modern capitalism" (Marx 1887/1996: 739; Mandel 1975: 54). It is within the conditioning situation of the uneven and combined development of different relations of production and through the specific class conflicts ascribed to processes of capital accumulation that the history of state formation can be related to conditions of passive revolution.

Gramsci cast the uneven and combined development of capitalism across the eighteenth and nineteenth centuries and subsequently as a series of "passive revolutions." As described in chapter 1, the condition of passive revolution was initially developed to explain the Risorgimento, the movement for Italian national liberation that culminated in the political unification of the country in 1860–1861. The notion of passive revolution was then subsequently expanded to encompass a whole series of other historical phenomena. As Fred Halliday (1999: 246) notes, "in the case of the uncompleted bourgeois revolution in Italy itself . . . [Gramsci] had a powerful example of the impact of combined and uneven development." Gramsci thus came to frame capitalist expansion as a world historical phenomenon within conditions of uneven and combined development through varied forms of passive revolution. While rooted in his writings on the crisis of the liberal state in Italy, the notion of passive revolution was also thus linked to historical transformations across Europe cast in the shadow of revolutionary French Jacobinism:

> The "passive" aspect of the great revolution which started in France in 1789 and which spilled over into the rest of Europe with the republican and Napoleonic armies . . . [gave] the old régimes a powerful shove . . . resulting not in their immediate collapse as in France but in the "reformist" corrosion of them which lasted up to 1870. (Gramsci 1971: 119, Q10I§9)

According to Gramsci, the French Revolution established a "bourgeois" state on the basis of national-popular support and the elimination of old feudal classes yet, elsewhere in Europe, the institution of political forms suitable to the expansion of capitalism occurred differently. Hence, highlighting "differences between France, Germany and Italy in the process by which the bourgeoisie took power (and England)," for, "it was in France that the process was richest in development, and in active and positive political elements" (Gramsci 1971: 82–83, Q19§24). This was indicative of mid-nineteenth-century European national unifications during which the masses became ancillaries of change organized from above based on elite-led projects. It was a process that in other parts of the world would take on a mimetic dimension, as "countries seeking to break through modernity are normally derivative and unoriginal in their ideas, though necessarily not so in their practices" (Hobsbawm 1975: 73, 166).[4] The result was a process of fundamental ruptural change that was nevertheless lacking national-popular appeal in founding bourgeois hegemony within the modern state. A passive revolution, concurrent with the discussion in the previous chapter, thus represents a blocked dialectic of progressive and reactionary elements, described as "revolution-restoration" or "revolution without revolution" (Gramsci 1992: 137, Q1§44). The point to underline here is the need to appreciate specific state effects within conditions of passive revolution or, "the significance of a 'Piedmont'-type function . . . i.e. the fact that a state replaces the local social groups in leading a struggle of renewal" (Gramsci 1971: 105–6, Q15§59). In the case of Italy, the theory exposed a situation whereby the "bourgeoisie obtained economic-industrial power, but the old feudal classes remained as the government stratum of the political class" (Gramsci 1971: 83, Q19§24). It is this weakness in the "function of Piedmont" that then becomes the analogue to state-building attempts elsewhere marking the history of nineteenth- and twentieth-century state formation processes. Passive revolution is therefore a condition that reveals continuities and changes within the order of capital, or processes that exemplify the inability of a ruling class to fully integrate the masses through conditions of hegemony. Hence a situation when "more or less far-reaching modifications . . . into the economic structure of the country" are made in a situation of "'domination without that of 'leadership': dictatorship without hegemony" (Gramsci 1995: 350, Q10I§9; Gramsci 1971: 106, Q15§59). That is why the concept of passive revolution, according to Gramsci, applies not only to Italy but also to various state formation processes confronted with the lack of established bourgeois hegemony (Gramsci 1996: 232, Q4§57).

As a general criterion of interpretation, then, the theory of passive revolution can be identified with various concrete historical instances when aspects of the social relations of capitalist development are constituted. This can proceed in two ways. First, with reference to a revolution without mass participation, or a "revolution from above," involving elite-engineered social and political reform that draws on foreign capital and associated ideas while lacking a national-popular base. At the same time, however, the notion of passive revolution should not be limited to this understanding. It is equally used in a linked but alternate, second, sense to capture how a revolutionary form of political transformation is pressed into a conservative project of restoration. In this second sense, passive revolution is linked to insurrectionary mass mobilization from below while such class demands are restricted so that "changes in the world of production are accommodated within the current social formation" (Sassoon 1987: 207; see Femia 1981: 260n.74). A passive revolution therefore becomes a technique of statecraft that an emergent bourgeois class may deploy by drawing in subaltern social classes while establishing a new state on the basis of the constitution of capitalism (Riley and Desai 2007). It is in this second sense that the outcome of the Mexican Revolution can be referred to as a period of passive revolution.

This means recognizing how the modern state comes to impose itself on society and space through an attempt to homogenize relations of power. This "statifying" tendency of power to equalize and mediatize social development animated Henri Lefebvre (1991: 23) when he noted how "the modern state is consolidating on a world scale . . . imposing analogous, if not homologous, measures irrespective of political ideology, historical background, or the class origins of those in power." As David Harvey (2003a: 101) clarifies, "the molecular processes of capital accumulation operating in space and time generate passive revolutions in the geographical patterning of capital accumulation." In sum, the strategy of "passive revolution becomes the historical path by which a 'national' development of capital can occur without resolving or surmounting those contradictions" of capital (Chatterjee 1986: 43). It not only represents the type of emergent class strategy undertaken in establishing and maintaining the expansion of the capitalist state but also the ways in which capitalism is subsequently forced to revolutionize itself *whenever* hegemony is weakened or a social formation cannot cope with the need to expand the forces of production (Sassoon 1987: 210). "To sharpen it," adds Chatterjee (1986: 30), "one must examine several historical cases of 'passive revolutions' in their economic, political and ideological aspects."

HEADACHES FOR HISTORIANS

The contradictory blend of conservative and revolutionary elements that constituted the Mexican Revolution continues to provide, as Alan Knight (1994a: 393) has commented, headaches for historians. The issues that divide historians range from disagreement about the *processes* that influenced political mobilization during the revolution, to dispute about the overall *outcome* of the Mexican Revolution, to divergences over the era most pivotal to the development of capitalism in Mexico. Did the Mexican Revolution elicit genuinely popular political mobilization? Was real sociostructural change wrought as a result of revolutionary upheaval? What was the function of the revolution in furthering conditions for patterns of capitalist development? The headaches are made worse, however, if we agree with Adolfo Gilly that the massive operation of dispossession wrought by the primitive accumulation of property ensued through the growth of capitalist relations under Porfirio Díaz (1876–1911), exemplified among other developments by the influx of foreign capital and the expansion of the railway as "the very symbol of capitalist penetration in the territory of Mexico" (Gilly 1971/2007: 40–45).[5] Or, if we accord with John Foran's (2005: 7, 34–46) analysis of the Mexican Revolution, as a "success" case in the history of revolution. My argument in this book is that an alternative historical interpretation of the social relations of capitalist development in Mexico is provided by drawing from the notion of passive revolution and relating it to the outcome of the Mexican Revolution.

A clear point of departure is evident here from the "pan-capitalist" thesis of dependency theory and world-system analysis (see Harris 1978: 5). This is because it would be mistaken to assume *either* the capitalist character of colonial Mexico linked to *hacienda* production *or* that the history of the Porfiriato similarly revolved around the propulsion of national capitalism through the *hacienda* system. Clarification of this point is necessary given the recent claim that "many of the ideas raised by the dependency writers of the 1960s and early 1970s continue to retain a contemporary validity" (Slater 2004: 118). In relation to dependency theory, it is argued that the principal flaw is a confidence in the logic of commercialization on latifundia as emblematic of the practices of capitalism (see Frank 1969a: 14). In addition, the assumption that these practices of colonial capitalism "made their appearance in Latin America in the sixteenth century" to initiate underdeveloped development in colonial metropolises and structural underdevelopment in satellite peripheries is equally problematic (see Frank 1969a: 14–15; Frank 1969b: 20, 27; Cockcroft et al., 1972: xi, xvii). The reasoning here is because capitalist development is presumed to be always-already nested within the means of appropriation specific to the practices of precapitalist land tenure arrangements in Mexico and Latin America based on the commercialization of agriculture within a world mercantile capitalist system (see Frank 1979: 5–7, 78–84). Additionally, dependency theory has been criticized for its inattentiveness to an analysis of substantive instances of social agency in terms of the relations of class formation and class struggle (Henfrey 1981: 32–34).

With reference to world-system analysis, problems similarly arise in delineating the *differentia specifica* of capitalist development due to the predominant focus on efficient and expanded productivity by means of a *world market* mechanism supported by expanded territorial state sovereignty rather than transformations in property relations in the sphere of production (Wallerstein 1974: 36–38). The genesis of capitalism is therefore held to be "production for sale in a market in which the object is to realise the maximum profit" (Wallerstein 1979: 15). The basic expansion of capitalism is then regarded to be the transformation of trade in surpluses through commodity exchange linking different regions based on a predominant division of labor between formerly "free" wage labor in the core, sharecropping in the semiperiphery, and forced (coerced cash crop) labor in the periphery (Wallerstein 1974: 91). Despite world-system analysis viewing capitalism as a combination of free and coercive labor within the capitalist system (therefore differing from the more rigid "developed metropole-underdeveloped satellite" division of labor of dependency theory), the long-standing critiques of both these perspectives can confidently be reasserted. These are that both approaches (1) recall neo-classical political economy with their emphasis on market relations and end up "assuming away the fundamental problem of the transformation of class relations" by assimilating the emergence of markets and merchants within the trade-centered impulses of commercial development (Laclau 1971/1977: 46; Brenner 1977: 39); and (2) result in a "descriptive gap" between the international division of labor posited and the history of labor and surplus extraction in Latin America all of which combines to mask the rupture of capitalist development in the region (Stern 1988: 865–66). Overall, with regard to both dependency theory and world-system analysis, "capitalism is simply more trade, more markets, more towns, and above all, a rising 'middle class'" (Wood 1991: 7).

Instead, colonial land tenure arrangements in Latin America are held to revolve around (1) the large estate or latifundia that represents a form of the early encomienda and later slave plantations, generally characterized by the utilization of various forms of labor exploitation based on extraeconomic co-ercion (labor-rent, rent-in-kind); (2) sharecropping based on payment through labor services; and (3) smallholder communities based on subsistence pro-duction. From these social property relations, the agrarian sector comes to represent (but not mirror) feudal or semifeudal arrangements (Fernández and Ocampo 1974: 44–46). In Mexico, the Spanish colonial regime inherited from its Aztec predecessor certain features of surplus extraction based on the appropriation of surplus product in the form of tax or labor services in kind. This entailed surplus extraction through the substitution of pre-Conquest patterns of political authority by the Spanish Crown (a tributary form) *and* the creation of heritable latifundia worked by dependent peons based on the private appropriation of surplus in the form of rent or labor services in kind (a landlord form). From the point of view of social property relations, colonial Mexico was a "feudal" creation of a feudal Spain (Knight 2002a: 183–84,

200). What this means is that the economy cannot be simply regarded as capitalist, given that the mass of the labor force was subject to extraeconomic coercion, or was unfree, and at the same time was producing for the market in which the main goal of landowners was commodity exchange (Steenland 1975: 49–58). The above social property relations marked the Habsburg colony as well as its successor Bourbon New Spain albeit with major social and political changes throughout the mid-seventeenth-century processes of introverted development (*desarrollo hacia adentro*) and the export-led growth (*desarrollo hacia afuera*) era of the later eighteenth century (Knight 2002b: 202–6). Despite the stirrings of a commercial economy and the political ambition of forging a strong centralized state, the Bourbons could not set off capitalist dynamism in New Spain. While national independence was set in motion in 1810 this eventually took the form of a conservative transformation leaving the old socioeconomic order intact; although the Liberal reform of 1857 did significantly result in further expropriation of church properties and concessions to landowners in northern Mexico as well as the dispossession of Indian village lands to existing and new *latifundistas* (Otero 1999: 34–35). Overall, postcolonial Mexico was bequeathed a centralized state that reflected the essential hallmarks of feudal social property relations in which the agrarian economy was predominantly based on surplus extracted from direct peasant producers by the landed class; subsistence production coexisted with production for the market; and the mobility of factors of production was limited (Knight 2002b: 185–201, 240–69; but see Semo 1993: 141–57, for a conflicting view).

Elements of these land tenure arrangements and the traits of state centralization endured throughout the Porfiriato. The internal structure of agrarian social property relations in Porfirian Mexico was based on *hacienda* production centered around a combination of direct extraeconomic coercion through continued forms of debt-peonage and labor-rent, whereby peons received plots of land in return for work on the demesne alongside payments in kind, contract labor, and subsistence agriculture, which all inhibited a shift toward free wage labor (Knight 1985: 20–21). As Marx (1887/1996: 178n.2) adds, "in some states, particularly Mexico . . . slavery is hidden under the form of *peonage*. By means of advances, repayable in labour . . . not only the individual labourer, but his family, become, *de facto*, the property of other persons and their families." The uneven development of Mexican agriculture, however, created an important regional heterogeneity in such property relations and class structures (Otero 1999: 9). In central and southern Mexico under Spanish colonial power, so-called free villages existed under the jurisdiction of *corregidores* (Spanish officials in charge of overseeing Indian populations), different from *hacendados* controlling peon producers, that continued to exist after colonial rule but became subject under the Díaz regime to large-scale expropriation and political subordination (see Katz 1981: 5–21). These conditions differed from the northern frontier states of Sonora, Chihuahua, and Coahuila that under the Spanish crown were subject to military settlement aimed at pacifying Apache incursions. By 1885 the Mexican frontier region was secured in this respect while the northern military communities became subjected to the expropriation of land and the suppression of traditional rights including municipal autonomy. The Yaqui Indians, inhabiting the fertile regions of Sonora including the Yaqui Valley, also experienced a concentrated offensive to seize their lands and were defeated by the Díaz regime in 1908. Both groups, the frontiersmen and the Indians, thus experienced expropriation of lands during the Díaz regime. Elsewhere, on northern *haciendas* in the Laguna area of Coahuila and Durango, producers came to experience debt peonage less directly, with the *tiendas de raya* (company stores) used more as supplementary incentives to increase production than as a means to ensure debt servitude as in the center of the country. These permanent resident peons on northern *haciendas* would later revolt together with their *hacendados* during the Mexican Revolution. "Like medieval lords in Europe, some of the landowners of Sonora and the Laguna even led their well-paid and well-treated peons into battle" (Katz 1981: 14).

The Porfiriato therefore pushed Mexico's rural population along a continuum that extended from the peon to the free peasant (on some *haciendas*) and dependent proletarian status, albeit with representatives of the latter concentrated in enclaves dominated by foreign capital (in railway construction, raw materials extraction, petroleum production) rather than by capitalist society as a whole (Hodges and Gandy 1979: 9, 76–77; Katz 1981: 12; Hodges and Gandy 2002a: 14–15; Knight 2007: 159). Capital was therefore to a considerable extent of foreign origin imported into Mexico. This meant that the growth in market relations was not accompanied by the spread of productive free wage labor, that forms of debt peonage and sharecropping continued to thrive, and that the domestic market remained limited thus restricting the scope for capital accumulation (Knight 1990a: 187). Thus, as "injections of foreign capital into the economy brought spurts of uneven development" (Hodges and Gandy 1979: 9), the Porfiriato was marked by the dominance of capital from abroad. Despite the expropriations of the liberal reforms of 1857 or the later dispossession of colonists and frontiersmen by *hacendados* during the Porfiriato, the development of capitalism in Mexico followed less the route of the "junker road"—based on the slow transformation of landholdings (*haciendas*) into capitalist enterprises that was blocked—and more the route of the "farmer road"—based on the violent destruction of estates (*latifundia*) and the breakup of the dominant traditional landowning classes through revolution and land reform (Lenin 1907/1962: 241–43, 422). The "farmer road" entailed far-reaching social differentiation in the countryside through the creation of an emerging rural petty bourgeoisie, rural producers, and/or propertyless proletarians compelled to sell their labor through the "non-political" or "purely economic" means of social power mediated by the market (Bartra 1975: 126–27; de Janvry 1981: 106–9). As Knight (1985: 20) summarizes, "capitalist development required kulakisation and/or proletarianisation not just on definitional grounds, but also as a practical prerequisite of the creation of a domestic market, of capital accumulation, and of industrialisation" in Mexico. For, as outlined in chapter 1, Marx specified that the historical conditions of the existence of capital are constituted not by the mere circulation of commodities but by the condition of the "free" laborer, which comprises a world's history. "Capital, therefore, announces from its first appearance a new epoch in the process of social production" (Marx 1887/1996: 180). It is to this new epoch, the age of capital, in Mexico that attention now turns and to the specific configuration of class forces linked to capitalist social property relations arising as a consequence of the Mexican Revolution, which is understood as a blocked dialectic of revolution-restoration or as a passive revolution.

THE FAIRY STORIES OF "BOURGEOIS REVOLUTION"

At its apogee between 1910 and 1915 the Mexican Revolution was a popular agrarian- and peasant-based movement that led to widespread agrarian and social reform in the postrevolutionary era, especially during the administration of Lázaro Cárdenas (1934–1940). Accounts of the "institutional" phase of the revolution are part of longer narratives of sociopolitical change linked to either a popular-revolutionary outcome or a qualified bourgeois outcome that may well be variations on a well-worn theme akin to fairy stories (Knight 1990a: 198). The institutions constructed during the Díaz regime were physically shattered by the revolution, and this led to the emergence of social class forces, through nascent peasant leagues and trade unions and the circulation of state elites and changes in political rhetoric (Knight 1985: 17). "By 1940 a complete land reform had smashed the semifeudal landowning class and issued in a capitalist society" (Hodges and Gandy 2002a: 37). However, the period 1920–1940 should not be seen as a simple saga of state formation, nation-building, and capital accumulation. The program of radical reform in the 1930s was the outcome of broad peasant rebellion during the Mexican Revolution based on the possession of powerful rural visions that sustained overlapping class struggles in a situation of multiple sovereignty (Knight

1985: 9–10, 17). It therefore went beyond the mere consolidation of neo-Porfirian elites or the construction of a cynical, centralizing state (Knight 1992a: 172–73).

Concurrently, a complex mix of Constitutionalist generals, Obregón's senior officers, and other functionaries and politicians emerged. Additionally, "as at the time of the French Revolution, the old possessing classes punished by the revolution grew ever more brazen in pursuing family ties with the self-seeking new bourgeoisie" (Gilly 1971/2007: 146). As Gilly (1971/2007: 208) continues to detail, "they would enrich themselves with a voracity comparable to that of the bourgeoisie in the Great French Revolution, constituting a layer of new *latifundistas* and 'revolutionary' *nouveaux riches* later represented by the government of the Mexican bourgeoisie, and fusing with the remnants of the Porfirian oligarchy through a variety of deals, marriages and other such business contracts." Examples here would include the Banco Nacional de México, formed in 1884 and controlled by French capital in the form of the Banque de Paris et des Pays Bas, that survived the Porfiriato and became managed in the 1920s by the Legorreta family; the Barcelonnette group, individuals and families who emigrated from the French province of Barcelonnette to Mexico and collaborated with the Banque de Paris et des Pays Bas to form the Société Financiere pour l'Industrie au Mexique—key to commercial, financial, and real estate operations in Mexico including the establishment of major department stores such as El Puerto de Liverpool and El Palacio de Hierro; or the case of Aarón Sáenz who made the transition as a member of the general staff within the Constitutionalist Army to hold sub-cabinet and cabinet posts in the 1920s and 1930s to become a member of the national bourgeoisie (see Córdova 1973: 376–77; Hamilton 1982a: 38–44; Hamilton 1982b: 46–9, 87–90).

Therefore, while the peasantry became an active agent in the revolution, it did not bring it to fruition because of the entrenched interests just described, the development of a national bourgeoisie, and the ambiguous role played by the emergent urban/industrial working class, which precluded an alliance between proletariat and peasantry (Hamilton 1982b: 143). As Knight (1986a: 433) states, "there was no grand alliance between peasant and proletarian." Thus, despite the fact that the peasant armies of Francisco "Pancho" Villa and Emiliano Zapata united after the Aguascalientes Convention (1914–1915) and gained control of Mexico City and two-thirds of the country, any wider proletariat-peasantry alliance was thwarted by the competing Constitutionalist Army of Venustiano Carranza and Álvaro Obregón. By 1919, Zapata was assassinated and the Constitution of 1917 made limited concessions to subaltern social classes by recognizing the collective social and political rights of workers and peasants represented by Article 27 concerning land reform and Article 123 concerning workers' legal and social protection. Yet, while the constitutional program would strengthen the development of capitalism, "it is not enough . . . to say that the 1917 Constitution was a bourgeois constitution. Undoubtedly it was, and under its protection the bourgeoisie and capitalism would undergo development in Mexico. But it is also an indirect, remote—in short, constitutionalist—testimony to the conquests of the mass struggle" (Gilly 1971/2007: 259). During the course of the revolution, an agreement between the Constitutionalist Army and the workers of Casa del Obrero Mundial succeeded in separating workers and peasants. In 1918 the formation of the first labor organization in Mexico, the Confederación Regional Obrera Mexicana (CROM), heralded the future of close relations between an interventionist state and "official" co-opted labor organizations. The failure to develop a cohesive revolutionary program increased the tactical marginalization of popular classes despite their participation in the reformist aspects of the "revolutionary" outcome (see Hesketh 2010b). The resulting relative stabilization of conditions, under the tutelage of the Constitutionalist Army in Sonora led by Obregón, Plutarco Elias Callés, and Adolfo de la Huerta and supported by the CROM, led to the election of Obregón in 1920 for a four-year presidential term. With sharp historical sociological acumen, Gilly (1971/2007: 352) reveals that, overall:

> The postrevolutionary bourgeoisie developed through this peculiar system of primitive accumulation (already proven by the European bourgeoisie centuries before), that soon invested its gain in banking, industrial and commercial concerns and went on enriching itself by the normal mechanisms of capital accumulation.

Therefore, despite the institutional and agrarian changes wrought by the revolution, it also led to enhanced capitalist social property relations, labor mobility, capital accumulation, and the formation of an integrated national market. Thus it was in some sense a "bourgeois revolution" (Knight 1990a: 182–83), "not because it was the conscious work of the bourgeoisie (still less the national bourgeoisie) . . . but rather because it gave a decisive impulse to the development of Mexican capitalism and the Mexican bourgeoisie" (Knight 1985: 26). This does not mean that the Mexican Revolution was consciously made by capitalists, but it does mean that it ushered in changes in property relations and a shift in state power as "the precondition for large scale capital accumulation and the establishment of the bourgeoisie as the dominant class" (Callinicos 1989: 124). This analysis avoids the assumption that "the bourgeoisie's rise to power is quasi-automatic" or that an already existing bourgeois form of society was constitutive of capitalism (Brenner 1989: 280). "It is more sensible . . . to judge a bourgeois revolution by the degree to which it succeeds in establishing an autonomous centre of capital accumulation, even if it fails to democratise the political order, or to eliminate feudal social relations" (Callinicos 1982: 110).

The broad aims of the Porfiriato (state-building and national development) were therefore continued, albeit haphazardly, under radically changed circumstances. Thus a combination of widespread peasant rebellion and popular mobilization safeguarded agrarian reform that was congruent in its consequences with subsequent twentieth-century Latin American patterns, for instance in Guatemala (in 1952), Bolivia (in 1952), and, to some extent, in Venezuela (in 1959) (de Janvry and Ground 1978: 91–2). The preoccupation of the nascent Mexican state was reconstruction alongside radical reform that benefited industry, deepened the domestic market, dispossessed the peasantry of their land and created propertyless wage laborers through processes of primitive accumulation, rendered agriculture more efficient, and transferred resources from countryside to city (Knight 1985: 27). The formation of the revolutionary state was not, however, a smooth passage toward the construction of a "Leviathan on the Zócalo" (see Córdova 1973: 236–47; Benjamin 1985). The state was far from established as the sole legitimate power in the provinces and was actually confronted with various social bases of agrarian violence between 1920 and 1940 (Tutino 1986: 341–47). Throughout the period, state formation was the historical product of experiences molded from above and below, based on a mix of peasant insurrection and elite reformism (Knight 1990a: 186–90; Knight 1994a: 401). Yet, "only at isolated times and places . . . were the masses able to transcend the globally bourgeois character of the revolution" (Gilly 2005: 331). Thus, in its program and outcome the Mexican Revolution can be correctly located among the classic bourgeois revolutions of historical sociology. "What emerges from bourgeois revolution is the political rule of a minority class and the development of capitalism. Yet, its rule is won by collective action" (Wolfreys 2007: 57). Evident in the Mexican Revolution, this logic grants "it a place in world history on the frontier between the last bourgeois revolutions and the first proletarian revolution, that of October 1917 in Russia" (Gilly 1979: 50). It was also, in its contradictions, the first passive revolution of the twentieth century in Latin America.

As argued above, the notion of passive revolution can be extended to a variety of historical developments (see also chapter 1). In Mexico, while agrarian reform was inaugurated and the popular masses did go through a "revolutionary" experience, there was still the constitution of political forms that suited the organization of capitalist social property relations. As Gramsci (1992: 150–51, Q1§45) once counseled, "the class relations created by industrial development induce the bourgeoisie not to struggle against the old world but to allow that part of the façade to subsist which would serve to conceal its domination." As Arnaldo Córdova (1978: 21) summarizes on the Mexican Revolution itself, "in practice the social reforms were employed as instruments of state power," to the degree that subsequent Mexican populism would have counterrevolutionary roots based on the domination and manipulation of the masses behind the façade of revolutionary rhetoric. This conservative character was reflected in the destruction of the great *haciendas* while the *hacienda* system, at least to some extent, persisted, reflecting the differences between northern and center-south agrarian property relations outlined earlier (Knight 1991a: 74, 96, 102–3). The old agrarian order was severely weakened but not entirely displaced; the old feudal classes maintained some political influence (Knight 1986b: 464–65). The "passive" aspect of this process consists in its absorbing the revolutionary potential of class forces through the state and changes in social property relations by inducing consent, exercising coercion, and engaging in co-option. Changes are accommodated within the current social formation, although, of course, not necessarily in a "passive" way. The emphasis here is on the development of property relations through state intervention—through the inclusion of new social groups within a conservative political order. There is no expansion of mass control over politics.

The state therefore comes to play an inordinate role in attempting to secure a dominant center for capital accumulation within the uneven and combined developmental conditions of the world economy. In the Russian historical context, "capitalism seemed to be an offspring of the state" (Trotsky 1919/2004: 173), and in the Mexican context "the final outcome of the revolution was expressed above all at the level of the state" (Gilly 1979: 43). The process of overcoming uneven and combined development—or "belated bourgeois development"—in colonial and postcolonial states is therefore spearheaded by social forces, including the intelligentsia, linked to state capitalism (Trotsky 1929/2004: 152; Cliff 1963/1999: 65).[6] Gramsci (1971: 58–9, Q19§24) argued that mobilization through passive revolution involved "the formation of an ever more extensive ruling class" through "the gradual but continuous absorption, achieved by methods which varied in their effectiveness, of the active elements produced by allied groups—and even of those which came from antagonistic groups and seemed irreconcilably lost." The state serves as the locus of accumulation and the construction of the political order of capital. A passive revolution is therefore secured through the political dominance of state capitalism (Callinicos 1982: 108–11; Callinicos 1989: 124, 160). In Mexico this meant maintaining "the constant state of violence, struggle and expropriation characteristic of the process of permanent primitive accumulation" (Bartra 1975: 141). A passive revolution was thus evident in the contradictions stemming from this process (Knight 1986b: 498, 500,

511). As Womack asserts (1978: 97), in capturing these contradictions, "the difference the so-called Revolution made to the country's modern history was therefore not a radical transformation but simply a reform, accomplished by violent methods but within already established limits." The bourgeois character of the Mexican state thus mystified principles of the Revolution in order to co-opt the radical demands of the popular classes to the point that counterrevolutionary ideological myths could then be propagated as a state-class strategy (O'Malley 1986: 7). Modernity in Mexico would therefore become characterized by a liminality primarily founded on a national identity oscillating between the indigenous peasant hero and the *mestizo* proletarian resulting in the incomplete and unfinished drama of capitalist consolidation (Bartra 1992: 93–94). There was a hybrid culture to Mexican modernity linked to the contradictions of capitalist expansion. "We have not had a solid industrialisation," states Néstor García Canclini, "nor an extended technologising of agricultural production, nor a socio-political ordering based on the formal and material rationality that . . . has become the common sense of the West." A result of this liminality was to be "an exuberant modernism with a deficient modernisation" (García Canclini 1995: 7, 41). In such circumstances, "the reification of the 'nation' in the body of the state becomes the means for constructing this hegemonic structure" of state power (Chatterjee 1993: 212). It is now time to focus on the further contradictions and antagonisms of continuity and change that resulted from the Mexican Revolution and the passive revolution of capital.

CONTINUITY AND CHANGE: TOWARD THE INSTITUTIONALIZED REVOLUTION

By 1920 the Sonoran generals of the Constitutionalist Army (Obregón, Calles, de la Huerta) had established a position as "victors" of the Mexican Revolution (1910–1920) over the competing factions led by Emiliano Zapata, Venustiano Carranza, and, eventually, Francisco "Pancho" Villa. This Sonoran dynasty was to preside over a period commonly recognized as the institutional phase of the revolution (1920–1940) during which the words "revolution" and "reconstruction" became synonymous (Meyer 1991: 204). Following the provisional presidency of de la Huerta, a peculiar brand of socialism was touted during the presidency of Obregón (1920–1924), who held the view that "the principal purpose of socialism is to extend a hand to the downtrodden in order to establish a greater equilibrium between capital and labour" (as cited in Cockcroft 1983: 105). The situation at the time, however, was far from stable with the state-building Sonorans having to counter the reactionary interests of the surviving Porfirian elites, contending military and civilian caudillos, and mass unrest. As a result, tactical alliances were forged with Mexico's lower classes and with U.S. interests. The 1923 Treaty of Bucareli guaranteed diplomatic recognition of the Mexican government and the exemption of U.S. capital from Article 27 of the constitution concerning the appropriation of land. An educational project led by José Vasconcelos involved the subsidization of a renaissance in the arts and literature often associated with the works of Diego Rivera and his proclivity to represent the Indian presence within Mexican modernity as an inert past or "dead world" (see Bonfil Batalla 1996: 55); although such projects had firm roots in the prerevolutionary era.[7] The budget of the Secretaría de Educación Pública (SEP) notably increased from 15 million pesos in 1921 in the year that it was established to 35 million in 1923 in an effort to bring about a reconstruction or change in *mentalité* (Meyer 1991: 208). As part of the project of state formation, the SEP assisted in building up popular support among peasants and workers for state policies. As Mary Kay Vaughan (1997: 20) has documented, the SEP helped to mobilize urban and rural society not only through notions of modernity linked to production and technology, but also through educational policies of secularism, patriotism, and popular culture by overcoming regional superstitions and practices to engender "a common language for consent and protest." By the mid-1920s, with the regime slightly more stable, a wider ideological and cultural struggle also began with an assault on the church. The promotion of deep-seated anticlericalism under President Calles (1924–1928) resulted in a violent phase of church-state conflict and the highly coercive Cristero War (1926–1929) (see Meyer 1976). This period incidentally caught the attention of Gramsci and was referred to as "Calles's Mexican Kulturkampf": a stage of anticlerical struggle that exemplified the emergence of the modern state (Gramsci 1992: 195–96, Q1§107; Gramsci 1996: 11–13, Q3§5, 207, Q4§49). This class struggle was also part of the wider effort to promote a "psychological revolution" in Mexico that would involve shifting the consciences of the people to create a "new national soul" (Knight 1994a: 402). The result of this effort, according to the novelist Carlos Fuentes (1988: 12–13), was a cultural perception of self-knowledge and national identity in Mexico that became one of the principal legacies of the Mexican Revolution. However, the attempt to integrate divergent sociopolitical and economic forces under the authority of the state was founded on continued co-optation with the prevalence of violence and coercion. Indicative of this was the assassination of Obregón in 1928 at the hands of a Catholic fanatic during the Cristero War.

A further characteristic feature of this effort to consolidate and institutionalize state-class power was the courting of the labor movement and the peasantry in the guise of class collaboration. This included fostering a close rela-tionship with trade unions, which would serve as a base of support, as well as a means of diluting more autonomous forms of class-organization. Thus the CROM was set up as a bulwark against rivals such as the Partido Nacional Agrarista (PNA), the Confederación General de Trabajadores (CGT), or the Confederación Sindical Unitaria de México (CSUM). Although the Partido Comunista Mexicano (PCM) was founded in 1919 it was relatively weak, fragmented, and caught up in syndicalist and libertarian ideas (Carr 1983: 277–305). Instead, officials of the CROM such as Luis Morones, who was ap-pointed head of the Ministry of Industry, Commerce, and Labour, developed into powerful regional and local government forces to the point that they were fully incorporated into the state apparatus (see Tardanico 1981). The virtual disappearance of the strike as a weapon of Mexican labor between 1924 and 1933 (Michaels 1970: 65–6) seems to be a strong indication of the institu-tionalization of class conflict within the emerging state, which would sub-sequently ensure political control, new social bases for the development of production, and beneficial conditions for increased capital accumulation (see Mackinlay and Otero 2004). However incomplete or porous, state dominance in this period still went beyond the fragility of the Porfiriato while maintain-ing the structural base of capitalist enterprise. As Nora Hamilton (1982b: 101–3) has argued, many of the dominant groups of the Porfiriato were able to reinstate themselves within the economic system alongside "capitalists of the revolution" who became the new bourgeoisie as wealthy *hacendados* and urban entrepreneurs (see also Tardanico 1982: 417). Restoration in postrevo-lutionary Mexico was perfectly captured in the novels by Carlos Fuentes, whose social function was linked to his position as one of the foremost cul-tural "theoreticians of the passive revolution" (Gramsci 1971: 109, Q15§11). While chapter 5 covers in detail the social function of this novelist as a pas-sive revolutionary, the general scene was depicted by him as one of "zoom-ing industrialists," such as Federico Robles in *La región más transparente* (Where the Air Is Clear, 1958), and revolutionary-cum-bourgeois parvenus, such as Artemio Cruz in *La muerte de Artemio Cruz* (The Death of Artemio Cruz, 1962). Overall, the classes of the *antiguo régimen* managed to maintain a political role while the institution of new forms of power proceeded to suit the expansion of capitalism under the tutelage of an emergent bourgeoisie. These are classic features of a situation of passive revolution.

While far-reaching modifications in Mexico's economic structure were in-troduced, those changes maintained the privileged position of principal elites, including the Sonoran dynasty that lacked any plans to transform society and, instead, sought to maintain the established order. This resulted in "a timorous, imitative, and thoroughly colonised Mexican bourgeoisie, which depend[ed] on state subsidies and patronage, easy concessions and profits without risk" (Aguilar Camín 1980: 122). Rule was maintained with coercive forms of political control and piecemeal absorption of opposition forces by the ruling elites. The way the CROM was courted epitomized these tactics (known as *trasformismo*), which involved incorporating potentially threatening leaders, alternative programs, and ideas until substantive differences could be dissolved (Gramsci 1971: 58n.8, Q19§24). At this time, then, the revolutionary elites under Calles exercised at best a fractured or minimal hegemony that was based on coercive control (see chapter 1). It was not the "'normal' exercise of hegemony . . . [that] is characterised by a combination of force and consent, which balance each other reciprocally, without force predominating excessively over consent" (Gramsci 1971: 80n.4, Q19§24).

In 1929 the Partido Nacional Revolucionario (PNR) was created by Calles, who perceived the creation of such a national party as essential to building a strong state, keeping both military and civilian elements under centralized civilian control, and ensuring the political stability necessary for economic modernization (Middlebrook 1995: 26–27). The creation of an official party was a crucial attempt to try and foster consensual unity among the revolutionary leaders. It established a selective form of inclusion to minimize division and the resort to coercion (Knight 1992c: 134–35). Yet the creation of a would-be vanguard party occurred *after* the revolution (Knight 1990a: 181–82). Similarly, nearly all of Mexico's contemporary labor unions emerged *after* the revolutionary regime was established, which contributed to an asymmetrical relationship between the state and labor (Whitehead 1991: 81). Gramsci (1977: 330–39) has argued that political parties created after "bourgeois revolutions" were unlikely to contribute to a radical challenge of capitalist society, and the CROM's arrogation to itself of the political functions of worker organization and the state's provision for this role parallels his analysis. Although the Mexican working class was still in the making in the postrevolutionary era, the mass of workers in modern industries—railwaymen, dockers, textile operatives, miners—entered political formations that were strongly reformist and pragmatic in nature. This acceptance of state authority by workers parallels labor movement reformism across Europe (Knight 1984: 68–69, 71).

Further evidence of passive revolution is apparent between 1928 and 1934 when, despite having left the presidency, Calles continued to have major political influence during the titular presidencies of Emilio Portes Gil, Pascual Ortiz Rubio, and Abelardo Rodríguez. This period became known as the *Maximato* because of Calles's praetorian influence as *jefe máximo* and due to the fact that social reform of any significance dwindled under the policies of this foremost ideologist of capitalism in Mexico (Cornelius 1973: 407).

By 1932 the CROM was in decline because it was unable to maintain its alliance with the increasingly conservative national government and because the Mexican working class no longer approved of its policies of governmental cooperation, nationalism, and curtailment of direct action (Michaels 1970: 65–66). In the same year the labor leader Vicente Lombardo Toledano declared, "We cannot proclaim or praise the dictatorship of the proletariat . . . because we are living under a period of organised capitalism" (as cited in Cockcroft 1983: 122). In 1933 he presided over the Confederación General de Obreros y Campesinos de México (CGOCM), which was to become the officially recognized national labor organization over its rival the CROM. Meanwhile social reforms of any kind began to stagnate and certain classes and class fractions (landless peasants, urban labor, and militant Catholics) became increasingly alienated from the Callista regime without being able to unite around a single leader or political program. These contending political interests were reflected within the structure of the PNR that came to revolve around the issues of agrarian policy, labor policy, church-state relations, and economic nationalism. Thus, "the situation in the country during the Maximato could be characterised as a case of acute incongruity between belief systems—the 'ideology of the Mexican Revolution,' as embodied in the 1917 constitution as well as in public statements by Calles and his collaborators since 1924—and the manifest allocation of goods and statuses" (Cornelius 1973: 406). This situation is indicative of the impasse of passive revolution that confronts a state incapable of including entire social groups within a hegemonic political and social ideology (Gramsci 1971: 210–11, Q13§23). As García Canclini (1995: 221) puts it, "when the new movement becomes the system, the projects for change follow the route of bureaucratic planning more than that of participative mobilisation. When social organisation is stabilised, ritualism becomes sclerotic."

Symptomatic of the condition of passive revolution and open class confrontation between contending social forces in Mexico, in the 1930s, was the rise of a native type of fascism in the shape of the Sinarquistas and the paramilitary "Gold Shirts," which raised the possibility of a rightist coup prior to consolidation under the Cárdenas administration. By 1933, however, a dominant class fraction made up of the old bourgeoisie, new "revolutionary" capitalists, and an emerging group of "agrarians" including state governors such as Lázaro Cárdenas (Michoacán), Adalberto Tejeda (Veracruz), Emilio Portes Gil (Tamaulipas), and Saturnino Cedillo (San Luis Potosí), supported by increasing peasant discontent, was taking shape. As Hamilton (1982b: 120) notes, the development of a national capitalist class was also formed in the context of world geopolitical competition. The statism of the New Economic Policy (NEP) in the Soviet Union and Franklin Roosevelt's New Deal in the United States helped to reinforce earlier conceptions of the "revolution-ary" state actively shaping the national context and led to greater willingness to intervene in production relations on behalf of peasants and the working class. The state-labor alliance was also extended as part of a program of popular mobilization, channeled through a multiclass party, which resulted in ideological and material organizational gains (Collier 1992: 25). Social prop-erty relations in Mexico at this time retained lineaments of the Díaz regime or, in Trotsky's felicitous terms, there existed "the orbits of old pre-capitalist cultures" (Trotsky 1936/1980: 27). Nevertheless, there was a "sea change" in political attitudes that was to be consolidated during the "solid achievements" of the 1930s (Knight 1984: 79; Knight 1994a: 394; Maxfield 1993: 238).

CARDENISMO: TOWARD "THE PHILANTHROPIC OGRE"

The rise of Cardenismo—perhaps suitably captured in Octavio Paz's (1979/1990: 377–98) description of the Mexican state as the "philanthropic ogre"—was the result of organic, relatively permanent social forces stem-ming from the Mexican Revolution interacting with specific conjunctural geopolitical factors related to the contradictions of capitalism and the world crisis in the 1930s (see Gilly 1994: 295–324). At the party congress of the PNR in 1933 a combination of internal struggles and external trends produced a coalition of forces that converged to support the presidential candidacy of Cárdenas. This "progressive" coalition would espouse "radical" notions of labor militancy and agrarianism within institutional parameters of political struggle. A six-year plan, also announced at the PNR convention, symbolized such elements. There was a reaffirmed commitment toward agrarian reform within a more *dirigiste* state that would actively direct and restructure society in the name of the masses, strengthen union organizations, and train workers and peasants. The objective was to foster a new sense of popular identifica-tion with the state and therefore lay the foundation for organized mass sup-port that was to transform both the social basis and the function of the state. A key feature of such "hegemonic activity" within conditions of passive revolution (see chapter 1) was Cárdenas's incessant traveling, especially as president, that included a total of 673 work days—nearly one-third of his term in office—away from Mexico City, traveling almost fifty-five thousand miles in 143 separate expeditions to all states and territories in Mexico (Cornelius 1973: 455).

Preceding the implementation of such changes, however, was a struggle in 1934–1935 among generals and *políticos*, especially Calles and Cárdenas. The consolidation of Cárdenas's influence was not ensured until 1937–1938, due to the constant threat of right-wing popular mobilization and the intransigence of *caudillos* with independent resource bases, such as General Saturnino Cedillo—described by Graham Greene (1939/2006: 46, 53) as an "obsequious capitalist" that "no other capitalist would trust." Nevertheless the changing class configuration of support for political actors did lead to the eventual marginalization of Calles. By 1936 Cárdenas had toppled the *Maximato* and brought an end to Sonoran rule by exiling Calles to the United States. Between 1934 and 1937 a process of labor organization and popular agrarian mobilization unfolded which balanced initiatives "from above" with thrusts "from below." In 1936 the CGOCM was renamed the Confederación de Trabajadores de México (CTM), with Lombardo Toledano as secretary general and Fidel Velázquez as organization secretary, which maintained the balance between capital and labor within the context of a capitalist system of production. Steps were also taken to *separately* organize peasant support under the auspices of the PNR, which would facilitate closer control over agrarian reform, leading to the founding of the Confederación Nacional Campesina (CNC) in 1938. This institutionalized segregation ensured against the possibility of an effective peasant-labor alliance. Once the CTM and CNC were created it was possible to restructure the basis of the governing party, and this resulted in the creation of the Partido de la Revolución Mexicana (PRM), also in 1938. The PRM had four sectors: labor (dominated by the CTM); peasant (represented by the CNC); "popular" (owners of small and medium-sized businesses, small landowners, teachers, middle-class professionals); and military (incorporating the armed forces). Within the popular sector, the Federación Sindicatos de Trabajadores al Servicio del Estado (FSTSE), established in 1938, became one of the core organizations linked to the state. It also contained the Sindicato Nacional de Trabajadores de la Educación (SNTE), founded in 1943, that was pivotal in promoting social consensus. By 1943 the Confederación Nacional de Organizaciones Populares (CNOP) was formed to take the place of the FSTSE, and it became the third principal arm of the ruling party constituting 33.7 percent of it, more than the labor sector of the CTM (30.4 percent), and comparable to the peasant sector of the CNC (35.9 percent) (Davis 1994: 101).

The intention was to broaden the social base of the PRM, more effectively linking the urban and rural masses to national decision making as a counterweight to disaffected conservative groups and enhancing the economic-corporate versus the class organization of the popular classes. "The creation of the PRM marked the high point of mobilised mass support for the post-revolutionary regime, and organised labour emerged as the central force within the party in the late 1930s and early 1940s" (Middlebrook 1995: 94). It was crucial in allowing the articulation of subaltern class interests and claims through the CNC and CTM while firmly entrenched within a framework of capitalist development (Vaughan 1997: 6). Popular demands, especially for land reform, were ever present here. The scope of agrarian reform was much wider during the Cárdenas administration than before, resulting in 810,000 peasants receiving land compared to 778,000 under all previous administrations combined, with between 17.9 million and 20 million hectares distributed compared to 8.7 million previously (Hamilton 1982b: 177; Cockcroft 1983: 132). Highly developed *haciendas* were also expropriated so that by 1940 *ejidos* represented 47 percent of cultivated land compared with 15 percent in 1930, the *ejidal* population had more than doubled from 668,000 to 1.6 million, and the landless population had fallen from 2.5 million to 1.9 million (Knight 1991b: 258). This can be seen as the culmination of the "progressive" element of the passive revolution and should not be trivialized. As Löwy (1981: 166) remarks, "the most advanced social measures of the Mexican Revolution were not granted by the bourgeoisie but rather violently arrested by insurgent peasant masses." The expropriation of the oil companies in 1938 can be seen in a similar light. On one hand, it was *el desquite* (the recovery) for territory lost to the United States during the war in 1846–1848 (Gilly 1994: 253–65). It can thus be regarded as the apogee of national cohesion and patriotic jubilation, with Cárdenas winning converts from various political constituencies—workers, peasants, and leftist activists—to become a heroic symbol of the nation against foreign capital (Knight 1992d: 109).[8] On the other hand, Trotsky (1940/1990: 15), writing in the period of expropriation, stated that "the nationalisation of railways and oil fields in Mexico . . . is a measure of state capitalism in a backward country which in this way seeks to defend itself on the one hand against foreign imperialism and on the other against its own proletariat." To summarize, the Cárdenas government successfully articulated the "relative autonomy" of the state with respect to the working class and the peasantry, the organization of labor, elimination of traditional forms of agrarian exploitation, and nationalization of the petroleum and railroad industries within the constraints of state capitalism and the international division of labor (Poulantzas 1975: 97; Hamilton 1982b: 240).

Yet the struggle of Cardenismo cannot accurately be said to reflect conditions of "normal" hegemony, as charted in the previous chapter, by "which a class or a fraction manages to present itself as incarnating the general interest of the people-nation" (Poulantzas 1973: 221). The agrarian reform or popular element of the passive revolution evident during the Cárdenas administration did generally expand the conditions for the emergence and growth of popular demands but the forms through which this found expression and projection—such as the CTM, CNC, and the CNOP—were conditioned by social relations organized through the state. As Gramsci might have put it, this was not a case of integral hegemony ("protected by the armour of coercion"), but more a case of the armour of coercion ("the state-coercion element") protecting the development of a minimal hegemony (Gramsci 2007: 75, Q6§88). Thus, in Cardenismo there was always a dialectic between continuity and change, or revolution-restoration. The myth of the Mexican Revolution was preserved at a time when the stability of the government was threatened. The agrarian reform, while producing widespread change, established the conditions for capitalist agricultural production, and even when Mexican nationalism was at its strongest expression, foreign capital was dominant (Hamilton 1982b: 179, 200). The number of privately owned farms increased by 44 percent between 1930 and 1940, and by 1940 over half the cultivable land consisted of estates of more than five thousand hectares (Cornelius 1973: 474; Cockcroft 1983: 135). Thus, rather than destroying capitalism, the intervention of Cárdenas bolstered capitalist development (Michaels 1970: 59). Cardenismo has been summarized as a radical movement that embodied substantial popular sup-port but also faced conservative resistance; incapable of always following its desired route, it was more jalopy than juggernaut (Knight 1994b).

The resurgence of right-wing opposition signified that the limits of Carden-ismo had been reached. As has been noted, the fascist-inspired Sinarquista movement drew considerable support from the rural sectors least benefiting from the redistributive and agrarian policies of the Cárdenas administration. Founded by Catholic laymen in 1937, the movement grew from an estimated five thousand adherents to more than half a million in mid-1940 (Cornelius 1973: 468). It included support from the previous Cristero unrest while right-wing opposition alternatively led to the creation of the pro-Catholic Partido Acción Nacional (PAN) in 1939. The Mexican Revolution clearly contained within its accommodating reach an amorphous variety of class movements. By 1940 some of the more reactionary elements were surfacing alongside increased opposition from organized labor that was to lead to the dominance of conservative forces in society. The dwindling support for Cárdenas and the institutional loyalty Ávila Camacho attracted as the new president (1940–1946) signified this triumph. The CTM's support for the candidacy of Ávila Camacho was to establish the pattern for subsequent labor participation in presidential successions (Middlebrook 1995: 95). The axis of conflict within Mexican society thus shifted from polarization based on class antagonisms to a struggle between coalitions dominated by conservative class fractions (Hamilton 1982b: 265).

Ávila Camacho and his successor, Miguel Alemán, were able to cultivate the kind of support that was to lead to an institutional counterrevolution in the 1940s and 1950s. This entailed, especially during the presidency of Alemán (1946–1952), the defeat of radical, syndicalist, and Cardenista elements and the dilution of class and ideological differences in the solvent of nationalism (Knight 1991b: 315). It is this period more than any other that saw the consolidation of a bourgeois minimal hegemony under the single state-party system. After the 1940s the mechanisms of Cardenismo were put to new purposes and a form of political co-optation began to prevail under the PRI (as the PRM was cosmetically renamed in 1946). Although a degree of genuine consensus did prevail, with the regime maintaining a level of legitimacy, authoritarian structures were also reinforced. For example, there was a greater prevalence of *charrismo*, the corruption and co-optation of labor leaders in return for political favors or advancement. The emerging basis of class rule articulated by the PRI was therefore not an expression of "normal" hegemony, as detailed in chapter 1, based on intellectual and moral leadership. The relationship established between the subaltern classes and the ruling elites by the PRI was maintained less by the organic unity of rulers and ruled than by the threat of coercion. Hegemony in Mexico between 1940 and 1970 has therefore been described as analogous to Swiss cheese: not a solid structure but a permeable complex (Knight 1992a: 175). This minimal hegemony had to be constantly renewed and re-created while defended and modified by "authoritarian and coercive interventions" (Gramsci 2007: 76, Q6§88). The handling of the labor crisis between 1947 and 1951, the coercive ending of the militant general strike of the Sindicato de Trabajadores Ferrocarrileros de la República Mexicana (STFRM), in 1959, or the murder of peasant leader Rubén Jaramillo, in 1962, were just a few prominent examples of the contested dynamics of hegemony during the subsequent period of *desarrollo estabilizador* (stabilizing development) and ISI (see chapter 3). There was constant need to renegotiate and reinforce this minimal form of hegemony with a degree of violence and repression under the PRI. Therefore, the specific form of minimal hegemony that prevailed in Mexico was based on an "inclusionary" ideology of the revolution but also monopolistically and coercively controlled political power and patronage to maintain a broad majoritarian coalition (Knight 1999: 118).

Overall, Cardenismo represented a dramatic break with the previous postrevolutionary regimes. Until the Cárdenas reforms of the 1930s the revolution had overwhelmingly resulted in piecemeal social change. The mass character and revolutionary logic of the revolution returned during the Cárdenas period and significantly contributed to forms of progressive social change. The notion of passive revolution captures these contradictions that permeated the formation of the social basis of the state in Mexico. Emblematic here was the status of the *ejido* sector as a specific variant of property ownership adapted to the requirements and constraints of dependent capitalism that acted as a "shock absorber" to the capitalist process (Bartra 1975: 128). As a result, social classes in Mexico founded a state that institutionalized social conflict over labor and the peasantry involving a mixture of structural reforms, re-pression, and co-optive measures that fostered specific relations of capitalist development. This dependent bourgeoisie used ISI and the protection of manufacturing industries with high tariffs and an overvalued currency to reduce the cost of imported components, as chapter 3 will demonstrate, to articulate a relatively weak or minimal form of hegemony throughout the 1940s and 1950s. While this model of development was to produce sustained growth over this period it had its state institutional and organizational roots in the Cárdenas era. Similarly, Cardenismo as a current in the history of Mexican state formation contributed to the building of a closer collabora-tive relationship with the United States (Knight 1987: 18–19). There was a marked increase in the United States' cultural influence between 1920 and 1940 that was matched by its growing capital investment in and industrial exports to Mexico (Hamilton 1982b: 73; Knight 1990b: 260). Therefore, as the social basis of the state was being consolidated in Mexico during the Cárdenas period, U.S. interests played an increasing role that established the limits of a dependent form of capitalist development (Hamilton 1981). The result meant that Mexico had "perhaps the most highly perfected bourgeois state machinery in Latin America" (Bartra 1993: 129). How this ISI model of capitalist development, the influence mediated by the PRI, and the growing global presence of the United States altered within a situation of structural change in the 1970s is best left for chapter 4, where a detailed analysis of this different context in the history of passive revolution in Mexico is taken up.

CONCLUSION: THE PASSIVE REVOLUTION OF CAPITAL

The fragmented process of Italian state formation considered by Gramsci prompted him to analyze the uneven development of state power in relation to specific geopolitical and territorial coordinates. These conditions of pas-sive revolution were summarized in a letter he addressed to the Fourth World Congress of the Third International, 20 November 1922 (Gramsci 1978: 129):

> The Italian bourgeoisie succeeded in organising its state not so much through its own intrinsic strength, as through being favoured in its victory over the feudal and semi-feudal classes by a whole series of circumstances of an international character (Napoleon III's policy in 1852–60; the Austro-Prussian War of 1866; France's defeat at Sedan and the development of the German Empire after this event).

It is striking that the process of state formation in Mexico was similarly marked by foreign interventions across a coeval period of geopolitical rivalry.

Indeed, it is not a stretch to say that the emergence of the modern state in Mexico and subsequent conditions of class struggle were shaped by "a whole series of circumstances of an international character": the United States' annexation and war in 1846–1848; the occupation of Veracruz by Spanish, British, and French forces in 1861; the installation by the French of Emperor Maximilian in 1863; the occupation by U.S. troops of Veracruz in 1914; and, one could add, the development of the "American Century" after this event (see Katz 1981; Hart 1987, 2002). These circumstances have been expressed in this chapter through an emphasis on the Mexican Revolution as a passive revolution in which there was an expansion of capitalist social property relations and the internalization of geopolitical factors within the dynamics of class struggle in Mexico. That seemingly distinct processes of state formation in time and/or space can be similarly affected by foreign interventions across coeval periods should not be too surprising (see Morton 2010b). As the conclusion to this book will tease out in more methodological detail (see chapter 8), state formation in Mexico can be seen as a differentiated outcome with certain peculiarities that is linked to a historically integrated process, or an uneven and incomplete modernity, in which "multiple logics of development" coexist (García Canclini 1995: 9). This specific profile of modernity—a hybrid culture of passive revolution—marked state forms in Latin America including those of Brazil and Argentina and in different ways shaped state forms in late-developing capitalism in Japan, Germany, Spain, and Italy (Löwy 1981: 162–66; Leal 1986: 32–33; Callinicos 1989; Riley and Desai 2007), all of which have involved developmental catch-up. Different historically distinctive national processes of passive revolution can thus be regarded as connected variants within the geopolitical conditions of world capitalism. The Mexican Revolution is therefore one such instance in the world history of the passive revolution of capital.

This conclusion is the result of an analysis of the social property relations that fostered certain conditions of capitalist development in Mexico after the revolution. A series of continuities and changes emblematic of state capitalism and passive revolution were thus present in Mexico throughout the period under consideration. While the revolution embodied numerous developmental possibilities or trajectories, a process of state formation unfolded after 1920 that involved institutionalized social class conflict under the guise of "revolutionary" class collaboration. This process was incomplete, resisted, challenged, and messy. Nevertheless, certain features of state–civil society relations began to emerge: in particular, the form that state-labor relations began to take and the role of the *ejidal* sector as a pivot of permanent primitive accumulation in expanding capitalist forms of production in agriculture and extending state policies to compensate for the disorder and conflicts that ensued, which resulted in the unstable reproduction of the peasantry, always threatened with proletarianization (Bartra 1982: 38–40). In the words of one historian, "the chief legacy of the revolution was a state which in its very structure was created to act as a substitute for and to protect the emerging hegemony of the national bourgeoisie" (Aguilar Camín 1980: 123). These are the very contradictions of the circumstances of passive revolution. The concept of passive revolution thus retains importance in its concrete expression of that phase of history known as the Mexican Revolution. It is now time to extend this analysis of passive revolution in relation to the period of capital accumulation, state formation, and class struggle commonly known as import substitution industrialization.

NOTES

1. Crucially, in addition to stating that the treatment would have to be original, Womack (1978: 123n.54) also notes that "the master" for the study of any analysis—relevant to the failure of the Mexican bourgeoisie to take shape as a ruling class and then having to resort to the state to conduct reform, evoke consent, and exercise coercion—is Antonio Gramsci; yet anybody undertaking such an endeavor should not attempt to "slough off" his or her share of the intellectual work.

2. Romagnolo's article elicited a number of responses in *Latin American Perspectives*, not least a barbed commentary from Michael Löwy (1975). These contentions and more are included in a fine collection of essays representing the diversity of debate on uneven development, see Chilcote (2003).

3. More recently the conditions of the permanent primitive accumulation of capital have been referred to as a process of "accumulation by dispossession" involving inter alia the commodification of land; changes in property relations; the appropriation of natural resources; and the use of national debt, the credit system, and the inflationary process as an expression of class struggle all of which are contingent upon the stance of the state (Harvey 2003a: 145).

4. This phrasing echoes the insight offered by Trotsky (1936/1980: 26) that, "A backward country assimilates the material and intellectual conquests of the advanced countries. But this does not mean that it follows them slavishly, reproduces all the stages of their past."

5. Although, as Lenin (1916/1964: 190, original emphasis) makes clear, "the uneven distribution of the railways, their uneven development—sums up, as it were, modern monopolist capitalism on a world-scale . . . *as long as* private property in the means of production exists."

6. Although the outcome of the processes in which state capitalism comes to predominate can be termed a "deflected permanent revolution" (Cliff 1963/1999: 65), or a "misdeveloped revolution" (Cockcroft 1974: 251), the overall conditions are consonant with the course of action of a passive revolution (Callinicos 1982: 111).

7. As early as 1910, under the Díaz administration, the minister of education, Justo Sierra, planned for a group of muralists known as the Society of Mexican Painters and Sculptors to decorate the Escuela Prepatoria (Ministry of Public Instruction) in Mexico City. Diego Rivera was a beneficiary of official patronage at this time and then caught the revolutionary spirit when the mural project was revived and presented as a "revolutionary" gesture after 1920, see Marnham (1998: 85, 169–70).

8. Once again Graham Greene (1939/2006: 91) demurs, noting that there would be pickings for everyone except the workers as a result of the oil expropriation.

Chapter Three

Capital Accumulation, State Formation, and Import Substitution Industrialization

As a theory of history, the concept of passive revolution was developed in the preceding chapter through an analysis of the Mexican Revolution. The outcome of the Mexican Revolution was understood as a contradictory amalgam of sociopolitical processes in which the strains of transformation were both displaced and accomplished.[1] In the words of Pablo González Casanova (1968: 470), "the Mexican Revolution managed only to take the step from a colonial pattern of development to national development of a semicapitalist type." Combining both mass mobilization as well as conservative modernization, the Mexican Revolution thus represented a passive revolution, or what has been described as a blocked dialectic of revolution-restoration (Buci-Glucksmann 1980: 315). Just as Antonio Gramsci captured the road to modernity in Italy as a combination of these elements, it was argued in chapter 2 that the passive revolutionary route to the modern world can explain the displacement of revolutionary impulses and the consolidation of capitalist class rule across comparable instances of postcolonial state formation. What has been termed as Antonio Gramsci's "eventful" concept of causality—developed through the analysis of passive revolution and the event of the Italian Risorgimento (McKay 2009: 134)—can thus inform alternative revolutionary events constituting twentieth-century capitalism.

Beyond the specific ruptures of a passive revolution, though, the thesis expresses not only a certain mode of class organization within the conditions of modern state formation specific to capitalism but also ongoing forms of capitalist class reorganization (see Morton 2010b). Passive revolution is therefore a mode of class rule associated both with ruptural conditions of state development, ushering in the world of capitalist production, and class strategies linked to the continual furtherance of capitalism (Sassoon 1987: 210; Thomas 2007: 71). "The thesis alone in fact develops to the full its potential for struggle," Gramsci stated, "up to the point where it absorbs even the so-called representatives of the antithesis: it is precisely in this that the passive revolution or revolution/restoration consists" (Gramsci 1971: 110, Q15§11). This means that the conditions of class struggle indicative of passive revolution encompass tendencies in the reorganization of capitalism linked to consolidations in the form of state. In such cases, "a passive revolution takes place when, through a 'reform' process, the economic structure is transformed . . . i.e., an economy in the space between the purely individualistic one and the one that is comprehensively planned" is established (Gramsci 2007: 378, Q8§236).

The task of this chapter is to focus on the class strategies in the reorganization and consolidation of the postrevolutionary state in Mexico during the initial phase of import substitution industrialization (ISI) (1940–1954) and the subsequent period known as *desarrollo estabilizador*, or stabilized development (1955–1972). This focus is essential in furthering the underlying argument of this book, which is an account of the historical sociology of modern state formation and uneven development in Mexico as a form of passive revolution. The emphasis on analyzing this context as part of the ongoing class strategies that have constituted and restructured the state and capital in Mexico adds several new dimensions to both state theory within the historical sociology of international relations (HSIR) and studies on the political economy of Mexico. Reinstating class at the center of the making of modern Mexico, shaping the origins and form of state, is one paramount benefit. Set against the conditioning situation of uneven development, the following account of ISI as a continuation of the politics of passive revolution in Mexico shifts the focus toward an appreciation of the differing class configurations central to state formation and the accumulation of capital. The framework of passive revolution contributes to grasping such class agency in constituting and reproducing the state within conditions of uneven development. Furthermore, viewing the passive revolutionary configuration of class conditions in Mexico under ISI assists in understanding such policy priorities as less the result of development "failures" and more a consequence of the "successful" emergence and strengthening of capitalist class processes in Mexico and Latin America (see Ruccio 2010: 188–213; and, also, Minns 2006; Radice 2008). The next chapter to come, on processes of neoliberal restructuring (see chapter 4), will equally highlight the "success," in the sense of deepening capitalism, of the class strategy of passive revolution. Subsequent analysis will then turn to questioning alternative forms of agency that have contested the class practices of passive revolution, in the second part of the book. For the present chapter, though, two questions shape the focus on the postrevolutionary state in Mexico and inform my argument: (1) what property relations and social class forces continued to shape the conditions of ISI and the form of state in Mexico?; and (2) how did these structures and actions further the "success" of the passive revolution of capital in Mexico and attendant cultural, political, and economic processes?

In tackling a class analysis of state formation and capital accumulation through the policies of ISI—as the continuation of the passive revolution of capital—this chapter is structured along three main interrelated lines of argument. After defining the economic strategy of ISI, the first section will detail the initial state theoretical elements shaping this chapter that support the aim of analyzing the reorganization of class rule under conditions of passive revolution within capitalism in the periphery. This then assists in highlighting the role and development of the spatial scale of state power as nodal, alongside dominant fractions within the capitalist class, as intrinsic to capitalist accumulation in Mexico (also see chapter 1), which is undertaken in section two. Building on the account of primitive accumulation and the Mexican Revolution in chapter 2, the aim across these first two sections is to explain the conditions under which certain fractions of capital emerged with particularized features of political organization in creating a form of state as an effectively delimited space for the movement of capital in Mexico. "Through the national state apparatuses the fractionated bourgeoisie organises state interventions of the most diverse forms in the world market movements of capital" (Braunmühl 1978: 174). The task is to delineate the distinct political forms embedded in the territorialization of capital that are nevertheless grounded in the global dynamics of accumulation. Specific fractions of capital—industrial, financial, and agrarian—came to play a principal role in furthering the conditions of passive revolution in Mexico. Yet these fractions of capital and the development strategy of ISI in Mexico emerged within the uneven developmental process of capital accumulation on a world scale. Passive revolution is therefore explained best as the expansion of capitalism through the internalization of bourgeois class interests between dominant fractions of capital and the state (Poulantzas 1975: 73–76). As will become apparent, such a stress on the internalization of class interests within the form of state further realizes elements of class agency rather than simply assuming the external imposition of dependent relations. Specific representations of space linked to the condition of passive revolution are also highlighted at this stage, in the third section of the chapter, notably in terms of how class inequalities become embedded in the spatial structures of the built environment and urban forms linked to state development. Architecture is revealed here as a projection of passive revolution embedded in a context that assists in realizing spatial relations specific to capitalism. The literal "architecture" of passive revolution is therefore pivotal as part of a particular production of space linked to the formation of the modern state. Hence a focus in this third section on aspects of architectural urban space and the extent to which it too can contribute to an understanding of passive revolution and the reproduction of the social relations of production in the era of ISI in Mexico. How these processes of state formation and capital accumulation resided within an "open frontier" of geopolitical interests on a global scale is then reaffirmed in the conclusion.

A STATE IN CAPITALIST SOCIETY
VERSUS A CAPITALIST TYPE OF STATE

The social property relations underpinning ISI were based on a social division of labor involving the production of nondurable goods (processed foods, beverages, tobacco products, cotton textiles) and some capital goods undertaken by domestic capital and the production of durable goods (household appliances and automobile assembly) produced by transnational corporations (TNCs). Infrastructure and basic goods (steel, electricity, telecommunications, water and sanitation, oil extraction and refining, air, road, rail, and port links) were provided by state-owned enterprises (SOEs), while state-owned development and investment banks also played a pivotal role in providing credit for the financing of industrial development and promoting strategies in support of a still maturing national bourgeoisie. Succinctly put, "ISI is an economic strategy based on the sequenced expansion of manufacturing industry, with the objective of replacing imports" (Saad-Filho 2005: 222).

Between 1950 and 1972, Mexico's growth in gross domestic product (GDP) averaged 6.3 percent (Ramírez 1986b: 41). Average GDP per capita (at 1960 prices) rose from 3,230 pesos in 1950 to 6,718 pesos in 1975; despite population growth more than doubling across the same time period from 26 million (1950) to just under 60 million (1975) (Nacional Financiera 1978: 4, 19). Taking macroeconomic real rates of growth from 1940 to 1975, Mexico experienced GDP growth of more than 8 percent per year between 1960 and 1970. On a per capita basis the rate exceeded over 3 percent over the same period. Furthermore, industrial production rose at a rate of at least 8 percent per year between 1940 and 1975, although agricultural production plunged from a significant growth rate of 8 percent in the 1940s, to roughly 4 percent during the 1950s and 1960s, to less than 1 percent per year in the 1970s (see table 3.1).[2] In 1950 the agriculture sector constituted just over 58 percent of the labor force and approximately 19 percent of GDP, while in 1975 the distribution of labor within this sector of the economy had dropped to about 34 percent and its share of GDP output had fallen to less than 10 percent. Across the same period, industry accounted for just 16 percent of the labor force in 1950 and about 27 percent of GDP, shifting to nearly 25 percent of the labor force and a more significant proportion of nearly 36 percent of GDP in 1975 (see tables 3.2 and 3.3). As a whole, the financing of capital formation by the state through public investment reached over 50 percent of total capital formation in the 1935–1945 period and declined to 33 percent in the 1955–1965 period (Fitzgerald 1977: 83). These transformations were wrought by the ongoing processes of primitive accumulation discussed in the previous chapter, with the transfer of the labor force from agriculture to industry indicative of the generation of propertyless individuals forced to sell their labor. At the same time, the state became the fulcrum of capital accumulation through ownership of surplus-generating sectors, furthering the expansion of the public sector through the support of financial groups (*financieras*), sustaining the management of credit and domestic manufacturing by the channeling of foreign exchange through state banks thus ensuring a mediatory role between domestic and foreign capital.

Masked by these aggregate transformations in the economy, the uneven development of capitalism in Mexico was expressed at this time through a high concentration of ownership of the means of production with modern commercial agriculture located predominantly in the northern part of the country supported by public investments in irrigation and complemented by public and private agricultural programs. In manufacturing, uneven geographical development was manifest in advanced industrialized zones of the country (Valley of Mexico, Monterrey), semi-industrialized zones (Coahuila, Chihuahua, Jalisco, Puebla, Veracruz), and "subindustrial" regions (Oaxaca, Chiapas).[3] Urban centers were bolstered by the drive of ISI (notably the Federal District, Monterrey, Guadalajara) while in the 1940–1950 decade those regions and states in Mexico most favored were

1. those initiating strategic industries for national development (iron and steel in Coahuila and Nuevo León; cement in the Federal District, Jalisco,

Table 3.1. Mexican Macroeconomic Indicators, 1940–1975
(real average annual growth rates, 1960 = 100)

Indicator	1940–1950	1950–1960	1960–1970	1970–1975
Gross domestic product	7.1	7.3	8.8	5.3
Population	3.4	3.2	3.6	3.1
Per capita product	3.7	4.1	5.2	2.2
Industrial output	8.0	9.0	12.0	6.2
Agricultural output	8.2	4.3	3.9	0.6

Source: Calculated from Nacional Financiera (1978: 19–45).

Table 3.2. Distribution of the Labor Force by Sector, 1900–1975 (thousands of workers)

Sector	1900 No.	1900 %	1910 No.	1910 %	1921 No.	1921 %	1930 No.	1930 %	1940 No.	1940 %	1950 No.	1950 %	1960 No.	1960 %	1970 No.	1970 %	1975 No.	1975 %
Agriculture[a]	3,177	69.5	3,596	68.3	3,490	71.5	3,626	70.4	3,831	65.5	4,824	58.3	6,097	54.1	5,004	37.5	5,676	34.7
Industry																		
Mining[b]	92	2.1	86	1.6	28	0.6	51	1.0	107	1.8	97	1.2	141	1.3	185	1.4	230	1.4
Manufacturing	542	12	674	12.8	524	10.7	614	11.9	670	11.5	973	11.7	1,553	13.7	2,251	16.8	2,889	17.7
Construction	124	2.5	144	2.7	102	2.1	91	1.8	106	1.8	224	2.7	408	3.6	592	4.4	771	4.7
Electricity	1	0	2	0	6	0.1	17	0.3	26	0.4	25	0.3	42	0.4	55	0.4	121	0.8
Total	759	16.6	906	17.2	660	13.5	773	15.0	909	15.5	1,319	16.0	2,144	19.0	3,083	23.1	4,011	24.6
Services																		
Trade	235	5.1	299	5.7	271	5.6	274	5.3	452	7.7	684	8.3	1,073	9.5	1,212	9.1	1,558	9.6
Transport and Communication	63	1.4	65	1.2	75	1.5	107	2.1	149	2.5	211	2.6	356	3.2	371	2.8	513	3.1
Others[c]	337	7.4	398	7.7	388	7.9	371	7.2	517	8.8	879	10.6	1,521	13.5	2,718	20.4	3,624	22.2
Unspecified	—	—	—	—	—	—	—	—	—	—	355	4.3	83	0.7	955	7.2	952	5.8
Total	635	13.9	762	14.5	734	15.0	752	14.6	1,118	19.0	2,129	25.7	3,033	26.9	5,256	39.4	6,647	40.7
Overall Total	4,571		5,264		4,884		5,151		5,858		8,272		11,274		13,343		16,334	

Source: Interpolation and extrapolation of population census data. Secretaría de Programación y Presupuesto (SPP: Ministry of Planning and Budget), General Bureau of Statistics (Nacional Financiera 1978: 13–14).

[a]Includes livestock raising, forestry, and fishing.

[b]Includes the petroleum industry.

[c]Includes government and private services.

Table 3.3. Gross Domestic Product (GDP) by Sector, 1950–1975 (millions of 1960 pesos)

Sector	1950 Pesos	%	1955 Pesos	%	1960 Pesos	%	1965 Pesos	%	1970 Pesos	%	1975 Pesos	%
Agriculture	15,968	19.2	20,841	18.7	23,970	15.8	30,222	14.1	34,535	11.5	37,511	9.5
Industry[a]												
Mining	1,739	2.1	2,011	1.8	2,306	1.5	2,429	1.1	2,859	1.0	3,406	0.9
Manufacturing	14,244	17.1	19,589	17.6	28,931	19.0	45,241	21.1	69,060	23.0	92,488	23.4
Construction	3,028	3.6	4,133	3.7	6,105	4.0	8,534	4.0	13,583	4.5	20,205	5.1
Energy	3,086	3.7	4,378	3.9	6,591	4.4	10,294	4.8	16,652	5.5	23,837	6.0
Total	22,097	26.5	30,111	27.0	43,933	28.9	66,508	31.0	102,154	34.0	139,936	35.4
Services												
Trade	24,001	28.8	33,855	30.3	46,880	30.8	67,368	31.4	94,491	31.5	121,777	30.8
Transport and Communication	2,709	3.3	3,560	3.2	4,996	3.3	6,443	3.0	9,395	3.1	15,089	3.8
Others[b]	18,529	22.2	23,304	20.8	32,251	21.2	44,063	20.5	59,592	19.9	80,671	20.5
Total	45,239	54.3	60,719	54.3	84,127	55.3	117,874	54.9	163,478	54.5	217,537	55.1
Overall total	83,304		111,671		152,030		214,604		300,167		394,984	
Adjustment for banking	−564		−1,076		−1,519		−2,284		−3,567		−4,684	
Gross Domestic Product	82,740		110,595		150,511		212,320		296,600		390,300	

Source: Banco de México annual reports (Nacional Financiera 1978: 26–43).

[a]Includes food, textiles, forestry, chemicals, metallic, and nonmetallic material industries.

[b]Includes government and banking, finance, and hospitality.

Nuevo León, and Chihuahua; paper in Jalisco and Chihuahua; petroleum in Veracruz and Tamaulipas; and refining processes in the Federal District and Guanajuato);

2. those that were beneficiaries of large-scale irrigation projects of more than a million hectares supported by large investments, technology, and modern equipment (Sinaloa, Sonora, Coahuila-Durango [La Laguna], Tamaulipas, and Chihuahua);

3. those with already established nodal cities (the Federal District, Nuevo León, Jalisco, and Puebla) as hubs of modernization;[4] and

4. specific urban centers, such as Toluca and Atlixco, that experienced "regional economic reanimation" linked to industrial investment (cement and textiles).

Between 1950 and 1960, northern and central states concentrated commercial agricultural production with technological advancement in Veracruz (coffee, tobacco, sugar cane, and beans), Sonora (wheat, rice), Sinaloa (tomatoes, rice), and Baja California (cotton), while in the south the states of Yucatán (henequen/sisal) stood out alongside Chiapas (coffee, cocoa) and Oaxaca (tobacco, coffee) (see Mendoza-Berrueto 1968: 98–99, 104). Viewed from the national scale, the result was a bimodal pattern of uneven development characterized by heavy public investments in industry and infrastructure as well as irrigation projects benefiting agribusiness in the northwest while the majority of *ejidatarios* specializing in the production of stable foodstuffs subsisted in southern states (Ramírez 1989: 76–77).

During the earlier postrevolutionary shift toward commercial agriculture and manufacturing, from 1925 to 1930, capital accumulation was marked by an average ratio of gross fixed capital formation to GDP of 5.3 percent with two-fifths absorbed by transport and commerce (roads and motor vehicles), one-fifth taken up by housing and urban infrastructure, and the balance invested in agriculture and industry. The state share of this fixed capital was 38 percent reflected in large-scale programs of public works geographically ordering the built environment through irrigation, roads, and railway transport (Fitzgerald 1984: 216). Notably, this was within a context of world economic crisis that witnessed a decline in Mexico's exports by 64.9 percent, between 1929 and 1932, and a fall in the terms of trade by 20.8 percent during the same period (Cárdenas 2000: 178). From 1926, when the Banco Nacional de Crédito Agrícola was founded to support commercial farmers, land irrigated with federal government waterworks increased from 827,425 hectares to 3,349,133 hectares in 1975 (Nacional Financiera 1978: 55–56). Between 1940 and 1979, irrigation works accounted for 70 percent to 99 percent of state investment in the agricultural sector principally concentrated in the key northern states of Sonora, Sinaloa, and Tamaulipas (Barkin 1990: 16). Investment in fixed capital such as the Morelos Dam, on the Colorado River in the northeastern section of the state of Baja California, or the Falcon Dam in the lower Rio Grande Valley, not only added thousands of acres "to the agricultural base of the nation, but also a series of hydroelectric stations [that] contributed to the tripling of Mexico's electrical output by 1952" (Meyer and Sherman 1987: 640, as cited in Ramírez 1989: 50). The kilometers of roads increased from 9,929 to 184,392 between 1940 and 1975. While, on the railroads, the kilometers of track remained reasonably constant (increasing from 23,329 to 24,912 kilometers between 1951 and 1975), commercial freight nevertheless increased from 21 million tons in 1951 to 62.5 million tons in 1975 (Nacional Financiera 1978: 79–82, 83–84). As David Barkin (1975: 69; 1983: 99–101) summarizes this spatial organization of agriculture and industry, regional disparities became "indelibly engrained on the Mexican socio-economic structure" as the state-led development and banking sectors reinforced such divisions, ensuring preferential treatment to specific industrial and/or agricultural regions, and the channeling of credit in ways that reinforced the dominant patterns of uneven development, as outlined in chapter 1. Both fixed capital and the creation of the built environment leading to specific spatial arrangements across a variety of state scales (local, regional, national) are thus essential features of the uneven development of capitalism (Harvey 1982/2006: 226, 235). The built environment for production (roads, railways, factories, warehouses, wharves, etc.) becomes "the geographically immobilised forms of fixed capital" central to the progress of capital accumulation and the geographical expansion of capitalist society (Smith 1984/2008: 159). Some of the detail of the historical geography of this uneven development will be dealt with in the subsequent section, tracing the specific fractions of capital that became dominant during the ISI phase of development. In tackling the historical specificity of the capitalist state, however, it is necessary to briefly outline some core distinctions that assist in understanding the state forms through which the political interests of capital are consolidated.

Rather than taking as given the separation of the "economic" and "political" in capitalism, a more fruitful approach to understanding the capitalist state is to begin by "asking what it is about the relations of production under capitalism that makes them assume separate economic and political forms" (Holloway and Picciotto 1977: 78). This entails viewing the development of the state form under capitalism as a particular manifestation of the capital relation, meaning economics and politics (state and civil society) are not posited in an exterior relationship but only appear as separate entities owing to the way production is organized in capitalism. Extending the framework outlined in chapter 1, under capitalist social property relations the direct extraction of surplus is accomplished through "nonpolitical" relations of power. Within capitalist social forms, then, surplus extraction is indirectly conducted through a contractual relation between those who maintain the power of appropriation, as owners of the means of production, over those who only have their labor to sell, as expropriated producers. Paraphrasing Marx (1857–1858/1973: 247–48), then, there is the *presupposition* of exchange value within capitalist relations of production that implies a *compulsion* over those individuals whose existence is historically and socially determined as producers. Direct producers are thus no longer in possession of their own means of subsistence but are compelled to sell their labor power for a wage in order to gain access to the means of production (Wood 1995: 31–36). Said otherwise, direct producers only have access to the means of production through the sale of their labor power in exchange for a wage, which is mediated by the purely "economic" mechanisms of the market. The market conditions of "civil society" are not therefore separate from the "state," as those mainstream approaches criticized in chapter 1 would have it, but are internally related forms of the capital relation compelling both appropriators and producers (capital and labor) to engage in the imperatives of competition, profit maximization, and survival (Wood 2002: 96–98, 102). However, this formal institutional arrangement of the "state" and "civil society," linked to the historical specificity of exploitative relations for capitalist purposes, is not identical with studying the historical constitution of different forms of state that emerge within capitalist societies in the periphery. Here there is a need to introduce a distinction between a *capitalist type of state* that is distinguished by its institutional separation from the economy characteristic of modern capitalism and a *state in capitalist society* that is still emerging as a modern representative state within a capitalist social formation in the periphery.

The peculiarities of these two state forms have been charted in the state theoretical analysis of Bob Jessop. Following this theory of the state, a *state in capitalist society* refers to the historical constitution of the state as an emerging capitalist social formation with the likelihood that class power is more transparently articulated in the interests of particular capitals. The form of state in capitalist society is not fully secure in organizing the requirements of accumulation but simply retains a functional adequacy. This means that the capacity of the state in capitalist society to secure the "economic" and extraeconomic (or purely "political") conditions for accumulation in a given conjuncture is yet to be consolidated. Policies are more or less functionally adequate to the reproduction of the requirements of the capital relation but the struggle to establish the institutional design of such policies means that class power is more transparent. Alternatively, a *capitalist type of state* is dominated by the logic of accumulation so that the form of the modern state is distinguished by its institutional separation from the economy and class power is more obscure. In this case, there is formal adequacy of a given state form in securing the capital relation so that the provision of an overall framework for capital accumulation is assured in securing political class domination within specific circumstances. As Jessop (2008: 140) argues, "the state forms through which the political interests of capital are initially pursued are formally inadequate and must be conformed to its changing economic and political interests through open political struggles aimed at achieving a modern representative state." As a result, there is no guarantee that a given state in capitalist society will consolidate its character as a capitalist type of state. Hence a need to focus on its specific forms, institutional architecture, and political design, based on two complementary strategies examining the outcome of class struggles over the historical and formal constitution of the state by: (1) analyzing how the exercise of state power by the agents of the state in capitalist society overcome problems of governance through various policies that are consistent with the expanded reproduction of capital; and (2) analyzing how the exercise of power in and through the capitalist type of state overcomes the problem posed by the institutional separation of the "economic" and the "political" through specific accumulation strategies and hegemonic projects. The remainder of this chapter will deal with the first strategy, by analyzing the attempts to secure the functional adequacy of the state in capitalist society and the expanded reproduction of capital in Mexico. The second task, considering the further consolidation of the capitalist type of state in Mexico through the articulation of specific accumulation strategies and hegemonic projects will befall chapter 4.

It seems appropriate at the same time to consider some criticisms of this state theoretical approach, not least the association with aspects of regulation theory. The arguments focusing on the development of "peripheral Fordism" have purchase on some of the issues and distinctions drawn above. Chief among these would be the focus on the uneven insertion of postcolonial states into international conditions of differentiation and developmental catch-up; the recognition that capitalism grew into territorialized spaces established within prior state structures; a stress on the internalization of forms of production and associated procedures, norms, and habits within social formations in the periphery; and recognition that the combined development of capitalist and precapitalist labor processes thwarts the straightforward construction of hegemonic political and cultural rule (Lipietz 1982: 46; Lipietz 1984: 73–74; Lipietz 1987: 55–77). Yet the extrapolation of Fordism as a mode of capital accumulation on a world scale—based on the extension of a labor process that combines recognition of productivity gains through rising real wages with the extension of mass consumption and coercive control—meets several problems. First, a binary line is drawn between "central Fordism" and "peripheral Fordism" with the latter regarded as unable to extend certain aspects of Fordist industrialization and its social labor processes and mass consumption norms. Second, the failure of agrarian reform to redistribute wealth, the failure of the manufacturing export sector, and the failure to incorporate mass consumption into a regime of accumulation are all emphasized. "*Desarrollismo* failed in Latin America" (Lipietz 1987: 63). This clearly undervalues the "successful" emergence, strengthening, and deepening of capitalist class processes through import-substitution strategies in Mexico and elsewhere in Latin America, as argued earlier. Third, the overriding focus on state classes not only flattens out the contradictions of class struggle but also neglects the wider role of the state in creating "hothouse" fashion the conditions for capitalism through primitive accumulation and investment in fixed capital, as stressed in this and earlier chapters. Finally, there is a tendency to analyze the functional prerequisites of capitalism so that the *necessary* political form of the state is taken as a given indicator of ISI based on the lawlike regularities of the expanded reproduction of capital. This underestimates the changing features of class struggle, contestations over hegemony, and the role of ideology and nationalism within which processes of accumulation, regulation, and the extraction of surplus value take place. As David Ruccio (2010: 314), who makes these last three criticisms, flawlessly puts it:

> Regulation theory, at the most general level, introduces a law of correspondence between accumulation and regulation and ultimately fails to theorise both the essential status which it attributes to capital accumulation and the role of the state. . . . [It] thus fails to elaborate the concepts necessary to theorise the uneven, contradictory emergence of the capitalist class process in the periphery.

By contrast, my argument is that recourse to the theorizing of political modernity offered by Antonio Gramsci and the notion of passive revolution better captures processes intrinsic to the emergence and rise of the state in capitalist society and the complexities of state power that emerged in Mexico.

FRACTIONS OF CAPITAL AND THE CONTRADICTIONS OF STATE ACCUMULATION

In developing a periodization of modern state formation in Mexico it has been argued by some that there was "an ongoing but often disrupted process of uneven capitalist development" from the early-to-late colonial period (1519–1770), with merchant capital the key stimulus to the development of capitalism, through to the early postcolonial period (1770–1880), when capitalism was consolidated (see Cockcroft 1983: 39–44, 45–57; Cockcroft 1998: 9–10, 76–80). This outlook is based on a commercialization account of agriculture viewing *hacendados* as an emergent agrarian bourgeoisie allied with mining and manufacturing interests setting in motion the transition toward capitalism from the seventeenth century onward (see Semo 1978: 83–87, 163–69; Semo 1993: 153–57). By extension, it has been stated that "the entire 1880–1940 period of capitalist economic development was structurally the same, based on agro-mineral exports and a strong insertion into the relations of world capitalism." The result, the argument continues, was a *re*consolidation of the capitalist state in Mexico between 1920 and 1940 (Cockcroft 1983: 111, 138–39). This timeless account of the onset of capitalism (a "pan-capitalism" thesis) and the rise of the modern Mexican state was critically assessed in the previous chapter. Instead, it was argued there that up to the end of the Porfiriato there was an enclave economy dominated by foreign capital, which controlled 97.5 percent of the mining sector, 100 percent of the petroleum sector, 87.2 percent of the electricity sector, 61.8 percent of railroads, 76.7 percent of banking, and 85 percent of industry (Villareal 1977: 68). However, the rupture of the revolution and processes of agrarian reform and industrialization set in motion during the Lázaro Cárdenas administration (1934–1940), partly accelerated by world economic crisis, laid the basis for the development of capitalism and the consolidation of the new state-information. The object of state capital accumulation in Mexico was to support a process of industrialization carried out by the emergence of dominant fractions within the national capitalist class alongside the expansion of the public sector and control over strategic resources. It is to the postrevolutionary era that attention must turn in developing a periodization of capitalism and the *modern* state in Mexico.

Following the founding of the Banco Nacional de Crédito Agrícola in 1926, the Banco Nacional Hipotecario Urbano y Obras Públicas was established to finance municipal infrastructure as well as road construction (1933). At the same time, Nacional Financiera, S.A. (NAFINSA) was formed as the government development bank focusing on long-term debt financing of sectors of the economy as well as involvement in infrastructure investment, such as electric power and railroads (1933). Then the Comisión Federal de Electricidad (CFE) was created granting the state direct participation in the generation of electricity through the construction and control of hydroelectric and hydraulic works, while Petróleos de México (Petromex) was established (1934) eventually leading to the forging of Petróleos Mexicanos (PEMEX) and the expropriation of foreign-owned petroleum companies (1938). Earlier, the Banco Ejidal was created to meet the lack of credit available to *ejidatarios* for agrarian reform (1935) and the Financiera Nacional Azucarera was subsequently established to channel investment capital to the sugar industry, protect employment, and boost production (1943). Prior to all this activity the state banking system was consolidated, centered on the founding of the Banco de México as the central bank (1925) so that taken as a whole these institutions "formed the basis of a new system of state finance which, in combination with the Banco de México, could provide finance for public sector investment and exert some leverage on private accumulation" (Fitzgerald 1984: 225). Between 1940 and 1950 the Banco de México accounted for 80 percent of the total claims of the banking system on the government sector, with the state running a steady public sector deficit (Ramírez 1986b: 46).

The first period of ISI (1940–1954) based on the substitution of consumer goods was characterized by two major overall policies: (1) tariff protection to entice domestic capital into import-substitution industries and encourage private sector investment, while low import duties were granted toward raw materials, and rates in excess of 100 percent were allocated to finished manufactures; and (2) an elaborate system of import licensing constituting the major control over imports with up to 80 percent of overall Mexican imports at the end of the 1950s subject to such licensing requirements (Hansen 1974: 48–49). The administration of Manuel Ávila Camacho (1940–1946)—hailed as signifying the "end" of the Mexican Revolution (Aguilar Camín and Meyer 1993: 159–61)—was particularly marked by these more "inward" strategies of developing industry through direct state intervention while supplying U.S. demand for mineral exports (zinc, copper, lead, mercury, cadmium) and, during World War II, petroleum and rubber to the Allied forces.[5] Notably at this time, as early as 1941, the U.S. Department of the Treasury and the Banco de México also agreed on a monetary stabilization package of $50 million to strengthen the peso-dollar parity (Cárdenas 2000: 185–86). Under the Miguel Alemán Valdés (1946–1952) administration, funds were then channeled to the building of irrigation projects, electric power, and more extensive communications and transportation networks. In addition, initiatives such as the Ley de Fomento de Industrias Nuevas y Necessarias (Law for New and Necessary Industries), in 1954, were launched in an attempt to facilitate the greater concentration of capital accumulation under ISI.

Movements in the exchange rate were also a principal mechanism used to adjust the balance of payments deficit, with devaluations resorted to twice, in 1948–1949 and 1954. Especially under the administration of Adolfo Ruíz Cortinez (1952–1958), a policy of devaluation and inflationary financing of public sector expenditures (rather than direct taxation) was pursued, supported by the Banco de México compelling capital through private *financieras* to supply the deficit financing required by the state (Ramírez 1986b:

48). This led to a "fiscal crisis" referring to the imbalance between the acceleration of state accumulation and its inadequacy in financing public sector borrowing requirements (Fitzgerald 1978: 280). Allied with the central bank controlling the aggregate supply of money and credit there was, then, an increased dependence on external financing of the public sector deficit. Due to this structural dependence on foreign capital (external loans and/or investment) the main mechanism of adjustment was therefore through devaluation, which resulted in the dollar rising in price by more than 200 percent. Devaluation—from 4.05 pesos/dollar in 1945, to 8.65 pesos/dollar in 1948–1949, to 12.50 pesos/dollar in 1954—resulted in the balance of payments shifting from a deficit of $49.6 million to a surplus of $72.5 million, in 1948–1949, and then a deficit of $32.6 million to a surplus of $34.9 million, in 1955–1956 (Villareal 1977: 71; Nacional Financiera 1978: 377–78). The timing of these devaluations at crucial junctures, following World War II in the middle of ISI and at the initial kick start of the era of stabilized development, adds credence to the view that devaluations can generally be regarded as a means to overcome crises of production and overaccumulation, so that capitalist accumulation can renew its course upon a new social and technological basis (Harvey 1982/2006: 200–202).

Organized labor, such as the teachers' movement, was rooted in these developments linked to the stagnation of real wages and inflationary pressures exacerbated by the 1954 devaluation. For example, a series of mobilizations began in 1956 by the Sindicato Nacional de Trabajadores de la Educación (SNTE) that was centered around demands for a 30 percent wage increase and a move to forge independent union representation outside the PRI. While it should be remembered that "the teachers wanted to fulfil the Mexican Revolution; they wanted to push the Mexican government forward, not aside," this labor struggle nevertheless was still subjected to state repression and control by the 1960s (La Botz 1988: 102). Earlier, in 1946, state coercion was also witnessed against the Sindicato Trabajadores de Petroleros de la República Mexicana (STPRM) and its attempt to establish labor union independence from the state-backed Confederación de Trabajadores de México (CTM). The result was a period of labor quiescence with the STPRM, between 1952 and 1958, dominated by leaders such as Joaquín Hernández Galicia—"La Quina"—controlling the *petroleros*. While again, in 1958, class struggle and labor militancy in the form of the rebellion of the Sindicato de Trabajadores Ferrocarrileros de la República Mexicana (STFRM) led to coercive suppression and the mass arrest of labor agitators. The overall outcome at this time was a dependent labor movement under the tutelage of the Mexican state so that "Mexico's new industrial policy, the substitution of imports, was predicated upon a compliant labour force and low wages" (La Botz 1988:

86). It would not be until the 1960s and 1970s that heightened class struggle, involving urban and rural guerrilla movements as well as renewed efforts to establish autonomous labor fronts alongside student protests, would be witnessed; mobilizations that resulted in large measure from both the uneven development of agriculture and the capital-intensive nature of exploitation within the labor process (Ramírez 1989: 72).

After 1955 the central bank shifted the burden of financing both government and public enterprises to credit institutions and *financieras* within the private sector. At the same time, the Banco de México also issued peso-denominated securities with high real rates of interest, convertible in dollars at any time at a guaranteed rate, which attracted foreign finance capital. This would subsequently present an increased reliance on foreign borrowing to cover public sector deficits. Up to the 1950s, cycles of devaluation and inflation were thus evident with the latter regarded as an expression of class conflict, meaning that inflation is as much a manifestation of the class character of the state in terms of its unequal impact on social conditions as it is a monetary feature (Barkin and Esteva 1982). Throughout the era of ISI, it is illustrative that the increase in wholesale prices in Mexico City averaged 76 percent, while across the period of stabilized development the increase was 39 percent (Nacional Financiera 1978: 231–33). Hence, "during the initial phase of ISI (1940–1954), the Mexican economy adjusted primarily via price increases, while later, during the stabilising adjustment period (1955–1972), increases in the real rate of interest became the mechanism of adjustment" (Ramírez 1986b: 49). In the second period of stabilized development to contain inflation and defuse class conflict, the substitution of intermediate and capital goods was promoted through a dependence on foreign capital, hence an increase in the current account balance of payments deficit due to the continued reliance on foreign investment and external loans. Illustrative here would be the plummeting of the balance of payments from a $34.9 million surplus in 1955 to a $761.5 million deficit in 1972 and then to a $3,692.9 million deficit in 1975 on the eve of the next major devaluation of the peso in 1976 (Nacional Financiera 1978: 379–83). Between 1960 and 1975 Mexico's external public debt, as a percentage of GDP, rose from 9.7 percent to 24.4 percent (Ramírez 1986b: 44). The enormous constellational shift in Mexico's spatial orbit of capital, toward the close of ISI and on the eve of the debt crisis, is revealed by figure 5.1, which appropriately closes the first part of this book after a consideration of the political economy of neoliberalism in chapter 4.

Across the ISI era, adjustments of the exchange rate subsidized the importation of capital-intensive technologies that decreased the relative price of capital in relation to labor and increased productivity but without resulting in growing employment. Put another way, the rate of exploitation of labor was increased during this period indicating the start of a shift from the production of absolute surplus value (extension of the working day, increasing work hours, rising activities performed by labor in the same period), to relative surplus value (technological changes inducing a reduction in the value of labor power and increasing productivity). The social reorganization induced by *desarrollo estabilizador* thus commenced the consolidation of capitalist accumulation not just on the basis of exploitation of labor through the extraction of absolute surplus value (or the formal subsumption of labor to capital) but also on the basis of the extraction of relative surplus value (or the real subsumption of labor to capital) (see Marx 1887/1996: parts III–V; Marx 1857–1861/1986: 267–91). While the unevenness of development meant that such features were not consolidated across the entire space economy of capitalism in Mexico, due to variegated historicogeographical conditions, these more intensive forms of exploitation within the labor process were experienced up to the mid-1960s ensuring increases in the profit rate through the value form (see Rivera Ríos 1986: 47–53). It would be the downward shift on such profit rates, as wage pressures on capital contributed to a slackening of private sector interest in productive accumulation, that would contribute to the subsequent crisis conditions up to the 1980s (Fitzgerald 1985: 220–21). As Miguel Ángel Rivera Ríos (1986: 48) puts it, "at the end of the 1960s, the prevailing conditions of capital accumulation and uneven development in Mexico acquired a character of central contradiction that contributed to a slowdown of economic expansion and reframed the falling rate of profit after the slight improvement experienced in the middle of the decade." The shakeout from the *docena trágica*—tragic twelve years—spanning the administrations of Luis Echeverría (1970–1976) and José López Portillo (1976–1982) is at the heart of the discussion in chapter 4. Attention now turns to analyzing the specific social relations that enabled these conditions of capital accumulation and the reconstitution of class power in Mexico. "History in Mexico," President Adolfo López Mateos (1959: 12) once commented, "has determined that the state many times assumes the role of a pioneer. Nacional Financiera has been the prime instrument in the execution of this policy, with the object of accelerating economic development." Given that NAFINSA directed most of the long-term financing for development throughout the 1940s and 1950s—as the origin of 56 percent of all the fixed capital formation from 1950 to 1970—and was intrinsic to the subsequent development of state agencies oriented to the accumulation of capital, analysis starts with its "hothouse" role in shaping industry and finance (Cypher and Delgado Wise 2010: 39–40).

Various fractions of the capitalist class coalesced in the postrevolutionary period in Mexico alongside the state taking on the role of coordinating capital accumulation. These fractions of capital are significant in that they reveal the concentration and centralization of capital in the drive for surplus value allowing for a more rapid expansion in the scale of production. While concentration proceeds through the process of primitive accumulation, centralization involves the clustering of capitals and, simultaneously, the destruction of one capital and the surge in valorization of another (Smith 1984/2008: 163). In Mexico, early indicators of the social centralization of fractions of capital included the formation of the Asociación de Banqueros Mexicanos (ABM), in 1928, and the foundation of the Confederación Patronal de la República Mexicana (COPARMEX), in 1929, based in Monterrey and constituted largely by the Garza Sada family. Under Ávila Camacho's presidential term, business associations were restructured, leading to the further emergence of the Confederación de Cámaras Nacionales de Comercio (CONCANACO), mainly associated with large commercial capital, and the Confederación de Cámaras Industriales (CONCAMIN), mainly associated with large industrial capital, in 1941. Importantly, within CONCAMIN, the Cámara Nacional de la Industria de Transformación (CANACINTRA) was also created, which was a semiautonomous "chamber" that elevated Mexico City–based industrialists to a more central position closer to the ruling PRI and the president. CANACINTRA became a locus of industrial fractions of capital in the 1940s, involved in state-led development that ensured the control of capital over labor while also acting as a bulwark against the larger confederations of CONCAMIN and CONCANACO. At the same time, "the development of a national bourgeoisie capable of carrying forward the project of economic growth was made possible by the successful reconstruction of the banking system" (Bennett and Sharpe 1982: 180). This included the nurturing and coordination of both the national bourgeoisie and finance capital through the Secretaría de Hacienda y Crédito Público (Ministry of Finance), the Banco de México as the central bank, and the development bank NAFINSA. This treasury–Banco de Mexico–NAFINSA complex became a key counterpart to a still maturing national bourgeoisie with numerous overlapping concerns connecting state and capital. This was epitomized by figures that could be considered "theoreticians of the passive revolution" (Gramsci 1971: 109, Q15§11), such as Luis Montes de Oca, director of the Banco de México, who was instrumental to the internalization of capitalist class interests within the state (Hamilton 1982b: 207, 284). It would also be true of architects of ISI and the stabilized development model, such as Antonio Espinosa de los Monteros, initial director-general of NAFINSA, or Antonio Ortiz Mena, minister of finance for a twelve-year period across the *sexenios* of Adolfo López Mateos (1958–1964) and Gustavo Díaz Ordaz (1964–1970).[6] As a result, a trend of capital accumulation was concentrated among fractions of the capital class, located within the complex of state–civil society relations. As Juan Felipe Leal (1974: 185) states: "all the governments that 'emanated from the revolution' have followed a political tendency favouring capital, particularly national, and within it established the hallmarks of state ownership." Consequently, a "process of private accumulation strengthened a small group of capitalists in relation to the dominant class as a whole and ultimately in relation to the state" (Hamilton 1982b: 215). Taken together, the fractions of classes linked to the bourgeois sector through the various confederations and allied with the state could "contain and channel the development of capitalism in Mexico in a global way" (Bartra 1993: 131). Following a restructuring in 1940, NAFINSA became the latest institutional form of the state that projected the interests of finance capital and promoted basic industry. Further, from 1942 on, "NAFINSA's intervention in foreign capital markets on behalf of credit-seeking private firms was perhaps as important as its own investments were in promoting industrial development" (Blair 1964: 211).

As the foregoing discussion has already mentioned, during the 1940s the bulk of NAFINSA's loans and investments went to public sector infrastructure projects in railroads, irrigation, electric power, and telecommunications. Its financing of transportation and communication sectors increased by over 500 percent between 1945 and 1952, at an average rate of 62.6 percent (Ramírez 1986a: 71). From 1950 onward, NAFINSA would come to account for between one-third and one-half of the banking system's total financing of industry (Bennett and Sharpe 1982: 183). Major instances of NAFINSA's role in hastening "hothouse fashion" processes of capitalist transformation would include the cases of Diesel Nacional (DINA), one of the first major companies involved in the automobile industry, using Fiat technology to produce diesel trucks, and Sociedad Mexicana de Crédito Industrial, one of the most important *financieras* (private banks) funding industrial projects in automobile assembly, household appliances, and the canning and fishing industries under the acquisition of the state. Practically all of the external credits received by public enterprises in Mexico were obtained with the intervention of Nacional Financiera. From 1958 to 1964, the sectoral distribution of such funds went, respectively, to transport ($190.5 million or 27 percent), electrification ($153.6 million or 22 percent), industry ($82.8 million or 12 percent), and irrigation, education, and public health ($145.7 million or 28 percent) (Ramírez 1986a: 102). Prominent among parastatal firms was the first integrated steel mill, Altos Hornos de México, at Monclova in the state of Coahuila, using Mexican coal and iron ore and expanding into investments in paper and cement as well as railroad construction. To help finance its founding, NAFINSA was instrumental in negotiating credits from the U.S. Export-Import Bank, in 1942, while loan transactions followed with the International

Bank for Reconstruction and Development (IBRD, or World Bank), in 1949, and the Inter-American Development Bank and the United States Agency for International Development (USAID) in the early 1960s. Between 1942 and 1959, NAFINSA obtained overseas credits of $992,443,000 from the Export-Import Bank, the IBRD, Bank of America, and the Chase Manhattan Bank for public works and industrial or public service enterprises, according to its director general from 1952 to 1970, José Hernández Delgado (1959: 19).

> NAFINSA co-operated with both the Mexican government, whose top financial officials were usually drawn from NAFINSA's board of directors, and private capital, including foreign investors, to whom it often made loans. U.S. bankers, through their status as NAFINSA's creditors and their purchases of state bonds issued by NAFINSA, were thus able to assert considerable influence over state economic decision making. (Cockcroft 1983: 184–85)

Indeed, as early as 1951, Nacional Financiera proposed that a combined working party be established with the International Bank for Reconstruction and Development "to assess the major long-term trends in the Mexican economy with particular reference to absorb additional foreign investments" (Combined Mexican Working Party 1953: ix). Based on a review of investments by Raul Ortiz Mena (Nacional Financiera), Victor L. Urquidi (Banco de México), and Albert Waterston and Jonas H. Haralz (both from the International Bank for Reconstruction and Development), the emphasis was on Mexico's capacity to absorb foreign investments by supplying "the essential foundations needed by the Mexican government to formulate a development program" (Combined Mexican Working Party 1953: vii). As Alfredo Navarrete, deputy-director of Nacional Financiera and a further "theoretician of the passive revolution," later summarized:

> Foreign capital, both public and private, participated in several of the key industrial promotions of Nacional Financiera in this period, notably in the establishment of enterprises to produce steel, copper, fertilizers, paper, synthetic fibres and electric equipment—industries oriented primarily to the substitution of imports . . . Thus foreign capital was able to assist in the active process of transformation of the productive structure necessary to economic development and growth. (Navarrete 1968: 78)

Between 1942 and 1967, Nacional Financiera received $4,218 million in foreign capital channeled to infrastructure projects and basic industries noted throughout this chapter (electric power, railroad transportation, highways, agricultural investments and irrigation, petroleum and petrochemicals, steel, and vehicle production). From 1942 to 1954, 79 percent of the amounts drawn by NAFINSA came from the United States, 19 percent from international institutions, and the remaining 3 percent from European and Canadian sources (Navarrete 1968: 82). Capturing the goal of creating "national" capitalists, Alfredo Navarrete has stated that "the action of the Revolutionary governments has not been at the expense of private Mexican investment. . . . In fact, public investment has filled the vacancy left by the massive foreign investment of the regime of Porfirio Díaz." Hence, national integration and productive expansion were at the core of this strategy of financing social development, "yesterday in violent and forceful stages, today in a more subdued and quiet manner" (Navarrete 1967: 128, 130).

Of course, it needs to be stressed that such a serene view of capitalist consolidation should be avoided while also remembering that the import-substitution process was continually subject to contradictions and improvisations throughout its progression (Cypher 1990: 64). It is also important to note that the ISI strategy was aimed at advancing agricultural transformations wrought by the processes of primitive accumulation, as observed in chapter 2, by increasing heavy investments in infrastructure and targeting domestic production of basic grains in order to achieve food self-sufficiency. As Marx (1894/1998: 792) indicates, a "portion of the surplus labour of the peasants, who work under the least favourable conditions, is bestowed gratis upon society" through the formation of value. Yet, as Roger Bartra (1993: 64) clarifies, it is the bourgeoisie as a whole that benefits from peasant surplus labor that is then "bestowed gratis upon society." It is tempting to agree with the view that "the collective *ejidos* were an aberrant form, struggling for survival in a capitalist society" (Hellman 1983: 90). However, such an assessment should be checked given that the *ejido* was a pivot of support for the legitimization of state policies and political stability under the PRI in Mexico (Chevalier 1967). More fundamentally, it should be recalled from chapter 2 that agrarian reform followed more the route of the "farmer road," based on the violent destruction of estates (*latifundia*) while leading to the proliferation of *ejido* land and small private property, rather than the "junker road" of slowly transforming landholdings (*haciendas*) into capitalist enterprises. The *ejido* is therefore better regarded, not just as a form of communal property, but also as a disguised form of private property situated in the context of capitalist production and articulated with combined developmental processes of precapitalist property relations (Bartra 1993: 94). While agriculture in Mexico grew at an annual rate of 5.7 percent from 1940 to 1955, by the end of the 1960s the overall rate of agricultural growth had fallen to 1.5 percent (Arizpe 1985: 206). At this time, food self-sufficiency had been maintained and the agricultural sector was directly financing the industrial and service sectors with the net transfer from agriculture to the rest of the economy estimated at some $250 million at 1960 prices (Hansen 1974: 59). There was, then, widespread "squeezing" of agriculture under ISI in order to finance new manufacturing industries, undertaken through price controls on basic foods, forms of taxation, and the control of wages in urban centers (Bruton 1998: 914).

The dominance and significance of state financing of agriculture is indicated by the early priority granted to the sector by NAFINSA during the primary phase of ISI. In 1940, financing granted by NAFINSA to the agricultural sector was 14.5 percent compared to 11.4 percent to industry (see table 3.4). By 1950 the level of NAFINSA's financing granted to agriculture remained roughly constant just below 15 percent, while the industrial sector had jumped to over 65 percent. More dramatically still, in 1960, the shake out from agriculture to industry was signified by the industrial sector receiving over 81 percent of NAFINSA's state-led developmental financing compared to the drop to below 10 percent granted to agriculture. By the 1960s the economy shifted to more intensive forms of labor processes within industry (and increased proletarianization) and agroindustrialization came to further the modernization of the food industry and transform the organization of production. This led to the transformation of basic grain production by *ganaderización* (livestock-oriented commercial production) involving the displacement of sorghum for corn and the industrial production of poultry and pork meat so that the agricultural productive process became increasingly controlled by industrial capital. As David Barkin (1990: 31) has detailed, "the distorted pattern of development of Mexican agriculture has resulted in a generalised move toward a demand-driven model of agricultural production" and a productive structure oriented toward animal feed (sorghum), luxury foods, and agroexports. This drive came to dominate the agrarian landscape in the 1970s albeit, at the time, with enhanced state support to halt the demise of food self-sufficiency, such as the Compañia Nacional de Subsistencias Populares (CONASUPO). The latter, set up in 1965, ensured that labor's urban consumption needs of basic foodstuffs could be met by maintaining cheap foodcrop supplies appropriated from peasant producers. CONASUPO ensured, then, the commoditization of the peasant economy by bringing *ejidal* production to the market (Bartra and Otero 1987: 343). Attempts to offset the crisis in the peasant economy also included expanded agrarian reform during the Díaz Ordaz administration, with the total surface of distributed lands amounting to 25,568,204 hectares, which was more than the 21,654,920 hectares distributed under Cárdenas (Nacional Financiera 1978: 53–54).[7] This partly explains the spike in NAFINSA financing granted to agricultural investments throughout the 1970s, shooting to just over 30 percent in 1970 and holding at 22 percent in 1975. Linked to this was also the prominence of new initiatives such as the Programa Integral para el Desarrollo Rural (PIDER), launched in 1973 with financing from the World Bank channeled through NAFINSA. The aim here was to promote a self-sustained development process within "micro-regions" by targeting livestock production and small-scale irrigation through the provision of agricultural credit, infrastructure support, and education facilities. As a result, specific "micro-regions" across varied climatic zones in the states of Puebla (Zacapoaxtla), Nuevo León (Sur de Nuevo León), Sinaloa (Cosala-Elota), Yucatán (Sur de Yucatán), Aguascalientes (El Llano), and Guanajuato (northeast Guanajuato) would be guaranteed access to goods and services while applying modern technology to increase crop yields on rain-fed smallholdings. As a result of PIDER, the World Bank claimed that "the Mexican Government has organised itself through both spatial (river basin and micro-region) and functional (credit, extension, irrigation, feeder road) programs for a major effort to address rural poverty" (World Bank 1975: 3). The three phases of World Bank funding covered a twelve-year period amounting to loans of $110 million (1975–1980), $120 million (1977–1983), and $175 million (1982–1987). In summarizing, the World Bank has stated that PIDER was instrumental in two main ways by: (1) assisting the Secretaría de Programación y Presupuesto (SPP) in building a decentralized institutional framework that formed the basis for subsequent major rural and regional development programs (World Bank 1986: 17); and (2) shifting the focus solely from infrastructure support "to an emphasis on productive investments to promote self-sufficiency and improve income distribution" and to tap into "unrealised productive potential" (World Bank 1990: vi).

From a different vantage point these development plans have been signaled as increasing the process of proletarianization alongside an array of props claiming to support agricultural producers (Hellman 1983: 96–97). By

Table 3.4. Nacional Financiera, S.A.: Financing Granted by Economic Sector, Selected Years, 1940–1976 (percent)

Sector	1940	1950	1960	1970	1976
Infrastructure[a]	14.5	14.9	9.6	30.5	22.3
Industry	11.4	65.3	81.5	69.4	77.6
Basic[b]	8.2	48.2	63.4	47.7	56.5
Other manufacturing[c]	3.2	17.1	18.1	21.7	21.1
Other activities	74.1	19.8	8.9	0.1	0.1
Total	100	100	100	100	100

Source: Calculated from Nacional Financiera (1978: 300–305).

[a]Includes roads, highways, and bridges as well as irrigation and agricultural investments.

[b]Includes mining and petroleum, iron and steel, nonferrous metals, cement and construction materials, and electric power.

[c]Includes food products, textiles and clothing, wood industry, cellulose and paper, and chemicals.

1980, the Ley de Fomento Agropecuario (Agricultural Development Law), announced in President José López Portillo's State of the Union address, signaled the future for agrarian reform. The main thrust was to guarantee private property ownership of land and the legal possibility for *ejidatarios* and agribusinesses to join together in "free association" to establish the introduction of large amounts of capital and technology to increase production. The final development along these lines was the Sistema Alimentario Mexicano (SAM), a further attempt to raise productivity among smallholding, subsistence, producers by providing price guarantees, credit, and discounts on agricultural producers of beans, maize, rice, and wheat. Introduced in 1980, SAM was projected to bring about food self-sufficiency by increasing maize production by 46 percent (from 8.9 million metric tons in 1979 to 13 million in 1982) and the production of beans by 135 percent (from 637,000 metric tons in 1979 to 1.5 million in 1981). Yet, prior to its collapse in 1983, the SAM was again a policy that followed in the footsteps of its contemporary agrarian reform counterparts, such as PIDER, by contributing to the separation of peasants from the land and their means of subsistence. So, while the aim was to increase agricultural production, the result was the extension of capitalist property relations into the countryside that accelerated proletarianization and the use of wage labor on *ejido* parcels (Bartra 1993: xiii–xv; Harris and Barkin 1982: 5–7).

These are the paradoxes of passive revolution whereby state agencies internalize the class interests and orientations of capital, inextricably tying the nurturing and consolidation of a national bourgeoisie to state intervention, within a world context dominated by foreign capital. Within conditions of uneven development in the periphery, the state in capitalist society comes to strengthen the national bourgeoisie while continuing to support processes of capital accumulation. In Mexico, state intervention through myriad institutions, such as NAFINSA that engendered and extended processes of primitive accumulation, was necessary to ensure national capitalist development albeit "articulated within the global rationality of specific core capitals" (Hamilton 1982b: 21, 186). While the consolidation of foreign capital would not be completed until the structural change of neoliberal reforms in the 1980s and beyond, something that will be traced in chapter 4, the expansion of capital nevertheless was secured through the internalization of capitalist class interests across various fractions of capital and the state form. Passive revolution is thus a central expression of the shaping and reshaping of class struggle through the "spatial fix" of state formation within the broader conditions of uneven and combined development (Harvey 1985/2001: 324–25).

ARCHITECTURING PASSIVE REVOLUTION

Yet, as Gramsci reminds us, within conditions of passive revolution, it is important to recognize that state formation is "further complicated by the existence within every state of several structurally diverse territorial sectors" (Gramsci 1971: 182, Q13§17). Equally, then, the spatial role of the state redounds across multiscaled contexts and a diverse set of hierarchical arrangements (local, regional, national, or international) through which classes and class fractions compete to profit from the flows of capital and labor (Harvey 1982/2006: 420). Gramsci further adds that recognizing how the "material structure of ideology"—meaning the social function performed by the built environment, including architecture, street layouts, and even street names—shapes social power would also "get people into the habit of a more cautious and precise calculation of the forces acting in society" (Gramsci 1995: 155–56, Q3§49). The urban economy and built environment in Mexico City can thus also be regarded as an additional essential element inscribing the class conditions of capital accumulation and national state formation under ISI. Just as Paris has been described, during its material transformation under Napoleon III and Georges-Eugène Haussmann in the 1850s, as "a capital city being shaped by bourgeois power into a city of capital" (Harvey 2003b: 24), then so can Mexico City be similarly described in the 1950s.

The spatial practices that transformed Mexico City through the expression of mimetic architectural forms and cultural monuments, of course, have a long history. The prevalence of *los afrancesados*—the Frenchified—among traditional ruling classes before and after the 1862–1867 French invasion and imposition of Archduke Maximilian of Austria as emperor was emblematic. While novelists at the time translated the mannerisms and mores of French society into a Mexican setting, thoroughfares such as Paseo de la Reforma (formerly Emperor's Road until 1877) were planned during Maximilian's rule (1864–1867), as a Champs-Élysées linking the city center around the Zócalo to Chapultepec Castle. Under Porfirio Díaz, Mexico City's department stores, such as El Puerto de Liverpool (1888) and El Palacio de Hierro (1891), were constructed by French architects and foreign capital; streets in the *colonias* of Cuauhtémoc and Juárez were named Rhine, Danube, Seine, and Berlin, Hamburgo, or Londres and built by finance minister José Limantour's links to foreign capital; buildings were designed by foreign architects such as the famous Central Post Office (completed 1907) and the stalled Palacio de Bellas Artes (begun 1904) by Adamo Boari; and national monuments such as the Column of Independence (completed 1910) were constructed—resembling elements of both the Place Vendôme column in

Paris and the Victory Column in Berlin, with its sculptures undertaken by the Italian artist Enrique Alciati, including El Ángel de la Independencia that sits atop the column. Mexico City's historical transformation under Díaz was marked by the "invasion of statues" (Monsiváis 1989: 118), reflecting a "mania" for statuary and symbolic buildings across Europe that peaked between 1870 and 1914 (Hobsbawm 1983: 273). As Michael Johns (1997: 22–23) details, in his coverage of Mexico City during this age, "Mexican architecture . . . was an expression of a city run by people who were looking to create their own culture while entirely dependent on the industry and ideas of Europe and America. They copied the places they envied, but those copies betrayed insecurity, anxiety, and inexperience." The Porfirian elite's obsession with Paris and its architecture, its urbanism and forms was expressed by practicing architects from the Academia de San Carlos in Mexico City, the equivalent of the French École des Beaux Arts, and its importation of metropolitan architectures, axial organization and placement of large avenues, and neo-Colonial style, resurrecting Churrigueresque, Renaissance, and Baroque elements (Carranza 2010: 5–7). In this period, up to the 1920s, the long-established spatial hierarchy in Mexico City was furthered with the western areas maintained as established locations of wealth but overlade with the real estate interests and, eventually, the California Colonial or Hollywood style of architecture, swapping the fashion of Emperor Maximilian for American-type influences (Garza 2006: 115; Olsen 2008: 11, 34). Generally, then, countries in the throes of rapid development have embarked on such imitative forms of architectural power, analogies of expression, resemblances, and mimesis, with the latter having a role and function in the domination of space (Lefebvre 1991: 309–11, 376). As González Casanova (1970: 6) notes, "in the underdeveloped nations creativity is stifled by appropriated foreign ideas and by imitation and adjustment."[8]

In Mexico City, there are various examples of the ways in which the spatial practices of passive revolution have become expressed through the modern urban economy and built environment. As Patrice Olsen (2008: xv, 20–29) details, "the ironies of the revolution were chiselled into the built environment" of the capital city, revealing fundamental contradictions in the Mexican Revolution itself as capitalist development was extended. Generally speaking, the conditions of capitalist transformation associated with modernity can be related to what has been called "the anguish of backwardness": the spatial ordering of urban landscapes within capital cities that conjoins the contradictions of national identity with imitative modernism. "The modernism of underdevelopment is forced to build on fantasies and dreams of modernity, to nourish itself on intimacy and a struggle with mirages and ghosts" (Berman 1982: 232). The presence of émigré architects, such as the

Bauhaus's Hannes Meyer, director of the Instituto del Urbanismo y Planificación (1942–1949) and designer of high-rise housing for unionized workers and state employees in Mexico City, or the Russian émigré architect Vladimir Kaspé and designer of the Súper Servicio Lomas building, built in 1948, raise compelling cases of the role of cosmopolitanism within Mexico's cultural patrimony (Davis 2009). The issue of mimesis is promoted by such architectural codifications, in the sense that foreign ideas come to play a prominent role in the representation of space and in legitimating state ideology. Within its own context, "the Bauhaus, just like Le Corbusier, expressed (formulated and met) the architectural requirements of state capitalism" (Lefebvre 1991: 304), something applicable to the passing of such representations of space to alternative modernist landscapes. Noteworthy in this context is the development of multifamily housing regarded as emblematic of the rationalization of urban growth in Mexico City, exemplified by the Centro Urbano Presidente Alemán (President Alemán Urban Housing Project), constructed between 1947 and 1949, by the architect Mario Pani, and the Centro Urbano Presidente Juárez (President Juárez Urban Housing Project), built between 1950 and 1952. Linked to the same architect, the well-known Ciudad Habitacional Nonoalco-Tlatelolco (Nonoalco-Tlatelolco Urban Housing Project), constructed between 1960 and 1964, combining 148 structures honeycombed with 15,000 apartments and the capacity to house between 75,000 to 100,000 inhabitants, came to represent the modernism of Mexico City. These monuments of *multifamilares* combined European forms, from Le Corbusier and the Bauhaus movement, and adapted them to Mexican culture and sensibilities that "took special account of the *modus vivendi* of Mexicans" (Noelle Merles 1997: 182).

Attention therefore needs to be cast to a "vernacular architecture," linking Mexican-based architects and practices to nationalist aspirations and modernist ideological styles, as significant in the built expression of the modern state (Ward 1990: 185–94). The completion of the Monument to the Revolution is especially instructive here in its spatial practices linked to its status as one of the country's most significant commemorative sites. Originally designed as one of the hallmarks of the Díaz era, as the Palacio Legislativo Federal, in 1897 by Italian architect Pietro Paollo Quaglia and then French designer Èmile Bernard, it was transformed into the triumphal arch of *la Revolución* following its completion in 1938. Thoroughly modified by the Mexican architect Carlos Obregón Santacilia, the monument carries four sculptures by Oliverio Martínez, renowned for his earlier statue of Emiliano Zapata in Cuautla, that stand at the base of the monument representing National Independence, Reform, the Redemption of the Peasant, and the Redemption of the Worker. With these Mexican figures, Indian and mestizo, and partial funding through national subscription, El Monumento has become the spatial base for honoring and remembering the heroes of the Mexican Revolution through official ceremonies as well as the site for significant protests (see Benjamin 2000: 127–36).[9] "The Monument to the Revolution acts as a 'gateway,' an urban portal, and a pure space of transition" (Mijares Bracho 1997: 157). The placement of the ashes and the remains of rival leaders such as Madero (1960), Calles (1969), Cárdenas (1970), and Villa (1976) in the pillars of the monument reflect the attempt to legitimize state power and authority. Henri Lefebvre (1976: 88) captures this spatial dimension in stating:

> Architecture oscillates between monumental splendour and the cynicism of the "habit." The monumental consists of borrowings from bygone styles and displays of technicality. It attempts to conceal the meaning but only succeeds in proclaiming it: these are the places of official Power, the places where Power is concentrated, where it reflects itself, looks down from above—and is transparent.

This description of how the state binds itself to space transmits directly to the Monument to the Revolution, not only in terms of its borrowings and displays of style. State space itself has also been represented adjacent to the monument, by the offices of the Dirección Federal de Seguridad—Mexico's secret police force headed by Fernando Gutiérrez Barrios and instrumental in orchestrating the repression of the left in the "dirty war" of the 1970s—that once faced the Monument to the Revolution. Therefore, although, "the Monument to the Revolution was built, primarily, to heal the wounds of memory that divided revolutionaries and retarded and weakened the development of a new institutional political order" (Benjamin 2000: 135), it was equally surrounded by state power looking down from above. Literally, specific spatial practices, in the form of state codifications of architecture therefore contribute to the reproduction of the social relations of production and the construction of the modern state in conditions of passive revolution. In terms of synthesis and symbolism, then, "el Monumento a la Revolución" is best understood as "el monumento a la revolución pasiva" in Mexico. It represents the very institutionalization of the revolution, retaining the empty space of the old Porfirian structure, and stands as a monumentalization of Mexico's incomplete modernity (Olsen 2008: 128–33, 245–46; Carranza 2010: 198–99). In reproducing the urban form of the city and class inequalities, Peter Ward (1990: 231) states that "Mexico City's architecture is a very important medium whereby the reigning philosophy and ideology of development are read and made legible to the general public," especially through the state's commissioning of monuments. Later architects, such as Luis Barragán or Ricardo Legoretta, came to combine orthodox modernism with Mexican nationalism, from the 1940s through to the 1960s, in (literally) cementing specific spatial practices, social patterns, and behavior within the urban form and a dominant logic of capital accumulation.

Within the wider urban economy of Mexico City, during ISI, the governing role of Ernesto Uruchurtu through the Departmento del Distrito Federal as mayor of the city over a fourteen-year period (1952–1966) also reveals the consolidation of class and state power within this period of passive revolution. Importantly, Uruchurtu developed close ties with the fractions of capital analyzed earlier, represented through CANACINTRA that favored a "DF-centric" model of urban growth policies orchestrated by the PRI, while restricting urban squatter neighborhoods (*vecindades*) and targeting the removal of low-income population settlements. As Diane Davis (1994: 134–37) has detailed, the result was that migrants to Mexico City were displaced to the peripheral zones resulting in the spatial expansion of the metropolitan areas. Simultaneously, Uruchurtu co-opted specific sectors of the working population within the city through the Sindicato Único de Trabajadores del Gobierno del Distrito Federal (SUTGDF) for whom he built parks, installed kindergarten facilities, modernized clinics, and created special stores with clothing, furniture, and household goods. The spatial organization of the city also underwent radical change as land speculation fueled urban growth following the introduction of stabilized development in 1955. While street widening was one controversy under Uruchurtu's mayoralty, the pivotal project to grip urban renovation was the building of the underground transport system, the METRO, linked to real estate development interests and, increasingly, the influence of foreign capital through CONCAMIN. The drive behind the METRO project led by CONCAMIN and its links to international capital threatened to undermine Uruchurtu's political bases of support from nationally based capital within CANACINTRA, leading to the stalling of the development. As Davis (1994: 159) summarizes, the struggle over the METRO project "was a struggle over Mexico City's character, over the place and power of middle classes in local and national politics, and over the urban and industrial future of the nation." It was the struggle between these class fractions that ultimately led to Uruchurtu's demise and resignation and the acceleration of the METRO's construction under the administration of Gustavo Díaz Ordaz (1964–1970) in 1967. Uruchurtu fought *El Monstruo*, the Monster that is Mexico City, and lost (Ross 2009: 239). The conflicts between these fractions of capital—on one hand representing import-substituting industrialists and smaller manufacturers of national capital and on the other hand financial and banking interests linked to the internationalization of capital—would come "to haunt the PRI once again," whether on issues of urban growth, national development, or ultimately the restructuring of the economy under neoliberalism (Davis 1994: 173). The next chapter will pick up the analysis of the inertia experienced by the expanded reproduction of capital under ISI allied with a renewed focus on its crisis conditions and the conjunctural class alliances and conflicts that would come to reshape the uneven geography of capital accumulation and neoliberalism in Mexico.

The point to affirm within this chapter is that the modern state binds itself to space whether through forms of monumentality in architecture, investments in urbanization, or through the creation of development, banking, and credit institutions through which surplus value transfers are produced and allocated (see Lefebvre 1978/2009: 247). As explained above, such interventions become "statified" elements reflecting the structural conditions of passive revolution rather than society creating "for itself the revolutionary point of departure, the situation, the relations, the conditions under which alone modern revolution becomes serious" (Marx 1852/1979: 106). For Marx, the social basis of the blocked factional struggles between rival propertied interests was reflected in the historical condition that would, ultimately, be temporarily surmounted by the coup d'état in France of Louis Napoleon III. In this case, Marx stated that "instead of *society* having conquered a new content for itself, it seems shamelessly that the *state* only returned to its oldest form, to the shamelessly simple domination of the sabre and the cowl" (Marx 1852/1979: 106, emphasis added). In Mexico, institutions such as NAFINSA—perhaps not too dissimilar to its French counterpart of the 1850s, *Crédit Mobilier*—increased the fusion of financial and industrial capital within the constitution of the modern capitalist form of state to secure surplus value transfers. At the same time, sophisticated forms of spatial representation linked to *la Revolución*—such as the Monument to the Revolution—alongside ideological mechanisms of co-option and control aided the ruling PRI in performing its "world-historical necromancy" through which the sprits of the past could be conjured up to serve the present; hence "the resurrection of the dead . . . served the purpose of glorifying the new struggles; not of parodying the old" (Marx 1852/1979: 104–5). As one participant-observer to these processes, Leon Trotsky, summarizes, the state in Mexico gained "the possibility of a certain freedom toward the foreign capitalists" while "raising itself politically above the classes" and shoring up support through the "statisation of the trade unions" (Trotsky 1938/1979: 791; Trotsky 1939/1974a: 326; Trotsky 1934/1971: 512). In Nora Hamilton's (1982b: 4–25) view, this indicated the comparative weakness of the bourgeoisie so that the state came to act as the ultimate arbiter, assisting, stimulating, and completing capital accumulation with a degree of relative autonomy from dominant fractions of capital and subordinate classes (see also Cockcroft 1983: 145). This is not the same as positing the "rectorship" role of the state where it "gives life and reason to one unified national project which all social elements must take as their own; as the very incarnation of the interests of all" (Córdova 1974: 180; Cypher 1990: 18).[10] Instead, my argument has been that there was the active constitution and cohering in Mexico of the *state in capitalist society* through ISI, which secured the more or less adequate requirements of the capital relation by the late 1960s. Within the conditions of passive revolution that confront a state in capitalist society, due to the weakness of the bourgeoisie, there is "the fact that the state replaces the local social groups in leading a struggle of renewal" (Gramsci 1971: 105–6, Q15§59). It was a state with almost limitless repressive possibilities based on a divided bourgeoisie that was unable to articulate a case of integral hegemony, while nevertheless constantly readjusting capitalist development to global exigencies (Leal 1974: 190). The emergence in Mexico of a *capitalist type of state* dominated by the logic of capitalist accumulation, the appearance of the institutional separation of "economic" and "political" aspects, and the securing of class domination in a period of structural change from the 1970s onward is the topic of the next chapter.

CONCLUSION: THE "OPEN FRONTIER" SHAPING THE STATE AND CAPITAL ACCUMULATION

Within a passive revolution the action of the dominant classes is in response to the "popular masses" and there is a degree of hegemonic activity, with the former accepting "a certain part of the demands expressed from below" resulting in aspects of revolution-restoration (Gramsci 1995: 373, Q10II§41xiv). As noted above, the state comes to replace the mass character of the transformation of society, a situation where domination, or coercion, tends to predominate over leadership; when there is a situation of "dictatorship without hegemony" (Gramsci 1971: 105–6, Q15§59). Following the lead in chapter 1, state power in a situation of passive revolution is channeled more through authoritarian and coercive interventions, although hegemonic activity does also clearly exist. A passive revolution is therefore a case of minimal hegemony, in that the state-coercive element superintends the hegemonic activity, and coercive organization comes to dominate over the "normal" exercise of hegemony based on the development of an organic relationship between force and consent. Through this specific form of transition to capitalism "the hegemonic system is thus maintained and the forces of military and civil coercion kept at the disposal of the . . . ruling classes" (Gramsci 1995: 350, Q10I§9). The overall outcome is a "statisation" of class struggle within which "the counter-attack of capital" displaces political forms emanating from the base of society (Buci-Glucksmann 1979: 219, 223).

The foregoing discussion has traced the consolidation of passive revolution in Mexico across the linked contexts of ISI and *desarrollo estabilizador* within which the state secured the economic and extraeconomic conditions for capital accumulation. This involved a process of state and class formation in which a distinction was drawn between the historical constitution of the state within an emerging capitalist social formation (state in capitalist society) and the preeminence of the logic of capitalist accumulation evident in the apparent separation of the state as a social form from the economy (capitalist type of state). It will be recalled that this period in the organization and reorganization of passive revolution was associated with the constitution of a state in capitalist society, securing the requirements of the capital relation. This was the "success" of ISI as a passive revolution in terms of establishing and deepening the development of capitalist class processes. Summarizing the benefits accruing to the capitalist class as a whole at this time it has been noted that their taxes and their wage costs were low, their profits were high, and the expanding state infrastructure that supported the extraction of surplus value was extensive to the degree that it would be difficult to imagine a set of policies designed to reward bourgeois interests more than those evident in Mexico since 1940 (Hansen 1974: 87). However, this was also a structurally incomplete or "sinuous" entrance into modernity (García Canclini 1995: 54). The contradictions of capital accumulation at this time were reflected in at least two weaknesses. First, despite capitalism becoming more fully established it had still not founded its logical form, namely, bourgeois democracy (González Casanova 1970: 159–65). Second, the ongoing processes of proletarianization, the reproduction of the peasantry, and the mobilization of social movements all meant that the roots of class struggle and conflict in challenging the state remained. Later chapters on the political economy of democratization and democratic transition (chapter 6) and uneven agrarian development and spaces of resistance (chapter 7) will analyze these contradictions.

Overall, this chapter had as its central argument, first, that the policies of ISI were linked to a configuration of particular class forces, in the form of certain fractions of capital, which propelled capital accumulation through specific social property relations based on the expansion of manufacturing industry and agribusiness with the aim of replacing imports. Underpinning the provision of infrastructure and basic goods (steel, electricity, oil extraction and refining, telecommunications, water and sanitation) were prominent SOEs and development banks—notably Nacional Financiera—that provided credit and public financing for industrial expansion and developmental objectives. NAFINSA was especially significant in concentrating and organizing the passive revolution of capital and hastening "hothouse fashion" processes of capitalist transformation in Mexico. The participation of foreign capital was an important feature of ISI in the 1950s and 1960s and was instrumental in establishing key manufacturing industries, investment infrastructures, and state-owned heavy industry. "It seems," notes Werner Baer (1972: 109–10), "that many forget that a large number of the key manufacturing industries of Latin America were constructed by or with the aid of foreign capital." Second, factors linking the "spatio-temporal fix" of the state to the multiscalar context of uneven development across state, region, and city form were also discussed. Here, "more than ever, the class struggle is inscribed in space" (Lefebvre 1991: 55). The architecture of the state and spatial practices of passive revolution were therefore analyzed within the conditioning situation of uneven development, which included aspects of the built environment contributing, literally, to the architecture of passive revolution. Yet here, again, the conditions of passive revolution and the emergence of specific fractions of capital in Mexico were not bracketed off from the context of world capitalism. Rather the discussion stressed the interiorization of the interests of capital that became integrated into state policies and spatial representations that were linked to the presence of capitalist interests on a global scale. This has been called the "open frontier" shaping the process of state and capital accumulation in Mexico (Fitzgerald 1985: 229). The crisis of ISI and the structural change of capitalism, leading to the ascendancy of neoliberalism in consolidating a capitalist type of state, as well as the role of specific fractions of the capitalist class in abetting the internationalization of capital in Mexico are at the heart of the chapter that follows.

NOTES

1. The stress on passive revolution as a condition of rupture in which sociopolitical processes of revolution are at once displaced and partially fulfilled can be found in Callinicos (2010).

2. While reliant on substantiation through recourse to statistical evidence, caution always has to be noted in drawing from such sources. One of the most banal commonplaces, as Gramsci (1971: 192, Q13§30) counseled, is that numbers decide everything. "But the fact is that this is not true. . . . Numbers, in this case too, are simply an instrumental value, giving a measure and a relation and nothing more. And what then is measured? What is measured is precisely the effectiveness, and the expansive and persuasive capacity, of the opinions of a few individuals, the active minorities, the elites, the avant-gardes, etc.—i.e. their rationality, historicity or concrete functionality."

3. For an overview, see Comisión Económica para América Latina/Nacional Financiera (1971).

96   *Chapter Three*

4. Although, of course, within these city forms "the façade was rough hewn and centres of urban misery contrasted with opulence" (Barkin 1975: 77). Also, within the specific spatial structure of Mexico City, uneven development became entrained by the orientation of different types of industrial activity, nondurable consumer goods industries in inner areas, while the outer areas and the metropolitan periphery became directed, up to the 1970s, more toward capital goods and the production of consumer durables located along two key sectors in the northeast (Azcapotzalco, Tlalnepantla, Naucalpan, and Cuautitlán Izcalli) and the northwest (Ecatepec) of the city (Ward 1990: 21, 94).

5. During World War II, however, the expansion of U.S. demand meant that Mexican manufactured exports northward increased from 7 percent of total exports in 1939 to almost 38 percent in 1945, meaning that "Mexico's industrial expansion during the war was export-driven" (Cárdenas 2000: 183, 185).

6. While starting out as director of the Instituto Mexicano del Seguro Social (IMSS), from 1952 to 1958, followed by his role as minister of finance for the twelve-year period from 1958 to 1970, Antonio Ortiz Mena went on to unsuccessfully compete for the PRI's nomination for the 1970 presidential election. In 1971 he was appointed as president of the Inter-American Development Bank until 1988. Between 1988 and 1990 he served as the director of Banamex, one of the country's main commercial banks.

7. Although, it is noteworthy that only 2.4 million hectares, or 9.6 percent of the land, under the Díaz Ordaz redistribution was arable, in contrast to the almost 5 million hectares, or 25 percent of arable lands, constituting agrarian reform under Cárdenas (Bartra and Otero 1987: 350).

8. This is reminiscent of Leon Trotsky's (1936/1980: 26) comment, noted in chapter 2, "A backward country assimilates the material and intellectual conquests of the advanced countries. But this does not mean that it follows them slavishly, reproduces all the stages of their past."

9. Recent examples would include the mobilization of trade unionists and campesinos at the Monument to the Revolution, in support of the forty-four thousand sacked workers of the Sindicato Mexicano de Electricistas (SME) struggling against the closure of the state-owned Compañía Luz y Fuerza del Centro, since October 2009; see *La Jornada*, "Campesinos arribarán en caravan para apoyar al SME en la *toma* del DF" (2 December 2009): 8. But also the remodeling of the site surrounding the monument, the reopening of its museum, and its renovation as an official site of commemoration at a cost of approximately $21 million was evident during the centennial anniversary celebrations of the Mexican Revolution, on 20 November 2010, an event convoked by Marcelo Ebrard, as mayor of the city, and attended by other luminaries such as Cuauhtémoc Cárdenas and the novelist Carlos Fuentes; see *La Jornada*, "Reinaugura Marcelo Ebrard la Plaza de la República con llamado a nueva revolución" (21 November 2010): 8. The recent fifth "Lesbian March" for the respect of women's human rights, ending at the Monument on Plaza de la República, organized by the Comité Organizador de la Marcha Lésbica (COMAL) and twenty-two other feminist groupings, on 19 March 2011, is an alternative example of lived space and reveals another different claim on the right to the city, to not be excluded

from its centrality and movement; see *La Jornada*, "Marcha de lesbianas exige respeto a los derechos humanos de ese sector" (20 March 2011): 33. The Monument to the Revolution thus traverses at least two of the principal types of transformation of urban monuments outlined by Néstor García Canclini (1989: 217–25), in terms of (1) popular intervention as political commentary on the significance of the monument; and (2) neutralization or alteration of the monument's significance, due to a disruption in scale given its subordination to urban sprawl by surrounding buildings (see also García Canclini 1995: 212–22).

10. Due to limitations of space, the connection here to the condition of Bonapartism is left for ongoing research, but analysis of the merits and shortcomings of Bonapartism can be found inter alia in Benjamin (1985: 197), Knight (1985: 4–5), Knight (1992a: 178–79), Knight (2001: 192), Markiewicz (1993: 35–45), Mora (1979: 127–34), Mora (1982), Rodríguez Araujo (1979: 19–58), or Semo (1978: 279–98).

Chapter Four

Neoliberalism and Structural Change within the Global Political Economy of Uneven Development

One of the themes touched on in previous chapters in the first part of this book has been the manner in which the spatial scales of state power, in terms of its uneven and combined development, can be meaningfully addressed through the theory of passive revolution. A key argument of the book is therefore that the theory of passive revolution throws into relief processes of capital accumulation in Mexico shaping the state form that are embedded within the uneven and combined development of global capitalism. More explicitly, this chapter addresses the multiscaled context of Mexico's shift from the stabilized development model scrutinized in the previous chapter toward the creation of a new spatiotemporal fix for capital accumulation in the form of neoliberalism. This means analyzing how capitalism attempts to resolve continued surplus-value extraction through some form of temporary "spatial fix" to provide a relatively coherent geographical framework for capital accumulation across various scales (Harvey 1982/2006: 431; Smith 1984/2008: 174). It is argued that the blocked dialectic of revolution-restoration emblematic of the historical conditions of passive revolution and evident since the Mexican Revolution became assailed by class forces expediting and arbitrating the continued expansion of capitalism through neoliberal restructuring (see also Hesketh 2010b). Taking the state as nodal, the underlying responsibility of this chapter is to explain how particular fractions of capital, emerging through the reorganization and consolidation of the state during the period of stabilized development, *authored* neoliberalism (Panitch 1994). Put differently, a focus on state space, the spatial fix of the national scale, discriminates how the state is itself actively engaged in producing the spatial configurations of the accumulation process in terms of construction, reproduction, and contestation (Brenner 1997: 286). After all, as Neil Smith details, "the division of the world economy at the scale of national capital is the necessary foundation upon which capital can launch its aspirations to universality." At the same time, though, there is a scalar contradiction at the heart of the accumulation process in terms of how "capitalism inherits the global scale" and produces it anew, or how the law of value becomes universal through the equalization of transnational space as well as its differentiation (Smith 1984/2008: 181, 192). Hence the importance of assessing a hierarchy of spatial scales within the historical geography of capitalism that can address "the territorial dialectics of capitalism" (Murray 1971: 109).

The objective of embarking on a multiscalar analysis of the passive revolution of neoliberalism in Mexico is realized by developing a nodal, or punctual, analysis of the spatial scale of state power (see also chapter 1). As Henri Lefebvre details in highlighting the formation of new state spaces through a complex process of fission:

> No space disappears in the course of growth and development: the *worldwide does not abolish the local*. This is not a consequence of the law of uneven development, but a law in its own right. . . . Consequently, the local (or "punctual" in the sense of "determined by a particular 'point'") does not disappear, for it is never absorbed by the regional, national or even worldwide level. (Lefebvre 1991: 86–88, original emphasis)

This cue is adopted in order to embark on an analysis of state space that is taken as punctual, or nodal, in determining and socially producing the changing capital and territorial logics of power. Similarly, Gramsci was attuned to a spatial problematic that was "clearly evident in the spatial relations embedded in the social formation and in the particularities of place, location and territorial community" he considered (Soja 1989: 89–90; see also Jessop 2006: 31). Hence recognition of the spatial scale of state power as nodal, rather than dominant, when analyzing the structuring of capital and territory through conditions of uneven and combined development. This approach is at odds with arguments asserting the epochal dimension of globalization, meaning that the history of capitalism is witnessing the rise of transnational capital through the constitution of a transnational state. The scholarship of William Robinson has extensively asserted how current national and regional accumulation patterns in Latin America reflect certain spatial distinctions specific to an integrated global capitalist configuration of power and production (see inter alia Robinson 2003, 2004a, 2008). It is precisely this configuration that he sees as bringing together a transnational capitalist class and *transnational state* that is transcending the state-centrism and territorially bounded politics of space, place, and scale. In his words, "the state as a class relation is becoming transnationalised" (Robinson 2004a: 99–100).

In this chapter, then, the relevance of a theory of passive revolution that encompasses the interscalar articulation of state power will be set against the thesis of the transnational state. As Bob Jessop (2006: 38–39) counsels, this is not to argue for the simple rescaling of concepts from the "national" to the "transnational." Instead, it involves internalizing the method of interscalar articulation encapsulated in the theory of passive revolution in order to appreciate the reciprocal influence of specific spatial scales in understanding the dynamics of global capitalism. Concurrent with Hannes Lacher (1999: 357), it is argued that "national" economies are not simply governed by the political will of territorially defined constituencies but, at the same time, nor should one suppose that the imperatives of the world market alone are simply imposed on societies. As John Agnew has noted, one needs to avoid *both* the territorial trap of accepting the assumption of fixed state territoriality *and* the view that territoriality is becoming transformed into a globally undifferentiated transnational state. The critical issue, as he puts it, is "the historical relationship between territorial states and the broader social and economic structures and geopolitical order (or form of spatial practice) in which . . . states must operate" (Agnew 1994: 77). It will be argued that the theory of passive revolution promotes an understanding of states as "nodes" grounded in space and situated in time. This perspective on nodal spatiality has the promise of emphasizing how different scales between places relate to one another differentially over time (Agnew 2003: 13). The theory of passive revolution captures the dynamics of state power by highlighting the framing of the territorialization of surplus value as well as the deterritorialization of global capital within capitalist uneven and combined development. The structure of the chapter falls as follows.

First, the theory of the transnational state and global capitalism as proposed by William Robinson will be detailed and a critique elaborated. The latter involves developing three core problems within the theory of global capitalism and the transnational state, in understanding: (1) the historical relationship between territorial states and capitalism; (2) the relationship between globalization and uneven development; and (3) the spatial expression of capitalism and territoriality (see also Massey 2005). On the basis of these criticisms, a second section will reiterate briefly the relevance of the theory of passive revolution to a focus on both the world-historical context of uneven and combined development and its connection to the formative influence of states. This section returns to the extensive coverage of state formation and passive revolution in chapters 2 and 3. Linking back to chapter 3, especially, a focus on the distinction between a *state in capitalist society* and a *capitalist type of state* is further developed (see Jessop 2008). This chapter advances the second distinction to analyze how the exercise of class power in and through the capitalist type of state in Mexico overcame the problems posed by the institutional separation of the "economic" and the "political" through the specific accumulation strategy and hegemonic project of neoliberalism. How this capitalist type of state was consolidated through the class strategy of passive revolution, albeit within an alternative crisis period, is at the heart of the discussion that follows.

A third section then demonstrates the utility of a nodal analysis of state power by tracing the agency of particular class fractions in the constitution and reproduction of neoliberalism within the conditions of uneven and combined development in the global political economy. This is regarded as the most contemporary context of passive revolution in the history of modern Mexico shaping the present. At this stage of the discussion the clear emphasis on how "capital remains a force that by preference seeks to occupy the interconnections between separate political jurisdictions" (van der Pijl 2006a: 15) should be apparent. A detailed analysis of spaces of resistance to neoliberalism is beyond the purview of this particular chapter. However, the present chapter evidently highlights how the passive revolution of neoliberalism represents dominant forms of agency in the restructuring of capitalism. Part two of the book will then demonstrate how the notion of passive revolution moves beyond the "counter-attack of capital" to also encompass alternative spatial practices in the contestation of revolution and state in Mexico, not least "anti-passive revolution" strategies of resistance against neoliberalism (Buci-Glucksmann 1979: 223, 232).

CONTESTING THE TRANSNATIONAL STATE

The term *transnational* has been defined as referring to "forces, processes, and institutions that cross borders but do not derive their power and authority from the state." It is also argued that the term represents a decisive break from state-centrism by appreciating the globalizing practices of a transnational capitalist class regarded as the main driver of the global capitalist system (Sklair 2001: 2–3). Taking this further, Robinson has detailed a "global capitalism" thesis based on the view that "globalisation represents a new stage in the evolving world capitalist system that came into being some five centuries ago" (Robinson 2004a: 2). "The core of globalisation, theoretically conceived," he argues, "is the near culmination of the 500-year process of the spread of the capitalist system around the world, its extensive and intensive enlargement" (Robinson 2008: 6). Globalization therefore represents a qualitatively new epoch in the world-history of capitalism "characterised by the rise of transnational capital and by the supersession of the nation-state as the organising principle of the capitalist system" (Robinson 2003: 6). The singular feature of the "global capitalism" thesis, then, is the bold argument that "in the emerging global capitalist configuration, transnational or global space is coming to supplant national space," with the attendant view that the nation-state as an axis of world development is becoming superseded by transnational structures leading to the emergence of a transnational state (Robinson 2001a: 532; Robinson 2003: 19–20; Robinson 2008: 6–7). The nation-state is no longer regarded to be a "container" for the processes of capital accumulation, class formation, or development (Robinson 2001a: 533; Robinson 2004a: 89). In its stead is the constitution of a transnational state defined as "a particular constellation of class forces and relations bound up with capitalist globalisation and the rise of a transnational capitalist class, embodied in a diverse set of political institutions" (Robinson 2003: 43; Robinson 2004a: 99), or as "a loose network comprised of inter- and supranational political and economic institutions *together with* national state apparatuses that have been penetrated and transformed by transnational forces" without acquiring a centralized form (Robinson 2008: 34, original emphasis).

> The globalisation of production has entailed the fragmentation and decentralisa-
> tion of complex production chains and the worldwide dispersal and functional
> integration of the different segments in these chains. Yet this worldwide de-
> centralisation and fragmentation of the production process has taken place with
> the *centralisation* of command and control of the global economy. (Robinson
> 2004a: 15, original emphasis)

In sum, it is argued that a key feature of the epoch of globalization is not only the transformation of the state but its *supersession* as an organizing principle of capitalism by a transnational state apparatus consisting of transnational class alliances involving everything from transnational corporations (TNCs); to the expansion of foreign direct investment (FDI); to cross-national merg-ers, strategic alliances, capital interpenetration and interlocking directorates, worldwide subcontracting, and resourcing; to the extension of special eco-nomic zones and other forms of economic organization (Robinson 2003: 39). Local and regional accumulation patterns are assumed to reflect spatial dis-tinctions shaped by an increasingly integrated global capitalist arrangement (Robinson 2006a: 173).

> Latin America has become swept up in these transnational processes. The new
> dominant sectors of accumulation in Latin America are inextricably integrated
> into global accumulation circuits. . . . Capitalist relations are practically univer-
> sal now in the region. (Robinson 2008: 28)

There are three main ancillary claims attached to the theory of global capitalism and the transnational state that need to be highlighted prior to examining three different lines of critique that were outlined in the introduction to this chapter (see also Cypher 2009).

First, the assumption about the emergence and consolidation of transnational state practices affirms the view that states act as mere transmission belts for the diffusing aspects of global capitalism. National states are rather uncritically endorsed as transmission belts, or "filtering devices," of proactive instruments in advancing the agenda of global capitalism (Robinson 2003: 45–46; Robinson 2004a: 109). Stated directly, "national states remain important, but they become transmission belts and local executers of the transnational elite project" (Robinson 2003: 62). By way of example, so-called transitions to democracy are held as one such feature of adjustments in the political structures of state forms to the economic changes wrought by capitalist globalization (Robinson 2003: 54). The somewhat hollow process of democratization is here understood as the *promotion of polyarchy* referring to "a system in which a small group actually rules and mass participation in decision-making is consigned to leadership choice in elections carefully managed by competing elites" (Robinson 1996: 49). Much heralded "transitions" to democracy are thus "a political counterpart to the project of promoting capitalist globalisation, and . . . 'democracy promotion' and the promotion of free markets through neoliberal restructuring has become a singular process in U.S. foreign policy" (Robinson 2000: 313; Robinson 2008: 272–79). Transitions to "polyarchy," in this argument, are therefore characteristic of states acting as transmission belts of capitalist globalization. In any given case, the goal is "to organise an elite and to *impose* it on the intervened country through controlled electoral processes" (Robinson 1996: 111, emphasis added).

As pathbreaking as such scholarship is on the paradigm of democratic transition and the promotion of polyarchy, the problem here is that such broad claims neglect the differentiated outcome of specific class struggles within forms of state through which the restructuring of capital and sociospatial relations are produced. As chapter 6 will distinguish, the straight diffusion, or imposition, of transnational capital and polyarchic political structures needs to be considered critically in relation to struggles over the restoration and contestation of class power in specific forms of state. At the center of the argument of the state as transmission belt, then, is a disaggregation of politics and economics so that "class relations (and by implication, struggle) are viewed as external to the process of [global] restructuring, and labour and the state itself are depicted as powerless" (Burnham 2000: 14). This leads to the identification of external linkages between the state and globalization while the social production of globalization within and by social classes in specific forms of state is omitted (Bieler et al., 2006: 177–78). As later sections in this chapter argue, alternative state theoretical sources can better examine the very constitution and reproduction of the social relations of production as founded on the perpetuation of class contradictions. This is the case if stress is placed on the *internalization* of class interests within the state—albeit through the transnational expansion of social relations—rather than assuming that states have become simple "transmission belts" from the global to the national level (see also Bieler and Morton 2003: 481–89; Bieler et al., 2006: 155–75).

The second ancillary assumption linked to the thesis of the transnational state is that global class restructuring is leading to the accelerated prole-tarianization of peasant communities, the process of primitive accumulation by which peasants lose access to land and become workers leading to the creation of new rural and urban working classes (Robinson 2004a: 8). Put bluntly, "a major story of globalisation—worldwide—is the agonising death of the peasantry" (Robinson 2008: 169). The impact of globalization in Latin America is held as furthering the proletarianization of the peasantry particu-larly in light of the restructuring of traditional agricultural production toward nontraditional agricultural exports (NTAEs), such as fruits, cut flowers, or-namental plants, winter vegetables, and spices (see Robinson 2003: 252–58; Robinson 2008: 58–64). Again, though, in the case of depeasantization, the priority is granted to the project of capitalist transformation and the integra-tion of agriculture into *global structures* to the extent that "the structural power of the global economy is exercised through NTAE global commodity chains as a market discipline resulting in an intensified subordination of agri-cultural producers to transnational capital" (Robinson 2003: 189). What these broad claims tend to neglect is, precisely, the constitution and reproduction of peasantries through the dynamics of capital accumulation. The action of groups like the Ejército Zapatista de Liberación Nacional (EZLN) in Mexico and similar agrarian-based movements, such as the Movimento dos Trabal-hadores Rurais Sem Terra (MST) in Brazil calling for agrarian reform, would seemingly challenge the thesis about the inevitable demise of the peasantry, as explained in more detail in chapter 7.[1] Contemporary features of these rural movements in Latin America are neglected in the totalising assumption of depeasantization at the hub of the transnational state thesis.

Finally, among the ancillary claims on the emergence, consolidation, and diffusion of transnational state practices is the linked contention that the transnational model of development is *ending* conditions of primitive accu-mulation (Robinson 2003: 158). "There are no longer any frontiers to colonise in the epoch of globalisation" (Robinson 2008: 230).[2] Globalization is held as the culmination of capitalism's extensive enlargement to the degree that "capitalist production relations are replacing what remains of precapitalist relations around the globe. The era of primitive accumulation of capital is coming to an end" (Robinson 2004a: 7). Yet this assumption belies Ernest Mandel's (1975: 46, original emphasis) point that

> primitive accumulation of capital and capital accumulation through the production of surplus-value are . . . not merely *successive* phases of economic history but also *concurrent* economic processes. Throughout the entire history of capitalism up to the present, processes of primitive accumulation of capital have constantly coexisted with the predominant form of capital accumulation through the creation of value in the process of production.

Hence the need to distinguish between two separate moments in the history of primitive accumulation: (1) primitive accumulation whose historical origins in constituting propertyless producers divorced from their means of subsistence go back to the genesis of the capitalist mode of production; and (2) the distinct situation that defines processes of primitive accumulation that already occur within a capitalist world market (Mandel 1975: 47). Ongoing primitive accumulation of capital is therefore a persistent feature of capitalist processes of production, as argued earlier in this book notably in relation to the condition of permanent primitive accumulation (see chapter 2 and also consider Bartra 1982: 46; Bartra 1993: 29, 75–78; Perelman 2007). What is therefore elided is how "new rounds of primitive accumulation attack and erode social relations of production achieved through preceding rounds" (Harvey 1982/2006: 437).[3] The task of critique now turns to uncovering three additional dimensions that further undermine the transnational state argument. These focus on the historical relationship between territorial states and capitalism, the relationship between globalization and uneven development, and the spatial expression of capitalism and territoriality.

State Territoriality and Capitalism

"The nation-state system," Robinson argues, "is a relatively fixed set of historical structures whose foundations were laid in the seventeenth century (Robinson 2004a: 90). Territorial state sovereignty is presumed to have emerged as a consequence of the 1648 Peace of Westphalia *prior* to the subsequent unfolding of primitive accumulation of capital throughout the world. A case is then made that capitalism was a necessary condition for the development of the interstate system (Robinson 2004a: 102).

> The nation-state, or interstate, system is a historical outcome, the particular form in which capitalism came into being based on a complex relation between production, classes, political power and territoriality. (Robinson 2004a: 90)

It is this form of the state that is then presumed to be superseded by transnational capitalism "and with it the supersession of the interstate system as the institutional framework of capitalist development" (Robinson 2004a: 92). But, in Lacher's words, "the sovereign state . . . was *never* truly a container of society, and modern social relations always included crucial global dimensions" (Lacher 2003: 523, original emphasis).[4] As detailed elsewhere in this book (see chapter 2), capitalism was born into an anterior international system of state territoriality. Therefore changing configurations in the spread of the capitalist world market have had to adapt in specific ways to the international states-system that *preceded* the emergence of capitalism as a social totality (Lacher 2002: 161). The existence of territorial sovereign states and the presence of a system of states thus shaped the subsequent geopolitical expression of capitalism. "The 'modern' states, together with 'modern' conceptions of territoriality and sovereignty," argues Ellen Meiksins Wood (2002: 22), "emerged out of social relations that had nothing to do with capitalism." That is why, Lacher (2002: 159) argues, "capitalism came to exist politically in the form of an international system for reasons not directly driven by the nature of capital." The geopolitical presence of capitalism was thus organized politically through the medium of a system-of-states (see Teschke 2003).

Understanding the historical emergence of the geopolitical structure of capitalist political space is therefore advanced best through a methodology that can address the fragmentation of the capitalist polity into a states-system that structures relations between classes *both* nationally *and* transnationally (Lacher 2002: 160). By contrast, the argument that globalization marks an epoch in the history of capitalism that entails not only the rise of transnational capital but also the constitution and diffusion of a transnational state fails to adequately develop a history of capitalism, or to substantively historicize the relationship between the state and capitalism (see Robinson 2008: 4–9, 25–42). What this periodization of capitalism falls into is the "pan-capitalist" thesis of dependency and world-system analysis criticized in chapter 2, namely, the assumption that the practices of capitalism have been always nested within a mercantile system of commercial market relations. In this sense, statements such as "the nation-state and the interstate system are not a constitutive component of world capitalism . . . but a (the) historical form in which capitalism came into being" must surely be inaccurate (Robinson 2004a: 143–44). By extension, the transnational state thesis claims that there exists "a 'deterritorialisation' of the relationship of capital to the state" and that this results in "the 'pure' reproduction of social relations, that is, a process not mediated by fixed geopolitical dynamics" (Robinson 2001b: 191; Robinson 2004a: 141; Robinson 2004b: 149). This overlooks a point made earlier that state power plays a major role in offsetting crisis conditions in the accumulation of capital by providing a temporary "spatial fix" for surplus value extraction. The overall problem, then, is that there is an absence of a historical theory of capitalism that prevents a realization of how global capital is produced through the spatial scale of state power and how multiscalar relations are immanent to capitalism. The result is that the transnational state thesis is unsuccessful in avoiding a unilinear trope about the state's demise (Brenner 1997: 274–75; McMichael 2001: 203–5).

Globalization and Uneven Development

While, within the transnational state thesis, there is an emphasis on the geographical expression of global capitalism as a condition of uneven development, at the same time the unitary effect of capitalism is assumed to involve worldwide progression toward and diffusion of the presence of a transnational state. Rather than highlighting the *lack* of homology, then, between capitalism's effects through conditions of uneven development, instead Robinson argues that there is a transition toward the equalization of transnational state formation. Stated most clearly, the "particular spatial form of the uneven development of capitalism is being *overcome* by the globalisation of capital and markets and the *gradual equalisation of accumulation* conditions this involves" (Robinson 2004a: 99, emphases added). Behind this view of the gradual equalization of accumulation conditions lies the core weakness at the heart of the transnational state thesis. It is one that fails to keep in tension the contradictory tendencies of both differentiation entrained within state territoriality and simultaneous equalization through the conditions of production induced by global capital. As Neil Smith (1984/2008: 122–23, original emphasis) elaborates:

> Space is neither leveled out of existence nor infinitely differentiated. Rather, the pattern is one of *uneven development*, not in a general sense but as the specific product of the contradictory dynamic guiding the production of space. Uneven development is the concrete manifestation of the production of space under capitalism.

Whether it is the absolute space of state territoriality, or the partitioning of private property, "capital does not succeed in eliminating absolute space altogether" (Smith 1984/2008: 122–23). What this means is that the spatial form of the state has a basis rooted both within a given territoriality that is differentiated by the condition of uneven development while subjected to the leveling of such differences through the universalizing tendency of capital and the equalization of production.[5] As Lenin (1916/1964: 259) reminds us, "however strong the process of levelling the world, of levelling the economic and living conditions in different countries . . . considerable differences still remain."

To be sure, there is recognition within the transnational state thesis of "the disjuncture between nation-state institutionality and capital's new transnational space" and a stress on the continued territorial division of the world by a states-system that is a central condition for the power of transnational capital (Robinson 2008: 24, 36–37). However, the overriding emphasis is on how global capitalism is having a unidirectional impact on diverse historical and geographical state and class relations. "Transnational capital is the hegemonic fraction of capital on a world scale in the sense that it *imposes* its direction on the global economy and shapes the character of production and social life everywhere" (Robinson 2008: 26, emphasis added). The danger, then, is that this collapses into an assumption about the "homoficence of capitalism," meaning the unitary diffusion and impact of capitalism across different regions that overlooks the contradictions of uneven development expressed through the varied relations of capital in divergent state formation processes (Foster-Carter 1977: 57–58, 65). The corollary of this tendency, "realised to the hilt . . . is the complete levelling of spatial differences and the instigation of even development" (Smith 1984/2008: 157).[6] The consequence is that the conditions and contradictions of *un*even development are flattened out by the assumptions of the transnational state thesis. This leads to the omission of uneven development and the particularities of primitive accumulation and state formation in specific locations through the "levelling" of transnational capital (Kiely 2005: 34–38).

> The new locus of development is emergent transnational social space. There is no theoretical reason to posit any necessary affinity between continued uneven development and the nation-state as the particular territorial expression of uneven development. (Robinson 2001a: 558)

A realization of the contradictions of uneven development is thereby lost as are expressions of class struggle inhering across different state and geopolitical spatial scales. While there is no ultimate "spatial fix" to the contradictions of uneven development, "capital achieves a degree of spatial fixity organised into identifiable separate scales of social activity" within which the state is a crucial spatial form (Smith 1984/2008: 180). This oversight persists despite recognition that "the uneven development of the transnationalisation process is an important source of conflict," for here the driver of uneven development should surely be the contradictions of capitalism itself rather than transnationalization (Robinson 2004a: 134; see Robinson 2008: 47–48). The latter is more consequence than cause of uneven development. This confusion is itself the upshot of the problematic conception, outlined above, of the historical relationship between the rise of a territorial states-system and capitalism that is at the center of the transnational state thesis.

The Spatial Expression of Capitalism and Sovereign Territoriality

Finally, as a consequence of the argument that nation-states are no longer relevant "containers" of economic, social, political, and cultural processes it is also held that "transnational or global space is coming to supplant national spaces" (Robinson 2004a: 89, 92; Robinson 2008: 6–7). In the transnational state thesis, moreover, the contention is that states "are no longer the point of 'condensation' of sets of social relations. They are no longer *nodal points*" (Robinson 2004a: 143, emphasis added). As alluded above, the significant problem here, though, is the lack of appreciation of the articulation of capitalism through multiscalar relations. Capitalism does not simply supplant one spatial scale for another but instead works across spatial scales located within state forms and through global relations. The point is not to take the dominance of one spatial scale over another as a given but to appreciate the manner in which capitalism operates through nodal rather than dominant points. This means appreciating states as political nodes in the global flow of capital, while eschewing claims that the global system can be reduced to a struggle between states (Bieler et al., 2006: 162, 191). Instead, according to Robinson (2004a: 123), "decision-making and regulatory mechanisms emanating from supranational agencies and from local contingents of the transnational bourgeoisie are superimposed on national states, which themselves become absorbed into the emergent transnational state apparatus." The focus on nongovernmental organizations (NGOs) is indicative here with such networks situated within a structure linking local, national, and transnational space but transposed onto a restrictive top-down vertical hierarchy. What this presents is a series of "out-of-scale" transnational images that are supposed to be reorienting political processes while lacking discriminate contents (Said 1990: 8). The transnational state thesis therefore offers a *flattened ontology* that removes state forms as a significant spatial scale in the articulation of capitalism, levels out the spatial and territorial logics of capital accumulation, and elides the class struggles extant in specific locations.

In contrast to the transnational state thesis that produces out-of-scale transnational conceptions of social development, my argument is that the theory of passive revolution provides a method of analysis combining an appreciation of the contradictions in the expansion of capital and the universalizing of the law of capital alongside understanding the persistence of geographical differentiation in terms of state formation processes and uneven development (see Morton 2007a). After all, Gramsci recognized the spatial scales of capital to question "how the complex problem arises of the relation of internal forces in the country in question, of the relation of international forces, and of the country's geopolitical position" (Gramsci 1971: 116, Q10II§61). Within a situation of passive revolution, then, it becomes important to identify a hierarchy of scales at which different policies might serve to anchor class strategies within specific spatial and geographical territorial forms although "it is production in particular locales that is always the ultimate source of that power" (Harvey 1982/2006: 423). The production of spatial configurations is thus an active moment in the dynamic of capital accumulation to the extent that "there is . . . no 'spatial fix' [such as state power or the transnational state] that can contain the contradictions of capitalism in the long run" (Harvey 1982/2006: 442). The theory of passive revolution is therefore a nodal approach to the spatial division of uneven and combined development that throws into relief how certain factors of state formation and spatial scales are socially produced. It is now time to develop the theory of passive revolution in relation to processes of capital accumulation that shaped the construction of a capitalist type of state and thus the patterning of neoliberalism in Mexico.

THE PASSIVE REVOLUTION OF NEOLIBERALISM: A CAPITALIST TYPE OF STATE IN MEXICO

The foregoing chapters in this book have stressed that the notion of passive revolution captures the political rule of capital and how processes of state formation are embedded in the specifically capitalist circumstances of uneven and combined development. The theory places emphasis on ruptural aspects of revolutionary upheaval that become undermined resulting in the reconstitution of social relations within new forms of capitalist order. It is therefore an account of historical change that concentrates on the constitution and/or restoration of the social relations of capitalist development within a crisis period of modern state formation and class struggle. As detailed earlier (see chapter 2), within conditions of passive revolution "the important thing is to analyse more profoundly . . . the fact that a state replaces the local social groups in leading a struggle of renewal" (Gramsci 1971: 105–6, Q15§59). Such a situation unfolds when the ruling class is unable to fully integrate the people through conditions of integral hegemony, or when "they were aiming at the creation of a modern state . . . [but] in fact produced a bastard" (Gramsci 1971: 90, Q19§28). It is one of those cases when a situation of "domination without that of 'leadership': dictatorship without hegemony" prevails because it is possible for the state to dominate civil society, which is "shapeless and chaotic" as it is in "a sporadic, localised form, without any national nexus" (Gramsci 1971: 105–6, Q15§59; Gramsci 1992: 214–15, Q1§130). Hence, as detailed in chapter 1, through the expansion of state intervention, a partial or minimal form of hegemony may only prevail, limited to a narrow social group rather than the whole of society. This may have various "path-dependent" (determined but not deterministic) effects that shape and define the nature and purpose of state actions during particular phases of development (Jessop 2002: 40–42, 58). The conditions of passive revolution therefore differ from "the real exercise of hegemony over the whole of society which alone permits a certain organic equilibrium" (Gramsci 1971: 396, Q16§9). The contradictions of passive revolution reflect more an unstable equilibrium that contains within itself the danger of disintegrating into a catastrophic equilibrium (Gramsci 1971: 219–22, Q13§27; 245–6, Q6§81). Within these latter conditions, "events that go under the specific name of 'crisis' have then burst onto the scene" (Gramsci 1971: 220–21, Q13§27).

Connecting back to the discussion in the previous chapter, the specific form of passive revolution can refer either to the historical constitution of the state as an emerging capitalist social formation (state in capitalist society) or as a state form increasingly dominated by the logic of accumulation so that the appearance of the institutional separation of the economy within capitalism becomes consolidated (capitalist type of state). As observed in chapter 3, the exercise of class power by agents of the state in capitalist society was analyzed by tracing the various policies and mechanisms that ensured the expanded reproduction of capital within import substitution industrialization (ISI). The purpose of the present chapter, though, is to highlight certain continuities and contrasts in the exercise of class power in consolidating a capitalist type of state within the overall dynamic of capital accumulation under neoliberalism. The preceding chapter was concerned with the functional adequacy of the state in capitalist society defining and securing the requirements of capital under ISI. The complementary strategy of analyzing the capitalist type of state under neoliberalism is concerned with examining the formal adequacy of routinizing the overall dynamic of capital accumulation and class domination (Jessop 2008: 135–41).

One way of furthering this analysis of a capitalist type of state is to distinguish analytically between an accumulation strategy and the attempt to construct a hegemonic project in securing the capital relation and the institutional division of the state as a social form appearing as separate from the economy. An accumulation strategy defines a specific economic "growth model" including the various extraeconomic preconditions and general strategies appropriate for its realization. The success of a particular accumulation strategy relies upon the complex relations among different fractions of capital as well as the balance of forces between dominant-subordinate classes, hence the importance of a focus on struggles over a hegemonic project. This involves the mobilization of support behind a concrete program that brings about the unison of different interests within an integral hegemony (Jessop 1990: 198–99, 207–8). An *accumulation strategy* is primarily oriented at the relations of production and thus to the balance of class forces, while struggles over *hegemonic projects* are typically oriented to broader issues grounded not only in the economy but the whole sphere of state–civil society relations. It will be recalled from chapter 3 that these are not to be regarded as separate realms but two aspects of political action grounded in the same social relations of production. As Bob Jessop (1990: 201) highlights, "the crucial factor in the success of accumulation strategies remains the integration of the circuit of capital and hence the consolidation of support within the dominant fractions and classes," that is, class struggle over hegemony. My argument is that the passive revolution of neoliberalism in Mexico can be understood within these state theoretical terms. As Marx (1894/1998: 27) himself noted, there is a need to "locate and describe the concrete forms which grow out of the movements of capital as a whole" so as to "approach step by step the form which they assume on the surface of society, in the action of different capitals upon one another."[7] The conflicts of interest that eventually culminated in the accumulation strategy of neoliberalism, reflected especially in the presidency of Carlos Salinas de Gortari (1988–1994), were pursued while attempting to reconfigure a renewed hegemonic project of the then ruling Partido Revolucionario Institucional (PRI), which is now the subject matter of the next section.

THE HISTORY OF MEXICO SEEN AS A STRUGGLE OF PASSIVE REVOLUTION[8]

The Rise of a Neoliberal Accumulation Strategy in Mexico

In order to account for the period that Mexicans refer to as *la docena trágica*, the "tragic dozen" (1970–1982), a determinant factor in the transition from the ISI strategy of accumulation to that commonly referred to as a neoliberal strategy has been seen as a set of institutional changes within the organization of the state (Centeno 1994: 41). The crucial phase that laid the basis for this shift in accumulation strategy in Mexico was the period in the 1970s that set the stage for subsequent developments (Dussel Peters 2000: 45).

By the 1970s, during the *sexenio* (six-year term) of Luis Echeverría (1970–1976), the government needed to revive its deteriorating legitimacy and responded with a neopopulist program of political and social reforms. Hence the Echeverría administration embarked on a macroeconomic strategy of "shared development" within a supposed *apertura democrática* (democratic opening) to forge a populist coalition between national industrialists, peasants, urban marginals, disillusioned labor sectors, students, and the middle classes. Yet, faced by pressure from internationally linked industrialists, Echeverría was not capable of implementing sufficient tax increases in order to support public spending directed toward national industry and the working- and middle-class sectors. Unable to introduce tax increases on internationally linked capital, foreign borrowing therefore became the major source of financing for development policies (Davis 1993: 55). Also, due to expanded state intervention in the economy and the increasingly antiprivate sector rhetoric, the government began to lose the support of significant sectors of capital. Such state intervention increasingly alienated the private sector and as a result, "the alliance that ha[d] existed between state and national capital was severely strained" (Centeno 1994: 69). An indication of this was the rise of the private sector in vocally articulating its opposition, notably with the founding of the Consejo Coordinadora Empresarial (CCE) in 1975, that has been described as an attempt "to coordinate the major fractions of the big and medium-sized bourgeoisie in the process of consolidating monopoly capital's dominant influence on the state" (Cockcroft 1983: 272). It is important to note that while neoliberalism *had not* taken hold at this time crucial cleavages within the organization of the state were developing that would lead to shifts in capitalist accumulation.

Pivotal in preparing the conditions for such changes was the Mexican financial crisis of 1976, the impact and consequences of which are wonderfully captured by figure 5.1 that divides the first and second part of this book. As James Cockcroft (1983: 259) has put it, "capital flight, noncompetitiveness of Mexican products, dollarisation of the economy, and IMF pressures forced a nearly 100 percent devaluation of the peso in late 1976, almost doubling the real foreign debt . . . as well as the real costs of imported capital goods—to the detriment of nonmonopoly firms and the advantage of the TNCs." Yet the financial crisis can be seen to be as much related to the expansionary public-sector expenditure policies driven by the crisis of the PRI as the macroeconomic disequilibria driven by structural change in the globalizing political economy linked to U.S. inflation. While the IMF certainly imposed austerity measures and surveillance mechanisms on Mexico, it has been argued that these were less violatory than feared; although they did have a strong impact in altering the internal distribution of power between social classes in Mexico (Whitehead 1980: 846–47, 851).

At almost the same time, large oil reserves were also discovered which, by 1982, were estimated at 72 billion barrels with probable reserves at 90–150 billion and potential reserves at 250 billion, amounting to the sixth largest reserves in the world (Cockcroft 1983: 261). Hence the political economy of Mexico became dependent on petroleum-fueled development under the administration of José López Portillo (1976–1982) with the share of hydro-carbons in export earnings rising from 16 percent in 1976, to 40 percent in 1979, to 65 percent in 1980, and reaching 75 percent in 1981 (Hellman 1983: 79–80). While, simultaneously, attempts were made to balance the tensions between competing social classes, a coherent course capable of satisfying the interests of national and internationally linked capital in Mexico, was not set. By the time world oil prices dropped in 1981, leading to reduced oil revenues, accelerating debt obligations and a surge in capital flight, Mexico faced another financial crisis that initially led to the nationalization of the banks on 1 September 1982. This was a last-ditch effort to recoup revenues for the public sector and reassert some form of state autonomy, but it resulted in reinforcing private-sector opposition, capital flight, inflation, and balance of payment problems (Davis 1993: 61). "It would presumably not be an exag-geration," adds Nora Hamilton (1984: 9), "to note that by this time the values, interests, and operating principles of the private bankers had been completely internalised by their counterparts in the state financial sector."

Similar to the earlier crisis, the result of the 1982 debt crisis and the accu-mulated foreign debt of $80 billion was a combination of mutually reinforc-ing factors both within the global political economy and the form of state in Mexico.

The crisis was precipitated by the world oil glut, a world economic recession, and rising interest rates in the United States, but its root causes were domestic: excessively expansionary monetary and social policies, persistent overvaluation of the peso, over-dependence of the public sector on a single source of revenue (oil exports), a stagnant agriculture sector (at least that part which produced basic foodstuffs for domestic consumption), an inefficient and globally uncom-petitive industrial plant, excessive labour force growth . . . , a capital-intensive development model that made it impossible to create an adequate employment base, endemic corruption in government, and resistance by entrenched eco-nomic and political interests to structural reforms. (Cornelius 1985: 87–88)

This resulted in another IMF austerity program—involving reductions in government subsidies for foodstuffs and basic consumer items, increases in taxes on consumption, and tight wage controls targeted to control inflation—that the Mexican administration implemented by exceeding planned targets.[9] Therefore, the crisis arose as a result of a conjunction of factors that also included the rise of technocrats—under way throughout the 1970s—which led to the ascendancy of the accumulation strategy of neoliberalism. A crucial issue at this time was the institutional career paths of the elite which began to alter so that ministries associated with banking and finance planning provided the career experience likely to lead to the upper echelons of government. The relations of production were therefore reproduced by "a class of people which is capable of substituting itself for the capitalists and the bourgeoisie— competent, disinterested experts and practitioners, organisers of enterprises, of production and consumption, and ultimately of *space*" (Lefebvre 1976: 24, original emphasis). What eventually unfolded in Mexico were specific transnational fractions of capital that would come to fuse the concerns of state managers, sectors of the business elite, large conglomerates tied to the export sector such as the *maquila* (in-bond) strategy of export-led industrialization, and sectoral reform of agricultural production. Notably this was the context within which the Secretaría de Programación y Presupuesto (SPP) came to rise to institutional predominance as a pivotal *camarilla* (clique) within the organization of the state.

The SPP was created in 1976 and culminated the process of taking economic policy making away from the Secretaría de Hacienda y Crédito Público (SHCP). Overall, not only was direct control over the most important resources of information for plans and projects in the bureaucracy secured, but competing factions within the PRI could also be circumvented. Significantly, up to President Ernesto Zedillo (1994–2000), the previous three presidents all originated from agencies related to these changes with López Portillo (1976–1982) heralding from SHCP and Miguel de la Madrid (1982– 1988) and Carlos Salinas (1988–1994) from SPP. By 1983 almost 60 percent of all cabinet-level appointees had started their careers in these sectors and over 80 percent had some experience within them while in the Salinas cabinet 33 percent had experience in SHCP and 50 percent had worked in SPP (Centeno and Maxfield 1992: 74). The rise of such technocrats ensured that precedence was accorded to ministries of finance like SPP that would subordinate other ministries and prioritize policies more attuned to transnational economic processes. To cite Gramsci, it was a process whereby, "in the political party the elements of an economic social group get beyond that moment of their historical development and become agents of more general activities of a national and international character" (Gramsci 1971: 16, Q12§1).

A pivotal factor in the formation of this transnational capitalist class in Mexico was the move during the Echeverría presidency after the oil boom of 1975–1976 to expand scholarships to foreign universities as a method of integrating dissidents radicalized by the massacre of students at Tlatelolco on 2 October 1968 (Berins Collier 1992: 66). Thus, throughout the 1970s, not only was there a dramatic increase in the educational budget *within* Mexico, leading to a 290 percent increase in university students between 1970 and 1976, but the number of scholarships for study *abroad* increased even more dramatically (Centeno 1994: 152n25). It can therefore be argued that the dissemination of foreign ideas in Mexico increased as a direct result of the oil boom. This led to many *tecnócratas* adopting a more conservative ideology while becoming dependent on the president for their subsequent governmental position; hence resulting in the crucial rise of *camarillas* that shifted institutional loyalty from a particular ministry or subgroup within the bureaucracy to close political and personal links with the president. It was this technocratic elite that took for granted the exhaustion of the previous ISI development strategy and engendered a degree of social conformism favoring the adoption of a neoliberal accumulation strategy. Yet it was hardly questioned to what extent such structural problems were not intrinsic to ISI but rather related to a series of exogenous shocks, such as the oil crisis, combined with the class interests of new coalitions of domestic and foreign capital seeking to restructure the state. After all, one of the central pillars of claims against ISI has been that state-owned enterprises (SOEs) were a drain on state resources and a fiscal burden. Yet, between 1978 and 1991, there was a positive flow of resources from public enterprises to the government in Mexico, with SOEs contributing a net financial flow of approximately 3 percent of GDP to the state throughout the period (Medeiros 2009: 115–16). It is also worth remembering that a significant number of public enterprises established under ISI were the direct result of the state intervening to prevent the failure of private sector companies in oligopolistic sectors of the economy. Hence the conclusion that "the privatisation process is simply transferring the proceeds of what are now profitable operations to powerful private interests, making them even more profitable . . . but resulting in no apparent public benefit" (Ramírez 1994: 38). In sum, the policy of privatization, as one of the factors that signaled a shift from ISI to the accumulation strategy of neoliberalism, was shaped significantly by the rise of *tecnócratas* that reflected new capitalist coalitions advanced through links with transnational capital within the form of state (Cockcroft 1983: 217). "Structural change now became the watchword of the administration" (Cypher 1990: 182).

For example, during this period of structural change or the "reformation of capitalism" in Mexico, fractions of a transnational capitalist class became influential in shaping the *maquila* (in-bond) strategy of export-led industrialization fueled by foreign investment, technology, and transnational capital (Sklair 1993: 13–14). While the *maquila* industry has its roots in the Border Industrialization Program, introduced in 1965 after the United States ended the bracero program (which provided a legal basis for labor migration from Mexico to the United States), it was not until the 1970s that economic promotion committees began to bring to fruition the earlier visions of border industrialization, particularly under the auspices of the Secretaría de

Comercio y Fomento Industrial (SECOFI) within de la Madrid's administration. Between 1979 and 1985 *maquilas* increased by 40 percent and employees almost doubled (Sklair 1993: 70). At an early stage in this transformation
the interests of private capital were represented by organizations within
the Cámara Nacional de la Industria de Transformación (CANACINTRA).
Along with other fractions of capital—such as the Confederación de Cámaras
Industriales (CONCAMIN), the Confederación de Cámaras Nacionales de
Comercio (CONCANACO), and the Confederación Patronal de la República
Mexicana (COPARMEX)—the major fractions of large and medium-sized
manufacturers coordinated and consolidated capital's influence over the
state. This influence proceeded further, as mentioned earlier, when such
capitalist organizations regrouped through the CCE, in 1975, to represent
a united front of capital, working within and against the state, to promote
capitalist class interests. The *maquila* industry was thus promoted, nurtured,
and supervised by fractions of a transnational capitalist class in Mexico but
through processes of carefully managed state-labor-business relations within
the form of state that later developed into a full-blown export-led strategy of
industrialization (Sklair 1993: 227). However, the interests of transnational
capital also reached beyond the *maquila* industry to gradually secure the
integration of Mexico into the global political economy. Hence, "the official agricultural policies of the Díaz Ordaz and Echeverría periods [also]
promoted transformations which deepened the integration of local farmers
into a transnational system of agricultural production" (Gledhill 1996: 183).
One consequence of this effort to reproduce the accumulation strategy of
neoliberalism in Mexico was the 1992 reform of collective *ejido* landholdings
enshrined in Article 27 to the Mexican Constitution, undertaken as a prelude
to entry into the North American Free Trade Agreement (NAFTA) in 1994
(Craske and Bulmer-Thomas 1994). This led to the increased capitalization
of land—involving changing property relations and shifts from rank-based
social ties and communal commitments of civil-religious hierarchies to cash
derived from wage labor—that would impact on forms of resistance such as
the EZLN (see chapter 7).

   An additional feature that also became crucial in the struggle over the neoliberal accumulation strategy was the introduction of the Pacto de Solidaridad
Económica (PSE) in 1987. The PSE was initially a mixed or "heterodox"
program that aimed to tame the current account deficit and inflation based
on a commitment to fiscal discipline, a fixed exchange rate, and concerted
wage and price controls. It has been heralded as instrumental in achieving a
successful renegotiation of external debt following the debt crisis of 1982, in
line with the Baker (1985) and Brady (1989) Plans, and further radicalizing
the import liberalization program following Mexico's entry into the General

Agreement on Tariffs and Trade (GATT) (Urquidi 1994: 58). Overall, three components of the PSE were crucial: (1) the government's pledge in favor of the acceleration of privatization and deregulation, (2) the centrality awarded to the CCE, and (3) the use of large retailers' market power to discipline private firms and further ensure the participation of business elites (Heredia 1996: 138). The CCE—itself formed from a forerunner of big business private sector groups within the capitalist class known as the Consejo Mexicano de Hombres de Negocios (CMHN)—became pivotal in initiating and implementing the PSE (Whitehead 1989: 210). As indicated earlier, the class interests of the CCE became centered around a transnationalized segment of national capital including direct shareholders of large conglomerates tied to the export sector with experience in elite business organizations (Luna 1995: 83). Subsequently, many of the CCE leaders became more closely linked with the PRI via committees and employers' associations to increase interest representation within the state. Little wonder, therefore, that the class interests represented by the CCE had a huge impact on the policies implemented by the PRI, including increased privatization (Ugalde 1994: 230). One commentator has gone as far as to argue that the relationship between the private sector and the political class became part of a narrow clique exercising a "private hegemony" so that "it would be no exaggeration to say that this alliance was based on a carefully thought-out strategy to bring public policy in line with private sector demands, to effect a global reform of the relationship between the state and society, and hence to redesign Mexico's insertion into the emerging neoliberal global order" (Ugalde 1996: 42).

As a consequence, there was a shift in the PSE from a commitment to state-labor corporatist relations to a disarticulation, but not severing, of the state-labor alliance in favor of the overriding interests of capital. This has been variously recognized as a form of "new unionism" or neocorporatism, "an arrangement involving the reduction of centralised labour power and the participation of labour in increasing productivity" (Teichman 1996: 257). The privatization of Teléfonos de México (TELMEX) in 1990, one of the pinnacles of the privatization program, particularly reflected the strategy of "new unionism." This not only involved manipulation of the Sindicato de Telefonistas de la República Mexicana (STRM), one of the key labor organizations used to secure privatization, it also entailed Salinas permitting the leader of STRM, Hernández Juárez, to create an alternative labor federation, the Federación de Sindicatos de Empresas de Bienes y Servicios (FESEBES), to further facilitate privatization. Hence labor became more dependent on the PRI during the privatization of TELMEX, which generated new resources for corruption and clientelism and lessened union democracy within STRM (Clifton 2000). What is important here, then, is that the accumulation strategy associated with neoliberalism did not involve a wholesale retreat of the state nor did the state act as a simple conduit or "transmission belt" for global capitalism. As Centeno (1994: 195) has commented, "the pacto [PSE] demonstrated that the *técnocratas* were not generic neoliberals who applied monetarist policies indiscriminately but were willing to utilise a variety of mechanisms to establish control over the economy." What the case of Mexico does exhibit, though, is precisely the internalization of certain transnational class interests conducive to a specific reorganization of production relations and changes in the form of state. The state was itself actively engaged in producing the spatial configurations of the neoliberal accumulation process—whether through the *maquila* strategy or NAFTA—that meant structural shifts in the scale of class relations and new coalitions between and within domestic and transnational fractions of capital. One consequence in the past few years has been that at least 85 percent of Mexico's banks have fallen under foreign ownership.[10] Indeed, between 1994 and 2001, foreign control of bank assets in Mexico increased from 1 percent to 90 percent (Leiva 2008: 125–26). A form of hegemony based on dominating subaltern classes to the unification of the state therefore became replaced by that of transnational capital appearing as a promoter of all sectors in civil society (García Canclini 1995: 61). The analysis now turns from discussing the details of how the neoliberal strategy of accumulation privileged particular fractions of capital in Mexico to address how the struggle over hegemony impacted on the PRI.

The Changing Circumstances of Minimal Hegemony

Intrinsically linked to changes in the social relations of production stemming from the 1970s was an increase in the sources of political instability in Mexico. "Political struggles over national economic policy began in the early 1970s when problems associated with import-substituting industrialisation began to mount" (Cook, Middlebrook, and Horcasitas 1994: 18). These struggles were manifest in the *sexenios* of Echeverría (1970–1976) and López Portillo (1976–1982) to the extent that the PRI faced problems with its already weak political legitimacy following the Tlatelolco massacre in 1968, a discontented urban middle class, disaffection with the ISI accumulation strategy, the emergence of new opposition movements outside the officially recognized party system, the rise of new labor militancy, the additional emergence of urban and rural guerrilla movements, and the declining ability of the PRI to compete with registered opposition parties (Middlebrook 1986).

For instance, the Coordinadora Nacional de Trabajadores de la Educación (CNTE), founded in 1979, came to challenge, particularly in the peasant communities of Chiapas, the state-imposed and privileged position of the Sindicato

Nacional de Trabajadores de la Educación (SNTE), established in 1943 (Foweraker 1993). This was also the period when independent unions articulated a so-called *insurgencia obrera* (labor insurgency) to question the lack of autonomy and democracy of official unions and to articulate demands across a variety of sectors beyond purely economic concerns (Carr 1991: 136–39). Yet, as a harbinger of reforms under the neoliberal accumulation strategy, the López Portillo administration coercively suppressed many of these opposition movements and implemented economic reforms in favor of the private sector as a prelude to introducing the Ley Federal de Organizaciones Políticas y Procesos Electorales (LFOPEE) in 1977. Between 1976 and 1979 the dynamism of the *insurgencia obrera* faded and became dominated by the themes of economic crisis and austerity (Carr 1991: 137). At the same time, the LFOPEE became an attempt to manage political liberalization within the current of the *apertura democrática* (democratic opening) by enlarging the arena for party competition and integrating leftist political organizations while inducing them to renounce extralegal forms of action. The measures, for example, involved the Partido Comunista Mexicano (PCM) obtaining its *official* registration as a political party that led to its first legal participation, since 1949, in the elections of 1979. Subsequently, in 1981, the PCM merged with four other left-wing parties to establish the Partido Socialista Unificado de México (PSUM) (Carr 1985). Thus the PCM, the oldest communist party in Latin America at that time, effectively dissolved itself while attempting to electorally compete within the parameters of the LFOPEE reform (Cockcroft 1998: 265). The reform, therefore, was more than a simple act of *trasformismo*, or co-optation measure. It was designed to frame and condition the very institutional context of opposition movements and constituted the construction of a specific legal and institutional terrain that was capable of containing popular demands by defining the terms and fixing the boundaries of representation and social struggle (Foweraker 1993: 11–12). It thus epitomized the structures of passive revolution shaped by the unevenness of economic and social development: an attempt to introduce aspects of change through the state as arbiter of social conflict. In the words of Echeverría the political reform strived to "incorporate the majority of the citizens and social forces into the *institutional* political process" (as cited in Pansters 1999: 241, original emphasis). As Kevin Middlebrook (1995: 223–24) has argued, this was a limited political opening that was essential at a time of severe social and political tension in order to balance stringent economic austerity measures with policies designed to diffuse widespread discontent. The capacity of labor to articulate an alternative vision for Mexican economic and social development through either official or independent unions, evident in the 1970s, thus declined throughout the 1980s to become scarcely evident a decade later (Cook 1995: 77–94).

What was evolving in the form of state at this time in Mexico, therefore, within the context of structural change in the global political economy, was a shift in the minimal hegemony of the PRI. More accurately, the attempt at political reform in the 1970s was an indication of the PRI's ailing class hegemony. Unable to represent class-transcending interests, the PRI began to reorient the social relations of production toward a new hierarchy in favor of particular class forces. As a result it is possible to perceive the beginning of the end in the fraying and unraveling of the PRI's minimal hegemony from the 1970s onward. The LFOPEE political reform was a clear indication of an attempt to absorb the competing demands of subaltern classes with those of the private sector and transnational capital in Mexico. It was a response to the erosion of support for the basic structure of the political system.

Yet, drawing from chapter 1, it is not easily explained as the exercise of an integral, or "normal," hegemony characterized by a reciprocal combination of force and consent. Instead, the PRI became increasingly unable to conceal its real predominance and relied on more coercive measures. Rather than hegemony "protected by the armour of coercion," the state-coercive element exercised a more directive function in underwriting the restructuring of neoliberalism. This was a situation when the party turns "into a narrow clique which tends to perpetuate its selfish privileges by controlling or even stifling opposition forces" (Gramsci 1971: 189, Q13§36). It entails a shift in the threshold of power where coercive means indicative of state crisis and the disintegrative elements of an unstable equilibrium take hold in order to shore up whatever minimal hegemony exists. As a counterpart to the neoliberal accumulation strategy, the PRI began to increasingly reflect these traits of passive revolution throughout the 1980s. These features of passive revolution were articulated both ideologically, through limited hegemonic activity, as well as through new forms of coercive organization. Ideologically, during the Salinas *sexenio* attempts were particularly made to reconstruct history in order to naturalize radical neoliberal changes to the political economy, notably through new discourses of nationalism (see Salinas de Gortari 2002; O'Toole 2003). As a result, neoliberalism came to represent a "hegemonic shift" in the attempt to dismantle the nationalism of the Mexican Revolution linked to ISI and displace its political symbolism as a focal point of national consciousness (Powell 1996: 40). Yet the government's ideological use of the legacy of the Mexican Revolution was not merely a straightforward foil for neoliberalism but, instead, was adapted to specific conditions in Mexico. This fundamental effort to reconfigure state–civil society relations within Mexico and the PRI's minimal hegemony was particularly exhibited through projects like the Programa Nacional de Solidaridad (PRONASOL).

Following the continued crisis of representation facing the PRI and the tenuous majority Salinas received from the electorate in 1988, a significant attempt was made to try and redefine conditions of hegemony. A notable feature in this effort was PRONASOL, a poverty alleviation program combining government financial support and citizen involvement to design and implement community development and public works projects. As the PRI had failed as an inclusive party covering all segments of society, PRONASOL became emblematic of the attempt to shore up the gap in hegemonic acquiescence (Centeno 1994: 224). It combined material and institutional aspects focusing on social services, infrastructure provision, and poverty alleviation in order to rearrange state–civil society relations and the coalitional support of the PRI (Cornelius, Craig, and Fox 1994: 3). There were three main objectives of PRONASOL. First, it attempted to adapt the state's traditional social role to new economic constraints and redefine the limits of its intervention in the context of a neoliberal strategy of accumulation. Second, it attempted to diffuse potential social discontent through selective subsidies, accommodate social mobilization through "co-participation," and undermine the strength of left-wing opposition movements. Third, it attempted to restructure local and regional PRI elites under centralized control (Dresser 1991: 1–2). Clearly PRONASOL was therefore a targeted attempt to buttress both the accumulation strategy of neoliberalism and the minimal hegemony of the PRI that was under threat from those very changes.

Emanating from the Salinas *camarilla* that had dominated the SPP, PRONASOL was officially described as an attempt to modernize, pluralize, and democratize state–civil society relations in Mexico as part of the doctrine of "social liberalism": "a mode of governance that ostensibly seeks to avoid the worst excesses of both unfettered, free market capitalism and heavy-handed state interventionism, by steering a careful middle course between these 'failed' extremes" (Carlos Salinas as cited in Cornelius, Craig, and Fox 1994: 4). Usurping the language and mobilizing role of grassroots organizations, PRONASOL was itself portrayed as a "new grassroots movement," empowering citizens through "an experience of direct democracy," while also redefining members of traditional corporatist organizations as "consumers" of electricity, improved infrastructure, and educational scholarships (Carlos Salinas as cited in Cornelius, Craig, and Fox 1994: 6–7). This new style of thinking among state officials "was reinforced by ideas recommending the involvement of the poor and NGOs in anti-poverty projects promoted by many international actors, including international financial institutions such as the World Bank and the Inter-American Development Bank, the United Nations, and international donors and development specialists" (Piester 1997: 473).

Between 1989 and 1993, the World Bank directly lent PRONASOL $350 million to improve rural service provision and to support regional development in four of Mexico's poorest states—Oaxaca, Guerrero, Hidalgo, and Chiapas—while the bank also supported a health and nutrition pilot project (Cornelius, Craig, and Fox 1994: 16).

Despite the rhetoric, though, PRONASOL preserved and even reinforced presidential rule and complemented the established bureaucracy. As Denise Dresser (1991: 2) states, "the politics of PRONASOL sheds light on why hegemonic parties like the PRI can survive even when threatened by powerful alternative organisations, and why the party has apparently been able to revive after a period of crisis and decline." Essentially PRONASOL was crucial to maintaining the lagging effect of the PRI's minimal hegemony because it provided the political conditions for sustaining the neoliberal accumulation strategy notably through a modernization of populism and traditional clientelist and corporatist forms of co-optation. This was carried out through a process of *concertación*, understood as the negotiation of cooperative agreements between social movements and the state involving division and demobilization. The *concertación* strategies espoused by PRONASOL represented a convergence of interests between those of the popular organizations and the technocratic sectors within the PRI and the government (Dresser 1991: 32). Thus, while the Salinas administration presented neoliberalism as a hegemonic project in Mexico, it used PRONASOL as a vehicle of hegemonic activity to create a sense of inclusion and a durable base of support within civil society. This objective was also fulfilled within PRONASOL by denying the existence of class antagonisms while at the same time claiming to transcend class differences (Dresser 1994: 147).

By the time PRONASOL became institutionalized within the Secretaría de Desarrollo Social (SEDESOL), in 1996, it was clear that the program had been successful in sustaining the passive revolution of neoliberalism (see Soederberg 2001). This means that it was intrinsic in changing the correlation of forces in Mexico and the class project of neoliberalism—to supervise the "counter-attack of capital" through passive revolution—within which there was a transformation of the elite from arbiter of class conflict to ruling in its own interests (Veltmeyer, Petras, and Vieux 1997: 160–61; Hodges and Gandy 2002b: 246). PRONASOL incorporated potentially threatening leaders, alternative programs and ideas by nullifying substantive differences. Hence, despite the neoliberal accumulation strategy making it increasingly difficult to conceal the real predominance of its narrow basis of interest representation, the PRI still managed to exert some form of minimal hegemony albeit relying more on coercion rather than true leadership. As Wil Pansters (1999: 256, original emphasis) puts it, "the combined result of neoliberal economic adjustment, institutional malfunctioning and the decomposition of personalistic networks and loyalties [w]as . . . an increase in violence *at all* societal levels."

Hence my argument is that there was an ongoing crisis in the minimal hegemony articulated and present throughout the phase of neoliberal restructuring in the 1980s and 1990s in Mexico. It was a situation when "the ruling class has lost its consensus, i.e. is no longer 'leading' but only dominant, exercising coercive force"; it means "precisely that the great masses have become detached from their traditional ideologies, and no longer believe what they used to believe previously" (Gramsci 1971: 275–76, Q3§34). As the prominent novelist Carlos Fuentes—whose social function as an intellectual is taken up in chapter 5—expressed it at the time: "It is as though the PRI has gone out to kill itself, to commit suicide. There are Priístas killing Priístas. . . . What we see is the internal decomposition of a party, which has, in effect, completed its historic purpose" (*Mexico & NAFTA Report*, 8 December 1994). The PRI, to summarize in Gramsci's words, became a party that increasingly existed as "a simple, unthinking executor . . . , a policing organism, and its name of 'political party' [became] simply a metaphor of a mythological character" (Gramsci 1971: 155, Q14§70). Social order was increasingly regressive, to the extent that the party was "a fetter on the vital forces of history" so that it had "no unity but a stagnant swamp . . . and no federation but a 'sack of potatoes,' i.e. a mechanical juxtaposition of single units without any connection between them" (Gramsci 1971: 155, Q14§70; 190, Q13§36).

As a result, the changes inaugurated in Mexico that led to the promotion of neoliberalism can be understood as an expression of passive revolution operative within the structural conditions of uneven and combined capitalist development. Neoliberalism continued to reflect the incomplete process of state and class formation in Mexico that was never truly settled after the Mexican Revolution, in line with the argument in chapter 2. It represented a furtherance of particular path-dependent responses to forms of crisis and thus a strategy developed by the ruling classes to signify the restructuring of capitalism, or the "counter-attack of capital," in order to ensure the expansion of capital and the introduction of "more or less far-reaching modifications . . . into the economic structure of the country" (Gramsci 1995: 350, Q10I§9). Neoliberalism, therefore, can be summarized as less "tightly linked to a vast local economic development, but . . . instead the reflection of international developments which transmit their ideological currents to the periphery" (Gramsci 1971: 116, Q10II§61). In Mexico, the conditions of hegemony were limited to privileged groups based on a central core of dominant classes that enacted rhetorically "revolutionary" changes in the social relations of production, through the neoliberal accumulation strategy, alongside engineered social and political reform. The result of this passive revolution of capital in the form of neoliberal restructuring can be evidenced through the changing urban class structure in Mexico. As disclosed by table 4.1, based on estimates drawn from Comisión Económica para América Latina y el Caribe (CEPAL) data by Alejandro Portes and Kelly Hoffman (2003), the size of the capitalist class has remained low, constituting up to just 2 percent of the economically active population (EAP) according to the most recent indicators. Significantly, the subordinate classes, broadly defined, make up most recently nearly 85 percent of the EAP in contrast to a total for the dominant classes, including executives and professionals, of nearly 6 percent of the EAP. Additionally, at least two major trends emerge: (1) there is a consistent decline of the formal proletariat, and (2) there is the continued increase of the

Table 4.1.   Urban Class Structure in Mexico, 1984–2000 (percent)

	1984	1989	1998	2000
Dominant classes	6.4	9.5	7.5	5.7
Capitalists[a]	0.2	0.5	0.9	1.6
Executives and professionals[b]	6.2	9.0	6.6	4.1
Petty bourgeoisie[c]	3.3	4.4	5.8	9.4
Proletariat[d]	63.1	64.7	47.3	39.1
Nonmanual formal proletariat	—	—	—	13.7
Manual formal proletariat	—	—	—	25.4
Informal proletariat[e]	27.3	21.6	39.5	45.7
Unclassified	—	—	—	0.1
Totals[f]	100.1	100.2	100.1	100

Sources: Interpolation and extrapolation of data from Economic Commission for Latin America and the Caribbean (ECLAC), *Social Panorama of Latin America, 1999–2000,* Annual Report (Santiago de Chile: ECLAC, 2000: table 11); and International Labor Office, "Panorama laboral: la estructura del empleo urbano en el período 1990–1998," Report of the ILO Regional Office, http://www.ilolim.org.pc/panorama/1999: table 8-A (as cited by Portes and Hoffman 2003: 52, 55–59).

[a]Represented by owners of the means of production employing more than five workers; overestimating the overall proportion.

[b]Including executives and administrators in public agencies and private firms employing more than five workers and university-trained salaried professionals within corporate and government agencies; overestimating the overall proportion.

[c]Assumes a distinct form in the peripheral societies of Latin America, combining reference to public servants, salaried professionals, or skilled workers affected by neoliberal structural adjustment and thrust into a role as microentrepreneurs producing low-cost goods and services for consumers as well as inputs subcontracted by large-scale industry.

[d]Disaggregated comparable data are not available for the earlier periods. Nonmanual formal proletariat refers to salaried technicians and subordinate white-collar employees protected by existing labor laws and covered by a system of health care, disability, and retirement. The formal proletariat refers to those who only have their labor to sell as wage workers in small, medium, and large modern enterprises, which, in this case, are not covered by the national social security system.

[e]Represents workers in urban microenterprises (vendors), small rural enterprises, domestic servants, and unpaid family laborers, without social security or legal protections in industry, services, and agriculture procuring a living as unprotected workers through direct subsistence; underestimating the informal proletariat.

[f]The total figures do not all add up to 100 percent because they are approximations.

informal proletariat; features that are common throughout the regional class structures of Latin America.[11] One of the most significant conclusions, then, reflected specifically in the data on Mexico, and Latin America in general, is that *pace* Robinson "the numerically most important segment of the population in Latin American is that excluded from modern capitalist relations and which must survive through unregulated work and direct subsistence activities" (Portes and Hoffman 2003: 53). Needless to say, as the contradictions of neoliberalism become more apparent, the "path-dependent legacies of neoliberal errors" stemming from such class polarization will also need to be addressed (Jessop 2002: 169).

However, it should not be presumed on the basis of the above argument that both the accumulation strategy and the minimal hegemony of neoliberalism in Mexico entailed the erosion of state power or conversion into a transnational state. Neoliberalism did not entail the dismantling, or retreat, of the state, but the rearrangement of the spatial scales of state power in a new hierarchy. As Dresser (1994: 155) has commented,

> Even though neoliberal policy currents underscore the importance of reducing the economic power of the state, the Mexican case reveals that the imperatives of political survival will often dictate the need for continued state intervention through discretionary compensation policies.

The reconfiguration of the spatial scales of the state, rather than its dismantling, was based through PRONASOL on a "neo-corporatist" arrangement that was pivotal in bolstering the accumulation strategy and minimal hegemony of neoliberalism (Craske 1994). Such nuanced conclusions about the transformation and rescaling of the Mexican state emerge through a focus on how the state is itself actively engaged in producing the spatial configurations of neoliberalism, which are revealed by taking the state form as "nodal" within the restructuring of the uneven and combined development of neoliberal capitalist accumulation.

CONCLUSION: THE SHIFTING SANDS OF MINIMAL HEGEMONY

One of the contentions of this chapter has been that the process of historically specific class struggles reflected in the transition from ISI to neoliberal capitalist accumulation is grasped better through a focus on how the spatial form of the state under global capitalism is socially produced, or authored, by particular class forces. The theory of passive revolution reveals the different scales of power and production under capitalist accumulation processes while

prompting one to take as nodal the capitalist type of state in tracing the geopolitical circumstances of uneven and combined development. The analysis
of passive revolution linked to the rise of a neoliberal strategy of capitalist
accumulation bears out David Harvey's (1982/2006: 33–4, 102–4) claim
that the progression of neoliberalism within conditions of uneven development proceeded more from the diversification, innovation, and competition
between different fractions of national capital than the straight diffusion of
global capitalism. As Ernest Mandel (1975: 332–33) affirmed some time ago,
"the counteracting force of the uneven development of capital prevents the
formation of an actual global community of interest for capital." It is on this
basis that the adequacy of the transnational state thesis has been challenged
as a suitable account of the relationship between space and development.
While it is acknowledged that a specification of the relationship between issues of space and territory is difficult (Robinson 2003: 326), my argument
has challenged three crucial conventions about the transnational state thesis.
Namely, (1) the problematic conception of the historical connection between
state territoriality and capitalism; (2) the assumption that global capitalism is
having a unidirectional impact on conditions of uneven development, referred
to as positing the homoficence of capitalism and evened development; and (3)
the ontological assumption of a transnational state that flattens out the spatial
and territorial logics of capital accumulation eliding class struggles extant in
specific locations. The thesis of the transnational state fails to avoid a depiction of the diffusion of transnational capital to different spatial and territorial
places and scales. One consequence is that a false dichotomy is then posited
between the state intervention of developmentalist capitalism and the liberalization of transnational capitalism (Robinson 2008: 177, 184). In contrast, my
argument in this and the previous chapter implies certain patterns of continuity cutting across the period of transformation from ISI to neoliberalism, not
least the importance of the spatial scale of state power and specific fractions
of capital in shaping capitalist restructuring (see also Martin 2007). Future
advances in debate on the uneven development of global capitalism would
most likely have to square the differences between a theory of uneven and
combined development and earlier arguments about the development of underdevelopment. "The essential difference between the two theories," notes
Ronald Chilcote (2000: 227), "is the latter's association of capitalism with
the conquest of the Americas and the former's assumption that the capitalist mode of production did not fully establish itself even in Europe until the
eighteenth century." These, stated succinctly, have been the arguments that
animated this chapter.

    As a result, it was possible to trace the shifting sands of minimal hegemony
linked to the rise of the accumulation strategy of neoliberalism in Mexico,

especially reflected in the era of *salinismo*, which seriously eroded the historical basis of the PRI. This bears out the view that granting priority to the accumulation function of the state can undermine its legitimation function leading to conditions of weakened hegemony (Cox 1982: 54). The demise of ISI and the rise of neoliberalism were accompanied by the exhaustion of the PRI's minimal hegemony. Since the phase of structural change in the 1970s, the historical and social basis of this minimal hegemony began to alter and seriously erode. Throughout the 1980s and 1990s, the PRI increasingly resorted to forms of dominance and coercion, reflecting an increasingly dwindling form of class hegemony. It is within this era of structural change that a crisis of hegemony unfolded.

> In every country the process is different, although the content is the same. And the content is the crisis of the ruling class's hegemony. . . . [Hence] a "crisis of authority" is spoken of: this is precisely the crisis of hegemony, or general crisis of the state. (Gramsci 1971: 210, Q13§23)

By thus tracing these shifting sands of minimal hegemony it was argued that the PRI was only hegemonic in a very narrow sense and it continued to lose a large degree of internal coherence and legitimacy from the 1970s onward. While the lagging effects of such class hegemony were evident during the restructuring of state–civil society relations within the accumulation strategy of neoliberalism, the historic purpose of the PRI was ended by the victory of Vicente Fox on 2 July 2000. It is beyond the scope of this chapter to determine whether a more cohesive form of hegemony can be refashioned within the "second generation" of neoliberalism in Mexico (see Middlebrook and Zepeda 2003; Middlebrook 2004a; Charnock 2006). Yet it was possible through the theory of passive revolution to emphasize variations or lags in hegemony and a minimal hegemony was discernible but increasingly recessive over the period under consideration since the 1970s. This helps to avoid either assuming the straightforward existence of hegemony or indulging in crude dichotomies between coercion and consent in understanding the role and influence of the PRI within the conditions of passive revolution and recurring crisis. Hegemony is not like a light switch, clicked on or off. Instead, struggles over hegemony entail a complex mix of state-coercive elements and hegemonic activity, the latter aiming to organically bind state-civil relations. More generally the above analysis of neoliberalism also highlighted the unfolding process of class struggle brought about by the *internalization* of the interests of capital that became integrated into policies within the emerging capitalist type of state in Mexico. The discussion of the PSE and PRONA-SOL, two coexisting measures both introduced to offset political instability resulting from the neoliberal accumulation strategy and the reconfigured minimal hegemony of the PRI, exemplifies this process of class struggle. The final point that the argument has raised is that the case of Mexico does not signify the straightforward reproduction of a transnational state thesis of neoliberalism. It would be inappropriate to assume, therefore, that the social production of neoliberalism in Mexico was brought about by a transnational state apparatus transmitting global restructuring. Part two of the book now raises the importance of alternative spatial practices in the contestation of revolution and state in modern Mexico.

NOTES

1. For representative works on the MST, see Petras and Veltmeyer (2002); Branford and Rocha (2002); or Desmarais (2007).

2. Although this neglects the ongoing drive behind imperialist aspirations, evident historically in Cecil Rhodes's attributed statement that the parceling out of the world under colonialism left only the stars: "These stars that you see overhead at night, these vast worlds which we can never reach! I would annex the planets if I could. I often think of that. It makes me sad to see them so clear and yet so far away" (as cited in Millin 1933: 138).

3. Again, recall here David Harvey's notion of "accumulation by dispossession" as a constant process of ongoing primitive accumulation involving inter alia the commodification of land; changes in property relations; the appropriation of natural resources; and the use of national debt, the credit system, and the inflationary process as an expression of class struggle all of which is contingent upon the stance of the state (Harvey 2003a: 145). A further earlier precursor would be Samir Amin's emphasis on mechanisms of primitive accumulation that "do not belong only to the prehistory of capitalism; they are contemporary as well" (Amin 1974: 3).

4. My attention to this quotation is indebted to the citation by Kiely (2005: 44).

5. Lefebvre (1991: 220) puts it thus: "We may wonder whether the state will eventually produce its own space, an absolute political space. Or whether, alternatively, the nation states will one day see their absolute political space disappearing into (and thanks to) the world market. Will this last eventuality occur through self-destruction? And must it be one or the other, and not perhaps, both?"

6. As Lenin (1916/1964: 295, original emphasis) implores, "the *even* development of different undertakings, trusts, branches of industry, or countries is impossible under capitalism." The phrase *evened development* also arises in Anderson (1983: 100).

7. This citation owes a debt to the reading of Harvey (1982/2006: 450).

8. The title deliberately paraphrases Gramsci's note, similarly entitled, on the history of state formation in Italy (Gramsci 1971: 118–20, Q10I§9).

9. The Miguel de la Madrid administration reduced the public-sector deficit to 8.3 percent of GDP in 1983—lower than the 8.5 percent targeted by the IMF—and the balance of payments deficit, standing at $12,544,000 in 1981, was turned into a

$3 million surplus in 1983 due, largely, to a surplus in the trade balance linked to a decline in imports (Hamilton 1984: 26).

10. *The Economist* [London], "Won't Lend; Mexican Banks" (12 October 2002): 98.

11. While figures may differ slightly, due to the definitions in use, the evidence on class stratification in Mexico for the ten-year period from 2000 to 2010 follows a similar trend; namely, an overall decline in the dominant class, a decline in the formal proletariat, and a leap in the ranks of the informal proletariat (see Cypher and Delgado Wise 2010: 22–26).

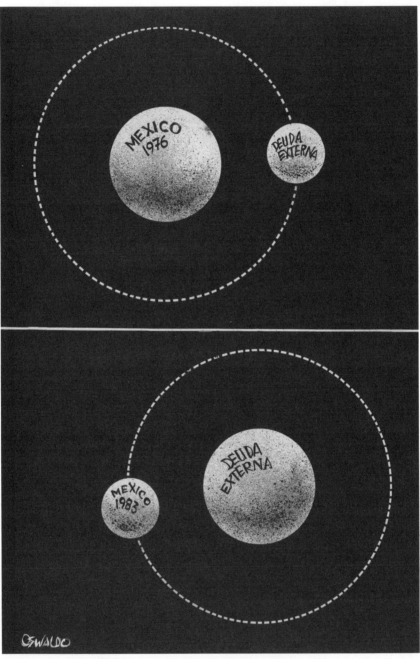

Figure 4.1. Oswaldo Sagástegui, *Orbitas* [Orbits] cartoon, *Excélsior* (Mexico City), 9 March 1983, ink drawing. Private collection of the author.

Part II

CONTESTING REVOLUTION
AND STATE IN MODERN MEXICO

Chapter Five

Intellectuals and the State

A Critical Social Function or in the Shadow of the State?

Arising from "the anguish of backwardness," mentioned in chapter 3, and the modernism of uneven development, there holds a brilliance and depth within the "living modernism" of art that struggles to capture, express, and process the temporalities and configurations of capitalism (see Berman 1982: 232). In this context, the works of Carlos Fuentes, among others, have been heralded as indicative modernist masterpieces "but we seem to have forgotten how to grasp the modern life from which this art springs" (Berman 1982: 24). Flanking this history of modernity have been the convulsions in the rise of capitalism itself, distinguished by the "constant revolutionising of production, uninterrupted disturbance of all social conditions, everlasting uncertainty and agitation" so that "all fixed, fast-frozen relations, with their train of ancient and venerable prejudices and opinions, are swept away, all new-formed ones become antiquated before they can ossify. All that is solid melts into air" (Marx and Engels 1848/1976: 487).

Previously in this book, the route to modern state formation has been analyzed through the ruptural instance of the Mexican Revolution as both the displacement and consolidation of capitalist social relations. Central to the construction of the modern state in Mexico has therefore been a blocked dialectic of revolution-restoration emblematic of the historical conditions of passive revolution. Across the first part of the book, then, there has been both analysis of the specific rupture of the Mexican Revolution as a passive revolution and subsequent class strategies linked to the furtherance, expansion, and consolidation of capitalism in the forms of import substitution industrialization (ISI) and neoliberalism within the conditions of uneven and combined development. In turning to an examination of the contestation of revolution and state in Mexico, in the second half of this book, attention is initially cast toward one of the focal social sources of ideology, namely, the "living modernism" captured within literature. "Literature," according to Terry Eagleton (1976/2006: 101), "is the most revealing mode of experiential access to ideology that we possess. It is in literature, above all, that we observe in a peculiarly complex, coherent, intensive and immediate fashion the workings of ideology in the textures of lived experience of class-societies." At the same time, literature itself has to be inserted within the context of capitalist uneven and combined development. This was suggestively apparent in the *Manifesto of the Communist Party*, when Karl Marx and Friedrich Engels noted:

> The bourgeoisie has through its exploitation of the world market given a cosmopolitan character to production and consumption in every country. . . . And as in material, so also in intellectual production. The intellectual creations of individual nations become common property. National one-sidedness and narrow-mindedness become more and more impossible, and from the numerous national and local literatures, there arises a world literature. (Marx and Engels 1848/1976: 488)

Differences between modern states and their subjection to capital have also been noted, if somewhat clumsily, by Jean-Paul Sartre who touched on how "in the conquered or ruined countries literature has recently begun to be considered as an article for export" (Sartre 1948/2001: 186). More generally, the history of art and literature is not simply one of material abundance but also of the uneven development of the forces of production within certain class-specific and ideological forms (Eagleton 1976/2006: 182). This chapter thus aims to grasp the contestation of revolution and state in modern Mexico by focusing on the "living modernism" apparent in the artistic form of literature, through an examination of the specific literary and political activity of Carlos Fuentes. Following the lead in chapter 1, the conditions of passive revolution find their expression across the politics and culture of state power internally linking architecture, literature, and art to modern state formation. As a result, the key argument here will not only reveal the contribution of Carlos Fuentes as a novelist of the conditions of passive revolution in Mexico but also delve into issues of literary aesthetics and form to expose his wider social function as a "passive revolutionary" in shaping modern state formation and state–civil society relations.

A critical stance toward the outcome and legacy of the Mexican Revolution has been a persistent, indeed archetypal, theme throughout the writings of Carlos Fuentes. This theme, for example, is acutely evident within *The Years with Laura Díaz* (*Los años con Laura Díaz*, 1999), one of his relatively recent novels.[1] Juan Francisco, husband of the main character Laura Díaz, has trouble living up to ideals founded on the myth of the Mexican Revolution.

Francisco changes from an "energetic and generous labour tribune in the Revolution to second-rate politico and functionary." He also takes his eldest son, future business luminary and wearer of black Gucci loafers, Danton López-Díaz, to the offices of the Confederación de Trabajadores de México (CTM) to experience the flaccid life of politics in 1940s Mexico based on corruption and control of the labor unions. As Francisco states, "You have to realise . . . that the government's raison d'être is to ensure stability and social peace in Mexico. That, today, is what revolutionary means" (Fuentes 1999/2000: 297, 435, 303, 312). It is this social landscape, the accommodation between both the new society created by the Mexican Revolution and the aristocratic and impoverished society of the *antiguo régimen*, which Fuentes captures within his sociohistorical criticism of Mexican politics. Moreover, it is a social landscape that marks both the conditions of passive revolution and, indeed, the role of intellectuals in Latin America as figures who have acted as critical substitutes for the structures of civil society and/or as reactionaries much more interested in creating self-legitimating roles that have perpetuated social order within the "shadow of the state" (Camp 1985; Miller 1999). These twin aspects will be discussed in order to subject, to detailed scrutiny, the "living modernism" within the social function of Carlos Fuentes in Mexico. Attention is drawn to Fuentes, in particular, because of his prominence as a key intellectual figure in considering issues of national identity, history, and culture within the wider problematic of modernization (Boldy 1987: 157). As a participant in the so-called boom generation of the Latin American novel, he has also been a pivotal intellectual in Mexico from the 1950s to the present. The national epics of Carlos Fuentes locate him as a *cronista* of modern Mexico, or one of its key *pensadores* (intellectuals-at-large), providing a vision of culture on a national scale, accompanying the community, guiding it through its dilemmas, consoling it in grief, and sharing in its triumph, albeit at times as an authorized voice of the state (Lomnitz 1992: 11–13; Lomnitz 2001: xi). The breadth of output and continued conduct of this social function licenses such a detailed focus, in contrast to considering some of his late contemporaries (i.e., Rosario Castellanos, Ricardo Garibay, Octavio Paz, Jaime Sabines), additional counterparts (i.e., Gustavo Sainz, Guadalupe Loaeza, Christina Pacheco, or Paco Ignacio Taibo II), or literature of *la generación del "crack,"* a more recent mid-1990s movement initiated by a younger group of authors breaking with the boom generation and its literary conventions (i.e., Ignacio Padilla, Jorge Volpi, Eloy Urroz, Pedro Ángel Palou, or Ricardo Chávez-Castañeda). The argument is structured into three main sections.

First, adding to the theoretical innovations that mark each previous chapter in this book, the forms of cultural and literary criticism developed by both

Antonio Gramsci and Leon Trotsky will be detailed. In essence, these combine attentiveness to the links between sociohistorical content and aesthetic form within literature, which have been relatively neglected and underutilized in discussions on art and literature.[2] These social categories and distinctions of literary criticism will then be positioned within wider cognate insights on Marxist aesthetics and form. Here it will be argued that "Marxism seeks . . . the social roots of the 'pure' as well as of the tendentious art. It does not 'incriminate' a poet with the thoughts and feelings that he expresses, but raises questions of a much more profound significance, namely, to which order of feelings does a given artistic work correspond in all its peculiarities?" (Trotsky 1922–1923/2005: 143).

The second section then deploys these insights on aesthetics and form through an examination of the concrete political and literary activity of Carlos Fuentes. Stemming from the 1950s, an overview will therefore be provided of the political and literary dimensions of Fuentes's role as an intellectual and, in particular, his prolonged critique of the iniquities of the Mexican political system and the social conditions that arose in the aftermath of the Mexican Revolution. This will involve not only tracing his activity through political journalism and the production of a series of novels but also entail a discussion, on the basis of personal interviews, of Fuentes's own conception of his social and political responsibility. Overall, attention in this section will be drawn to Fuentes's *critical* activity as an intellectual engaged in more immediate national-popular state processes in his attempt to demystify the ideology of the Mexican Revolution.

A third section then focuses on tensions between national and cosmopolitan cultural stances within Fuentes's work by exploring in more detail the attitudes he presents in a variety of novels. This does not mean simply equating an author's views with the content of a text but, instead, refers to recognizing representations within a novel as, nevertheless, ideological social constructions that accrue distinct political significance. It will be noted that beyond a literary style, laden with elitist irony, a haughty attitude and the elaboration of cultural stereotypes toward people from lower social classes is evident within Fuentes's work. Indeed, it will be argued that the common concern for Fuentes has predominantly been the interior life of the upper classes in Mexico, a feature that has characterized the Mexican novel in the twentieth century more generally (see Monsiváis 1975). Hence the importance of reflecting on whether certain contradictions within Fuentes's literature have ultimately conspired to limit his impact in challenging the prevailing Mexican political system, to the extent that the overall effect of his cultural practice has been, rather, to sustain the minimal hegemony of the once-ruling Partido Revolucionario Institucional (PRI). This will assist in elaborating in conclusion on the overall social function of Carlos Fuentes as an intellectual, the degree of connection he has had with class forces in Mexico, and thus on his role as a frequent mediator for the minimal hegemony of the PRI in the construction and contestation of modern Mexico.

THE SOCIAL FUNCTION OF THE INTELLECTUAL AND PASSIVE REVOLUTION: FORM AND CONTENT

Within his analysis of literature, Trotsky outlines and sketches the lineaments of a social method of literary criticism that focuses on the social basis of art connected to aesthetics. Rather than accepting the binary opposition of "form" and "content," a dialectical appreciation of the aesthetic and the ideological is affirmed. "The relation between form and content (the latter to be understood not simply as a 'theme' but as a living complex of moods and ideas that seek artistic expression) is determined by the fact that [it] . . . has its roots in society" (Trotsky 1922–1923/2005: 191). Elsewhere, he balks at the suggestion that Dante's *The Divine Comedy* should be analyzed in terms of its class content, or understood as an expression of certain class conditions limited to an epoch for "to put the matter that way means simply to strike out *The Divine Comedy* from the realm of art" (Trotsky 1924/1970: 70). Rather, there should be an aesthetic relationship between artistic creation and historical criticism capable of situating problems of aesthetics within a broader historical and philosophical canvass refracted through a rootedness in social purpose.

> The architectural scheme of the Cologne cathedral can be established by measuring the base and the height of its arches, by determining the three dimensions of its naves, the dimensions and the placement of the columns, etc. But without knowing what a medieval city was like, what a guild was, or what was the Catholic Church of the Middle Ages, the Cologne cathedral will never be understood. (Trotsky 1922–1923/2005: 151; cf. 155–56)

This method has been described as "adjacentism" referring to the placing of an isolated detail in relation to wider social historical conditions (Eagleton 1976/2006: 171). However, Eagleton argues that although this approach moves toward theorizing the productive relations between aesthetic form and sociohistorical content and grasps their unity it struggles within the categories it is attempting to overcome. The task, then, remains "a matter of analysing how the text constructs itself as a wholly 'aesthetic' product on the basis of its *internal relation* to the ideological" (Eagleton 1976/2006: 178, emphasis added). Given that this philosophy of internal relations is a core feature of this book's approach to state theory in general (see chapter 1), this avenue will be pursued in more detail.

In avoiding a simple opposition between form and content, Eagleton argues that there is a complex, mutual articulation between the ideological and the aesthetic whereby aesthetic modes become ideologically saturated. The significations worked into literature are thus already representations of reality rather than reality itself, so the text is "the product of certain signifying practices whose source and referent is, in the last instance, history itself" (Eagleton 1976/2006: 75). The result is a position that eschews posing the relation between aesthetic form and social content as an extrinsic one, as two externally related phenomena. Instead, the presence of the text within ideology is posited as an inherent constituent of ideological reproduction. It is this philosophy of internal relations between aesthetic form and social content— or the interweaving of materiality and meaning—that also denotes cognate contours within Marxist aesthetics (see Jameson 1971; Adorno 1974b; Williams 1977; Marcuse 1978). The task then becomes one of analyzing how a text is an aesthetic product on the basis of its internal relation to the ideological (also consider Bieler and Morton 2008).

Following Gramsci, "the intellectual function cannot be cut off from productive work in general, and the same is true for artists" (Gramsci 2007: 25, Q6§29). Similar to the arguments presented above, Gramsci's focus on the aesthetic form of a novel involved appreciating the specific sociohistorical conditions within which a writer exists so that political criticism can focus on how the contradictions and problems within society may be evident in the interests and activity of the writer (Gramsci 1985: 91–93, Q23§1). The social element of a work, in terms of practical tendencies and class sentiments, therefore becomes significant but as a wider aspect, or structure of feeling, associated with hegemonic forms (Williams 1977: 132–33). Attitudes present in a work of art can then be appreciated from an aesthetic point of view while also subjecting the same to critique in terms of ideological content. Thus the two tendencies of the aesthetic ("pure art") and the politicocultural ("pure politics") are combined in an appreciation of a writer on the basis that art cannot be understood solely as the product of individual expression but also as part of concrete activity within a specific society (Gramsci 1985: 108–10, Q15§38; 112, Q14§28). "Our research," states Gramsci in a note directly on "Popular Literature: Content and Form," "is thus into the history of culture and not literary history as a part of a broader history of culture" (Gramsci 1985: 205, Q14§72). An insistence on social content therefore promotes analysis of the "specific conception of the world" in a piece (Gramsci 1985: 203–6, Q14§72). Yet it widens the reach of literary criticism to consider a broader history of culture and incorporates a consideration of the specific moral and intellectual content of a work going beyond issues of "beauty" associated with "the literature of the aesthetes" (Gramsci 1985: 264–65, Q21§4; 273–75, Q6§29).

This coherent approach to the politics of literature was then deployed by Gramsci to engage with a variety of novelistic forms—popular serials, detective, Gothic romance, science fiction—as well as other forms of cultural production such as architecture, the theater, and cinema (Dombroski 1986; Gramsci 1994a: 260–63). The latter included commentary on "the urban 'panorama' . . . in the broader sense of an architectural complex with streets, squares, gardens, parks, etc." in which the architectural "building is the social externalisation of art, its 'dissemination'—just like the printed book, it gives the public the chance to participate in its beauty" (Gramsci 1996: 125, Q3§155). Methodological criteria were also brought to bear in producing an interpretative reading of specific texts, such as Dante's *Inferno* (see Gramsci 1996: 246–58, Q4§78–§88), while the popularity of foreign serial fiction among Italians was also crucial for Gramsci because it conspired to limit the influence of national literature and the educative role this could play in forging a "national-popular" alliance between opposition forces. Consequently, the Italian people experienced the hegemony of foreign ideas because intellectuals there had increasingly become a caste disconnected from everyday aspirations. This resulted in the non-national-popular or cosmopolitan character of Italian intellectuals who were predominantly divorced from lay culture (Gramsci 1985: 118, Q15§20; 206–12, Q21§5).

One of the key works that was expressive of such non-national-popular traits was the influential historical novel *The Betrothed*, published in revised form in 1840, by Alessandro Manzoni (Manzoni 1997). In contrast to other historical novelists, such as Anton Chekhov who was regarded as a "progressive" writer or Leo Tolstoy described as a "world" writer who managed to arouse popular interests in works of aesthetic "beauty" (Gramsci 1994b: 360–61), Manzoni tended to side with the upper classes of society in his works (Gramsci 1985: 288–91, Q23§51). There was thus an "aristocratic" character to the people in *The Betrothed* to the extent that the lower social classes were represented as "the humble," as popular caricatures, who were usually humiliated and insulted (Gramsci 1985: 291–96, Q7§50). Therefore, while subaltern classes were depicted as having no history, the narrative tended to value the interior life of the nobility and their "complex" psychology, feelings, and ambitions. Hence a supercilious attitude towards "the humble" and a concern with peasant life that was more apparent than real (Gramsci 1985: 294, Q14§39). Moreover, the jargon used by Manzoni as well as the "finesse" and "intellectual minutiae" evident in *The Betrothed* was limited in appeal to specific groups of the literati (Gramsci 1985: 296–97, Q15§37). As a result,

Manzoni conveyed a non-national-popular attitude and failed to appeal to the popular classes in Italy.

Overall, then, Gramsci's literary criticism always linked possibly abstract issues to concrete expressions, reconciling the intrinsic and the extrinsic in terms of aesthetic form and sociohistorical content (Gramsci 1985: 108–10, Q15§38; 112–15, Q23§36). Yet the concern was not just directed to narrow literary aspects but to the "objectification" and material aspects of the production of art and literature relative to the history and culture of a particular society. The task of the social literary critic thus becomes one of analyzing how a text is an aesthetic product on the basis of its internal relation to struggles over hegemony. As Herbert Marcuse subsequently came to illuminate, aesthetic form refers to the transformation of a given content (actual, historical, personal, or social facts) into a self-contained whole (poem, play, novel). The critical function of art then resides in the aesthetic form, by the content having become form, in an inexorably mediated fashion. "The aesthetic transformation is achieved through a reshaping of language, perception, and understanding so that they reveal the essence of reality in its appearance. . . . The work of art thus re-presents reality while accusing it" (Marcuse 1978: 8).

Finally, the pertinence of this critical practice to assessing the meaning of materiality comes to the fore in the functions exercised by intellectuals across the social, political, economic, and cultural fields. According to Gramsci, the most important forms of intellectuals are the traditional and the organic. On one hand, traditional intellectuals are those who consider themselves to be autonomous but, more accurately, can be related to preceding socioeconomic structures belonging to a different period of historical time. Examples would include the clergy and idealist philosophers, or "ivory tower" intellectuals, who "can be defined as the expression of that social utopia by which the intellectuals think of themselves as 'independent,' autonomous, endowed with a character of their own etc." (Gramsci 1971: 8, Q12§1). Traditional intellectuals therefore represent "the culture of a restricted intellectual aristocracy" that is "given by the man of letters, the philosopher, the artist" (Gramsci 1971: 9, Q12§3: 9; 393, Q16§9). On the other hand, although it has been inferred that some traditional intellectuals can perform functions organic to the rise of new ruling classes (Sassoon 1987: 144, 214), the category of organic intellectual was predominantly reserved for those intellectuals that stood as the mediators of the capitalist class. Such intellectuals have the function of organizing the hegemony of a ruling class, and thus forms of consensual leadership, beyond the coercive apparatus of the state (Gramsci 1996: 200–201, Q4§49). Hence, organic intellectuals are engaged in active participation in everyday life, acting as an agent or constructor, organizer and "permanent persuader" in forming hegemony (Gramsci 1971: 9–10, Q12§3). The specialism of an organic intellectual can therefore entail a connection with the active formation of hegemony by particular class forces that constantly construct and maintain a social order. Alternatively, it can entail a connection with opposing initiatives attempting to forge an alternative hegemony by connecting many different forms of struggle. By producing certain ideas, intellectuals can therefore play an essential mediating function in struggles over hegemony by acting as "deputies" or instruments of hegemony, or by performing a valuable supporting role to subaltern classes engaged in promoting social change (Gramsci 1971: 5–23, Q12§1, §3; 52–55, Q25§2, §5).

Again, what this amounts to is a conception of the "real dialectical process" between the ideological and the social relations of production, or the internal relation between form and content, in sustaining and contesting state–civil society relations (Gramsci 1971: 12, Q12§1; Gramsci 2007: 340, Q8§182). It is a focus that links the social function of intellectuals to the world of production within capitalist society, without succumbing to economic determinism, while still offering the basis for a materialist and social class analysis of intellectuals (Vacca 1982: 63). Cultural aspects, including literature, clearly play a significant role within this conception of organic intellectuals wherein literature is understood as a material social product and the social function of the author is endowed with political significance. The task therefore becomes one of revealing the social functions and attitudes of intellectuals within the complex web of state–civil society relations. As a result, one aspect of the focus on the social function of the intellectual involves analyzing particular ideologies within literature by combining an appreciation of both aesthetic form and sociohistorical content. It is now time to pose these particular issues in relation to the social function of Carlos Fuentes as an ideator of passive revolution in Mexico.

THE FORMATION OF THE *CRITICAL* SOCIAL FUNCTION OF CARLOS FUENTES

Fuentes himself has admitted that he comes from what could be described as "typical petit bourgeois stock" (Harss and Dohmann 1967: 281) with clear links to the social and political elite in Mexico. In the words of Richard Reeve (1982: 41), "he was not simply a witness of the changing face of Mexico, but a participant in its inner circle." In the 1950s this initially included involvement in a youthful grouping of intellectuals from elite circles that organized parties to reflect on philosophical issues, known as the Basfumismo group. The group attempted to act as some sort of vanguard movement but promoted little more than the opportunity to organize social gatherings and exclusive parties. Interestingly, though, it has been conjectured that this social setting provided the background for Fuentes's subsequent examination and critique of the national intellectual, political, and cultural scene to be discussed shortly (Reeve 1982: 41–42). Also significant for later discussion was Fuentes's role, in 1955–1957, as founder and editor—along with Emmanuel Carballo—of the *Revista de Mexicana de Literatura*. This journal embarked on a sustained attempt to promote a cosmopolitan view of Mexican culture and hinted, perhaps, towards Fuentes's future cosmopolitan bias and distaste for narrow forms of cultural nationalism. It was following the publication of a collection of short stories, *The Masked Days* (*Los días enmascarados*, 1954), that these and many other factors emerged within Fuentes's literary and political writings throughout the 1950s and early 1960s.

As a recipient of a fellowship from the Rockefeller-sponsored Centro Mexicano de Escritores, Fuentes began full-time work on his first novel, which was published as *Where the Air Is Clear* (*La región más transparente*, 1958). This was soon succeeded by the publication of *The Good Conscience* (*Las buenas consciencias*, 1959) and *The Death of Artemio Cruz* (*La muerte de Artemio Cruz*, 1962). It is within this context that Fuentes's *critical* social function was formed, which would then shape his subsequent literary career. This entailed enduring criticism of Mexican bourgeois society, the iniquities of the Mexican political system, analysis of the unfulfilled promises of the Mexican Revolution, and an ongoing critique of the PRI. These particular aspects of social criticism not only emerged within this period but were also to have a bearing on subsequent political and literary endeavors. Hence, in terms of a critical social function, Fuentes has consistently highlighted how certain class forces thwarted the progressive aspects of the revolution to culminate in the reorganization of capitalism in Mexico. In short, how a social formation adapted and subverted potentially revolutionary aspects of social change in order to further the survival of capitalism, defined as a "passive revolution." Note here that this refers to "the fact that 'progress' occurs as the reaction of the dominant classes to the sporadic and incoherent rebelliousness of the popular masses—a reaction consisting of 'restorations' that agree to some part of the popular demands and are therefore 'progressive restorations,' or 'revolutions-restorations,' or even 'passive revolutions'" (Gramsci 2007: 252, Q8§25). Given that Fuentes portrays in novelistic form this complex historical process of the blocked dialectic of the Mexican Revolution, of both revolution and restoration, he can be described as *the* novelist of passive revolution in Mexico. "Fuentes' version of the Mexican Revolution," notes fellow writer Keith Botsford, "is that it is entirely corrupted, because, to a large measure, it has succeeded."[3]

Commenting in the 1960s, the cultural and literary critic John Brushwood (1966: 16) declared that "it is not possible to understand recent Mexican fiction without knowing that the country passed through a social revolution that did not create utopia." This context was at the heart of the discussion in chapter 2. As also detailed in chapter 3, from the 1940s onward a distinct capitalist model of development was promoted in Mexico with substantial social and economic growth succeeding the populist administration of Lázaro Cárdenas (1934–1940), which was then driven by the more conservative probusiness administration of Miguel Alemán (1946–1952). The cultural political economy of this milieu was exceptionally captured in *Where the Air Is Clear* (*La región más transparente*, 1958). The book is particularly, but not solely, a totalizing novel offering a representation of the postrevolutionary state and its national-popular ideology, including issues of modernization and the gulf between social classes within the bustling urban expansion of Mexico City in the 1950s (Long 2008). It is Mexico City itself, as "the capital of underdevelopment," that is the backdrop to this social panorama of modern state formation (Fuentes 1984/2001: 16).

The opening scenes of the novel are dominated by a depiction of the inner life of Mexico's upper classes that are all present at an exclusive party hosted by the character Bobó and surveyed by the elusive figure Ixca Cienfuegos. This may well be a snapshot of the interior world of the Basfumismo group, mentioned earlier. Various aspects of the rising bourgeoisie are therefore represented in the novel. There are "soaring lawyers," such as Licenciado Librado Ibarra; "zooming industrialists," such as the key figure Federico Robles; and young literati like the intellectual Manuel Zamacona and the poet Rodrigo Pola (Fuentes 1958/1971: 20–21).[4] It is through such characters that the rise and fall of the bourgeoisie in Mexico are examined alongside a discussion of the relentless divisions between social classes. Ixca Cienfuegos is both witness and victim of the various cycles of prosperity and sacrifice experienced by these characters. He seems to be both surveyor (judge) as well as conveyor (narrator) of Mexican history from the panoramic to the quotidian.[5] It is in dialogue with Cienfuegos that the revolutionary, turned millionaire banker, Federico Robles notably reflects on the lasting legacies of the revolution.

Robles, as a *mestizo* and protagonist in the revolution, personifies the heritage and national character of Mexico while also representing its contradictions and compromises. Throughout *Where the Air Is Clear* one understands that although Robles fought, almost by accident, in the Mexican Revolution he actually sided with General Álvaro Obregón, who defeated the Northern Division of Francisco "Pancho" Villa at the battle of Celaya (1915). In the years succeeding the revolution—throughout the "institutional" phase (1920–1940)—Robles became a lawyer and beneficiary of relative progress and bourgeois stability established under the presidency of Plutarco Elías Calles that "laid the foundation for Mexican capitalism" (87). To be sure, in contrast to the dictatorship of Porfirio Díaz (1876–1910), progressive aspects of the revolution are highlighted. For instance, Librado Ibarra, supposed friend and alter ego of Robles, acknowledges to Cienfuegos that the new postrevolutionary government pulled in everyone including workers, capitalists, campesinos, intellectuals, professional men, and "even Diego Rivera." A form of hegemonic political organization is acknowledged. "Unlike Díaz, who had organised from above downward, the Revolution first gathered in all the living forces of the nation" (140). Yet, as a member of the rising bourgeoisie—who persistently attempts to disguise the Indian within himself with cashmere and cologne—Robles pronounces to Cienfuegos, "Only we know what a revolution is . . . and every revolution ends with the creation of a new privileged class" (87). Hence the aim of creating a stable middle class after the revolution, which was allied with defending merely rhetorical revolutionary principles (86). Key administrations, including that of President Lázaro Cárdenas (1934–1940), therefore sought after bourgeois stability by applying protective legislation to the workers while still striving to build a capitalist economy. "Mexican capitalism is indebted to two men: Calles and Cárdenas. Calles created the foundation. Cárdenas brought it to life. . . . If Cárdenas hadn't given the labour movement an official character, administrations since would not have been able to work peacefully and increase national production" (89).

Later in the novel similar commentary on the fledgling nature of the bourgeoisie in Mexico can also be found. The lives of the privileged seem to revolve around frequenting fashionable stores, such as Sanborns, where money and social position are on display. Mexico is thus described as a country of adventurers and social climbers. It has "none of the gestation which gives the European bourgeoisie a certain class," because "the bourgeoisie in Europe *is* a class" (136, original emphasis). In contrast, in Mexico, "there is [a] caste without tradition, without taste and without talent. . . . They're an approximation to bourgeois . . . playing in imitation of the great bourgeoisie" (136). Along with the church, referred to as "the petty Mexican priesthood" (136), the social strata of intellectuals in Mexico receive further critical attention. This is again articulated through Robles but this time in dialogue with the intellectual Manuel Zamacona.

Zamacona wants to search for solutions to Mexico's predicament more suited to concrete local conditions rather than imitating foreign models of development. Hence he is both critical of the positivism of the *antiguo régi-*

men and the outcome of the Mexican Revolution. After all, "Díaz and his collaborators thought that for us to become European, all we had to do was wear clothing cut by August Comte, live in a mansion designed by Haussmann" (221). Subsequently, though, only half solutions are apparent because "the only concrete result of the Revolution had to be the rise of a new privileged class, economic domination by the United States, and the paralysing of all internal political life" (221). Similarly, the poet Rodrigo Pola questions whether the revolution served only to create a new group of potentates (102). In sum, with an almost prescient forecast, Zamacona declares, "Only the bourgeoisie moves and moves again, works forward, takes the country over. In ten more years we'll be a country controlled by plutocrats, you'll see" (292). Yet there is common ground in the point of contact between the novel and state ideology. "The principal characteristic of *La Región* that ties it significantly to its context is its desire to establish and sustain a totalising representation, a desire that corresponds to the epistemological foundations of post-revolutionary state ideology and Mexicanist philosophy" (Long 2008: 21).

These facets also become apparent, albeit to different degrees, within Fuentes's next two novels: *The Good Conscience* (*Las buenas consciencias*, 1959) and *The Death of Artemio Cruz* (*La muerte de Artemio Cruz*, 1962). The former was set in Guanajuato, the epitome of provincial conservatism in Mexico, and is a typical *bildungsroman* centered on the character Jaime Ceballos. The Ceballos family was originally made up of poor immigrants who established a modest clothing shop after arriving from Spain in 1852. Through associations with Porfirio Díaz, government functionaries, businessmen, landowners, and "new industrialists," the Ceballos family's second generation in Mexico manage to diversify commercial interests and establish a *hacienda* with a lordly mansion. Although the hacienda was broken up during the revolution and the family mansion became semiderelict, the social status of the family survived. The novel then centers on the confused convictions of the central protagonist, Jaime Ceballos, who becomes "a kind of moral raw material" for his aunt and uncle, Asunción and Jorge Balcárcel (Fuentes 1959/1968: 24). The "new historical circumstances of the Revolution" are therefore very much the background setting for the novel representing a critique of the hypocrisy and contradictions of those laying claim to moral and spiritual superiority in the immediate postrevolutionary era (61). This is represented by Jaime's acquiescence to the "great expectations" of his class and social background despite his attempt to harbor and rescue the runaway miner, Ezequiel Zuno. Such social conformism also transpires despite a friendship with a young peasant, Juan Manuel Lorenzo, who brought about a critical sense in Jaime by educating him to read rebellious books and to submit authority to question. Jaime ultimately yields to the life and established order he inherited and becomes "the spoiled child of the Party of the Revolution in Guanajuato," content to live with his good conscience along with the wealthy and those of fine reputation (148). Significantly, toward the end of the earlier novel *Where the Air Is Clear*, Jaime Ceballos also appears as one of the participants of the new ruling elite who has supposedly distinguished himself by ambition and ability (347–54). A similar and probably more conspicuous expression of social criticism also pervades *The Death of Artemio Cruz*.

The publication of this novel in 1962 provided continued social criticism of Mexican social, political, and economic circumstances in the twilight of the Mexican Revolution but eschewed encompassing the large-scale social fabric evident in earlier novels. Written in the shadow of the Cuban Revolution (1959), the novel addresses feelings of disillusionment and atomization within the character of Artemio Cruz and his sense of *angst* toward the Mexican Revolution. In the present of the novel, according to Carol Clark D'Lugo, the revolution in Mexico has been stymied and social classes in the country are fragmented just like the central protagonist. There is thus a call for unification, to bring together diverse social and cultural groups in an attempt to break the pattern of power mongering in Mexico (Clark D'Lugo 1997: 115). The novel thus "absorbs many of the energies released by the Cuban Revolution, feeding consciously on a newly awakened spirit of solidarity and commitment to the struggle for greater freedom and self-determination in Latin America" (Fiddian 1990: 99).

The chronology of the novel is fragmented and structured around the life and imminent death of Artemio Cruz, another revolutionary-cum-bourgeois parvenu. Almost immediately indications are given of Artemio Cruz's material interests and "vast network of businesses" from control over the press; real-estate investment; heavy industry sulphur, mining, and logging concessions; administration of railroad loans; involvement in the hotel industry; shares in foreign corporations; and finance (Fuentes 1962/1991: 9–10). Much later, further indications of the opulence of Cruz's existence are also explicitly detailed—from the floor of Italian marble, the white-leather sofa decorated with gold fillet, the cognac and cigars, to the light silk tuxedo—all on display during decadent annual New Year's Eve parties (249–62). The source of this wealth and power derive from stealth, treachery, and betrayal that once again heralds from activity during the Mexican Revolution. Also significant is the presentation of Cruz's "tight relationship with President Alemán," and how he also benefited from the "twenty years of confidence, social peace, class collaboration . . . [and] progress after Lázaro Cárdenas's demagoguery" (10). As observed in chapter 3, it was under the administrations of Manuel Ávila Camacho (1940–1946) and Miguel Alemán (1946–1952) that Mexican finance and industrial capital was consolidated during the first phase of ISI. By highlighting the actions and desires of Cruz, Fuentes therefore discloses the complicity of some Mexicans in the consolidation of the modern state and its capitalist trajectory (Fiddian 1990: 107–8). Equally culpable and willfully immured within this process is, once again, the figure of Jaime Ceballos who appears toward the end of the novel as the heir-apparent to Cruz's empire (248, 249, 252, 258–61). Overall, it is clear that Fuentes provides a critical perspective on Mexican society within *The Death of Artemio Cruz*. As a result, the novel carries a social praxis by delineating and criticizing the corruption of the wealthy landowning class as well as the business connections between Mexican capitalists and their United States' counterparts (Manuel Durán 1994: 52).

At this stage of the argument it is worth noting the cross-fertilization between Fuentes's fiction and political journalism that has been described as "avowedly partisan writing" (Faris 1983: 102; van Delden 1998). According to Fuentes himself (1992a: 2), "the writer . . . appears on the political scene as a citizen with political options no more, and no less, than other professionals or workers within society." The main motive for writing was thus initially to counterbalance the weakness of civil society in Mexico, in Fuentes's own words, because the intellectual has responsibilities "foisted upon him," to become "transformed into a tribune, a member of parliament, a labour leader, journalist, a redeemer of his society in the absence of the functions that civil society should fulfill" (as cited in Castañeda 1994: 182). Indeed, this has been an unremitting theme in promoting the privileged expressive capacity of the novel in Latin America (see Fuentes 1969a). "By multiplying both authorship and readership," declared Fuentes more recently, "the novel, from the times of Cervantes to our own, became a democratic vehicle, a space of choice, of alternative interpretations of the self, of the world, and of the relationship between myself with others, between you and me, between we and they."[6] The social function of the intellectual according to Fuentes was therefore to "speak for others" and to "give voice to the voiceless" (MacAdam and Ruas 1981: 146; Baxandall 1962: 49). Hence Fuentes has been described as one of the leading figures who took from Jean-Paul Sartre the idea of the writer as an *engagé*—a politically committed individual—who "contributed the most to emphasising the social and political responsibility of the Latin American writer" (Williams 1998: 63). "I see no contradiction," says Fuentes, "between being an absolutely pure, distilled poet [or novelist] and having a political and social function" (King 1987: 151). Accordingly, it has been argued that Fuentes has attempted to reconcile the ideal of the autonomy of art with the social and political responsibility or authorial function of the intellectual (Wing 1982: 208). Hence the identification of Fuentes as an intellectual performing a *critical* social function in Mexico: articulating a critical sense or spirit of opposition by disputing prevailing norms about the Mexican Revolution. While Fuentes's œuvre makes significant contributions beyond a sustained criticism of the outcome of the revolution, it is his analysis of the circumstances of socioeconomic change in Mexico that is central. It also appears in novels such as *Holy Place* (*Zona sagrada*, 1967), *The Hydra Head* (*La cabeza de la hidra*, 1978), *Distant Relations* (*Una familia lejana*, 1980), *Burnt Water* (*Agua quemada*, 1981), *The Old Gringo* (*Gringo Viejo*, 1985), and *The Campaign* (*La Campaña*, 1990). It is as a result of these concerns that Fuentes can be described as a novelist who has grappled with that mode of state formation and transformation to modernity in Mexico that has been examined in this book as the condition of passive revolution. The constant theme, highlighted thus far in this chapter, that Fuentes returns to is a sustained critique of the social order that emerged out of the Mexican Revolution, the parasitic nature of the bourgeoisie in Mexico, and how the priority has been to try and imitate foreign models of social and economic development. Recalling that the condition of passive revolution relates to a process of social change and political order consonant with capitalist property relations, then similar propositions become apparent across *Where the Air Is Clear*, *The Good Conscience*, and *The Death of Artemio Cruz*. "We have a horrible bourgeoisie in Mexico," declares Fuentes, "a know-nothing bourgeoisie proud of being ignorant" (MacAdam and Ruas 1981: 161). While this bourgeoisie in Mexico did try to project and represent universal values and interests, "the truth of the matter is that they merely represent the private values of a certain class and they safeguard only these" (Fuentes 1969b: 13). This status as novelist of passive revolution in Mexico is perhaps assured when Fuentes asserts that the Mexican Revolution was a typical bourgeois revolution but one that occurred in a relatively underdeveloped country. It was based, he continues, on popular support—overcoming the land tenure system of feudalism, expropriating land holdings, and nationalizing the oil industry—but it led to the creation of a middle class and bourgeoisie in Mexico within a capitalist structure (Baxandall 1962: 52–53). The outcome of this "superimposed capitalism" is depicted as a cardboard façade behind which lies "a collapsed feudal castle" (Fuentes 1963: 12, 21). Even when affirming the progressive aspects of the Lázaro Cárdenas administration (1934–1940), Fuentes goes on to note that the equilibrium created would always be subject to crisis precisely because it was based on a bourgeois revolution and founded on class conflict (Baxandall 1962: 52; Harss and Dohman 1967: 292). Attuned to specific historical and cultural particularities, Fuentes has thus encapsulated the dialectical combination of progressive and reactionary elements in Mexico to emphasize the twin aspects of revolution-restoration. He has traced how "a particular ideology . . . born in a highly developed country, is disseminated in less developed countries, impinging on the local interplay of combinations" (Gramsci 1971: 182, Q13§17).[7] Therefore, Carlos Fuentes can be appropriately designated as *the* novelist of passive revolution in Mexico. Yet this is only one aspect of his social function as an intellectual.

THE RETREAT OF THE INTELLECTUAL WITHIN THE "SHADOW OF THE STATE"?

It was noted earlier that Fuentes has held a view of the writer as an *engagé* or socially and politically committed individual. Yet ambiguities do creep into this self-perception. Fuentes has made a clear distinction, for instance, between his literary and political obligations. The writer, he remarks, "should be creative when he is a writer, when he is a novelist or poet, and should be political when he is a political writer. The point is not to mix the two things" (Baxandall 1962: 49). Yet it would be a mistake to accept this distinction and assume that the writer is somehow free to pursue aesthetic concerns within the novel independent of politics and thus only engages in politics outside literary experience. This ambiguity, or contradiction, has crucial ramifications for the assessment of Fuentes's social function as an intellectual in Mexico. My argument is that deploying further some of the key conceptual innovations on aesthetics and form, outlined earlier, can assist in highlighting such an ambiguity or contradiction. This focus on the political dimension of literature involves analyzing the social element present in a writer's work. It also involves analyzing what Gramsci recognized as the "organisational and connective" links of the intellectual (Gramsci 1971: 12, Q12§1). By tracing these issues in relation to Fuentes's social function as an intellectual in Mexico it becomes apparent that the contradictions within his role arise from tensions between national and cosmopolitan issues. All these features unfold within a context that involves the increasing retreat of the intellectual within forms of literary experience and, crucially, within the "shadow of the state."

Toward the end of the 1960s and through the 1970s, the novel in Mexico generally began to follow a more exclusivist route, becoming more recondite and removed from everyday lived experience, to delight only a select group of privileged readers (Brushwood 1992: 80–81). This was part of a wider transition across Latin America based on a shift from the consideration of broad socioeconomic issues of modernization to a search for Latin American identity (Miller 1999: 95, 128–29). Clearly, the role of the intellectual varies over time according to changing historical circumstances. What is perhaps startling, however, is the way that this role was fundamentally recast and altered. In recent times, for example, Fuentes has commented on the social function of the intellectual as a "storyteller" to declare that "the sheer weight of social problems and quickened change in Latin America have effected and will affect our writing, but will not absolve us from the demand of shaping, giving form, giving speech and imagination *to* our societies." Yet while this is consistent with the earlier view of the social and political responsibility of the intellectual, it is immediately followed by the comment, "but as writers, our contribution to society lies less in political action . . . than in the two social needs that a writer is best prepared to fulfill: language and imagination" (Fuentes 1998: x). More starkly, while the political effect of a novel is seen to seep through civil society quietly, over the long term, "the level at which the novel deals with imagination and language is the first obligation. The social consequences, if they come, will come later."[8] It is also surprising to find Fuentes announcing that he was *never* in favor of the view of a writer as an *engagé* because, rather than being engaged, the writer engages the world through language and imagination.[9] As Nicola Miller (1999: 207) writes, this focus on language "came to seem an acceptable substitute for more tangible forms of action in protest against the imperialist practices to which twentieth-century Spanish America was subject."

This retreat of the critical intellectual became increasingly apparent in Fuentes's literary production throughout the 1960s and 1970s during which a discernible change emerged in the representation of issues linked to the subject of identity (Helmuth 1997: 21). It found expression in the novella *Aura* (1962), *A Change of Skin* (*Cambio de piel*, 1967), and the monumental *Terra Nostra* (1975), which heralded an intention to embrace the trend toward more complex (sometimes weary) self-referential literature and a move away from the documentary to the more fantastic dimension of "magical realism"[10] (Kerr 1980: 91–102; Standish 1986: 19–20; Faris 1995). Such works reflect a retreat within literary experience that can be regarded as homages to intertextuality, becoming preoccupied with the metaphorical representation of the world. Any transformative or critical practice is thus limited to individual consciousness (Gonzalez 1974: 11–13). Similarly, *Christopher Unborn* (*Cristóbal Nonato*, 1987) has been described as a novel within which the rhetoric is more revolutionary than the referents (Faris 1988: 282). One is thus left uncertain about the desire for social and political change especially as a dystopian perspective lies at the core of the novel which fails to provide any strong vision of political hope (van Delden 1998: 34, 179).[11] Put differently, sociohistorical content has been smothered by the form of such novels and the retreat within literary experience that they represent. Indeed a sense of anguish and anxiety over the separation between political and literary experience, theory and practice, culminated in *Diana: The Goddess Who Hunts*

Alone (*Diana, o la cazadora solitaria*, 1994), which has been described as an "autobiographical sin."[12] This novel conveys Fuentes's feelings of alienation and complicity following the Tlatelolco massacre of peaceful demonstrators on 2 October 1968 in Mexico City. By not undertaking a more direct involvement in politics he confesses that, really, "the traitor was me" (Fuentes 1994/1995: 59).

Yet of utmost significance is Fuentes's admission that "my writing is not political in the sense that it's pamphletary writing. . . . It's not even popular writing. It's rather elite writing, it takes a lot to get into my works and to win readers for my books" (Weiss 1991: 117). This stress was echoed in a particular exchange with Herman Doezema that led Fuentes to specifically acknowledge that he works within the limits of a cultural elite. To that extent, besides the issue of illiteracy, he admitted that his novels might have a small readership and thus resemble, for example, Chinese to a Tarahumaran Indian. In retort Doezema pointed out that they would *equally* resemble Chinese to a factory-owning industrialist in Mexico City. Fuentes then responds by reaffirming the very strict bias toward elite culture within his work. "I would be a demagogue and an idiot if I thought I were writing for the people! It would be a complete misunderstanding of the culture I'm working within" (Doezema 1972–1973: 500–501). Sometime later he would similarly declare that "I'm not going to pretend to be someone I'm not. Should I wear a Charro hat or peasant's sandals? No! I'm from the Mexican bourgeoisie, the Mexican upper class, and that's where I'll stay" (as cited in Brewster 2005: 31). It is this bourgeois culture, then, that he admits to both belonging to as well as criticizing (Harss and Dohmann 1967: 306). This bias can be further highlighted within Carlos Fuentes's social function as an intellectual. Hence the importance of a focus on the social element present in Fuentes's novels, the tension between his national and cosmopolitan social function, and his "organisational and connective" links beyond the realm of literary experience. As the novelist has himself stated, "for intellectuals who choose to live in Mexico, some direct or indirect association with the government is virtually impossible to avoid, whether they are employed at the university, in a government-funded research centre, or carry out intellectual work within the government or the party itself" (Fuentes 1971: 166).

As already discussed, one of the key literary works that Gramsci directed criticism toward was *The Betrothed* by Alessandro Manzoni. It will be recalled that *The Betrothed* tended to concentrate on the interior life of the nobility and their "complex" psychology, feelings, and ambitions while the lower social classes were represented as "the humble," as humiliated and insulted popular caricatures. By thus investigating Fuentes's representations, present in a variety of works, it might be possible to trace similar issues of ideological content. Indeed, Fuentes himself has commented that he tends to focus more on issues of personalization in order to write novels of inner life (Harss and Dohmann 1967: 308). A return to some of the novels discussed earlier might therefore reveal, in a dialectical manner, alternative themes related to the portrayal of such inner life.

Beginning with *Where the Air Is Clear* it is noteworthy that at the center of the novel are the wealthy characters while farther out on the periphery are portrayals of the "anonymous suffering masses" who tend to appear only once (Faris 1983: 19). The novel is a portrayal—as well as a critique—of the bourgeoisie and the *nuevos ricos* in Mexico. However, Brushwood points to a significant issue. "As pathetic as these revolting people are, they are hardly more so than the humble people who, on a different level, are equally lost in modern society" (Brushwood 1966: 38). In *Where the Air Is Clear* characters such as Galdys García, who spends her time as a prostitute "plodding the great street,"[13] or Juan Morales, a taxi driver who suffers an early death in a car crash, represent the lower social classes (Fuentes 1958/1971: 9, 50). Mexico City consists of futile lottery ticket vendors who are constantly returning unsold tickets; women who put "dabs of spit on their eyebrows and stockings"; and newspaper boys who share "a skimpy evening meal" before searching for a doorway bed (107). This attitude, on one hand, is refracted through the character Federico Robles, the revolutionary-cum-millionaire banker, who disdainfully surveys the wretched of the earth from his safely remote skyscraper environment (41). On the other hand, it is also reflected through the portrayal of lower-class characters like Beto, Tuno, and Gabriel. These figures are grouped in the novel under the heading "Maceualli," which is Nahuatl for "commoners" (146–75). These "commoners," or "the humble," of Mexico are presented as violent youths driven by alcohol and sex who tend to enjoy their typical Sunday afternoons by attending bullfights (306–8, 318–20). Overall, in relation to the marginalized characters in *Where the Air Is Clear*, "the reader never gains access to their thoughts, and perceives them only through the filter of the intellectual" that is Manuel Zamacona (Long 2008: 27).

Similarly, the collection *Burnt Water* contains numerous comparable representations of the humble of Mexico City. Federico Silva, in the story "The Mandarin," is ashamed that "a country of churches and pyramids built for eternity should end up contenting itself with a city of shanties, shoddiness and shit" (Fuentes 1980/1981: 155). It is at the hands of the "miserable beggars" and "filth," which he constantly ignores, that Silva finally meets his nemesis. In the same collection, "The Son of Andrés Aparicio" is the story of Bernabé, who used to live respectably until the rent was raised by Silva, to become "a shitty *lumpen*" (215). Bernabé cleans windshields with a rag at busy intersections during the hour of heaviest traffic and, with his uncles, frequents a "Sunday afternoon rodeo" of cheap sex with unknown women. Similarly, in *The Hydra Head*, the central character Felix Maldonado evokes thoughts about Mexico City as a place designed for gentlemen and slaves, but

> never for the indecisive muddle of people who'd recently abandoned the peasant's white shirt and pants and the worker's blue denim to dress so badly, imitating middle-class styles but, at best, only half successfully. The Indians, so handsome in the lands of their origins, so slim and spotless and secret, in the city became ugly, filthy, and bloated by carbonated drinks. (Fuentes 1978/1979: 7)

It is this image of resignation and anomie that fellow intellectual Carlos Monsiváis categorically rejects, arguing that the prophecies contained in such stories deprive Mexico City of the optimism and hope that is more characteristic, in practice, of everyday circumstances (Monsiváis 1997: 34–35).

Perhaps a more positive message can be found in the collection *The Crystal Frontier: A Novel in Nine Stories* (*La frontera de cristal: Una novela de nueve cuentos*, 1995). Yet there are further clear representations of the humble in Mexico whose lives are connected by Don Leonardo Barroso, a powerful industrialist and beneficiary of the North American Free Trade Agreement (NAFTA). Characters such as Marina Alva Martínez, a worker in the *maquiladoras* of Ciudad Juárez, is described as "the new arrival, the simplest, the humblest"; Lisandro Chávez, a dejected contract worker, might once have distinguished "the humble as inferiors," but he is resigned to accepting that now the majority of Mexicans are equally downtrodden; and Leandro Reyes, onetime tourist driver, accepts that it might be possible to chauffeur the wealthy "with dignity, with pleasure, without humbling himself," although he is robbed of any such chance following a tragic and fatal car crash (Fuentes 1995/1998: 132, 177, 203).

This attitude toward the lower social classes, or the humble, in Mexico has mixed importance. It could clearly be an attempt to convey the innumerable cultural meanings attached to the verb *chingar* in Mexico, as famously relayed by Octavio Paz in *The Labyrinth of Solitude* (*El laberinto de la soledad*, 1950/1990: 73–88). Yet while transmitting this culture through his novels, Fuentes more often appears to eschew any attempt to break such repetitive cycles of oppression. While occasional movement between social classes may be represented, or an abrupt end to the life of upper-class characters might occur, this often unfolds at the expense of others and there more often remains an inexorable distance between upper and lower social groups.

To illustrate, by returning to his bourgeois roots in *The Good Conscience*, Jaime Ceballos literally decides to live with his "good conscience," which belongs "to the just, to the wealthy, to those of fine reputation." By contrast it is "the poor and humble, the sinners, the abandoned and miserable, the rebels, everyone who was beyond the pale of gentility" that are left to Satan (Fuentes 1959/1968: 148). Significantly, "Most writers in Latin America," admits Fuentes, "that come from this [bourgeois] milieu have faced the options that Jaime faces in *The Good Conscience*" (Cooper-Clark 1986: 27). Hence, across a variety of novels, it is possible to find emasculating social messages alongside a persistent depiction of the lower social classes in Mexico as the humble, the humiliated and insulted. It is not difficult to therefore argue that Fuentes, like Manzoni, tends to side with the upper classes of society in his works. Moreover, because of the haughty attitude toward the humble, combined with the often complex nature of many of his novels, it is possible to see that Fuentes's appeal is more limited to the literati or, at the very least, he fails to establish truly national-popular appeal. A convoluted and wordy style, a reliance on caricatures of the lower social classes as "the humble," and an increasing disavowal of direct social and political criticism have all therefore conspired to dilute the critical social function of Carlos Fuentes. Hence, Claudio Lomnitz's (1992: 260) conclusion that "the characterisations of 'Mexican national culture' which the *pensadores* have developed are connected only very loosely (or vaguely) to the social groups that occupy the national space." "We do not believe the artist," states Néstor García Canclini (1995: 244), "who wants to build with illustrious grammar and is prepared to legislate the new syntax." Furthermore, in terms of his "organisational and connective" links, it becomes increasingly clear that Fuentes performs a function more organic to the ruling classes in Mexico that limits any fundamentally progressive potential. These links, which are considered next, raise further contradictions within his social function.

As a result of a sense of anguish following the Tlatelolco massacre in 1968, it is worth noting that, in the 1970s, Fuentes directly entered politics in Mexico by displaying support for the administration of Luis Echeverría (1970–1976). The rationale behind this was based on the belief that support for Echeverría would avert the takeover of the state by more right-wing elements. "Our choice," declared Fuentes, "is not between Echeverría and socialism, but between Echeverría and fascism" (as cited in van Delden 1998: 125). It was Díaz Ordaz that "brought force, repression, and fascism" to Mexico, according to Fuentes, both as presidential figure and earlier as minister of internal affairs under President López Mateos during the violent suppression of the railway workers (1958–1959), teachers and oil workers (1960), and telephone operators (1962), and it was Echeverría that lifted this veil of fear (Fuentes 1971: 162, 166). Besides political commentaries, arguing for a strong state and decrying utopian leftist visions of radical social and political transformation, Fuentes also accepted an appointment as Mexico's ambassador to France in 1975 (Janes 1979: 87–95). Yet, despite the putative *apertura* (opening) in the Mexican political system at this time, it is clear that Echeverría, as interior minister during the administration of Gustavo Díaz Ordaz (1964–1970), must have played a role in the 1968 massacre and subsequent crackdowns. However, Fuentes still decided to work within the constraints of the established Mexican political system (see Brewster 2005: 71–75). This period of direct involvement ceased when Díaz Ordaz was appointed ambassador to Spain at the beginning of the administration of José Lopez Portillo (1976–1982). In 1977 Fuentes therefore symbolically resigned from his diplomatic post although it is worth noting that during his diplomatic career he also found it impossible to write (MacAdam and Ruas 1981: 143–44). Earlier admissions by Fuentes that he works within the culture of the (upper) middle classes in Mexico while also trying to condemn this culture become increasingly important. Significantly, commenting on his socialization within the midcentury generation of Mexican diplomats, Fuentes proclaims, "I understand and want it to be understood that a man always belongs to the men and women with whom he was formed and with whom he acted together in life" (Fuentes 1994/1997: 178–79). It seems that, for Fuentes, serving this culture of elites and cosmopolitanism has become, over the years, increasingly more important.[14]

This is the conclusion reached by a particularly vehement analysis of Fuentes's social function by Enrique Krauze. According to Krauze, his novels have become increasingly verbalizing entities reduced to a literary exploration of language. Moreover, they contain parodies or caricatures of everyday lived experience which the writer is increasingly removed from. Hence a painfully rigid portrayal of the inner lives of themes and characters, which clearly strikes a chord with the way I have drawn attention to representations of "the humble." Overall, Fuentes is accused of "intellectual mimesis" by projecting antibourgeois ideological criticisms within the novel while simultaneously living a bourgeois lifestyle (Krauze 1988: 28–38). To be sure, this polemical assault has to be set within its own historical and political context.[15] Yet, discounting the tone of Krauze's commentary, it is still possible to discern a kernel of accuracy in his criticisms. Despite the verities of Fuentes's ongoing critique of the Mexican Revolution, for example, any break from the established political system in Mexico has been anathema to him. By the 1990s, for instance, statements were made by Fuentes celebrating the amorphous role of civil society as the central protagonist of history in Latin America (Fuentes 1992b: 355). Yet, crucially, when one of these protagonists, the Ejército Zapatista de Liberación Nacional (EZLN), embarked on concrete forms of resistance in Mexico, Fuentes rescinded an invitation to support the movement.[16] Instead he asserted the need to pursue dialogue through legal channels and was more concerned with neutralizing their arguments (Fuentes 1994/1997: 114–20, 130–31), thus reaffirming the view that there was a failure on his behalf to transfer initial sympathy for the EZLN into practical and substantive support (Brewster 2005: 180–92). In a rather beguiling fashion, Fuentes has responded to such criticisms by commenting, "I have intervened in Mexican politics as much as I can as a writer and as a commentator which is all I can do. If somebody wants me to take up a rifle and go into the hills I am not going to do that."[17] This sits rather comfortably with his confession that many members of the PRI have been "personal friends" and that Carlos Salinas, a figure reviled in Mexico toward the end of the 1990s, is "a very brilliant man, a very intelligent man who seized opportunities for Mexican development and Mexican business."[18] It is also consistent with his view that the benefits of NAFTA and neoliberalism can be harnessed as long as a "social chapter" can be added to avoid the worst excesses of "savage capitalism."[19]

Overall, then, it can clearly be asserted that Fuentes performs a social function that is organic to capitalism in Mexico as he has been fully assimilated into the capitalist project, which made anachronous any role he performed as a critical intellectual. He displays an "organic quality" closer to the ruling classes in Mexico in exercising social hegemony—as a member of the "caviar left" (Apuleyo Mendoza et al., 1996/2000: 169–70)—rather than constituting a direct expression of popular interests (Gramsci 1971: 12, Q12§1; 330, Q11§12).[20] As Richard Gott surveys the situation, there has been a shift in Fuentes from pillar of progressive writing in Latin America, early supporter of the Cuban Revolution, to propagator of jaundiced views on Latin America's revolutionary traditions, and supporter of figures such as the Venezuelan magnate Gustavo Cisnero, rather than Hugo Chávez (Gott 2006). The result is a projection of cosmopolitan interests that, albeit not without merit (Wilson 1989: 181–82), have reinforced his "transnational" authorial location and further undermined any likely national-popular social function (Romano 1989: 167–98). As Roger Bartra (1992: 167) puts it, "to make possible a national-popular sphere for literature and art, it is necessary that popular sentiments (or sentiments attributed to the people) be revived and appropriated by the intellectual class, as Gramsci noted." Hence the importance of remaining wary of the social utopia by which intellectuals think they can survey history without becoming enmeshed in it.[21] By demystifying Fuentes's social function it is possible to describe him as an organic intellectual who has provided a sense of homogeneity and awareness to the PRI and the state-party in Mexico across the social, political, and economic fields. While not a party cadre, he has nevertheless acted as a member of a cadre class that has maintained social cohesion and shaped new patterns of class relations by providing a degree of moral and intellectual social criticism while ensuring more favorable conditions of existence for the ruling classes. His essential activity has been to generate the literary "gastric juices" to assist the process of digesting or absorbing potentially disruptive elements (Gramsci 1994b: 182). Hence, his social function stands as a worthy comparison to that type of intellectual Gramsci described as "a kind of lay pope and an extremely efficient instrument of hegemony—even if at times he may find himself in disagreement with one government or another" (Gramsci 1994b: 67).[22] As Fuentes himself stated in the wake of the student movement of 1968, "I want to make it clear . . . that criticising Caesar is not criticising Rome. . . . The Mexican government is not the personification of the country, but its temporary representative" (as cited in Brewster 2005: 63). Rather than maintaining contact with everyday concerns, Fuentes's writings have become "devoted to creating a specialised culture among restricted intellectual groups" (Gramsci 1971: 330, Q11§12). A form of intellectual caste or priesthood has unfolded that is more cosmopolitan than national-popular and less rooted in the organic expression of everyday lived experience in Mexico. If Fuentes's social function is analyzed in this way it is no wonder that he has admitted to disliking the idea of an "organic intellectual" to confess that the very two words "terrify him."[23] As Gramsci summarizes, the social function—or "mode of being"—of the intellectual cannot just comprise eloquence but also "active participation in practical life, as constructor, organiser, 'permanent persuader' and not just [as] a simple orator" (Gramsci 1971: 10, Q12§3). Hence Fuentes is best described as an intellectual critic of power but one "albeit adapted to suit government interests" (Brewster 2005: 67, 201). As relayed by one character, Xavier "Seneca" Zaragoza, in one of Fuentes's recent novels, *The Eagle's Throne* (*La Silla del Águila*, 2002), "the PRI's soft dictatorship was mollified by a certain degree of tolerance for the Mexican elite. . . . Poets, novelists, the occasional journalist . . . our ineffable muralists, were allowed to say, write and draw more or less what they wanted. It was a case of the intellectual elite criticising the governmental elite, a very necessary escape valve" (Fuentes 2002/2006: 33). It remains to be seen whether Fuentes's social function will again vary and change over time, in light of different national circumstances in Mexico and new literary output, but a preoccupation with imagination and memory seems to presently far outweigh more overtly political concerns (see Fuentes 2000; Fuentes 2008; Fuentes 2009).

CONCLUSION: AN INTELLECTUAL HYDRA WITH INNUMERABLE HEADS

Gramsci once commented on the cosmopolitan character of Italian intellectuals, predominantly divorced from lay culture, to declare that they had "a deep *distrust* of the people, feeling them to be foreign, fearing them, because, in reality, the people were something unknown, a mysterious hydra with innumerable heads" (Gramsci 1985: 257, Q3§82, original emphasis). With an uncanny echo, this comment could, perhaps, be extended—with due regard to changing historical and cultural circumstances—to the social function projected by Carlos Fuentes in Mexico. Yet it would be too simple to dismiss or criticize this social function by reducing it to one single dimension. Again evoking the title of one of his own novels—*The Hydra Head*—the above argument has demonstrated more than anything else that Carlos Fuentes himself is an intellectual hydra with innumerable heads. He has performed a shifting social function that has varied over time in both constructing and contesting revolution and state in modern Mexico.

   The chapter has analyzed this social function by focusing on a combination of factors linked to both aesthetic form as well as sociohistorical content. Hence two crucial moments were highlighted in the social function of Carlos Fuentes as an intellectual within state–civil society relations in Mexico. First, throughout a series of early novels, alongside the prevalence of similar themes in later works, it was demonstrated how Fuentes's social function can be understood within the mold of a *critical* intellectual challenging the blandishments of the ruling PRI and the iniquities of the Mexican political system. A critical sense was thus projected against institutions of power and authority within Mexican society in a style of opposition rather than accommodation. The most outstanding feature of this critical social function was a fictionalization of the conditions of passive revolution in Mexico. By attempting to remain socially and politically engaged, efforts have been made by Fuentes to engender a critical consciousness within the reader to thereby question prevailing socioeconomic conditions, especially those that arose after the PRI had constructed a minimal form of hegemony in the 1940s, as detailed in chapter 3. Most concretely, Fuentes has understood socioeconomic change in Mexico as a combination of popular demands alongside the consolidation of the class strategy of the bourgeoisie who gave a decidedly capitalist imprint to social relations in Mexico and ensured the creation of an institutional framework consonant with the interests of capital. As a result, Carlos Fuentes was cast in this chapter as *the* novelist of passive revolution, combining elements of the blocked dialectic of revolution-restoration.

   Second, it was noted how contradictions and ambiguities have arisen during the pursuit of this varied social function. Stemming from a context in the late 1960s and increasingly from the 1970s onward it was argued that a shift became apparent. This involved a frequent appeal by Fuentes to distinguish between his literary and political obligations leaving him somehow free to pursue aesthetic innovations within the novel independent of politics. The prospect of making such a move was rejected. Instead, the autonomy of the intellectual was discarded by, once again, highlighting the social function of the intellectual in the construction and contestation of revolution and state in modern Mexico. This involved deploying key criteria drawn from Marxist aesthetics based on analyzing the social element present in Fuentes's work and, also, highlighting his "organisational and connective" links. By proceeding along these avenues attention was drawn to the way Fuentes came to promote principles of accommodation much more frequently than a critical sense of opposition. As Marx might have put it, within the "grand performances of state," ideologists involved in securing a social basis of support increasingly come to include such "philosophers of fusion" (Marx 1852/1979: 166). This is the absorptive logic of passive revolution in which intellectuals themselves become the mediating scribes of the bourgeoisie; a logic in which Carlos Fuentes himself becomes a *passive revolutionary*. Hence Fuentes increasingly began to perform a function organic both to capitalism and the maintenance of the PRI's minimal hegemony in Mexico, whether in the contexts of ISI or neoliberal capitalist accumulation assessed earlier in chapters 3 and 4. Besides highlighting his "organisational and connective links," this role was also emphasized by indicating the paternalistic attitude toward "the humble" in Mexico that he has conveyed throughout many novels. Such an attitude reflects the interests of an intellectual who is more concerned with cosmopolitan rather than national-popular issues. Any "organic quality" is restricted to an elite culture, or a social and intellectual caste, rather than reflecting an expression of wider social interests.

The overall conclusion to be drawn from this argument is that, through a focus on the social function of Carlos Fuentes, it becomes possible to distinguish the role intellectual activity can play in the construction and contestation of revolution and state in modern Mexico. Most crucially, the argument prompts a consideration of the social sources of ideology and the agency of intellectuals organically tied to particular class forces functioning throughout state–civil society relations. Put differently, through a detailed analysis of the social function of Carlos Fuentes, the argument confirms the view that the specific spaces for intellectual production characteristic of modernity in Mexico and Latin America have been shaped by the state's capacity to absorb intellectual agents (see García Canclini 1995: 47; Lomnitz 2001: 208–11). In other words, intellectuals have been "collective accessories rather than advisers to the Prince" to the extent that "it was the blueprints of the politicians, not the visions of the intellectuals, that prevailed" in Latin America (Miller 1999: 245, 246). While the social function of Carlos Fuentes has been ambivalent, consisting of a mixture of critical opposition and accommodation, the overriding interpretation is that such intellectual agency has predominantly performed a function organic to dominant class forces within the state. The social function of the intellectual in this case is therefore certainly cast within the "shadow of the state." The discussion that follows in the next chapter will deliberate whether the emergence of wider contestatory forces and struggles over democratization in Mexico—beyond the role of specific intellectuals— has broken the blocked dialectic of revolution-restoration characteristic of passive revolution.

NOTES

1. Note on translations: Following the convention outlined by Martin (1989), I provide the title of works in English, followed by the original Spanish title and date of original publication in parentheses. Information given on translations then cites up-to-date versions.

2. On Gramsci, see Boelhower (1981); Buttigieg (1982–1983); Davidson (1977); Dombroski (1982–1983); on Trotsky see Knei-Paz (1978); Geras (1986); Slaughter (1980); Wald (1995).

3. Keith Botsford, "My Friend Fuentes," *Commentary* (February 1965): 64–67, located in the University of California Riverside, Chilcote Archive, Intervention Box #30, "Mexico: Left and Chiapas"; accessed 15 January 2008.

4. Unless otherwise indicated, page references in the text will always refer to the book under principal discussion.

5. For commentary on the importance of Ixca Cienfuegos, within a wider analysis of Fuentes's prose, see Paz (1967/1983: 40–45).

6. Carlos Fuentes, "In Praise of the Novel," inaugural speech at the International Literature Festival, Berlin (6 September 2005), available at www.opendemocracy.net; accessed 16 January 2006.

7. In describing the European phenomenon of futurism, Trotsky—if a little more crudely—presents the traits of uneven development and ideological hegemony thus: "A phenomenon was observed that has been repeated in history more than once, namely, that the backward countries that were without any special degree of spiritual culture, reflected in their ideology the achievements of the advanced countries more brilliantly and strongly" (Trotsky 1922–1923/2005: 112).

8. Carlos Fuentes, "Imagining Power," interview by Isabel Hilton (10 February 2006), available at www.opendemocracy.net; accessed 12 January 2010.

9. Author's interview with Carlos Fuentes; Mexico City (12 March 1999). Also see the Isabel Hilton interview with Carlos Fuentes, BBC Radio 3's *Night Waves* (2 May 2001), when he again affirms that "every writer has a social function . . . and that function consists in maintaining [*sic*] language and imagination alive."

10. See Henri Lefebvre's caustic reception of "magic realism" as a form of art, believing that the real world is transposed, rather than transformed, by it (Lefebvre 2008 vol. 1: 110–23).

11. For an alternative view see Ortega (1988: 285–91).

12. Author's interview with Carlos Fuentes, London (28 August 1998).

13. According to Ryan Long, a rereading of Gladys García reveals her importance in standing for the need to recognize injustice and to incorporate Mexico's marginalized into the national imaginary but yet she remains beyond representation, is never reconciled within the totalization narrative of the novel, and is always outside incorporation. Thus, while the novel's reading of the Mexican Revolution is a complex narrative of redemption, in the form of Gladys García, "the novel's ground for the inclusionary promise of national fulfillment is exclusion" as this character always remains outside the representative identities deemed constitutive of the nation. "Gladys García emerges as the constitutive outside of the novel's appropriate foundation . . . the ever-excluded marginal figure, and thus the ever-constructed subaltern." This character is thus a representational microcosm of Fuentes's much broader denigrating portrayal of Mexico's popular classes (see Long 2008: 43, 46–47).

14. Roger Bartra also raises the pertinent question as to whether, following Gramsci, a national-popular literature actually exists in Mexico. His discussion of *apretados*, members of the bourgeoisie with patronizing traits of snootiness who hold power and prestige as the dominant class and thus dignity, refinement, and courtesy in contrast to *relajientos*, those lower-class members marked by a spirit of dissipation, laxity, disorder, or mess, may also bear relevance here (see Bartra 1992: 141–42).

15. Significantly, Krauze was a close collaborator with Octavio Paz in the publication of the magazine *Vuelta*. By the 1990s a conflict between Fuentes and Paz emerged publicly in Mexico and Krauze's image of Fuentes can be seen as a precursor of this tussle. For an outline of the disagreement see Williams (1996: 42–43), for a rebuttal of Krauze's arguments see González (1989: 98–102), and for a polemical intellectual genealogy of Krauze see Lomnitz (2001: 212–27).

16. This stance tends to contradict his own earlier assertions that indigenous demands and impulses for local democracy, embodied by Zapata, might play a redemptive role in Mexican politics (see Fuentes 1969c; 1973; 1988).

17. Author's interview with Carlos Fuentes, London (28 August 1998).

18. Author's interview with Carlos Fuentes, London (28 August 1998).

19. Carlos Fuentes, "Mexico's Democratic Transition," BBC World Lecture, The Royal Society for the encouragement of Arts, Manufactures & Commerce (16 June 1998, London). I would like to thank Zina Rohan for a recording of this lecture.

20. Critical geopolitical denunciations of U.S. foreign policy have long since disappeared, such as Carlos Fuentes, "For Too Long, America Has Cast a Blind Eye on Its Southern Neighbor," *Los Angeles Times*, part IV (4 January 1981), located in the University of California Riverside, Chilcote Archive, Intervention Box #29.2, "Mexico General"; accessed 14 January 2008.

21. One interesting historical incident involves the effort the CIA made to turn PEN, the World Association of Writers, into a designated tool through the Congress for Cultural Freedom. Linked to this aim was the organizing of a large PEN Congress that took place in Bled, Yugoslavia (July 1965), at which Carlos Fuentes and additional key intellectuals, such as Wole Soyinka, attended on the basis of receiving expenses from the Farfield Foundation, a now defunct CIA front organization. These participants, together with other delegates, elected Arthur Miller as PEN's new

president, under whose tutelage the view of the intellectual as an "independent spirit" became widespread (see Saunders 1999: 365–66).

22. An indicative spat with government was colorfully illustrated by the onetime labor minister, Carlos Abascal, claiming that Fuentes's writing was corrupting to women, see *Mexico & NAFTA Report*, "The Abascal Row: Censorship?" (RM-01–05, 1 May 2001): 5.

23. Author's interview with Carlos Fuentes, London (28 August 1998).

Chapter Six

The Political Economy of Democratization and Democratic Transition

On 5 September 2001, President Vicente Fox Quesada received the Annual Democracy Award from the National Endowment for Democracy (NED) at a Capitol Hill ceremony in Washington D.C. The award was heralded as marking the end of an era in Mexican politics due to the successful "transition" to democracy following the elections on 2 July 2000. As Fox himself remarked at the ceremony, "It is now required that we not only deepen the values that are part and parcel of democracy, but also promote a form of economic development that serves all and benefits all . . . within the framework of responsible economic management."[1]

It would be churlish to deny the impact and significance of the end of one-party dominance by the Partido Revolucionario Institucional (PRI) on the landscape of politics in Mexico, given that the ruling party was in continual power in one form or another for over seventy years. Certainly, the victory by Vicente Fox, backed by the Partido Acción Nacional (PAN), can be seen as both dramatic and historic, winning as the candidate for the Alianza por el Cambio 42.5 percent of the votes cast compared to Francisco Labastida, receiving 36 percent (representing the PRI), and Cuauhtémoc Cárdenas receiving 16.6 percent (representing the Alianza por México consisting of the Partido de la Revolución Democrática (PRD) and smaller parties such as Convergencia Democrática, Partido del Trabajo, Alianza Social, and Sociedad Nacionalista). At the time, the PRI also lost its position as the biggest party in the lower house of congress, with 211 seats compared to the 223 seats held by Alianza por el Cambio and the 66 seats held by the PRD and its allies.[2] However, it would also be precocious to assume that the passage of procedural elections in 2000 had ensured either democratic "transition" and/or "consolidation" in Mexico (as argued by Schedler 2005). Not the least significant here is what David Slater (2004: 110–12) has recognized as the process of geopolitical intervention embodied by market-based democracy and how this came about in Mexico given the interest of the NED and additional United States' foreign policy agencies in supporting the proliferation of human rights and democracy networks in the country. Perhaps the vocal action of the NED reflects and continues the earlier hubris of studies on democratization after the heady theories on "transitions" to democracy in the 1980s and democratic "consolidation" in the 1990s. Yet, on the other hand, it has been acknowledged that administrations across this period, most significantly starting with Ronald Reagan, did not initially extend their democracy promotion efforts to U.S.-Mexican relations (Carothers 1991: 10). Indeed, it is significant that the United States did not directly aid opposition parties in Mexico during the reign of the PRI leading to the claim that "it appears the United States goes after unlevel playing fields [only] when the ruling party is one the United States . . . does not like" (Carothers 1999: 147). The purpose of this chapter is to therefore further explore this mix of factors and provide a detailed analysis of the somewhat specific process of democratic transition in Mexico that, it is argued, is understood best as a quintessential feature of passive revolution shaping the construction and contestation of state and class power. The passive revolution of democratization refers here to the attempt to fully establish bourgeois democracy as the corresponding political form of capitalist social relations (see González Casanova 1970: 160). The passive revolution of democratization can be thus situated within a crucial distinction introduced earlier in this book. Following the lead in chapter 3, this was the contrast established between a *state in capitalist society*, referring to the historical constitution of the state as an emerging capitalist social formation, and a *capitalist type of state*, relating to the prevalent and dominant logic of capitalist accumulation so that the form of the modern state is posed around the formal institutional separation of the "economic" and the "political" thereby obscuring the relations of class power (see Jessop 2008). It will be argued that democratic transition in Mexico is embedded in this struggle to become a capitalist type of state, meaning the increasing domination of the logic of accumulation so that the appearance of the institutional separation of the economy within capitalism becomes both consolidated but also increasingly contested. In this way, democratization becomes a further feature of the passive revolution of capital, which was also a key theme addressed in chapter 4. Three main sections bring the argument into focus.

The first section situates democratization studies within more general theories of social and political change by developing a critique of such literature revolving around issues of democratic transition and consolidation. Vital attention is cast toward the supposed process of transition from instances of *dictablandas* (limited openings of liberalization without altering structures of authority under the tutelage of authoritarian rulers) to cases of *democraduras* (democratization without excessive expansion of freedoms so that restrictions remain) (O'Donnell and Schmitter 1986, vol. 4: 9). Second, the chapter turns to consider a more critical alternative to understanding the political economy of democracy that views democratization as a wider process implicated in *both* Cold War geopolitical structures of power *and* contemporary conditions of neoliberal restructuring. This alternative approach is more cognizant of the normative social content of democracy promotion, focusing on the underlying class interests at stake in the constitution of liberal democracies, while going beyond the elite-driven view that democracy is something practiced within the internal remit of sovereign states. As Gramsci reminds us, "it is strange," he says on the parliamentary system of government, "that it should not be criticised because the historical rationality of numerical consensus is systematically falsified by the influence of wealth" (Gramsci 1971: 193, Q13§30). The third section then relates this more critical understanding of democracy promotion to the case of Mexico. The analysis includes a broader set of issues and actors involved in the process of democratization by situating the role of geopolitical institutions alongside more local counterparts involved in democracy promotion in Mexico. This section draws on semistructured interviews conducted at such institutions, including the U.S. Agency for International Development (USAID), the National Endowment for Democracy (NED), the International Monetary Fund (IMF) and World Bank, the United Nations Development Program (UNDP), the Comisión Económica para América Latina y el Caribe (CEPAL), as well as key protagonists—such as the Instituto Federal Electoral (IFE), nongovernmental organizations (NGOs) such as Alianza Cívica, labor groups, and trade unions—all involved in the struggle for democracy in Mexico.

Several contributions are made toward understanding the advance and current progress of democratization as endemic to the condition of passive revolution in Mexico. Principally, democratic "transition" has ensured the institution of political forms intrinsic to the furtherance and expansion of capitalism. Democratization in Mexico is therefore an archetypal aspect of passive revolution in which capitalism has been reorganized on a new institutional basis ensuring the survival of class power. As such, the passive revolution of democratic transition is presented as less the product of direct intervention by the United States and more as a consequence of the internalization of the interests of capital that became integrated and contested across a scalar matrix combining local, state, and geopolitical levels. This means that the passive revolution of democratization has to be situated within the internalization of specific moral and cultural values, codes of conduct, and ideological transformations in Mexico linked to the coexistent shift toward neoliberalism (see also chapter 4). Perhaps one of the most significant issues worth questioning is this very process of internalization that has changed the connotation of the political economy of Mexico. In this sense, democratization can be seen as part of a wider geopolitical process linked to the absorptive logic of passive revolution and hegemonic control (Grugel 2002: 118). The internalization of specific interests in Mexico, linked to both changes in the social relations of production and associated cultural and ideological forms of democratic practice embedded within the rise of neoliberalism, is presented as a potent expression of geopolitical power relations. By way of conclusion, conjecture is then raised about the challenges facing democracy in Mexico and the conditions of class struggle articulated against the renewal of capitalism.

DEMOCRATIZATION STUDIES: RENOVATING MODERNIZATION THEORY?

By the 1980s concerns about "democratization" began to replace those of "development" within the mainstream literatures of political science as well as in the fashioning of United States' political development assistance. In practice the Reagan administration launched Project Democracy in 1982 that grafted a democracy focus onto political development assistance programs. The project was initially based on a $65 million proposal to be managed through the State Department, USAID, and the American Federation of Labor-Congress of Industrial Organizations (AFL-CIO), although it floundered due to a lack of congressional support. More modestly, perhaps, USAID subsequently obligated approximately $20 million per year for human rights and democracy promotion activities by the late 1980s, to total approximately $100 million during the years of the Reagan administration, with the funds almost exclusively granted to recipients within Central America (Carothers 2001: 126). In 1983 the NED was also created, an ostensibly private nonprofit organization with an independent board of directors, management, and staff based on a bipartisan structure. The latter consists of four separate organizations that claim policy autonomy: the Center for International Private Enterprise (CIPE), the Free Trade Union Institute (FTUI), the National Democratic Institute for International Affairs (NDI), and the National Republican Institute for International Affairs (NRI). The initial grant was $18 million with the annual budget ranging between $15 and $21 million across 1984–1988 and funds to Latin America amounting to approximately $25 million over these years, or about one-quarter the size of the United States' democracy assistance programs in Latin America as a whole (Carothers 1991: 226–27). The annual budget of the NED is something in excess of $30 million (Carothers 1999: 30). While the 1980s was marked by direct U.S. interventions identified as "democracy by force" (Nicaragua, Grenada), the shift toward different instruments of political development assistance has been regarded as one of promoting "democracy by applause" (Carothers 1999: 7–8). What this means is that the political component gained ascendancy over the military component so that U.S. foreign policy in Latin America seemingly began to break with the anticommunism of the Cold War. According to Jean Grugel (2002: 125), "by the 1990s pro-democracy strategies were about creating hegemonic control in the developing and post-communist world through consensual agreement or co-optation with key domestic elites."

The architecture of modernization and development theory also underwent modifications and shifts of emphasis within the academy. Most prominently the transitions to democracy paradigm emerged by advocating the construction of vibrant civil societies as supposedly autonomous realms of individual freedom and association through which democratic politics could proceed. Key foundational texts in this literature would include the collections *Transitions from Authoritarian Rule: Prospects for Democracy* (1986) and *Democracy in Developing Countries* (1989) that have been linked to associations within the government-university nexus in the United States (see O'Donnell, Schmitter, and Whitehead 1986; Diamond, Linz, and Lipset 1989; and, on the statecraft link, Robinson 1996: 44–45, 392n49). Moreover, a series of continuities can be established between this literature and earlier political development theory.

A central continuity is the preoccupation with safeguarding elite power and maintaining relatively quiescent political subjects within stable states. This commonly manifests in a counterposing of "state" and "society" within conditions of political order (see Huntington 1968), which directly relates to the state corporatist literature critiqued in chapter 1. Emergent here, though, was a doctrine for political development that was "always policy oriented; . . . [that] always valued political stability more highly than democracy; and . . . always saw mass participation in . . . new states as a *problem*" (Cammack 1997: 37, original emphasis). Subsequently this focus on stability became a concern about ensuring and consolidating *formal* democracy—holding clean elections, introducing liberal individual rights, creating participatory citizenship—which was distinguished from *popular* democracy—based on the introduction and extension of socioeconomic rights. The overriding stress in democratization studies was thus one of constituting an empirical (putatively) nonnormative definition of democracy limited to the descriptive, institutional procedures of electoral rights and democratic government, understood in a limited sense of the processes of state machinery and party politics. Joseph

Schumpeter's (1942/1975: 269) legacy is pivotal here in stating that "the democratic method is that institutional arrangement for arriving at political decisions in which individuals acquire the power to decide by means of a competitive struggle for the people's vote." A similarly canonical set of designations can be found in the work of Robert Dahl who outlined "polyarchy" as an institutional arrangement for the resolution of conflicts among dominant groups so that democracy is, at best, seen in a truncated way facilitating the setting up of the rule of law and judicial reform to strengthen contract rights based on individual autonomy (see Dahl 1954: 63–89; Dahl 1971: 17–32). As Schumpeter (1942/1975: 284–85) adds, "democracy does not mean and cannot mean that people actually rule in any obvious sense of the terms 'people' and 'rule.' Democracy means only that the people have the opportunity of accepting or refusing the men [sic] who are to rule them." It is this minimalist standard of democracy that is then taken as the locus for constructing democratic governance in Latin America (see Shifter 2008).

In this definition, there is a sharp separation of politics from economics within the gradual extension of formal associational life through democratization measures under elite control, which can be critiqued on four counts. Given the similar set of contributors to both the literature on democratic transition and state corporatism, as detailed in chapter 1, it should not be surprising that these four lines of criticism expand that earlier analysis. The first significant problem of democratization studies is the very division itself between state (politics) and market (economics). Indicative here is Juan Linz and Alfred Stepan's separation of five main arenas in democratic transition and consolidation: civil society is seen as "free and lively"; political society is regarded as relatively autonomous; independence is granted to the rule of law; the impartiality of a bureaucratic state apparatus is assumed; and the protection of property rights is paramount within economic society (Linz and Stepan 1996: 7). Larry Diamond, Juan Linz, and Seymour Martin Lipset have also explicitly crafted this sentiment within the democratization studies literature.

> We use the term democracy . . . to signify a political system, separate and apart from the economic and social system. . . . Indeed, a distinctive aspect of our approach is to insist that issues of so-called economic and social democracy be separated from the question of governmental structure. (Diamond, Linz, Lipset 1989: xvi; see Robinson 1996: 54)

By accepting such clear divisions, the shortcoming is that state (politics) and market (economics) are taken as ahistoric starting points of analysis (also see chapter 3). The state is perceived to be in an exterior relationship with the market, controlling it separately from the outside. Yet the counterargument is that state and market only appear as separate entities due to the way production is organized around private property relations in capitalism. This implies that the extraction of surplus value is indirectly conducted through a contractual relation between those who maintain the power of appropriation over those who only have their labor to sell, as expropriated producers, rather than by direct political enforcement (Wood 1995: 29, 31–36). By neglecting the central importance of the social relations of production, democratization studies thus overlook the historical specificities of capitalism and the vital internal links between state and market, with the former securing private property within civil society to ensure the functioning of the latter. As Philip Oxhorn and Graciela Ducatenzeiler (1998: 8) clarify, "the historical coincidence between economic liberalism and political democracy has allowed for certain facile conclusions concerning the consequences that this type of economic model would have for the political systems found in Latin America." The risk, then, is that a historically specific understanding of liberal democracy is formalized and institutionalized in a universal manner, leading to depoliticization as the economic sphere is removed from political control. Hence a failure to question the class structuring of civil society and/or relate liberal democracy to the historically contingent conditions of capitalist development. By extension, there is an undertheorization of the state that discounts a more social conception, meaning a conception of the state as a material condensation of the social relations of production formed by historically derived class struggles (Smith 2000: 29).

Second, within the liberal idiom of democratization studies, analysis is commonly domestically bound thus failing to think outside the boundaries of the state. At best, there is a clear demarcation and separation of the "internal" (national) and "external" (international) levels of analysis. The archetypal example of this can be found in the transitions literature where it is clearly stated that "the reasons for launching a transition can be found predominantly in domestic, internal factors . . . [and] it seems to us fruitless to search for some international factor or context," which thus leads to a neglect of social power relations beyond territorial states (O'Donnell and Schmitter 1986, vol. 4: 18). Even in the consideration of the "international dimensions of democratisation" there is a clear division of levels of analysis leading to a reification of "external actors" that are regarded as distinct from the system of government within "a separate, domestically driven process" of established national boundaries held as determinative (Whitehead 2001: 8–9, 16–17; Middlebrook 2004b: 8–11, 21–22). The system of territorial states is therefore abstracted from the bounds of capitalism, which are global in scope. By ascribing separate logics to the state and the international sphere, the opportunity to understand how the state has been restructured and penetrated by conditions of uneven and combined capitalist development is foreclosed. Most recently, this would include how the system of territorial states is being modified by processes immanent to conditions of global restructuring as indicative of the current phase of capitalism, as observed in chapter 4. Much heralded transitions to democracy are a central element to the passive revolution of capital and the constant reorganization of state and class power that is entrained. Put another way, neoliberalism remains bound to the exploitation of spatial contradictions extant to both state territoriality and globalization. Democratic transition is, then, a specific state spatialization strategy linked to the organization and reproduction of abstract space by dominant class practices. A passive revolution of democratic transition is an additional feature in the ongoing reconfiguration of ruling class interests and the spatial form of the state and cannot be adequately grasped without regard for the uneven geographical development of capital. Therefore the spread of capitalism and liberal democracy are linked through the exploitation of unequal contexts inscribed in space (Görg and Hirsch 1998: 588). The point that democratization processes themselves need to be conceived as variegated practices embedded within the spatially uneven context of development in Latin America thus requires greater emphasis.

Third, there is a closed design that underpins the transitions under scrutiny within the democratization studies literature. Thus, "no small amount of democratic teleology is implicit in the transition paradigm, no matter how much its adherents denied it" (Carothers 2002: 7). This is conceived around a "democracy template" involving top-down change through elections and state institutions that are again separated from bottom-up change through the strengthening and diversification of an independent civil society, literally leading to assumptions about a transition from authoritarianism (*dictablanda*) to the consolidation of democracy (*democradura*). Therefore "democracy is consolidated when under given political and economic conditions a particular system of institutions becomes the only game in town" (Przeworski 1991: 26). As Ronaldo Munck (1993: 8) has put it, "history in these models takes second place to an intricate game played by disembodied actors."

All this leads, fourth, to the assessment that such institutional modeling is disconnected from social power relations in which institutions are rooted: the very structures of power, authority, interests, hierarchies, and loyalties that make up socioeconomic and political life. In this vein George Philip (2003: 197–98) indicates that the importance of the political transition to democracy in Mexico is in the fact that it did not unhinge the pattern of economic reform so that neoliberalism and the North American Free Trade Agreement (NAFTA) became "the only rules in town." Overall, it is as a result of the division of state (politics) from market (economics), the separation of national and international spheres of analysis, the teleology embedded within assumptions about democratic transition, and an aversion to revealing questions of social power and interests in the struggle over democracy that one can establish connections between democratization studies and earlier theories. As Arturo Escobar (1995: 42) has argued, "although the discourse has gone through a series of structural changes, the architecture of the discursive formation laid down in the period 1945–1955 has remained unchanged, allowing the discourse to adapt to new conditions." The historical role of political development theorists has thus been crucial in renovating similar assumptions in democratization studies. In accord with Irene Gendzier's (1998: 57–58) view:

> In spite of the end of the Cold War, the logic driving development policies in the 1990s remained the extension of corporate liberalism, while the arguments used to justify it . . . served much the same function of legitimation that they did in the 1960s.

Albeit with a significant shift of emphasis, then, from the state as the center of social control to the support for the construction of conformist civil societies as supposedly autonomous spaces of individual association, there are lasting legacies of political development theory.

It should thus be no surprise that commentators have noted that institutions such as the NED still have a Cold War outlook marking its direction and substance (Carothers 1994: 137). This is best exemplified by avatars of global capitalism, such as Larry Diamond (2002), extolling the need to win the "new Cold War on terrorism" through the extension of a global governance imperative linked to the promotion of liberal democracy. Hence the importance of focusing on underlying social power interests that are contested within and through democratization processes. The next section now turns to a more critical alternative in understanding the political economy of democracy. The approach here, following the discussion in chapter 3, focuses on the state as constituted by specific social relations of production and the convergence of particular class interests as intrinsic to the promotion of neoliberalism, which is the backdrop to the analysis of democratization processes in Mexico.

THE POLITICAL ECONOMY OF DEMOCRACY, GLOBALIZATION, AND POLYARCHY

The tenor of democratization studies has been depicted so far as one that has continued some of the assumptions of political development and modernization theory due to an overriding preoccupation with maintaining political order in stable states. Furthermore, it has been noted that the identification of capitalism and democracy within such work is held to be a matter of natural law, "rather than as a specific product of historical conditions, conflict over the pursuit of interests and class struggle" (Gills, Rocamora, and Wilson 1993: 5). Democratization can therefore be understood as the *promotion of polyarchy* (or low intensity democracy) in terms of the attempt to secure institutional arrangements for the resolution of conflicts between dominant groups. Accordingly, promoting polyarchy in William Robinson's appraisal refers to "a system in which a small group actually rules and mass participation in decision-making is consigned to leadership choice in elections carefully managed by competing elites" (Robinson 1996: 49). Polyarchy represents the institutional definition of democracy present within mainstream democratization studies as well as the practices of United States' political development assistance and foreign policy. From within this perspective, the spread of polyarchies is upheld as representative of "'really existing' democracies" that, although falling short of idealized conceptions of democratic theory, nevertheless "provides the baseline for the contemporary debates about democratisation" (Whitehead 2002: 26; see also Foweraker, Landman, and Harvey 2003: 35–37, 40). This is most starkly visible when commentators such as Laurence Whitehead bemoan the fact that abruptly extended political rights may feed "weeds and thorns" as well as "gardens and manicured lawns," referring in the former to the recent and outright repudiation of *democradura* principles in Latin America (Whitehead 2002: 89; Whitehead 2008: 31–32). This stance is best summed up by Huntington's warning to "never introduce democratisation measures in response to obvious pressure from more extreme radical opposition groups" (Huntington 1991–1992: 602).

What this view indicates is, first, a preference for polyarchy understood as political contestation among elite factions for procedurally free elections—an attenuated or hollow form of democracy—which displaces more emancipatory and popular demands. Second, once the move to separate the economic and political spheres has been made, there is a contradictory tendency to then reconnect them by claiming a natural affinity between democracy (free elections) and capitalism (free markets). In the testimony of the *Economist*, "There is now no alternative to the free market as the way to organise economic life. The spread of free-market economics should gradually lead to a spread of multi-party democracy, because people who have got free economic choice tend to insist on having free political choice too."[3] Therefore, "promoting polyarchy is a political counterpart to the project of promoting capitalist globalisation, and . . . 'democracy promotion' and the promotion of free markets through neoliberal restructuring has become a singular process in US foreign policy" (Robinson 2000: 313). Liberal democracy is thus seen as a vulgarization of representation and accountability through which authority actually constrains freedom while imposing obligations and sanctions on those involved. Hence, to cite Antonio Gramsci:

> Democracy, the attempt to moralise domestic and foreign political relations by making of each human individual a citizen responsible for social life, initiator and free agent of historical activity, is an ideology that cannot fully establish itself in capitalist society. The part of it that can be realised is liberalism, through which all men [*sic*] can become *authority* from time to time as minorities circulate. (Gramsci 1918/1975: 81–82, original emphasis)

What is emphasized here, then, is the organization of the division of state and civil society as well as domestic and foreign relations within capitalist society. The institutions of law and private property are precisely presuppositions of the state in civil society through which the principles of individualism can be constituted and consolidated. As Karl Marx outlined, "the separation of the political state from civil society appears as the separation of the deputies from their mandators. Society delegates only elements from itself to its political mode of being" (Marx 1843/1975: 123). Hence the "isolation effect" of state policies that facilitate the fragmentation and atomization of social agents through the capitalist labor process (Poulantzas 1973: 130–37).

It is not therefore surprising to witness that primary among some of the wider components deemed essential to the constitution of polyarchy and thus a full transition to a market economy is that of the rule of law and property rights. These factors have been "suddenly considered indispensable for democracy, economic success, and social stability" (Carothers 1999: 164). Hence the rule of law is upheld as a bulwark for the effective administration of justice and emboldened legislatures within larger processes of democratization (Unger 2002). The conventional wisdom is that while "aid officials assert that the rule of law is necessary for a full transition to a market economy—foreign investors must believe that they can get justice in courts, contracts must be taken seriously, property laws must be enforceable" (Carothers 1999: 164). Participation in liberal democracy, after all, is dependent on the ownership of property.

The challenge, however, is to situate this understanding of polyarchy within an account of the particular, and in some ways specific process, of democratic transition in Mexico. After all, democratization has unfolded in Mexico as an incremental process with a heavily organized political opposition for change across successive elections since as early as the 1970s. This history not only breaks the paradigm of democratic transition theory—based on sudden democratic breakthrough, national elections, new democratic institutions—but also questions arguments about the promotion of polyarchy. Generally, William Robinson's assertion that the goal of U.S. policy in any given case is "to organise an elite and to *impose* it on the intervened country through controlled electoral processes" requires critical reflection (Robinson 1996: 111, emphasis added). Specifically, Robinson's additional claims that Mexico demonstrates the pattern of transition to polyarchy and that "US strategy was therefore to provide strong and consistent support for an authoritarian state even while prodding it to complete a transition to fully functioning polyarchy" necessitate some unpacking (Robinson 2006b: 110–11). Such an engagement also adds several new dimensions to the criticisms at the center of discussion on global capitalism and the transnational state thesis in chapter 4.

At issue here is, first, the somewhat exceptional status of democratic transition in Mexico compared with processes of democratization in other Latin American states. As Judith Adler Hellman (1994: 125) has astutely recognized, "the attempt to shoehorn the Mexican case into models designed principally to explain the military domination or democratization of the Southern Cone and Brazil has frequently brought Mexicanists to grief." The Mexican case does not demonstrate a change from military authoritarianism to democratization evident in so-called third wave transitions in Argentina, Chile, Uruguay, or Brazil from the 1960s and 1970s onward (see Huntington 1991). Nor does it relate to the conditions in Central America of widespread civil war, dictatorship, or popular revolution respectively experienced in El Salvador, Guatemala, and Nicaragua, in the 1970s and 1980s. The Mexican experience of dominant and continuous single-party rule under the auspices of the PRI for over seventy years, while consistently contested by labor movements, popular student movements, and the initial social movement logic of the Frente Democrático Nacional (FDN) that fed the emergence of the PRD, also sets it apart from the rule of elite-pacted democracies in Colombia and Venezuela that unraveled in the 1970s and 1980s and Costa Rica that has sustained pluralist liberal democracy since the 1950s. It was pointed out above that there is a need to recognize how democracy promotion is itself inscribed within divergent spatial conditions across the globe. The uneven development of democracy promotion is therefore one of the basic principles of capitalist expansion (Munck 1989: 20). Failure to recognize divergent spatial and temporal patterns in the promotion of polyarchy can thus be seen as one additional consequence of transnational state theorizing, which was critically challenged in chapter 4 (see also Massey 2005).

Second, the promotion of polyarchy in some of these states has involved comparatively large doses of United States' political development assistance funds. For example, in Chile between 1984 and 1991 the United States allocated $6.2 million through the NED and a further $1.2 million through USAID for an array of programs in support of moderate political parties, labor unions, and women's, youth, business, academic, and civic groups. Regional Latin American programs also involved a further $5 million to such groups in Chile with Christian Democrat leaders placed at the head of every "civil society" organization and project organized by the NED (Robinson 1996: 175–80). In Nicaragua $9 million was approved by the U.S. Congress prior to the pivotal 1990 elections, with $5 million allocated to the Unión Nacional Opositora and other anti-Sandinista groups, $2.9 million for discretionary NED spending, and a further $1 million for observer groups. The United States publicly acknowledged spending $12.5 million on the elections themselves, through the NED, although when various amounts of "circuitous spending" are totaled, which passed through conduits, the figure nears $30 million. Following the elections, a two-year $540 million assistance package was approved by the United States consisting of at least $10 million in political development assistance channeled through USAID and $3 million in new NED funding (Robinson 1996: 223–36, 231–36). Naturally, all this is outside the consideration of anterior forms of United States' intervention involving covert operations of destabilization against the government of Salvador Allende in Chile or the logistical support of low-intensity warfare granted to the Contras against the Frente Sandinista de Liberación Nacional. As we shall see, the circumstances of such democratization assistance and the level of funding are both different and comparatively larger than in the case of Mexico. Hence the important task of questioning whether the claims about the promotion of polyarchy are perhaps "too broad-brush" (Grugel 2003: 266). This task is all the more important considering recent conjecture about inflating the presence of the United States' democracy promotion institutions within Latin America by ascribing too much importance to their role in epochal events. For some, "the NED is neither monster nor saviour but rather a modest-sized organisation making a modest but real contribution to democratic transitions" (Carothers 1994: 137). Others would, of course, demur not least in light of the NED's role in funding opposition movements in Venezuela, notably surrounding the April 2002 coup against Hugo Chávez (see Gollinger 2007).[4] For these reasons the chapter now considers issues linked to democratization processes, or the promotion of polyarchy, in Mexico. The aim here is to appreciate and recover a focus on the *internalization* of practices and social relations at the heart of the promotion of polyarchy, rather than the stress on the direct *imposition* of such electoral processes, that seem more relevant to the experience of democratization in Mexico. This involves highlighting three *challenges* to the promoting polyarchy argument springing forth from the Mexican case in question as well as three *contributions* made to the very same argument stemming from the analysis of geopolitical institutions and more local counterparts involved in the struggle over democracy.

THE CASE OF MEXICO: FROM THE "PHILANTHROPIC OGRE" TO "FECKLESS PLURALISM"?

There has been a long history of social struggle in Mexico in the name of democracy that can, at least, be dated back to the emergence of the modern state itself during and after the revolution of 1910–1920 as well as clearly including political caesuras such as organized labor struggles in the 1940s and 1950s; the student movement and Tlatelolco massacre in 1968, notably captured in Elena Poniatowska's classic *La noche de Tlatelolco* (see Poniatowska 1971/1975; also Monsiváis 1990); the renewed *insurgencia obrera* (labor insurgency) and disaffection among the middle classes with import substitution industrialization (ISI) in the 1970s; the emergence of new opposition movements following the Ley Federal de Organizaciones Políticas y Procesos Electorales (LFOPEE) in 1977; the additional prevalence of urban and rural guerrilla movements in the same decade; and the emergence of the leftist coalition of the FDN that led to the institutional opposition of the PRD formed by Cuauhtémoc Cárdenas in the 1980s (see Bruhn 1997). In 1988, the crisis of representation facing the PRI culminated in the fraudulent electoral majority Carlos Salinas de Gortari claimed as the presidential candidate with 50.7 percent of the vote, while granting 31 percent to Cárdenas. Since that time, there has also been a proliferation of civic associations, human rights, and democracy networks in Mexico aimed at harnessing popular movements for change. Finally, by the 1990s, there were indications of stronger political party competition in the midterm elections on 6 July 1997 when the PRI lost its majority in the federal Chamber of Deputies; when key governorships went to the center-right PAN (in the states of Nuevo León and Querétaro); when the first election for the head of the Federal District went to Cárdenas as the center-left PRD candidate; and when competitive party-systems continued to emerge at the subnational level through state or municipal elections and with opposition parties defeating the PRI in gubernatorial elections in seven states between 1994 and 2000 (Baja California, Baja California Sur, Guanajuato, Jalisco, Nuevo León, Querétaro, and Tlaxcala) (see Cornelius, Eisenstadt, and Hindley 1999). This all suggests that democratization in Mexico followed a path far more complex than many explanations might appreciate. Starting with this complexity, three specific challenges are thrown up by the procedure of democratization in Mexico for those arguments focusing on the promotion of polyarchy.

Challenging the Case for the Promotion of Polyarchy in Mexico

First, in more detail, it is clear that even under the period of the so-called philanthropic ogre—an era supposedly leading to the rise of state power as detailed in chapter 2—there has been a long legacy of democratic social struggle in Mexico (Paz 1979/1990: 377–98). It is therefore vital to not neglect this history of political struggle and the efforts and sacrifices that have been made in the struggle for democracy. To do so would commit the mistake of assuming that there was a straightforward transmission of imposed principles and practices in Mexico linked to wider policies of United States' political development assistance, thus dismissing the long duration of social struggle. These struggles were particularly manifest in the student movement of 1968 surrounding the *sexenio* of Gustavo Díaz Ordaz (1964–1970) as well as throughout the *sexenios* of Luis Echeverría (1970–1976) and López Portillo (1976–1982) when the state attempted to revive its minimal hegemony by responding, at least initially, with a neopopulist program of political and social reforms. Hence the attempt to embark, under Echeverría, on a macroeconomic strategy of "shared development" within a supposed *apertura democrática* (democratic opening) to forge a populist coalition between national industrialists, peasants, disillusioned labor sectors, students, and the wider middle classes. One response, as noted above, was the *insurgencia obrera* that was aimed at autonomizing unions based on the principles of *autogestión* (self-management) through direct democracy and *formación* entailing ongoing education, consciousness raising, and worker advice (see Hathaway 2000). At the same time, as observed in chapter 4, the LFOPEE came to stand as an attempt to manage political liberalization within the current of the "democratic opening" by enlarging the arena for party competition and integrating leftist political organizations while inducing them to renounce extralegal forms of action. It will be recalled from chapter 4, that such measures involved the Partido Comunista Mexicana (PCM) obtaining official registration as a political party and participation in elections in 1979. It subsequently merged with the Partido Socialista Unificado de México (PSUM), a move that effectively led to the dissolution of the PCM. Yet the reform was more than just a simple co-optation measure. Referring back to chapter 4, it can be described as the quintessence of passive revolution in terms of its design to frame and condition the institutional context of opposition movements. The historical context of social struggle for democracy in Mexico and the subsequent institutional ensnaring of this process is therefore not easily read off as an imposition of policy priorities deriving from the political development assistance initiatives led by the United States.

Second, the role of the NED in Mexico must be placed in context. To be sure, as Denise Dresser (1996b) has noted, the NED has played a role in supporting various NGOs in Mexico, from the Comisión Mexicana de Defensa y Promoción de los Derechos Humanos, to the Movimiento Ciudadano por la Democracía, the Academia Mexicana de Derechos Humanos, and Alianza Cívica, the latter coming to act as a national coordinator for the other organizations. Yet, direct funds from the NED and USAID to organizations such as Alianza Cívica have been comparatively low when compared to the Chilean and Nicaraguan cases, discussed earlier. This is the case in spite of the difficulty of tracing additional "pass-throughs" for final recipients and acknowledging the point that publicly released budgets may be deceptive. In broad outline, from 1962 to 1971 loans and grants from USAID to Mexico as a whole totaled approximately $70 million, which was the lowest on a per capita basis for any state in Latin America. From the start of the 1970s, USAID missions were closed, to then reopen with a focus on population programs in 1977, but they were run through a minimally staffed and low-profile office out of the U.S. embassy. Between 1985 and 1991, nearly half of the NED's total grants to Mexico went to private sector business organizations, adding to the dominant rise of specific fractions of capital, as observed in chapter 4, linked to the Confederación Patronal de la República Mexicana (COPARMEX), the Confederación de Cámaras Nacionales de Comercio (CONCANACO), and the Consejo Coordinadora Empresarial (CCE). As Tom Barry (1992: 325) states, "in contrast to its policy in countries such as Nicaragua, where US pressures for internal political reforms were increased to full throttle, Washington did not make Mexico's movement toward democracy a condition of other assistance or of further relationships." The strategy, then, was one of supporting NED activities through U.S. foreign policy arms—such as the NDI and NRI—in order to convince Mexican organizations to unite. According to Jacqueline Mazza (2001: 113), "USAID and the State Department reached a decision on two key activities: to provide funds to Alianza Cívica though NDI and to fund an official observer/witness delegation through NDI and NRI." These initial activities totalled about $1.2 million.

In more detail, between 1994 and 2000, Alianza Cívica received $755,000 from the NED amounting to 20 percent of all its funding, along with a linked additional $377,632 from the NDI amounting to just over 10 percent of its funding, while the largest and most significant donor was the UNDP providing $1,786,790 amounting to 48 percent of all its funding (see table 6.1). These figures are low given claims that total U.S. State Department spending under the auspices of democratic development assistance, including USAID and NED programs, increased from $682 million in 1991, to $736 million in 1992, to $900 million in 1993, or the fact that the NED's budget increased by nearly 40 percent under the Clinton administration in 1993 from $35 million to $48 million (Robinson 1996: 100). The funds disclosed in table 6.1 also contrast markedly with the support granted, for example, to environmental projects by USAID, totalling some $6 million in 2000 (Fox 2004: 470–71). As Sergio Aguayo Quezada, leading figure in the National Co-ordination

Table 6.1.   Total Funding Granted to Alianza Cívica, 1994–2000

Foundation	Total US$	%
United Nations Development Program (UNDP)	1,786,790.00	48.04
National Endowment for Democracy (NED)	755,420.00	20.31
National Democratic Institute (NDI)	377,632.00	10.15
Trusteeship for Democracy	331,764.00	8.92
Inter Pares (Canada)	185,422.00	4.99
International Center for Human Rights and Democratic Development (Canada)	140,872.00	3.79
Development and Peace (Canada)	43,665.00	1.17
Ford Foundation (Mexico Office)	18,352.00	0.49
Different donations	17,647.00	0.47
The Angelica Foundation (United States)	17,500.00	0.47
Department of Education and International Affairs: Fund of Social Justice (Canada)	14,510.00	0.39
Threshold (United States)	13,035.00	0.35
Project Counselling Service (Costa Rica)	6,994.46	0.19
Counsel in Projects and Services (Guatemala)	6,784.00	0.18
Banco Obrero	1,470.00	0.04
Banco Mexicano de Comercio Exterior	1,548.00	0.04
Total	3,719,405.46	100.00

Source: Sergio Aguayo Quezada, "El financiamento extranjero y la transición democrática Mexicana: El caso de Alianza Cívica" (2001), http://www.laneta.apc.org/alianza/Conferencia; accessed 11 April 2002.

of Alianza Cívica, has indicated there was never a "relation of exclusivity" established with single donors such as the NED or USAID.[5] This means that even during the period of activity in 1994, at which time Alianza Cívica received a large injection of funds as the backdrop to the presidential elections, the largest grant was received from the UNDP. The breakdown of figures for 1994 alone indicate that the UNDP provided $1,277,087, or just over 71 percent of total funding received in this single year by Alianza Cívica, while

Table 6.2.   Total Funding Granted to Alianza Cívica, 1994

Foundation	Total US$	%
United Nations Development Program (UNDP)	1,277,087	71.2
Trusteeship for Democracy	331,764	18.5
National Endowment for Democracy (NED)	155,000	8.6
Different donations	17,647	1.0
National Democratic Institute (NDI)	8,941	0.5
Banco Mexicano de Comercio Exterior	1,548	0.1
Banco Obrero	1,470	0.1
Total	1,793,457	100.0

Source: Sergio Aguayo Quezada, "El financiamento extranjero y la transición democrática Mexicana: El caso de Alianza Cívica" (2001), http://www.laneta.apc.org/alianza/Conferencia; accessed 11 April 2002.

the NED directly provided $155,000 or 8.6 percent of total funding (see table 6.2). Yet, despite the large presence of the UNDP in this instance, representatives have notably downplayed their own role, emphasizing the organization as an "insignificantly minor actor."[6] As Sergio Aguayo has stated, "the NED never *imposed* any political conditionality, nor required information that was beyond the justification of how resources were spent." Additionally, he claims that the majority of funds during 1994, amounting to 90 percent of total funding, came from Mexican sources, if one accepts his point that the funding received from the UNDP directly relates to a grant given to the UN by the Mexican state (Aguayo Quezada 2001). Across the board, then, it has been admitted that U.S. or global governance institutions have had less prominence in Mexico than might normally be expected in other Latin America countries (see also Fox 2004: 471).[7]

These inferences are also further borne out by a study of all NED funding to grantees in Mexico between 1994 and 2007, which totaled just below $10 million across the period. Alianza Cívica directly received a declining amount over this duration, for example, from a peak figure in 1997 (the midterm election year) of $271,323; funds dipped to $246,530 in 2000 (an election year);[8] then dropped to $63,696 in 2001; remained similar at $63,000 in 2002, and then slipped to $52,000 in 2003 prior to ceasing all together. NED funding across this period, to Alianza Cívica, amounted to $1,080,249 or 11.5 percent of the total. This compares starkly with the NED funds awarded to the CIPE, linked to key fractions of capital (namely, leading business confederations, such as COPARMEX and CONCANACO); funds granted to amenable labor organizations linked to the American Center for International Labor Solidarity (ACILS); and funds channeled through the foreign policy arms of NDI and NRI that, in combination, amounted to $2,140,088 or 22.8 percent of the total (see table 6.3). In rather self-deprecating fashion, however, US-AID representatives have been at pains to highlight the "exceptionalism" of Mexico, meaning that their programs were very small and based on far more partnership and mutual support in deference to issues of "state sovereignty."[9] Representatives from the NED itself have also downplayed their role in promoting democratic transition in Mexico. Carl Gershman, president of the NED, has indicated that precedence must always be given to "national" processes of maturing democratic demands.[10] While in the World Bank the role of multilateral institutions impacting on the democratic transition in Mexico has been regarded as "close to zero" as events were perceived to have been shaped more by "national" conditions.[11] One even bolder affirmation made from within the Organization of American States (OAS) has been that the democratic transition in Mexico should be credited to the political parties themselves rather than activist groups within civil society.[12] There is clear dissonance here between those views holding that the "national" context was determinate and the argument that the Mexican case underscores the United States' objective to promote polyarchy through the imposition of specific institutions and procedures (Robinson 2000: 317–18; Robinson 2006b: 110–11).

The third difficulty thrown up by the procedure of democratization in Mexico for those arguments focusing on the promotion of polyarchy is linked to pivotal institutions such as the IFE breaking the pattern of U.S.-based geopolitical institutions directly funding democracy promotion networks, due to the financial and operational autonomy it established by the mid-1990s. This is exhibited by their undertaking of "South-South co-operation" projects, through which democratization programs of their own are conducted across the developing world (e.g., in East Timor, Bolivia, Ecuador) and the very fact that in any election year the IFE's budget is $80 million.[13] In 2006 alone, the IFE disbursed $572 million for political campaigns with 70 percent of that money used by political parties to buy advertising time in the electronic media, guaranteeing profits for Televisa and TV Azteca (Dresser 2008: 246). In this instance specific IFE funding is comparatively larger than parallel U.S. democracy assistance programs to NGOs in Mexico. Ordinarily, taking these points at face value, one might be led to the conclusion that the argument concerning the direct intervention of U.S. democracy promotion activities in Mexico is inflated. However, a more nuanced stance can be developed, namely, that the process of democratization in Mexico is less the product of direct U.S. intervention and more a passive revolutionary development springing from the internalization of specific economic, moral, and cultural values; codes of conduct; and ideological transformations in Mexico resulting in a process of democratization from above. Three clusters linked to this theme of internalization can be elaborated, which advance in a subtler way the central tenets of the polyarchy argument.

Advancing the Case for the Promotion of Polyarchy in Mexico

First, on the issue of funding, it is worth noting what has been termed the "cultivation of fig leaves" by the U.S. State Department, not only through the UNDP but also through the funding of NDI and NRI democracy promotion programs (Mazza 2001: 113). As a result, officials involved in USAID democracy and governance programs have directly acknowledged that efforts in Mexico gained greater significance over the years, leading to a recent switch in priorities from the bottom third in terms of USAID's financing to the top third.[14] While it was admitted that, in comparison with other "missions," the financing of groups is comparatively small in Mexico, the USAID-led

Table 6.3.   Total NED Funding in Mexico, 1994–2007

Year	Grantee	Total US$
1994	Democracía Solidaridad y Paz Social, A.C. (Demos Paz)	120,000
	Democracía Solidaridad y Paz Social, A.C. (Demos Paz)	60,000
	Democracía Solidaridad y Paz Social, A.C. (Demos Paz)	35,780
	Alianza Cívica	155,000
	Comision Mexicana de Defensa y Promocion de los Derechos	45,000
	Consejo para la Democracía	95,000
	Consejo para la Democracía	32,000
	Consejo para la Democracía	186,710
	Frente Civico Potosino	65,000
	Movimiento Ciudadano por la Democracía (MCD)	95,000
	Movimiento Ciudadano por la Democracía (MCD)	31,000
	Democracía Solidaridad y Paz Social, A.C. (Demos Paz)	95,000
	American Institute for Free Labor Development (AIFLD)	113,400
1995	Center for International Private Enterprise (CIPE)[a]	111,506
	Democracía Solidaridad y Paz Social, A.C. (Demos Paz)	88,000
	Democracía Solidaridad y Paz Social, A.C. (Demos Paz)	110,000
	National Democratic Institute for International Affairs (NDI)	84,625
	Council for Democracy Association of Civic Groups for Democracy	72,154
	Council for Democracy	60,000
	Frente Civico Potosino	55,000
	Mujeres en Lucha por la Democracía (MLD)	80,000
	Free Trade Union Institute (FTUI)[b]	176,400
	Alianza Cívica	105,000
	Centro Civico de Solidaridad (CECISOL)	211,420
	Frente Civico Potosino	81,163
	Comision Mexicana de Defensa y Promocion de los Derechos Humanos	50,000
	Mujeres en Lucha por la Democracía (MLD)	44,000
	Presencia Ciudadana Mexicana	26,500
1996	Alianza Cívica	95,700
	Presencia Ciudadana Mexicana	40,000
	Comision Mexicana de Defensa y Promocion de los Derechos	50,000
	Alianza Cívica	98,944
	Escuela de Capacitación Cívica	86,568
1997	Centro Cívico C.A.: Asociación Nacional Cívica Femenina (ANCIFEM) (formerly CECISOL)	274,907
	Alianza Cívica	121,323
	Alianza Cívica	150,000
	Movimiento Ciudadano por la Democracía (MCD)	74,000
	American Center for International Labor Solidarity (ACILS)[c]	278,221
	Comision Mexicana de Defensa y Promocion de los Derechos	45,000
	Escuela de Capacitación Cívica	60,000
1998	Movimiento Ciudadano por la Democracía (MCD)	70,000
	Presencia Ciudadana Mexicana	60,000
	Equidad de Genero: Ciudadana, Trabajo y Familia	52,000
	Center for International Private Enterprise (CIPE)[d]	34,032
	Alianza Cívica/Academia Mexicana de Derechos Humanos	100,000
	National Democratic Institute for International Affairs (NDI)[e]	86,935

Table 6.3. *(Continued)*

Year	Grantee	Total US$
	Asociación Nacional Cívica Femenina (ANCIFEM)	252,489
	Alianza Cívica	108,898
	Comision Mexicana de Defensa y Promocion de los Derechos	50,000
1999	Equidad de Genero: Ciudadana, Trabajo y Familia	55,000
	Centro de Apoyo al Movimiento Popular Oaxaqueño (CAMPO)	20,000
	Alianza Cívica	78,000
	Movimiento Ciudadano por la Democracía (MCD)	70,000
	Presencia Ciudadana Mexicana	70,000
	Equidad de Genero: Ciudadana, Trabajo y Familia	55,000
	Democracía Solidaridad y Paz Social, A.C. (Demos Paz)	60,000
2000	Universidad de las Américas (UDLA)	70,000
	Alianza Cívica	90,000
	Equidad de Genero: Ciudadana, Trabajo y Familia	22,000
	Asociación Nacional Cívica Femenina (ANCIFEM)	270,407
	Alianza Cívica	156,530
	Frente Indígena Oaxaqueño Binacional (FIOB)	30,000
	Presencia Ciudadana Mexicana	87,900
2001	Acción Popular de Integración Social	79,000
	Alianza Cívica	63,696
	Fundación Información y Democracia	47,000
	Comision Mexicana de Defensa y Promocion de los Derechos	40,000
2002	Acción Popular de Integración Social	43,000
	Universidad de las Américas (UDLA)/Universidad Iberoamericana	70,000
	Alianza Cívica	63,000
	Fundación Información y Democracia	70,000
	Asociación Nacional Cívica Femenina (ANCIFEM)	160,000
2003	Universidad de las Américas (UDLA)	50,000
	Alianza Cívica	52,000
	Fundación Información y Democracia	42,000
	Instituto para la Seguridad y la Democracia (INSYDE)	55,000
	Democracia, Derechos Humanos y Seguridad	50,000
2004	Acción Popular de Integración Social	45,000
	Center for International Private Enterprise (CIPE)[f]	49,683
	Centro de Encuentros y Diálogos, A.C. (CED)	36,724
	Democracia, Derechos Humanos y Seguridad (DDHS)	68,900
	Instituto para la Seguridad y la Democracia (INSYDE)	65,380
	Libertad de Información México	50,000
	National Democratic Institute for International Affairs (NDI)[g]	114,000
2005	American Center for International Labor Solidarity (ACILS)	183,315
	Center for International Private Enterprise (CIPE)	51,196
	Centro de Encuentros y Diálogos, A.C.	40,000
	Colectivo de Investigación, Desarrollo y Educación entre Mujeres (CIDEM)	32,100
	Democracia, Derechos Humanos y Seguridad (DDHS)	76,530
	Due Process of Law Foundation (DPLF)[h]	65,140
	Instituto para la Seguridad y la Democracia (INSYDE)	60,714
	Libertad de Información México (LIMAC)	51,000
2006	American Center for International Labor Solidarity (ACILS)[i]	233,175
	Centro de Encuentros y Diálogos, A.C. (CED)	54,347

Table 6.3. *(Continued)*

Year	Grantee	Total US$
	Colectivo de Investigación, Desarrollo y Educación entre Mujeres (CIDEM)	45,250
	Democracia, Derechos Humanos y Seguridad (DDHS)	84,717
	Due Process of Law Foundation (DPLF)[j]	70,000
	Instituto para la Seguridad y la Democracia (INSYDE)	65,000
	International Republican Institute (IRI)[k]	150,000
	Libertad de Expresión México (LIMAC)	52,750
	National Democratic Institute (NDI)[l]	150,000
2007	American Center for International Labor Solidarity (ACILS)[m]	500,000
	Centro de Derechos Humanos Asesoría a Pueblos Indígenas (CEDHAPI)[n]	34,550
	Centro de Encuentros y Diálogos, A.C. (CED)	48,100
	Colectivo de Investigación, Desarrollo y Educación entre Mujeres (CIDEM)	56,200
	Consejo Regional Indígena Popular de X'pujil (CRIPX)	30,000
	Libertad de Información México (LIMAC)	57,000
	Seguridad Ciudadano	45,510
	Servicios para una Eduación Alternativa (EDUCA)[o]	40,000
Total		9,399,489

Source: National Endowment for Democracy (NED) annual reports (1990–2007), http://www.ned.org.

[a] To enable one of Mexico's leading business confederations, Confederación de Cámaras Nacionales de Comercio (CONCANACO), to improve the capabilities of individual chambers of commerce in their advocacy efforts on behalf of the private sector.

[b] FTUI received NED support to provide Mexican unions with the information, training, and specific data necessary to lodge complaints effectively under the procedures set out in the NAFTA labor side agreement and in International Labour Organization (ILO) conventions.

[c] In former guises as the FTUI, the ACILS sought to improve the protection of freedom of association and collective bargaining, enhancing the implementation of Mexican labor law, and increasing the number of Mexican workers who participate in authentic democratic unions. To achieve these goals, two joint education programs were sponsored between U.S. and Mexican unions in the same sectors.

[d] CIPE, in cooperation with the Confederación Patronal de la República Mexicana (COPARMEX), conducted a technical assistance program to develop the government relations and advocacy capabilities of key private sector business organizations.

[e] NDI received funding to organize a series of seminars with the Center for the Study of State Reforms (CERE) in order to help the new multiparty majority in the Chamber of Deputies develop democratic practices. Through these seminars and consultations with party leaders, international experts were provided comparative information on issues of importance to the internal organization and policy-making role of the Chamber of Deputies. NDI aimed to disseminate the lessons of the seminars to state legislatures in Mexico and throughout the region.

[f] To build consensus within a coalition of representative labor unions and business organizations to advocate for labor reform. CIPE and its partner COPARMEX aimed to meet with federation and union leadership to strengthen the alliance between business and labor groups and meet with members of congress and congressional committees to assess attitudes in congress about labor reform. Finally, COPARMEX aimed to organize an international labor forum in which employers, workers, public officials, and civil society organizations could discuss the benefits of reforming the labor law.

[g] To generate further discussion within Mexican political parties regarding reforming party structures, NDI aimed to strengthen party training institutes in Mexico through a program that would include a national workshop, follow-on technical assistance, and materials distribution.

[h] To defend human rights of indigenous citizens in the justice system, DPLF aimed to prepare a cadre of indigenous and nonindigenous lawyers to serve as public defenders in criminal proceedings of indigenous

communities and in support of their human rights. DPLF also aimed to work with the state's human rights commissioner to reform the criminal justice system for indigenous communities.

i To improve the capacity of unions and labor-support organizations to organize workers and bargain collectively with employers in the auto-parts sector. This program also strived to strengthen internal union democracy by promoting rank-and-file participation and leadership in organizing and bargaining campaigns. ACILS also aimed to continue supporting the independent union movement in Mexico by conducting workshops, providing technical assistance, and facilitating communication among unions in the auto-parts sector.

j To strengthen the capacity of the Centro de Derechos Humanos Asesoría a Pueblos Indígenas (CEDHAPI), a local indigenous NGO. CEDHAPI aimed to present cases to both national courts and international bodies, and help bring Mexican practices concerning indigenous human and civil rights in line with international treaties and conventions. Through training, workshops, and meetings, DPLF aimed to mentor CEDHAPI on organizational practices and information-gathering skills, as well as provide technical assistance.

k To increase women's participation in, and the number of female candidates for, positions in the local and national government. IRI aimed to hold a series of trainings at the local level for women on political participation, campaign strategies, and media training. In addition, IRI aimed to work with the main political parties to develop a plan to increase women's participation in politics at all levels.

l To contribute to increased transparency in the Mexican electoral process. NDI aimed to work to identify real or potential challenges in the electoral process and, in turn, offer viable recommendations to these problems. NDI also aimed to place particular emphasis on enhancing civil society's ability to share information on electoral observation results and facilitating greater society-wide dialogue on electoral reform.

m To strengthen democratic and independent worker organizations that reflects the composition of the workforce and represents the concerns and interests of workers in the auto-parts, telecommunications, and ports sectors. ACILS aimed to conduct workshops, provide technical assistance, and facilitate communication among unions. Additionally, ACILS aimed to improve the capacity of independent unions to use international labor rights instruments and share experiences and skill building with key international allies.

n To promote human rights among the Chatino indigenous group of Oaxaca State. Through a series of intensive workshops, Centro de Derechos Humanos Asesoría a Pueblos Indígenas (CEDHAPI) aimed to train a network of human rights defenders to serve as references for their communities. The human rights defenders, it was argued, would gain the ability to disseminate information about human rights, to document human rights violations, and to access experts about protection of these rights.

o To encourage indigenous participation in municipal government in Oaxaca. EDUCA aimed to conduct workshops to train participants to use existing citizen participation tools and provide tailored technical assistance to four indigenous municipalities. EDUCA also aimed to coordinate a study of indicators of indigenous participation so that municipalities and NGOs could more effectively target reforms to increase citizen participation.

Democracy and Governance Program has nevertheless established its largest team in the country over its twenty-year history. For instance, it now has the organizational support and infrastructure of twenty-six officials, in contrast with other projects elsewhere in Latin America that sustain sixty to eighty officials or, for example, El Salvador that has several hundred. At the same time, despite lower funding figures in Mexico, USAID in its own words, received "considerable bang for their buck."[15] This means that greater impact could be sustained with relatively smaller funds due to an attributed lack of "civic culture" and citizen responsibility in Mexico.[16] While it was admitted that the U.S. state could act at times like a "300 pound gorilla" it was also emphasized that a more subtle and indirect form of financing was preferred by USAID endeavors.[17] Additionally, the wider and emerging involvement of agencies such as the Ford Foundation, the Inter-American Foundation

(IAF), the presence of the European Union (EU), and the interest of the Open Society Institute all has to be noted in terms of establishing "democracy and governance" programs in Mexico.

Notably, the IAF contributed levels of funding to Mexico in excess of the NED's, averaging approximately $2.3 million per year throughout the 1990s (Fox 2004: 471). The Ford Foundation has itself also claimed a larger presence than the NED in recent years announcing that it is now "one of the principal counterparts" on local governance and civil society projects. A conservative indication of such work covers a base budget in Mexico and Central America of $2 million per annum, although this is capable of rising to $5 million, with over 70 percent directed toward Mexico program funding activities, for example, local governance support, civil society and public sphere assistance, or increasing the participation of multicultural communities within civil society.[18] This is allied with the encouragement of microfinancing enterprises including access to financial services for low-income groups in urban and rural areas. As one program officer for Development Finance and Economic Security at the Ford Foundation put it:

> Access to financial services is regarded as part and parcel of democratisation because full participation in economic, social and political terms cannot proceed without full participation in financial institutions and having access to such resources.[19]

Similarly, a major grants program linked to the European Institute for Democracy and Human Rights has recently focused on human rights, the consolidation of the rule of law, and reform of the state through the strengthening of ombudsmen. Globally this EU scheme amounts to €100 million per annum covering thematic priorities and focus countries, with Mexico counting as one of the thirty-one focus countries receiving program grants of just below €3 million for NGO proposals (focusing on the abolition of the death penalty, defense of indigenous rights, strengthening the rule of law, and democratization). Similarly there is the funding of a microprojects program for one-year plans again covering the themes of indigenous peoples' rights and strengthening the rule of law for grants up to €50,000 and, lastly, there are large target projects linked to multilateral organizations such as the UN and the OECD. These aim to ensure "best practice" on international human rights standards running for two-year periods in liaison with the MacArthur Foundation for grants set at €640,000. With forthcoming agreements on strengthening the modernization and administration of justice and law enforcement it is claimed that the EU Commission is set to become "the major donor in this area."[20] Finally, the interest of the Open Society Institute has been recently marked in Mexico with a tripartite approach to democratization involving the support of projects focused on NGO assistance; technical assistance on issues of criminal justice reform, discrimination issues, human rights, and anticorruption policies; and freedom of information and reform of the media. Across Latin America, the budget for such activities is set at $15 million with approximately $2 million targeted toward democratization in Mexico, to be indefinitely continued as long as the annual global budget of the institute normalizes between $250 and $300 million.[21]

The fact remains that in both qualitative and quantitative terms such funding has been central to adapting civil society activism in Mexico to the context of formal and increasingly institutionalized liberal democracy controlled from above. Key figures central to the activities of NGOs such as Alianza Cívica as well as officials within the IFE have also noted that the sort of external financing in the 1990s from organizations such as the NED and the UNDP was absolutely essential to their democracy promotion activities.[22] It is then perhaps surprising, but still disappointing, to witness established authorities at the NED candidly stating that William Robinson's argument about the promotion of polyarchy in Latin America is "sheer crap, it is just a joke with flow charts and scatter diagrams that are just cooked up out of some conspiracy theory" that have no scientific basis.[23] There is clearly more to the argument than this asinine dismissal, which adds credence to the view that anybody critically challenging the "common sense" of the transition paradigm comes to be presented as a "crazed heretic" (Robinson 2006b: 97). After all, even Sergio Aguayo has gone so far as to explicitly confirm that "the problem of polyarchy" exists in Mexico "in a form of alienation from the institutionalised process of democracy."[24]

Second, the condition of polyarchy has received growing and explicit attention in Mexico. It has not only been regarded as *the* optimal situation to strive for by representatives of U.S. democracy promotion activities, such as at the NED and elsewhere, it has also been deemed the "basic aim."[25] As described by one Latin America specialist at the Carnegie Endowment for International Peace commenting on the democratic transition in Mexico:

> Polyarchy is the right system but it should deepen itself over time so that citizens feel that there is some real connection between their interests and their participation within the system and the change within that system and their daily lives.[26]

Another expert for Grupo de Economistas y Asociados, a consultancy firm founded in 1990 by Jesús Reyes Heroles, has added that the differences between political parties in Mexico are budgetary not ideological.[27] The circulation of political parties and elites, notes one field representative for the AFL-CIO in Mexico—from within the NED-funded ACILS as evidenced in table 6.3 above—does not amount to a transition.[28] These are all points that vitiate claims made from within the Secretaría del Trabajo y Previsión Social (STPS) that a plurality in Congress is a definite "guarantee" of democratic practice.[29] It is this problem of polyarchy that was most graphically exposed by the 2006 presidential election leading to the victory, again, of the PAN's candidate, Felipe Calderón, by an official margin of 0.56 percent, or no more than 238,000 votes, against the candidacy of Andrés Manuel López Obrador of the PRD. This is despite the widespread accord on the evidence of electoral fraud consisting of the double-counting of pro-Calderón precincts, collusion between PRI and PAN governors, and highly suspect processes of political corruption charged against the IFE and suspect processes of electoral review conducted by the Tribunal Federal Electoral (TRIFE) as the supreme electoral authority (Giordano 2006). The political landscape then witnessed López Obrador embarking on a populist bid to energize protest against the outcome of the 2006 election as the "Legitimate President" and ignite a social movement dynamic of support for his AMLO campaign with such currents having ongoing import and relevance (see Grayson 2007).[30]

Hence the *problem* of polyarchy, as a restrained form of popular participation, is regarded as one of the main challenges or threats to substantive democracy in Mexico by some of the actors involved in continual support for democratic change. For instance, coordinators at trade unions such as the Frente Auténtico del Trabajo (FAT) have upheld that there has been no advance of democracy in Mexico in terms of social development. Similarly, coordinators at the Sindicato Mexicano de Electricistas (SME) have balked at suggestions that any such democratic "transition" has effectively occurred in Mexico in the wake of the year 2000 elections, particularly given that proposed labor reforms were seen as disciplining workers according to regional drivers such as NAFTA and the Free Trade Areas of the Americas (FTAA).[31] Commencing with pointers during the Fox administration, moves to privatize the electrical system and energy sectors in Mexico have gained increased opposition from the SME and factions within the Sindicato Unico de Trabajadores Electricistas de la República Mexicana (SUTERM), which have been at the center of forming the Front Against Privatisation of the petroleum and electric power industries in order to articulate a more significant demonstration of wider democratic struggle in Mexico.[32] This focus became highly significant following President Felipe Calderón's decree to coercively liquidate the state-owned Compañía Luz y Fuerza del Centro (LyFC) in October 2009, seize its facilities with federal police, and sack forty-four thousand workers of the militant SME in an attempt to weaken the power of organized labor and establish a new round of investor growth in the energy sector, while leading to general strike mobilizations by the SME facing a struggle for its survival. Equally, since 2007, Calderón's administration has targeted the

Sindicato Nacional de Trabajadores Mineros, Metalúrgicos y Similares de la República Mexicana (SNTMMSRM) in an attempt to break its strike across three mines (including the historically symbolic Cananea works), consisting of thirteen thousand miners in total. Democracy is therefore seen across these mobilizations as less a "measured two minutes" in an electoral vote and more as the conduct of radical labor and social movement spaces of resistance to challenge, if not restructure, the political economy of class rule in Mexico.[33]

Third, one of the most significant conditions in shifting the debate about democratic transition and the promotion of polyarchy in Mexico is the issue of internalization that transpires from the above analysis. Time and again attention has been drawn to the internalization of particular democratic discourses, moral and cultural values, codes of conduct, and ideological transformations in Mexico. Not to be discounted in this process of internalization is the very alignment of interests brought about by neoliberalism (Bruhn 1997: 17). As Sergio Aguayo has indicated "democracy emerged in Mexico that was in some way linked to the neoliberal agenda of globalisation."[34] Yet the connection is not a simple equation between "free markets" and "free elections." The long-term emergence of neoliberal capitalist accumulation in Mexico, as traced in chapter 4, from the 1970s and 1980s onward has been accomplished in part by constituting a set of internalized rules and social procedures. Put another way, neoliberalism has induced a reorganization in the social relations of production in Mexico that has led to the internalization of certain class interests across state–civil society relations. It will be recalled from chapter 4, that neoliberalism emerged in Mexico as a process of change initiated from above based on a set of institutional processes within the organization of the state, especially reflected in the Salinas administration (1988–1994). Notably this was the context within which ministries such as the Secretaría de Programación y Presupuesto (SPP) came to rise to institutional predominance within the state alongside the dominance of fractions of capital represented by organizations such as the Consejo Coordinadora Empresarial (CCE) that included direct shareholders of large conglomerates tied to the export sector, the rise of the *maquila* (in-bond) strategy of export-led industrialization fueled by foreign investment and technology, and the sectoral reform of agriculture that integrated local farmers into a transnational system of agricultural production (see Centeno 1994; Fox 1993; Sklair 1993). After all, as Nicos Poulantzas (1975: 73) forewarned, "the international reproduction of capital under the domination of American capital is supported by . . . various national states, each state attempting in its own way to latch on to one or other aspect of this process." In Mexico the result was the emergence of a neoliberal state attuned to establishing a series of mechanisms conducive to resolving political disputes within the remit of a polyarchic

system. A counterpart to the passive revolution of capital in the form of neoliberal restructuring is therefore a resultant process of democratization from
above. In Kathleen Bruhn's (1997: 307) words, in the 1980s "the PRI-state
shaped the conditions for competition in such a way as to reduce the PRD
threat, salvage the PRI's electoral dominance, and ensure the implementation of the Salinas economic program." The limits of the passive revolution
of neoliberalism and democratic transition are revealed by the continued
separation of politics and economics, maintaining the division between the
political sphere and democratic control, so that crucial aspects of capitalism
are not overcome but reproduced in new forms (Sassoon 1980: 89). As John
Williamson (1993: 1331) clearly outlines "economic policy and democracy
will benefit if all mainstream politicians endorse the universal convergence
and the scope of political debate on economic issues is *de facto* circumscribed
in consequence."

In practice this has been evident in Mexico whether in the form of an
emphasis on the "enabling environment of arrangements such as NAFTA"
in terms of ensuring contract and property rights conducive to democratic
principles, or in the stressing of "civil society diplomacy" linking global
governance institutions to the constitution of certain values about democracy, freedom, and liberty based on the rights of the individual and the free
market.[35] Not surprisingly, this stress also came through Mexico-specialist
officials at the IMF and World Bank indicating that the so-called second
generation of neoliberalism, targeting small and medium-sized businesses as
well as energy privatization in the form of Petróleos Mexicanos (PEMEX)
and LyFC restructuring, would deepen the identification with formal democratic practices.[36] This is where initiatives led by the Ford Foundation and
the EU become so pivotal due to the tying of the rule of law and property
rights agreements to democracy assistance programs. The EU, it is claimed,
is not aiming to "impose any models" although "the rule of law is an integral
part of the democratic transition as democratic countries make better trad-
ing partners."[37] Similarly, the Ford Foundation's goal is to build "financial
literacy" at the local level through microcredit (lending) and microfinancing
(credit, insurance, savings) in order to further realize the internalization of
neoliberalism.[38] As USAID representatives have reaffirmed, democracy promotion is less about the imposition of "our" system and more the acceptance
of "universal rules of the democratic game" consisting of investment-related
rule of law, enforcement of contracts, collecting on collateral and bankruptcy,
and overcoming corruption.[39]

In sum, this stress on internalization bears out the point made earlier that
U.S. democracy promotion is based on the separation of politics from economics and it is the normalization of this doctrine of democratization that is

linked to the compulsion of states to conform to each other in their internal arrangements wrought by the uneven geographical development of capital (see Levy and Bruhn 2001: 10, 269). Hence the importance of emphasizing *both* the induced reproduction of capital brought about by neoliberal globalization *and* the political mediations of this internalization process linked to the shaping of common conceptions about democratization that are constitutive of the conditions of passive revolution in Mexico. One of the most salient contemporary challenges of democratization can therefore be described as the problem of "feckless pluralism": an extreme variant of neoliberal polyarchies linked to an inability to extend democracy beyond plural and competitive elites that are profoundly cut off from the electorate rendering politics a hollow enterprise (Carothers 2002: 11).

CONCLUSION: THE "ISOLATION EFFECT" OF DEMOCRATIZATION AS INDIVIDUALIZATION

"As it has transited rather painlessly from seven decades of rule by the PRI to a competitive democracy," exalts the *Economist*, "[Mexico] has discovered a new stability. Problems and poverty remain, but thanks partly to the much-maligned North American Free Trade Agreement (NAFTA) . . . most Mexicans can now claim to be middle-class."[40] With a rather different diagnosis, this chapter has asserted that the course of democratic "transition" has furthered the institutional separation of "the economic" and the "political," characteristic of a capitalist type of state and the accumulation strategy of neoliberalism, as observed in chapter 4. As a consequence, the process of democratization has been exposed as an element in the class strategy of passive revolution shaping the ongoing reorganization and expansion of capitalism. As a restorative strategy, democratic transition is an aspect of passive revolution in which the class relations of capitalism are reorganized on a new basis within the uneven developmental conditions inscribing state space. As Gramsci states, "the counting of 'votes' is the final ceremony of a long process, in which it is precisely those who devote their best energies to the state . . . who carry the greatest weight" (Gramsci 1971: 193, Q13§30). Yet the ritual of such vote counting—or what Marx (1852/1979: 161) would have recognized as "parliamentary cretinism"—reveals the threshold of liberal democracy and should not be the singular basis for assessing democracy. In sum, this chapter has argued that the canon of democratic transition is based on the limits of a class-based elitist focus on the role of the electoral system in the representation of the electorate that requires embeddedness within the uneven conditions of capitalism (see Santos and Avritzer 2007: xxxvi).

Hence, with "the word 'democracy' . . . what matters is that a bond is being sought with the people, the nation, and that one considers necessary not a servile unity resulting from passive obedience, but an active unity, a life unity, whatever the content of this life may be" (Gramsci 1985: 206, Q14§72). One of the many remaining challenges facing democratic transition in Mexico is therefore common to most of the region of Latin America. It is the problem of ignoring the contingent relationship between capitalism and democracy leading to the condition and "isolation effect" of extreme individualization, which has been criticized throughout this chapter as emblematic of liberal democracies. The main contribution offered here is the analysis of democratic transition that is linked to the reorganization of capitalism and state power on a world scale through neoliberal restructuring. As observed in chapter 1, this geopolitical context is that of the uneven and combined process of developmental catch-up that often compels, "under the whip of external necessity," forms of structural change. Yet, here, the stress has been a little more subtle: the necessity of transformation was borne more from the internalization of democratization, which was intrinsically linked to the passive revolution of neoliberal restructuring in Mexico. The result, as presciently envisaged some time ago by commentators on Mexico's crisis conditions, is that some of the most intense pressure for democratization has come from rightward institutional processes of opposition, which have resulted in the PAN as an obvious beneficiary of democratization from above (see Hellman 1983: 258–59; Otero 1996: 242). This sober assessment reminds one of O'Donnell and Schmitter's brazen normative stance that:

> Put in a nutshell, parties of the Right-Centre and Right must be "helped" to do well, and parties of the Left-Centre and Left should not win by an overwhelming majority. (O'Donnell and Schmitter 1986, vol. 4: 62)

More recently, in Mexico's July 2009 midterm elections for the Chamber of Deputies, similar trends are emerging where the PRI fared better than predicted, carrying 37 percent of the total vote over the 28 percent earned by the PAN. The PRD garnered just 12 percent of the vote after coming within less than a percentage point of winning the presidency in 2006. In Congress the PRI more than doubled its seats with an increase from 106 to 241, or 49 percent of seats, and will hold a majority through an alliance with the Partido Verde Ecologista de México (PVEM), which took 3 percent of seats. The PAN slipped somewhat from 206 seats to 147, leaving it just under 29 percent of seats, but the PRD will have only 14 percent of seats. The PRI also took governorships that were in the hands of the PAN (Querétaro, San Luis Potosí), and reaffirmed its control of Nuevo León. With the PRD reduced to having no meaningful role in the Chamber of Deputies, President Calderón will have to negotiate all legislation directly with the PRI in Congress. This balancing act between the PRI and the PAN in Congress will, no doubt, be a factor in shaping the 2012 presidential campaign and establishes, in practice, the narrow nature of supposed "transitions" from authoritarian rule, criticized above.[41] The fact that the PRI lost three significant state elections in 2010, in Puebla, Sinaloa, and Oaxaca—the latter witnessing the departure of the repressive governor Ulises Ruiz Ortiz—which it had controlled for eighty-one years, does not diminish the point about the limited nature of the democratic transition.[42] The problem, then, can be cast differently by recognizing the limits to democracy in Mexico imposed by *its own* institutional emergence signaled ever since the reforms from above of the 1970s. What needs to be questioned is the managed and measured institutional emergence of democracy in Mexico and the role U.S.-based geopolitical institutions have played in the process. After all, it has been noted that U.S. interest in democratic transition in Mexico has never been sought at the expense of jeopardizing elite rule itself, which has always been more interested in maintaining the basic order and controlling populist-based change (Carothers 1999: 147; Robinson 1996: 113). By contrast, in an intriguing note on "Hegemony and Democracy," Antonio Gramsci (2007: 345, Q8§191) wrote:

> Among the many meanings of democracy, the most realistic and concrete one, in my view, is that which can be brought into relief through the connection between the concept of democracy and hegemony. In the hegemonic system, there is democracy between the leading group and the groups that are led to the extent that the development of the economy and thus the legislation which is an expression of that development favours the molecular transition from the groups that are led to the leading group.

These conditions clearly differ from the factors of passive revolution and minimal hegemony revealed in this chapter in which capitalism has been reorganized and reformed through democratization processes. What it necessitates is consideration of the agenda of "anti-passive revolution" strategies or spaces of resistance articulated against the renewal of capitalism (Buci-Glucksmann 1979: 232). Clearly, challenges remain over the contestation of state power in Mexico, not least the attempt to reclaim alternative conceptions of popular democracy by widening the democratic canon (see Santos and Avritzer 2007: xlii). The next chapter thus raises the importance of considering alternative processes of popular democracy from below (*los de abajo*) absent from mainstream accounts that favor, somewhat similar to Gramsci's ambition, the transformation of the relation between "leaders" and "led." Among other factors at issue, in the chapter to come, is whether the principle of *mandar obedeciendo* ("govern by obeying") and the extensive struggle of the Ejército Zapatista de Liberación Nacional (EZLN) can shape the form of "anti-passive revolution" strategies and spaces of resistance against neoliberalism and therefore the further contestation of revolution and state in modern Mexico.

NOTES

1. President Vicente Fox Quesada, Remarks on accepting the 2001 Democracy Award from the National Endowment for Democracy, Washington, D.C. (5 September 2001), http://www.ned.org; accessed 17 January 2002.

2. All figures are from *Mexico & NAFTA Report*, "Fox Wins, Stunning Pollsters and Delighting Supporters and Markets," 11 July 2000 (RM-00–07).

3. *The Economist* [London], "The Hole He Left Behind" (21 December 1991): 9–10.

4. Revealingly, at the time, one senior NED official stated to me: "A coup, is a coup, is a coup . . . and it is a mistake to remove even an authoritarian government by undemocratic means, by using the military which is arbitrary and will always lead to the polarization and evasion of the rule of law. But what is being lost in the backlash to the U.S. administration's own declarations is the fact that the Chávez government was not democratic, it had closed down the media, there was a massive march of 350,000 people to protest the policies, and then Chávez did give an order to shoot some people." Author's interview with senior program officer for Latin America and the Caribbean, National Endowment for Democracy (NED), Washington D.C. (17 April 2002). It is quite clear, then, to see where the NED stood in relation to the coup.

5. Author's interview with Sergio Aguayo Quezada, National Co-ordination, Alianza Cívica (1994–1999), Mexico City (17 May 2002).

6. Author's interview with resident assistant representative, United Nations Development Program (UNDP), Mexico City (13 May 2002).

7. Author's interview with assistant director, United Nations Economic Commission for Latin America and the Caribbean (ECLAC), Mexico City (13 May 2002).

8. It is noteworthy that a senior NED authority confirmed that the figure in 2000 to Alianza Cívica combines a $90,000 grant from the NED and a $156,520 grant *initiated* by USAID but passed through the NDI due to concerns about "close ties" to the U.S. embassy; Author's interview with Carl Gershman, president of the NED, Washington, D.C. (17 April 2002).

9. Author's interviews with program officer for Latin America and the Caribbean, USAID, Washington, D.C. (18 April 2002) and senior program officer for Latin America and the Caribbean, USAID, Washington, D.C. (18 April 2002).

10. Author's interview with Carl Gershman, president of the NED, Washington, D.C. (17 April 2002).

11. Author's interview with economist, World Bank, Finance, Private Sector and Infrastructure for Latin America and the Caribbean Region, Washington, D.C. (19 April 2002).

12. Author's interview with ambassador, Mexican permanent representative to the OAS, Washington, D.C. (15 April 2002).

13. Author's interviews with director of international liaisons and political affairs, IFE, Mexico City (25 April 2002) and principal officer and general coordinator of the UNDP, Assistance to Electoral Observation, Mexico City (13 May 2002).

14. Author's interview with regional municipal finance advisor, USAID, Regional Urban Development Office, Latin America and the Caribbean (RUDO/LAC), Mexico City (24 April 2002).

15. Author's interview with regional municipal finance advisor, USAID, RUDO/ LAC, Mexico City (24 April 2002).

16. Author's interview with team leader, Democracy and Governance Program, USAID, Mexico City (24 April 2002).

17. Author's interview with regional municipal finance advisor, USAID, RUDO/ LAC, Mexico City (24 April 2002).

18. Author's interview with director of Democracy Program for Mexico and Central America, The Ford Foundation, Mexico City (14 May 2003).

19. Author's interview with program officer for Development Finance and Economic Security, The Ford Foundation, Mexico City (23 May 2003).

20. Author's interview with rule of law project officer, European Union Commission in Mexico, Mexico City (13 May 2003).

21. Author's interview with Open Society Institute, Latin America Program, Mexico City (16 May 2003).

22. Author's interviews with director of international liaisons and political affairs, IFE, Mexico City (25 April 2002); member of the Electoral Council, IFE, Mexico City (25 April 2002); and Silvia Alonso Félix, executive secretary, national coordination, Alianza Cívica, Mexico City (16 May 2002); and Sergio Aguayo Quezada, national coordination, Alianza Cívica (1994–1999), Mexico City (17 May 2002).

23. Author's interview with senior program officer for Latin America and the Caribbean, NED, Washington, D.C. (17 April 2002).

24. Author's interview with Sergio Aguayo Quezada, national coordination, Alianza Cívica (1994–1999), Mexico City (17 May 2002).

25. Author's interviews with regional municipal finance advisor, USAID, RUDO/ LAC, Mexico City (24 April 2002) and team leader, Democracy and Governance Program, USAID, Mexico City (24 April 2002).

26. Author's interview with codirector of the Democracy and Rule of Law Project, Global Policy Program, Carnegie Endowment for International Peace (CEIP), Washington, D.C. (16 April 2002).

27. Author's interview with correspondent, Grupo de Economistas y Asociados, Mexico City (14 May 2002).

28. Author's interview with AFL-CIO field representative, ACILS, Mexico City (29 April 2002).

29. Author's interview with STPS, International Affairs Section, Mexico City (30 April 2002).

30. See http://www.amlo.org.mx and http://www.regeneracion.mx for further details.

31. Author's interviews with national coordinator, FAT, Mexico City (29 April 2002) and international affairs officer, SME, Mexico City (30 April 2002).

32. Author's interview with national coordinator, Red Mexicana de Acción Frente al Libre Comercio (RMALC), Mexico City (29 April 2002).

33. Author's interviews with project organizer, Mexico Solidarity Network (MSN), Washington, D.C. (15 April 2002) and national coordinator, MSN, Mexico City (15 May 2002). At the time of writing (early 2011), events are still continually unfolding in relation to the war on labor in Mexico. Dan La Botz provides extremely useful updates and columns at *Mexican Labor News & Analysis*, see http://www .ueinternational.org/MLNA/index.php.

34. Author's interview with Sergio Aguayo Quezada, national coordination, Alianza Cívica (1994–1999), Mexico City (17 May 2002).

35. Author's interviews with resident assistant representative, UNDP, Mexico City (13 May 2002) and chief of staff of international affairs, IFE, Mexico City (25 April 2002).

36. Author's interviews with senior economist, IMF, Policy Development Review Department, Washington, D.C. (18 April 2002) and economist, World Bank, Finance, Private Sector and Infrastructure for Latin America and the Caribbean Region, Washington, D.C. (19 April 2002).

37. Author's interview with rule of law project officer, European Union Commission in Mexico, Mexico City (13 May 2003).

38. Author's interviews with director of Democracy Program for Mexico and Central America, The Ford Foundation, Mexico City (14 May 2003) and program officer for Development Finance and Economic Security, The Ford Foundation, Mexico City (23 May 2003).

39. Author's interviews with program officer for Latin America and the Caribbean, USAID, Washington, D.C. (18 April 2002) and senior program officer for Latin America and the Caribbean, USAID, Washington, D.C. (18 April 2002).

40. *The Economist* [London], "Mexico's Mid-Term Election" (11 July 2009): 18.

41. *The Economist* [London], "After Mexico's Mid-Term Election" (11 July 2009): 37.

42. *The Economist* [London], "Joining Forces" (10 July 2010): 49.

Chapter Seven

Uneven Agrarian Development and the Resistance of the EZLN

The historian Eric Hobsbawm has for some time heralded "the death of the peasantry" as the most dramatic and far-reaching social change to mark the twentieth century resulting from transformations in agricultural production. In his trilogy on the "long nineteenth century" (from the 1780s to 1914), he argued that the peasantry as a social class is destined to fade away, a possibility that became more actual by the late twentieth century. Across Latin America the percentage of peasants halved, or almost halved, in twenty years in Colombia (1951–1973), Mexico (1960–1980), and Brazil (1960–1980), while in the Dominican Republic (1960–1981), Venezuela (1961–1981), and Jamaica (1953–1981) the decline was by almost two-thirds (Hobsbawm 1987: 137; Hobsbawm 1994: 289–91). As observed in chapter 3, the social reorganization induced by *desarrollo estabilizador* kick-started the consolidation of capitalist accumulation on the basis of exploitation in the labor process through heightened proletarianization, up to the mid-1960s, which ensured increases in the profit rate through the value form (see Rivera Ríos 1986: 47–53). It was then the downward shift on such profit rates, as wage pressures on capital contributed to a slackening of private sector interest in productive accumulation, which contributed to the subsequent crisis conditions up to the 1980s, as taken up in chapter 5. For Hobsbawm, this means that in Latin America by the 1970s there was *no* country in which peasants were not a minority, whereas sub-Saharan Africa, South and continental Southeast Asia, and China stood as the only regions of the globe still essentially dominated by rural production. Accordingly, it has been stated that the epochal significance of this transformation is clear.

The mere fact that the peasantry has ceased to constitute the actual majority of the population in many parts of the world, that it has for practical purposes disappeared in some . . . and that its disappearance as a class today is quite conceivable in many developed countries, separates the period since the eighteenth century from all previous history since the development of agriculture. (Hobsbawm 1999: 198)

Stemming from this he proposed that the specific variety of subalternity, poverty, exploitation, and oppression encapsulated by the peasantry and its relation to land and production would lead to the gradual political disintegration of its class identity. Peasants, in his view, would become more and more incapable of enforcing their class interests, or organizing themselves as a class through representative organizations; although Hobsbawm has nevertheless stepped back from indicating their complete dismissal as a current of political agency (Hobsbawm 1999: 219–22). Elsewhere, one can find similar additional support for the claim about the gradual erosion of the peasantry as a social class. For example, in terms of transnational patterns of production and consumption making the peasant anachronistic and creating postpeasant identities (Kearney 1996). Or, similarly, in terms of the ways in which a proletarianization of the peasantry has ensued in light of the restructuring of traditional agricultural production by transnational capital toward nontraditional agricultural exports (NTAEs), such as fruits, cut flowers, ornamental plants, winter vegetables, and spices (Coates 2000: 256; Cammack 2002: 126–27; Robinson 2003: 252–58). These developments have led the UN Food and Agriculture Organization, at the annual Regional Conference for Latin America and the Caribbean, to state that the rural population in the region is doomed to disappear.[1]

What these claims tend to neglect, though, is precisely the constitution and reproduction of peasants through the dynamics of capital accumulation, which were fundamental to the discussion in chapter 2. The insight that the peasantry would be confronted with conditions of "multilineal evolution," neither constantly residing as direct producers nor moving inevitably through capitalist social relations, has been seemingly overlooked (see Hewitt de Alcántara 1984: 162). After all, following the onset of capitalism, the process of uneven and combined development is complicated by the way in which the organization of human sociality becomes overlain with different extractive relations of production (Wolf 1997: 73–75). There is a risk, then, that emergent processes in not only transforming but also in maintaining and resisting these relations of production in capitalist society and modern state formation are neglected. This is a problem that equally bedevils theorizing on the conditions of passive revolution. It was something that Antonio Gramsci was acutely drawn to consider in his realization of the utility and dangers of the thesis of passive revolution "as an interpretation of the Risorgimento, and of every epoch characterised by complex historical upheavals" leading to transformations to capitalist modernity. Hence "danger of historical defeatism, i.e., of indifferentism, since the whole way of posing the question may induce a belief in some kind of fatalism" (Gramsci 1971: 114, Q15§62). In order to retain the concept as a dialectical one, then, the articulation of new forms of struggle against the renewal of capitalism have to be considered and proposed, which is the purpose of this chapter in probing the agenda of "anti-passive revolution" strategies and spaces of resistance in Mexico (Buci-Glucksmann 1979: 232). While, therefore, the trend at the heart of claims about the "death of the peasantry" *may* be evident, it is important to avoid a view of defeatism or fatalism. This is so because the processes of class formation evident in the transformation of the peasantry through which a range of productive activities are combined means that there are forms of purposeful agency articulated by the peasantry as a subaltern class linked to their spatial (re)constitution within the changing dynamics of capital accumulation (see Bernstein 2000). In Mexico, the action of groups like the Ejército Zapatista de Liberación Nacional (EZLN) would seemingly challenge the thesis about the inevitable demise of the peasantry and warn against the fatalism inherent in the thesis of passive revolution. Specific attention to the EZLN is merited given that its emergence and continuance is notably shaped by the enduring conditions of uneven and combined capitalist development, "combined because capitalism forms a system on a world scale . . . [and] uneven because development is not linear, homogenous, and continuous" (de Janvry 1981: 1). At the same time, these features also resonate with familiar motifs of peasant movements in earlier transitions to capitalism, thus raising new issues about the old "agrarian question" (Bernstein 2002; Brass 2002).

The aim of this chapter is to retrace the novel form of political agency characterizing the EZLN and thus its antipassive revolution strategies and spaces of its resistance. This movement is significant for three main reasons. First, the EZLN was itself cognizant of the historically uneven and combined development of capital accumulation in Mexico and how this has impacted on regional conditions in the southern state of Chiapas, to be discussed below. This context of uneven and combined development has an enduring contemporary significance given that, throughout the period 1994–2003, foreign direct investment in Chiapas came to no more than $8.94 million, tiny in comparison to the $127,000 million that entered Mexico in the same period (Villafuerte Solís 2005: 476). It would therefore be erroneous to assume that transnational capital is universally transforming the rural landscape in Chiapas and penetrating "every nook and cranny" (see Robinson 2007: 143). Following the lead in chapter 4, one needs to be more circumspect about the contemporary configuration of global capitalism and its supplanting of local space.

Second, the crisis in the rural economy has witnessed the exodus of peasants to labor markets in the north of Mexico and the United States, with remittances close to $500 million per year in 2004–2005, comparable to the value of basic grains and the local state's three principal export commodities (coffee, bananas, and mangoes) (Villafuerte Solís 2005: 478–79). It would be mistaken, though, to assume that this exodus is simply leading to the proletarianization of the peasantry given that peasants in Chiapas have responded to the changing dynamics of capital accumulation with a range of productive activities and novel forms of agency, as detailed shortly.

Third, the focus on the EZLN is all the more important in order to avoid the exclusion of class solidarities from other forms of collective agency, commonly associated with ethnic, gendered, or racial identities. It would be mistaken to draw a binary line between class solidarities and ascriptive collective identities. Hence the importance of recognizing how class content "subsists" in the mobilization of social movements along with other identities (Foweraker 1995: 40; Hellman 1995: 170–71). My argument is that the EZLN is understood better as a resistance movement to neoliberalism linked to *class struggle* over the exploitation of the natural and social substratum, which has to be grasped in terms of its novel and purposeful form of political agency. After all, "rural movements today constitute the core nucleus of opposition to neoliberalism and the most important sources of democratic transformation in national and international politics" (Moyo and Yeros 2005: 6, 9). Consequently, the EZLN is granted detailed attention in this chapter in contesting the modern state in Mexico not least because it has acted as an intersection for wider movements of resistance, as the subsequent discussion will elaborate. Understanding the Zapatista experience is therefore pivotal to reconsidering the construction and contestation of the modern state in Mexico as a passive revolution. After all, as Luis Lorenzano (1998: 154) frames it, this condition of state formation is marked by the "incompletion of modernity" within which spaces of resistance are always present.

In order to realize this focus the chapter investigates the dynamics of anti-passive revolution strategies and spaces of resistance through a focus on the EZLN with three principal sections organizing the argument. The first section considers the peasantry as a *subaltern class* by unraveling Antonio Gramsci's own methodological criteria in understanding the history of subaltern classes to analyze instances of resistance and the interplay of ruler and ruled (see also Gilly 2006: 80–86). What emerges from this is a consideration of the growth of radical peasant organizations in Chiapas linked to transformations in property relations within the context of the restructuring of capital and the rise of neoliberalism on a global scale. Content is therefore added here to John Ross's (1995: 292) comment that "to the politilogue, the EZLN is located much closer to Antonio Gramsci than Karl Marx." In this section, the response of the EZLN is situated within the era of structural change in the 1970s, also considered in chapter 4, in which the logic of capitalist social relations shifted toward neoliberal policy priorities and when a capitalist type of state became more dominant. The roots of the rebellion are therefore analyzed by focusing on the changing forms and relations of production in Chiapas during the 1970s, which led to a growth of radical peasant organizations that would influence the formation of the EZLN. As a result of this analysis, issues arise concerning the intersection of class-based and indigenous forms of identity asserted by the EZLN. Hence appreciating how the movement is situated within the recomposition of labor and class struggle in Mexico (Veltmeyer 1997; Veltmeyer 2000). There are territories in revolt in Mexico and indigenous movements for autonomy are demanding the refounding of the state itself by expressing a class antagonism aiming to bridge *los de abajo* (Gibler 2009: 203–4).

In the second section, the more contemporary context of the rebellion is then discussed in relation to the restructuring of capital represented by the rise of neoliberalism. The latter is most significantly epitomized by the coexistent implementation of the North American Free Trade Agreement (NAFTA) in Mexico. Yet here the emphasis is on demonstrating how spatial practices of resistance are embedded in dimensions of territoriality that are not simply global but also local in form (see Bobrow-Strain 2007; Stahler-Sholk 2008). The spatialization strategies of the EZLN are articulated across multiple scales in asserting space for self-organization and in attempting to territorialize itself into a movement at national and global scales. In the third section, the innovative spaces of struggle developed by the EZLN are then analyzed within the context and categories of resistance developed by Antonio Gramsci. The forms of political representation developed by the EZLN in resisting neoliberal restructuring are thus analyzed in relation to how they have pressed claims and asserted autonomy within a critique of social power relations in Mexico. Attention is drawn specifically to what is termed here the three spaces of its autonomous practice of resistance, based on (1) alternative economy organizing, (2) self-sufficient educational projects, and (3) health care provision. The account therefore encompasses both specific changes to production relations that affected the rise of the EZLN while embedding these within the geopolitical conditions of uneven and combined development. What emerges, in conclusion, is an appreciation of the peasantry as a subaltern class that in the case of the EZLN also focuses on the subjective implications of political consciousness, processes of agency in contesting spaces of neoliberalism, and therefore the role that the peasantry still plays as a social class in the modern world.[2]

SUBALTERN CLASS AGENCY AND CHANGES TO THE
SOCIAL RELATIONS OF PRODUCTION

Through an emphasis on the sociocultural interplay between ruler and ruled, Antonio Gramsci advocated a focus on class struggles within which both domination *and* resistance could be analyzed. It is an emphasis also shared by Walter Benjamin in wanting to draw attention to history that was written less from the standpoint of the "victor" and more from that of the class struggle and "anonymous toil" of their contemporaries (Benjamin 1940/1970: 246–48). Here, Gramsci's own methodological criteria on the history of subaltern classes are useful as a point of departure in order to analyze alternative historical and contemporary contexts (Gramsci 1971: 52–55, Q25§2, Q25§5). According to Gramsci, the specific history of subaltern classes is intertwined with that of state–civil society relations more generally. It is therefore important to try and unravel such contestations. One way of doing so is to identify the "objective" formation of subaltern social classes by analyzing developments and transformations within the sphere of production (Gramsci 1971: 52, Q25§5). This advances an understanding of the "decisive nucleus of economic activity" but without succumbing to expressions of economism (Gramsci 1971: 161, Q13§18). Historical and contemporary research therefore needs to incorporate, as much as possible, a consideration of the mentalities and ideologies of subaltern classes, their active as well as passive affiliation to dominant social forms of political association, and thus their involvement in formations that might conserve dissent or maintain control (Gramsci 1971: 52, Q25§5). Additionally, such a method entails focusing on the formations that subaltern classes themselves produce (e.g., trade unions, workers' cooperatives, or peasant associations), which press claims or assert autonomy within the existing "relations of force." Questions of historical and political consciousness expressed by subaltern classes can then be raised. As Adolfo Gilly (2006: 83) puts it, "in the Gramscian conception . . . each form of state or state community is a complex field of forces and in constant movement and conflict." Or, as Gramsci writes, "the history of subaltern social groups is necessarily fragmented and episodic," to the extent that "subaltern groups are always subject to the activity of ruling groups, even when they rebel and rise up" (Gramsci 1971: 54–55, Q25§2). What emerges, then, is a methodology of subaltern class analysis embedded within a historical materialist political strategy of transformation (Green 2002: 19–20). These methodological insights can be useful in tracing the combination of developments that exacerbated the agrarian landscape in Chiapas to precipitate social mobilization.

Chiapas, as a region, has been inserted into capitalist relations of uneven and combined development affecting Mexico as a whole since, at least, the Mexican Revolution (1910–1920). Following the 1920s, land reform in Chiapas forged political compliance among indigenous highland communities that engendered exploitation of the peasantry and promoted dependent capitalism. Resident laborers (*acasillados*) that were previously tied to the land had a legal claim to property after the Mexican Revolution but labor exploitation shifted to sharecroppers (*aparceros*), day laborers (*jornaleros*), and seasonally contracted workers (*enganchados*) that were all excluded from agrarian reform (Rus 2004: 215). In Chiapas, by 1940, there still existed 773 large estates (*latifundios*) of more than 2,500 acres; 21 of these were made up of more than 100,000 acres and a further 9 had more than 175,000 acres (Rus 2004: 214). Across Mexico, once the original claims of redistribution made by Emiliano Zapata in Morelos had been invalidated by the policies of Álvaro Obregón, land reform was undertaken in the name of the state (Collier 1987: 95). As observed in chapter 2, land reform was regarded as an instrument of social control to pacify rebellious campesinos and create communities of cheap workers near commercial farm operations (Barry 1995: 20). At the local level in Chiapas, the institutionalization of clientelistic practices formed the basis for an authoritarian state assuring the concentration of land and capital by private owners in, or beyond, the central highlands albeit with local differentiations. This radical dispossession ensured an increased labor supply for agricultural expansion and the extension of the extraction of surplus value under the tutelage of the state (Lorenzano 1998: 152; Rus et al., 2003: 3).

In Chiapas, then, even during the administration of Lázaro Cárdenas (1934–1940), agrarian reform left almost intact the power of the regional elite to the extent that redistribution did not disguise the capacity of large landowners to resist many of the "revolutionary" programs (Serrano 1997: 78). By the 1940s, the process of penetrating and willingly binding Indian communities in Chiapas to the reformist party-state was complete. As Jan Rus (1994: 281, emphasis added) comments: "By the time the PRM [Partido de la Revolución Mexicana] became the PRI . . . in the mid-forties [1946], the former self-defensive, closed communities of the Chiapas highlands had become *integral parts* of the party's local machine." This situation was maintained by a series of ties connecting dominant family elites in Chiapas and bilingual indigenous *caciques* (powerbrokers) in the region, known as scribe-principales, who positioned themselves between class fractions of the Partido Revolucionario Institucional (PRI) and local elites. As a result, Chiapas has been described as an internal colony providing the rest of Mexico with oil, electricity, timber, cattle, corn, sugar, coffee, and beans. Up to the 1980s, while only having 3 percent of the total population, the region as a whole produced 54 percent of the country's hydroelectric power, 13 percent of Mexico's maize (corn), 13 percent of the country's gas, 5 percent of the timber, 4 percent of the beans, and 4 percent of its oil (Collier with Quaratiello 1994: 16). Despite changing political climates, then, Chiapas has been aptly described as a rich land consisting of poor people (Benjamin 1996).

Changing Forms and Relations of Production: Structural Change in Chiapas

It was particularly from the 1970s onward that a conjunction of several factors proved particularly crucial in precipitating social mobilization in Chiapas. A combination of migrant flows influenced by changes in production and land demands, the expansion of cattle ranching forcing the relocation of peasants, ambitious state projects negatively impacting on peasant subsistence, an energy boom skewing peasant and commercial agriculture, and the subsequent impact of neoliberal policies on state programs and policies of support all exacerbated the agrarian landscape in Chiapas. Therefore, rather than peasants being unaccustomed to change, communities underwent constant readjustment during this period that led to a crucial reorganization of local social organization (Rus 1995: 71–89). "But this purported 'modernisation,'" writes Gilly (1997: 57), "occurred without any substantial change in the corporatist political structures upon which were based the domination and reproduction of the national and local political régime." Yet the reaction to the dynamics of capitalism and fundamental changes to the way of life for certain communities in Chiapas would pose challenges that eventually began to undermine the minimal hegemony and institutionalized control of social conflict organized through the PRI, with peasant movements experiencing a greater degree of autonomy.

During the 1950s and 1960s agrarian reform laws began to promote an influx of indigenous immigrants into eastern areas in Chiapas, notably in the Selva Lacandona (Lacandón jungle), which were then followed by a second wave migration of cattle ranchers from Tabasco and Veracruz (Nations 1994: 31–33). Areas, principally in the Lacandón jungle and Simojovel in the eastern parts of the state, became settlement or colonizing frontiers so that "by the 1970s, immigrants from other areas of Mexico joined the flow of highland Indians into the east [of Chiapas] under Luis Echeverría's populist promotion of colonisation" (Collier 1994a: 372). According to George Collier (1994b: 110), around 57 percent of land in the southeast of Mexico came to be held in the tenure of *ejidos* or agrarian collectives by the 1970s. Yet these were primarily marginal, rain-fed lands leaving developed and irrigated lands relatively unaffected by agrarian reforms in the hands of private commercial agriculture. The distinction is important because communities became dependent on migratory labor for economic survival, due to the very marginal nature of land titles, which increased their vulnerability to the series of crises that impacted on agriculture in Chiapas during the 1970s and 1980s.

It is with reference to energy development and the linked oil boom in the 1970s that material and social bases of community existence in Chiapas particularly began to alter. A crucial consequence of this form of development was the impact of the Organization of Petroleum Exporting Countries (OPEC) oil crisis on communities in Chiapas that skewed production away from the fragile agricultural sector toward large-scale development projects (Rus 1995: 78). One of the roots of the Zapatista rebellion can therefore be linked to the pernicious impact the oil boom had in restructuring the social relations of production in Chiapas.

> After the OPEC oil crisis in 1972, Mexico borrowed internationally to expand oil production for export and to finance ambitious projects of development. During the resulting development boom, Mexico's agriculture declined from 14% of GDP in 1965 to just 7% of GDP in 1982, as resources for production flowed into other sectors. Mexico, propelled by energy development, became more and more oriented towards foreign markets and away from food self-sufficiency. (Collier 1994c: 16)

A feature of this was an expansion of Gulf coastal and inland oil production facilities in Tabasco, Campeche, and adjacent areas to Chiapas while huge hydroelectric dam projects were added along the Grijalva river basin at Las Peñitas, La Angostura, and Chicoasén. The populist promotion of agricultural policies during the Luis Echeverría administration (1970–1976) was then succeeded by the oil-led boom of the López Portillo administration (1976–1982) so that Chiapas became the productive source of 50 percent of Mexico's electric power and most of its petroleum (Collier, Mountjoy, and Nigh 1994: 398–407). Significantly, Petróleos Mexicanos (PEMEX) became responsible for 45 percent of all government expenditures in Chiapas in 1975, an amount that itself was three times the level all branches of government had spent in Chiapas in 1970 (Cancian and Brown 1994: 23). One result was the emergence of a class fraction of interests, termed the "Southeastern Cartel," that linked the old dominant political class, the *familia chiapaneca*, to modern forms of agroindustrial capital, construction, and resource extraction as well as elements of money laundering and narco-trafficking across Chiapas and Veracruz, Tabasco, Campeche, and Yucatán (see García de León 1994/2003: 26).

The above state-led projects of development had several consequences in the central highlands of Chiapas, principally drawing peasants into off-farm wages and entrepreneurial opportunities in transport and commerce, linked to the energy industry, or out of agriculture and into wage-work as unskilled laborers in construction (Collier 1994b: 115). These changes in the social relations of production resulted in distinctions being drawn between subsistence-producing peasants and those involved in wage labor. In particular, productive relations became more class based while gender and generational differences were also heightened by new meanings associated with work. This change in the social relations of production signified a move away from the politics of rank-based forms of organization, based on community hierarchies, to the politics of class-based forms of organization in Chiapas (Collier 1994d). It was an emergent process of class formation, to draw from E. P. Thompson (1978), whereby particular communities experienced new structures of exploitation and identified new points of antagonistic interest centered around issues of class struggle, even though forms of class consciousness—involving a conscious identity of common interests—may not have immediately formed.

In Chiapas, these issues of class struggle arose when peasant communities sought to resolve antagonisms less through the rank-based social ties and communal commitments of civil-religious hierarchies and more through cash derived from wage-work or through factions associated with political parties (Collier 1994d: 9–16). Yet this transformation did not simply equate with the death of the peasantry as a social class and thus as a form of political agency. Instead the situation was a mix of agricultural petty commodity production alongside the exchange of wage labor and other economic activities (Kovic 2003: 61). For instance, the attractiveness of wage-work over peasant agriculture during the 1970s did draw communities in Chiapas into a capitalist social division of labor but this became an especially vulnerable and acute situation after the collapse of Mexico's oil-fueled development in 1982. This meant that peasants had to then return to agricultural production alongside developing a mix of economic activities within the context of growing class stratification and changing processes of capitalist accumulation. Under these conditions of recomposition, peasantries experience processes of semi-proletarianization combining wage labor with a range of agricultural petty commodity production (Kay 2000: 130–31). As peasants became further excluded from processes of capitalist accumulation and detrimentally affected by rapidly changing social relations of production they began to embrace new forms of political organization. These increasingly emerged outside the minimal hegemony of the PRI. Drawing from the above methodological insights, this raises the importance of analyzing, beyond the sphere of production, the increasingly class-based conflict represented by the growth of new peasant organizations in the 1970s. Hence attention turns to the formations that subaltern groups themselves produced, which were constituted through radical consciousness-raising efforts, prior to the appearance of the EZLN.

Consciousness Raising and the Growth of Radical Peasant Organizations

It has been argued, without presumably wishing to overstate matters, that the formation of the EZLN movement is only intelligible if related to the pastoral and community work of Bishop Samuel Ruiz García (MacEoin 1996: 19).[3] Ruiz was the bishop of San Cristóbal diocese from 1960 to 1999 and cultivated contacts with French and Italian intellectual priests, clerical sociologists, and anthropologists of development throughout the 1960s (Womack 1999: 27–28). As a result, there were efforts in Chiapas to promote forms of social action and consciousness raising within the diocese. According to John Womack (1999: 23) an emphasis was placed on a form of critical reflection that involved taking cognizance and questioning received faith, wisdom, and conventions as a move toward becoming active subjects in response to changing material circumstances. At first, this approach in Chiapas reproduced vertical or top-down power relations based on the pedagogical position of lay preachers or catechists (Harvey 1998: 72). However, due to the central importance placed on constant reflection, there was a dialectical relation between the raising of a critical consciousness among the people of Chiapas and the very role of lay preachers or catechists (MacEoin 1996: 29). As Samuel Ruiz himself put the transformation, "I came to San Cristóbal to convert the poor, but they ended up converting me" (as cited in Womack 1999: 27). It was a situation whereby, following Gramsci (1971: 350, Q10II§44), "every teacher is always a pupil and every pupil a teacher." What emerged, therefore, was a different, more reciprocal and participatory, relationship between leaders and led.

Importantly, the consciousness-raising efforts carried out by catechists in Chiapas operated within the overall context of liberation theology and the growing influence of *comunidades eclesiales de base* (Christian base communities) across Latin America. Gaining impetus from the organizational work of the Medellín Council of Latin American Bishops (Colombia, 1968), there followed a rise in indigenous deacons in Chiapas throughout the 1970s that created community leaders who inspired new forms of collective political and economic action targeted toward land and political rights (Harvey 1998: 73–76). Within this context, the pivotal role played by Bishop Samuel Ruiz in shifting people's ideas about the changing social situation can be understood as the agency of an organic intellectual. As noted in chapter 5, this refers to the action of somebody organically connected to social class forces with the task of "systematically and patiently ensuring that this force is formed, developed, and rendered ever more homogeneous, compact and self-aware" (Gramsci 1971: 185, Q13§17). However, in contrast to the discussion of organic intellectuals earlier in this book (see chapter 5), the connectedness or "organic quality" of Samuel Ruiz was rather different, less institutionalized within the dominant form of state power. His social function broke with a conventional understanding of the role of the priesthood as a separate caste or that of a "traditional intellectual" detached from the people (Gramsci 1996: 173–74, Q4§33). Instead, awareness among the people of the exploitative nature underpinning social relations linked to changes in production was actively constructed and brought about through education and the development of a critical consciousness in an attempt to overcome everyday taken-for-granted attitudes.[4] Further, in an interview with Yvon Le Bot (1997: 132), Subcomandante Marcos has commented on the wider formation of leaders within the indigenous communities allied with the *mestizos* to become

> another movement that we could call an indigenous politicised elite, with great organisational capacity, with a very rich experience in political struggle. They were practically in all the political organisations of the left . . . [and] had figured that to address the problems of land, living conditions, and political rights, the only way out was violence.[5]

Indicative of such organic intellectuality were also Ruiz's ethical reflections on the causes of uneven development in Chiapas. For example:

> The objectives of the global economic system, and in particular the excesses committed under its processes of production, are causing irreparable damage to natural resources and must be transformed. This problem has emerged in Chiapas not because of anything particular to Chiapas, but because the uprising took place as concern was growing about the concrete global threat created by the productive system. (as cited in Rosen and Burt 1997: 43)

Equally crucial was the involvement of groups, such as the Línea Proletaria and later the Fuerzas de Liberación Nacional (FLN), in radical community organizing in Chiapas up to the 1970s that then further consolidated social and autonomous forms of peasant organization outside the minimal hegemony of the PRI (La Botz 1995: 34).[6] It was from within the complex waxing and waning of peasant organizations as well as the involvement of embryonic forms such as the FLN throughout the 1970s and 1980s that the EZLN would eventually emerge (see Harvey 1990; Harvey 1995: 39–73; Tello Díaz 1995: 62–85).

Overall, new peasant networks progressed with a less centralized structure and a more critical stance toward the role of conventional political parties while rejecting dependency on the leadership of particular individuals (Harvey 1988: 299–312). It was also a trend that was emblematic of a reconfiguration of state–civil society relations across Mexico in light of a crisis in the PRI's minimal hegemony and increased state-coercive elements, as discussed in chapter 4. "As mobilisation and land invasions increased, so did repression. The decade of the 1970s was dominated by forced eviction of invaded land, overt repression, massive arrests and assassination of agrarian leaders" (Serrano 1997: 90). The formation of radical peasant organizations within the context of changing forms of social relations of production in the 1970s also began to experience the assault of neoliberal restructuring in the 1980s. Hence, rather than a simple expression of fluctuating *conjunctural* events, resembling a coincidence of spontaneous or occasional responses, it is possible to situate the rise of the EZLN within a series of *organic* developments linked to the emergence of a neoliberal strategy of capitalist accumulation and the consolidation of a capitalist type of state. The clarification is important because whereas conjunctural movements stem from immediate circumstances, organic developments derive from more enduring predicaments.

> Conjunctural phenomena . . . do not have any far-reaching historical significance; they give rise to political criticism of a minor, day-to-day character, which has as its subject top political leaders and personalities with direct governmental responsibilities. Organic phenomena on the other hand give rise to socio-historical criticism, whose subject is wider social groupings—beyond the public figures and beyond the top leaders. (Gramsci 1971: 177–78, Q13§17)

Hence the importance of considering the significance of the "far-reaching socio-historical criticism" expressed by the EZLN in relation to the accumulation strategy of neoliberalism and the attempt to fully establish a capitalist type of state.

THE ACCUMULATION STRATEGY OF NEOLIBERALISM AND AGRARIAN REFORM

As observed in chapter 4, the administration of Carlos Salinas de Gortari (1988–1994) enacted a new phase of capitalist accumulation that involved neoliberal restructuring of the social relations of production. Efforts to reconstitute and redefine the old basis of minimal hegemony maintained by the PRI entailed reconstructing, but not dismantling, the previous form of state in Mexico (Nash and Kovic 1996). This particularly involved attempts at reconstituting old populist and clientelist forms of co-optation (or *trasform-ismo*) through new targeted social programs such as the Programa Nacional de Solidaridad (PRONASOL). Therefore, the recomposition of capital on a global scale under the rubric of neoliberal restructuring proceeded in Mexico along lines that involved attempts to rearticulate a minimal form of hegemony through a material and political discourse known as *salinismo* (see Salinas de Gortari 2002). The EZLN rebellion on 1 January 1994 was thus a response against both the global strategy of neoliberal capitalist accumulation as well as the specific discourse of *salinismo* in Mexico that peaked with the implementation of NAFTA (Zermeño 1997). Hence NAFTA was announced by the Zapatistas as a "death sentence" for the ethnic peoples of Mexico and Subcomandante Marcos declared that the rebellion "isn't just about Chiapas—it's about NAFTA and Salinas's whole neoliberal project."[7] It was therefore no coincidence that the EZLN rebellion was orchestrated on the very same day that NAFTA came into effect.

One of the principal measures of neoliberal restructuring in Mexico was reforming the agrarian sector. During the 1970s increases in state revenues from petroleum exports helped to sustain agricultural subsidies, which became embodied within the Sistema Alimentario Mexicano (SAM) in 1980. However, although annual subsidies stimulated national maize production among peasant producers, the international market for oil prices and the debt crisis eliminated the financial base of SAM and the attempt to implement redistributive food policies (Fox 1993). During the administration of Miguel de la Madrid (1982–1988), rather than public programs to stimulate maize production, marketing, and consumption,

> the Mexican government reaffirmed its commitment to meet its international financial obligations, thus committing a major proportion of the federal budget to debt servicing, and began a process of crisis management, oriented toward markedly reducing the level of subsidies and cutting back social services, selling off state-owned enterprises and postponing investment in the physical infrastructure of the country. (Hewitt de Alcántara 1994: 8)

Between 1987 and 1989 the price for maize plummeted, contributing to a deepening recession in the countryside while those maize producers operating at a loss increased from 43 to 65 percent between 1987 and 1988 (Hewitt de Alcántara 1994: 12). Within the context of neoliberal restructuring and the move to secure a capitalist type of state there was, linking back to the discussion in chapter 4, an overhaul of the agricultural sector that involved the privatization of state-owned enterprises and the withdrawal of price supports and subsidies associated with World Bank demands (Gilly 1997: 63). Notably the state-owned Instituto Mexicano del Café (INMECAFÉ), established in 1958, was also dismantled under the privatization policies of *salinismo* that meant a withdrawal from purchasing and marketing functions and the reduction of technical assistance. The collapse of world coffee prices by 50 percent in 1989 compounded this withdrawal and exacerbated the plight of rural communities with small-holders in the areas of Ocosingo, Las Margaritas, and Los Altos in Chiapas abandoning production between 1989 and 1993. The restructuring of the state and the reconfiguring of the PRI's minimal hegemony, as part of the rise of the accumulation strategy of neoliberalism, therefore also included fundamental reform of the agricultural sector. Among other issues, this reform involved altering the pivotal status of collective *ejido* landholdings.

This entailed reforming Article 27 of the Mexican Constitution of 1917 that ostensibly enshrined the *ejido* as central to collective land ownership. Yet the *ejido* also ensured a form of political and organizational state control because it became the principal vehicle for state regulation of peasant access to land and therefore helped to maintain political control over the peasantry (see chapter 2). However, under the *ejido* reform, lands could be legally sold, bought, rented, or used as collateral for loans; private companies could purchase lands; new associations between capitalist developers and *ejidatarios* (*ejido* owners) were allowed; and provisions for peasants to petition for land redistribution were deleted, formally ending the process of land distribution, with primacy given to private property relations (N. Harvey 1996: 194–95). Yet conclusions asserting the wholesale destruction of rural communities on the basis of changes to the *ejido* agrarian code should be muted. The collective status of such landholdings was more apparent than real as there was an ongoing capitalization of rural production even before the reform of Article 27, as also noted in chapter 3. The symbolic break, though, with past agrarian reform was pivotal and destroyed any future hope of land redistribution among the peasantry (Harvey 1998: 188). This loss of hope would be compounded by the realization that reform of the agrarian code would *accelerate* the capitalist transformation of agricultural productive relations (Collier 1994b: 124). The gradual elimination of restrictions on maize imports initiated over a fifteen-year period, under NAFTA—with average yields of maize in Mexico at 1.7 tons/hectare compared to 6.9 tons/hectare in the United States—would tend to support this view and thus agricultural land would become increasingly abandoned by small-holders (DeWalt, Ress, and Murphy 1994: 56).

One result of this neoliberal restructuring of the agrarian sector was that social and institutional bases of peasant representation linked to the *ejido* system were fundamentally altered (de Janvry, Gordillo, and Sadoulet 1997). This meant that, as the privatization of communal *ejido* landholdings proceeded, alternative institutional organizations had to be constructed in an attempt to reestablish and redefine the class rule of passive revolution. Yet this proved increasingly difficult as more autonomous forms of peasant mobilization in Chiapas, discussed earlier, developed outside the institutional organization of the PRI. In response, the PRI resorted to attempts to define and limit the conditions within which peasant associations could emerge to ensure their continual absorption, disaggregation, and neutralization. With such aims in mind, as a consequence of the gradual elimination of price subsidies within NAFTA, a new support program for the Mexican agricultural sector was announced in 1993 known as the Programa Nacional de Apoyos Directos al Campo (PROCAMPO). As the first disbursements were initiated just prior to the 1994 national elections it was clear that PROCAMPO subsidies were really only a palliative. They not only resulted in benefiting local merchants and private intermediaries rather than rural producers but they also, over the medium to long term, excluded small peasant producers (Harvey 1998: 183). At the same time, PRONASOL funds were also allocated for similar purposes amounting to some $15 billion throughout the whole period of the Salinas *sexenio* (Cornelius 1996: 59). Notably Chiapas itself was targeted with more PRONASOL funds than any other state, receiving $192 million in 1993 (Cornelius 1995: 148). However, such funds were diverted by the clientelistic politics of state governor Patrocinio González Garrido (1988–1992).

During this neoliberal phase of restructuring conflicts between and within peasant groups in the highland communities of Chiapas were also encouraged, especially during the governorships of Absalón Castellanos (1984–1988) and Patrocino González Garrido (1988–1992) (García de León 1995: 10–13). This indicated that the old basis of PRI rule was becoming increasingly undercut by neoliberal restructuring to the agrarian sector. The subsequent "crisis of authority" in Mexico faced by the PRI is appropriately captured in the following comment from Gramsci:

> The separation of civil society from political society: a new problem of hegemony has been posed; in other words, *the historical basis of the state has been displaced*. There is an extreme form of political society: either to combat the new and preserve what is tottering by consolidating it coercively or, as an expression of the new, to smash the resistance it encounters in its expansion. (Gramsci 2007: 178, Q7§28, emphasis added)

In an attempt to redefine the historical basis of the state in Mexico, social and institutional bases of peasant control were altered through the implementation of policies such as PRONASOL and PROCAMPO. Yet the recourse to violent repression at this time was indicative of the coercion directed through the state and the relations of minimal hegemony characteristic of passive revolution. A policy of impunity to human rights violations also particularly emerged in Mexico throughout the 1980s and 1990s.[8] Between 1994 and 1996, this manifested itself in Chiapas with the assassination of over one hundred activists linked to the center-left Partido de la Revolución Democrática (PRD) (Kampwirth 1998: 47n11). Estimated troop deployments in Chiapas since 1994 have ranged from 12,000 to 74,000 with the latter representing at least a third of the total Mexican Federal Army.[9] This has resulted in the militarization of over one-third of Chiapas including seventeen major military barracks, forty-four semipermanent military installations, and the deployment of one soldier for every three or four inhabitants of every community (Stephen 1997: 10–11). One report put together by a group of human rights organizations in Chiapas, including the "Fray Bartolomé de las Casas" Human Rights Centre established by Samuel Ruiz in San Cristóbal in 1989, noted that the annual cost of this deployment was conservatively estimated to be $200 million. The report also raised suspicion about nightly low-level flights to spread marijuana seeds in the conflict area as a pretext to justifying an escalated military campaign against narco-trafficking.[10] The result was a stark increase in paramilitary activity that involved groups such as Los Chinchulines, Tomás Munster, Movimiento Indígena Revolucionario Anti-Zapatista, Másacara Roja, Fuerzas Armadas del Pueblo, and, the largest, Paz y Justicia. A local PRI deputy, Samuel Sánchez Sánchez, admitted to being the spokesperson and leader of Paz y Justicia, while the Movimiento Indígena Revolucionario Anti-Zapatista had reported links to PRI federal deputy Norberto Santiz López.[11] The participants of such paramilitaries were commonly made up of young men divorced from the means of production, with no land or reliable means of subsistence, the result therefore of the government's agricultural policies of neoliberal restructuring (Aubry and Inda 1998: 9; Barmeyer 2003: 132–34).

Notably it was this climate of violence and the problems of internal divisions within excluded communities that came together in the massacre of forty-five people in Acteal in the highlands of Chiapas, twelve miles north of San Cristóbal, on 22 December 1997. These people belonged to a group called Sociedad Civil las Abejas who had close links to Samuel Ruiz but were nonviolent EZLN sympathizers that had fled the nearby Zapatista bulwark of Chenalhó in an effort to escape paramilitary violence (Nadal 1998a: 18–25). Following the Acteal massacre the official state justifications for a policy of coercion were shifted from a "war on drugs" to preventing further acts of "inter-ethnic war" (Gall 1998: 531–44). "From this point onwards," Antonio García de León (2005: 520) has explained, "the state was no longer able to control Chiapas without a strong policy of militarization, which made it impossible to sustain the electoral triumph of the PRI in the region." As

Luis Hernández Navarro (1998: 8) has added, "within the logic of counterin-
surgency, the massacre also serves as exemplary punishment for those who
dare to challenge the local and national hegemony of the ruling party." This
was coupled with the arbitrary exclusion of foreign citizens known as a policy
of "political cleansing." Between 1996 and 1997, immigration authorities
expelled 60 foreigners with a further 141 "invited" to leave, while in January 1998 the International Committee for the Red Cross (ICRC) was ordered
to cease operations in Chiapas (Nadal 1998b: 20–22). These expulsions included the director of Mexico Solidarity Network (MSN), Tom Hansen, and
Michel Chanteau, the former French Catholic priest of the Tzotzil community
of Chenalhó, who was expelled after thirty-five years of service in the community.

   Several issues emerge from the above discussion, which are worth highlighting before analyzing further the EZLN's antipassive revolution strategies
and spaces of resistance. Most significantly, the specific struggle in Chiapas
signifies generally the degree of conflict and coercion present at the level of
subnational politics that has entailed hard-line Priísta leaders exercising impunity to ensure their tenure (Cornelius 1999: 11). It is difficult to therefore
argue that the PRI articulated "normal" conditions of hegemony, as outlined
in chapter 1, "characterised by the combination of force and consent, which
balance each other reciprocally, without force predominating excessively over
consent" (Gramsci 1971: 80n4, Q19§24). Rather than an organic equilibrium
based on a relationship between leaders and led, rulers and ruled, expressive of these conditions of hegemony, the PRI became increasingly unable
to conceal its real predominance and relied much more on the state-coercive
element. The situation reflected more the traits of passive revolution in which
the armor of coercion superintends the minimal forms of hegemonic activity (see chapter 1). "As soon as the dominant social group has exhausted its
function," within such conditions of passive revolution, "the ideological bloc
tends to crumble away; then 'spontaneity' may be replaced by 'constraint' in
ever less disguised and indirect forms" (Gramsci 1971: 60–61, Q19§24). Or,
citing a comment from one of Carlos Fuentes's (1987/1990: 29) novels: "The
obvious truth about Mexico is that one system is falling apart on us, but we
have no other system to put in its place" (see chapter 5 on this intellectual's
specific social function in Mexico as a "passive revolutionary").

   The resistance of the EZLN is thus embedded in the history of passive
revolution linked to processes of state formation and the conditions of uneven
and combined development in Mexico examined throughout this book. It is
a reflection of the minimal or "fractured hegemony" marking modern state
formation in Mexico (Van der Haar 2005: 493–96). The struggle of the EZLN
rebellion is best inserted within the history of passive revolution in Mexico,

marked by the attempts of developmental catch-up and its incomplete achievement of modern state formation. As Luis Hernández Navarro (1998: 9) has put it, the crisis in Mexico resulted from "contradictions between a set of political institutions based on top-down corporatist and clientelist relations on the one hand, and an increasingly mature civil society which seeks full participation on the other." It is within this crisis period that the resistance of the EZLN was articulated through various "spatial movements" linking the occupation of physical space with articulations across the spatial sites of the political, the symbolic, and the discursive, both inside and outside Mexico (Gilly 1997: 92). Emerging publicly on 1 January 1994, with a mass base of support and a well-organized army of over three thousand initial combatants, the EZLN occupied the towns of San Cristóbal, Ocosingo, Las Margaritas, Altamirano, Chanal, Oxchuc, and Huixtán. In one statement it was declared to tourists in Chiapas, "The Palenque road is closed—we have taken Ocosingo. I'm sorry for the inconvenience but this is a revolution."[12] The "First Declaration of the Lacandón Jungle" [2 January 1994] announced the demands of work, land, housing, food, health, education, independence, freedom, democracy, justice, and peace (see EZLN 2003, vol. 1: 35). While the decision to resort to armed conflict did not draw a consensus from within the EZLN movement, it nevertheless prevailed as a final option. "We spoke out, but there was no echo," Samuel Ruiz stated. "It took a suicidal peasant insurrection for anyone to pay attention."[13] The following section now highlights further aspects of the EZLN to examine it in relation to its practices of antipassive revolution strategies and spaces of resistance.

EZLN RESISTANCE BEYOND
THE POLITICS OF PASSIVE REVOLUTION

"The ethnic identity of an oppressed people—the Maya—is embraced proudly," observes Bill Weinberg (2000: 193), "but not exalted to the exclusion of common class concerns." At a time when utopias across Latin America were declared by Jorge Castañeda (1994) as unarmed,[14] the EZLN initiated a military offensive against the above processes of neoliberal restructuring, which raised new questions about the options and innovative techniques open to resistance movements. Almost immediately there was a mobilization of different weapons, fusing the materiality of armed struggle with the symbolic importance of particular images and discourses. Various forms of resistance can be combined in challenging the structures of passive revolution, which are ultimately conditioned by the "relation of forces" shaping contending class fractions (Gramsci 1971: 177–85, Q13§17). Specifically, Gramsci differentiated between those based on a "war of manoeuvre" and those involving a "war of position," although these should not be regarded as different extremes or mutually exclusive options but, rather, possibilities located on a spectrum. A "war of manoeuvre" is analogous to a rapid assault targeted directly against the institutions of state power, the capture of which would only prove transitory. Alternatively, a "war of position" is comparable to a form of trench warfare involving an ideological struggle on the cultural front of civil society: to overcome the "powerful system of fortresses and earthworks" requiring a concentration of hegemonic activity "before the rise to power" in an attempt to penetrate and subvert the mechanisms of ideological diffusion (Gramsci 1971: 59, Q19§24; 238, Q6§138). Thus the initial military assault by the EZLN begun in 1994 was a transitory phase in a "war of manoeuvre" signified by their intention to advance onto the capital of the country and defeat the Mexican Federal Army (EZLN 2003, vol. 1: 34). Yet, as Gilly (1997: 84) clarifies, "the rebels had risen up with an objective: to unleash a popular war and demolish the federal government. . . . The opposite in fact occurred." Since this phase, although the armed option has been present but limited, it is possible to highlight the strategy of a shifting "war of position" conducted by the EZLN. This has involved asserting intellectual and moral resistance to confront both the minimal hegemony of the PRI but also wider material social class interests in Mexico that have subsequently been supportive of the accumulation strategy of neoliberalism. Hence, "while Marcos has never declared himself a Gramscian, it is impossible to believe that he has had no exposure to Gramsci" (Bruhn 1999: 44). Within this war of position, various novel features have been adopted by the EZLN to articulate an antipassive revolution struggle of resistance. Five points in this struggle stand as particularly noteworthy: (1) the activation of national and international civil society, (2) the aim to address and establish indigenous rights, (3) the appeal to collective interests beyond the ascriptive identities of ethnicity, (4) the campaign for wider democratization from below, and (5) the constant goal of innovation through new spatial forms of governance within the communities of Chiapas.

First, in terms of the activation of civil society, the EZLN has promoted various forms of mobilization and new forms of organization to gain wider national appeal. This, of course, has included recourse to the media and the Internet, although the effectiveness of the latter has to be assessed in a measured manner (see Hellman 1999). Such civil society activity initially included calling for a Convención Nacional Democrática (CND), in the "Second Declaration of the Lacandón Jungle" [12 June 1994], which was part of the strategy of building up an overall movement within civil society to challenge existing power relations. Ambitiously, it was followed in the "Third Declaration of the Lacandón Jungle" [2 January 1995] by the call for a national liberation movement (EZLN 2003, vol. 2: 187–93). As Javier Elorriaga formulates it: "The idea was: Cardenismo + CND + Zapatismo + EZLN = National Liberation Movement."[15] In the Zapatistas' own spatial formulation:

> The revolution will not end in a new class, faction of a class, or group in power. It will end in a free and democratic "space" for political struggle born above the fetid cadaver of the state-party system and presidentialism. A new political relationship will be born, based not in the confrontation of political organisations among themselves, but in the confrontation of their political proposals with different social classes. (EZLN 2003, vol. 1: 273)

As a result, the CND was organized between 6 and 9 August 1994 in San Cristóbal and a place in the Lacandón jungle renamed Aguascalientes which brought together more than six thousand delegates to deliberate on the need for a transitional government and strategies to promote democracy and develop a coordinated national project (Stephen 1995: 88–99). Despite ultimate failure in influencing the outcome of the national elections on 21 August, this was a clear effort to mobilize civil society as a site of popular antagonism and to try and develop an increase in the spatial growth of the movement across a variety of scales.

Similarly, the aim of activating civil society has been expressed across both national and international scales, for example, represented by the attempt—announced in the "Fourth Declaration of the Lacandón Jungle"—to form an additional political force, on 1 January 1996, called the Frente Zapatista de Liberación Nacional (FZLN). Although described as a "weak-sister political action front" (Ross 2006: 63), the FZLN's aim was to support the EZLN "as a site for citizen political action where there may be a confluence with other political forces of the independent opposition, a space where popular wills may encounter and co-ordinate united actions" (EZLN 2003, vol. 3: 87). In contrast to the processes of democratization from above examined in chapter 6, the Fourth Declaration was "a radically democratic proposal that questioned the illusions of democracy rather than its ideals" (Esteva 2003: 263). The aim was to establish "a political force which does not aspire to take power. A force which is not a political party" (EZLN 2003, vol. 3: 87). Globally, this emphasis of the EZLN impacted on broad "anti-capitalist" resistance movements, with Luca Casarini, the main spokesperson of autonomist resistance active within the European Social Forum (ESF), confirming that inspiration has been drawn from the EZLN (see Hernández Navarro 2004: 3–4). Various international meetings convened by the EZLN both in Mexico (July–August 1996) and in Europe (Spain, July–August 1997), known as intercontinental meetings against neoliberalism, have demonstrated the spatial insertion of such resistance within the global conditions of neoliberalism.

Albeit with modest outcomes, the EZLN became a backstop for the global justice campaign and set precedents for the "anti-capitalist" movement, leading to the subsequent targeting of initiatives such as the Free Trade Area of the Americas (FTAA). There are now over eighty EZLN solidarity communities in Europe and approximately fifty such communities in the United States, which have supported the autonomous municipalities in Mexico while simultaneously campaigning closer to home against neoliberalism. Many of the characteristics of anticapitalist resistance are thus seen as debuting in the rebellion of the EZLN in Mexico with the latter consistently demonstrating an ability to mediate between the particular and the universal to forge a global consciousness of solidarity (Olesen 2004; Olesen 2005: 102–26).

The second area of importance in the expression of spaces of resistance has been the EZLN's involvement in peace talks and the assertion of indigenous rights at San Andrés Larráinzar, a small town in Chiapas, with two intermediaries in dialogue with the state, the Comisión de Concordia y Pacificación (COCOPA) and the Comisión Nacional de Intermediación (CONAI). The peace process hoped to address a series of issues revolving around indigenous rights and culture, negotiations on democracy and justice, land reform, and women's rights. It resulted in the San Andrés Accords on Indigenous Rights and Culture, signed on 16 February 1996, which laid the groundwork for significant changes in the areas of indigenous rights, political participation, and cultural autonomy. Concretely, this inspired the founding of the Congreso Nacional Indígena (CNI) in 1996 as representative of Mexico's indigenous peoples, approximately thirteen million people or between 10 to 14 percent of the country's population. While, again, advances such as the CNI and the San Andrés Accords should be seen as limited in terms of securing substantive gains for the indigenous communities in Mexico, they should not be totally discounted. For instance, some have swayed toward the former stance by drawing a comparison between talks with the EZLN and the overall process of electoral reform in Mexico. "Everyone agrees the dialogue must be pursued, there is a broad consensus regarding the worthiness of the cause," averred Jorge Castañeda (1995: 258), "but few are terribly excited either about the outcome itself or its urgency. As long as the process continues, there is little concern about its results, or absence thereof." Thus it can be agreed that little progress has been made since the San Andrés Accords were signed on 16 February 1996. However, presaging a continuation of resistance after the national elections on 2 July 2000—which, as chapter 6 detailed, witnessed the defeat of the PRI and the presidential victory of Vicente Fox backed by the center-right Partido Acción Nacional (PAN)—the EZLN have embarked on renewed forms of resistance to assert indigenous rights. On 21 March 1999 both the EZLN and FZLN organized a strategically important

"Consulta for the Recognition of the Rights of the Indian Peoples." This was a mobilization of five thousand Zapatista delegates consisting of teams of two people—one male, one female—visiting every municipality across Mexico to promote participation in a referendum on the peace "process" and the future of the EZLN. The consulta resulted in some three million votes with 95 percent of the participants voting in favor of honoring the San Andrés Accords, recognizing Indian rights, and supporting military withdrawal from Chiapas. The Zapatistas also subsequently set the date of 25 February 2001 for the "March of Indigenous Dignity" to leave San Cristóbal in Chiapas, to cross through various states, and arrive in Mexico City on 6 March, in order to promote support for their latest demands. This was designed to mount increasing pressure in support of the fulfillment of the San Andrés Accords and the bill on indigenous rights that followed the original COCOPA legislative proposal. Between 28 April and 2 May 2001, Congress approved a watered-down version of the original COCOPA bill on indigenous rights and culture. This failed to recognize communities as legal entities and their rights to natural resources or to hold communal property, which could have threatened the property rights of landowners. Hence the conservative view that there will be a return to the status quo *ante-bellum* in Chiapas.[16] Although the outcomes might seem disappointing, the attempt to constantly innovate with new forms of political mobilization and expressions in the name of indigenous rights is itself significant.

What these tactics have meant in practice is, third, an endeavor to appeal to various forms of identity as the basis for common points of convergence grounded in capitalist relations of exploitation.

> The EZLN in Chiapas has created a counter-hegemonic discourse in Mexican national culture that draws on the past hegemonic culture of the revolution but radically reinvents it by invoking the mediating figure of Zapata as a bridge to current social issues. (Stephen 1997; see also Stephen 2002)

Primarily, the ambiguities of identity have been embraced by constructing and mobilizing ethnic identity while also maintaining a degree of anonymity through the wearing of masks. This helps to project issues of ethnicity while creating new social spaces within which alternative forms of identity coexist. At one level this has involved making an equation between indigenous identity and poverty to recognize that socioeconomic exclusion has an ethnic dimension (Nash 1995). At another level it has involved promoting indigenous identity within the context of Mexican nationalism and appeals to the workers' movement and trade union struggle in Mexico (Earle 1994: 26–30; Roman and Velasco Arregui 1997: 98–116). Additionally, there have been attempts to reinvent group identities by emphasizing the struggle against gender inequalities and by affirming sexuality rights (Harvey 2000: 158–87; Rovira 2000; Hernández Castillo 1995; Eber and Kovic 2003). However, this does not mean that the new discourses and challenges to power relations have become part of everyday practice or that there is complete internal democratization within the communities of Chiapas. Also, it remains crucial to note that a struggle conducted on the basis of ethnic identity does not exclude intraclass conflict within and between communities, alongside interclass conflict between peasant producers in indigenous communities (Brass 2005: 660–61). At the same time, though, it is too dismissive to conclude that the location of the EZLN within a strategy of indigenous identity politics has become a "one-way street" (Pitarch 2004: 310–11). This is a position that the EZLN would itself clearly reject.[17] It can also be easily acknowledged that the struggle has transcended some of its particular aspects to engender a wider movement of Zapatismo in and beyond Mexico (Leyva Solano 1998). As Marcos himself has stated, explicitly critiquing neoliberal globalization, the EZLN struggle is a search for "a world in which there is room for many worlds. A world capable of containing all the worlds."[18]

The fourth area that the EZLN has promoted since the beginning of the rebellion has thus been the rallying cry for democracy from below in Mexico. As noted above, initial communiqués signaled the demand for work, land, housing, health, education, independence, freedom, democracy, and justice. It has also been possible to witness the EZLN's contribution, along with other civil society organizations in Mexico, to the cleanliness of elections, the importance of electoral monitoring, the transparency of civil servant practices, the need for independent media reporting, and the popularization of civic participation (Gilbreth and Otero 2001). "The PRD is a vote," the late Mexican cultural critic Carlos Monsiváis once declared, but "the Zapatistas are a cause."[19] However, the historic defeat of the PRI and the victory of Vicente Fox seemingly drained some of the potency away from this demand, in terms of the official democratic "transition" in Mexico. Greater circumspection, though, needs to be raised about the formalistic degree of such democratic "transition," the unspecified nature of such a hollow form of democracy, and the equation of democracy with the periodic circulation of elite classes, as discussed in chapter 6. Most significantly, the fact that neoliberalism can be upbraided as a thoroughly undemocratic common denominator, in both a national and international context, is significant. The Zapatista pursuit of democracy, however, may have resulted in a series of missed opportunities.

> Simply to call for the adherence on the part of the Mexican social formation to a systematically non-specific form of democracy, as the EZLN have done, without simultaneously calling into question the class structure which gives expression to the way in which (and for whom) political democracy operates

within this wider context, negates their own demand for social justice in Chiapas. (Brass 2005: 670; see also Vilas 1996: 277–81)

In Chiapas itself, the election of a new state governor on 20 August 2000 led to the victory of Pablo Salazar, representing an eight-party "Alliance for Chiapas," which again would seemingly detract from the EZLN cause of democratization. The sanguine view is that these polls have been turning points in the Zapatista conflict because peace proposals—backed by a "democratic" mandate—would be difficult to rebuff.[20] Likewise, Luis H. Alvarez, the coordinator of governmental peace efforts in Chiapas under the Fox administration, announced the partial withdrawal of the army in Chiapas in December 2000, although the army still maintains a large presence throughout the state alongside paramilitaries. Breaking their silence with the new administration, the Zapatistas embarked on a whole series of new initiatives from 2002 onward with new demands focusing on "three signals." These were (1) fulfilment of the San Andrés Accords, following the COCOPA legislative proposal; (2) release of all Zapatista prisoners held at Cerro Hueco state prison in Chiapas and in the states of Tabasco and Querétaro; and (3) a large process of demilitarization that would go beyond prevailing troop movements. While there has been partial compliance with these three signals—Chiapas state interior minister, Emilio Zebadúa, even acknowledged that the autonomous municipalities in Chiapas created by the EZLN represent legitimate aspirations that could be regularized through constitutional means—there are still major stumbling blocks to such negotiations. Not the least is the fact that there are a minimum of twenty thousand refugees in Chiapas internally displaced by armed conflict. This condition has been exacerbated by the decision of the ICRC to close its office in 2004, leading to the possible end of food distribution to eight thousand refugees in the communities of Pohlo and Chenalhó.

Yet, picking up the common national and international denominator of neoliberalism, the Zapatistas roundly criticized development proposals promoted by the Vicente Fox government, with Marcos stating that "although there is a radical difference in the way you came to power, your political, social and economic program is the same we have been suffering under during the last administrations" (EZLN 2003, vol. 4: 476). Perhaps more ominously, Marcos went on to state in an interview with the national newspaper *La Jornada*, "I don't know if our plans are terribly subversive, I don't believe so, but I do know that, if this isn't resolved, something terrible is going to explode, even without us."[21]

Fifthly and finally, therefore, the EZLN has continued to innovate with new forms of governance to challenge the Mexican state alongside pursuing tactics of land occupation. This initially led Richard Stahler-Sholk (1998: 14) to observe that "the real challenge to PRI hegemony lies in the Zapatistas' development projects, including collective agriculture, building local infrastructure, piping water from streams, training health promoters and starting up small enterprises." Since the Zapatista uprising in 1994, land seized by various peasant organizations and indigenous communities has been estimated to be between 60,000 and 500,000 hectares with government distribution in reaction to such seizures amounting to 180,000 hectares, although retaliation by landowners has reduced these figures (Barmeyer 2003: 133–34).

This brings to the fore the three spaces of autonomous resistance conducted by the EZLN, based on (1) alternative economy organizing, for example, linked to the Mut-Vitz coffee cooperative, that at one time had about six hundred members prior to folding, as well as artisan production; (2) self-sufficient educational projects; and (3) health care provision. Linked to these spaces, the Zapatistas have created since August 2003 five *caracoles* (or "spirals") in the communities of Chiapas (La Garrucha, Morelia, Oventic, La Realidad, and Roberto Barrios) to replace the former autonomous municipalities that covered more than thirty townships. These *caracoles* are based on five Juntas of Good Government in an attempt to further redefine and assert autonomy as well as promote economic development. The *caracoles* cover the Guatemala border region, the southern and northern canyons, the northern zone, and the highlands of Chiapas. They are responsible for carrying out legal, judicial, and economic policies across the range of education, health care, justice, and development. "These non-market alternatives to the neoliberal model were an effort to create material conditions for the support-base communities to hold out while inspiring a broader movement capable of changing state policies" (Stahler-Sholk 2008: 123). The *caracoles* can therefore be understood as a territorialization strategy that entails moving from, organizing in, and dominating place to *commanding space* as the EZLN endeavor to transcend their own militant particularism (see D. Harvey 1996: 324).

In Oventic, for example, all three spatial dimensions have been evident within the municipio of San Andrés de Sakamchen de los Pobres (see figure 7.1). Located within this highland *caracol* are self-sufficient cooperatives centered around artisan production as well as autonomous community governance structures and a health care clinic that is the most advanced of Zapatismo performing fifty surgeries a year. The production of artisan crafts is coordinated between three cooperatives in Oventic (Mujeres por la Dignidad, Nichim Rosas, and Xulum Chon Dinosaurio) consisting of six hundred to one thousand women producers selling wares locally and internationally (see figures 7.2 and 7.3). The sense of autonomy comes from the fact that the decisions and labor of the women are not appropriated by others. Significantly, a regional autonomous primary school—the Escuela Primaria Rebelde Autónoma Zapatista (EPRAZ)—as well as a similar secondary school—the

Escuela Secundaria Rebelde Autónoma Zapatista Primero de Enero (ESRAZ) are both located in Oventic, served by up to fifty educational promoters involved in establishing "the next generation of Zapatistas"[22] (see figures 7.4, 7.5, and 7.6). These are supplemented with a language center for Tzotzil and Spanish—the Centro de Lenguas Tsotsil y Español (CELMRAZ)—that is pivotal in diffusing links internationally through study programs. Taken together this growing system of autonomous education aims to continue constructing a shared and liberating form of resistance through the education "of those from below, but without submission."[23] Overall, Zapatistas have relocated from isolated communities in the Montes Azules bioreserve to move to lands with easier access to the regional Juntas of Good Government to establish better access to such education and health care facilities. While the EZLN has difficulty in protecting, defending, and expanding development initiatives and land redistribution in Chiapas, it would again be precocious to simply dismiss such efforts. The autonomous communities no longer recognize government-imposed authorities but democratically install their own community representatives. Within the newly created municipal structures,

Figure 7.1.   Caracol II: Oventic, Chiapas (May 2008). Main educational complex containing the Escuela Secundaria Rebelde Autónoma Zapatista Primero de Enero (ESRAZ) and the Centro de Lenguas Tsotsil y Español (CELMRAZ). Photo by author.

Figure 7.2.   Caracol II: Oventic, Chiapas (June 2008). Artisan cooperative complex. Photo by author.

the Zapatista communities name their authorities and commissions for various spheres of duty such as land management, education, health, justice, and women's rights (Barmeyer 2003: 135; Baronnet 2008: 117). It is to these endeavors that the achievements of the EZLN should be recognized while remaining open as to what further lasting effect it will have on the terrain of social struggle in Mexico (see Otero 2004a).

Figure 7.3.   Caracol II: Oventic, Chiapas (June 2008). Office of the "Women for Dignity" cooperative. Photo by author.

Figure 7.4.   Caracol II: Oventic, Chiapas (June 2008). Building notice of the Escuela Primaria Rebelde Autónoma Zapatista (EPRAZ). Photo by author.

Figure 7.5.   Caracol II: Oventic, Chiapas (June 2008). Building edifice of the Escuela Primaria Rebelde Autónoma Zapatista (EPRAZ). Photo by author.

Figure 7.6.   Caracol II: Oventic, Chiapas (June 2008). Building edifice to the Escuela Secundaria Rebelde Autónoma Zapatista Primero de Enero (ESRAZ) and the Centro de Lenguas Tsotsil y Español (CELMRAZ). Photo by author.

All of the above features of antipassive revolution spaces of resistance were most recently present in the initiative launched on 1 January 2006, when a delegation of the EZLN departed from Chiapas to visit all Mexico's thirty-two states. This marked the first step in a new Zapatista political initiative known as *La otra campaña*. The Other Campaign—timed to coincide with the 2006 Mexican presidential race—aims to build a program of struggle capable of constructing democracy from below along with national and international organizations resisting neoliberalism. Permeated with the principles of *mandar obedeciendo* (govern by obeying) the goal is to build a national program of struggle, to forge an "anti-capitalist" alliance, "from below and to the left" in Mexico.[24] It is to this forum and its future that additional social movements have looked to combine through similar principles of radical democracy, autonomous organizing, and direct action (see figure 7.7). This includes important associated struggles over a similar duration such as the Asamblea Popular de los Pueblos de Oaxaca (APPO) threaded together by a combination of extraparliamentary opposition, electoral participation, and autonomous self-governance against the corruption represented by former state governor Ulises Ruiz Ortiz (see inter alia Esteva 2007; Rénique 2007; Hesketh 2010b).[25] It would also include urban social movements such as the Frente Popular Francisco Villa-Independiente (FPFVI)—located across two sites of self-help settlement in Mexico City, the first in Polvorilla in the southeast within the Delegación Iztapalapa, accommodating some 650 families, and the second in Pantitlán, in the eastern sector within the Delegación

Figure 7.7.   FPFVI *manifestación* supporting *La otra campaña* held in the Plaza de la Constitución, Mexico City (June 2008). With the government offices of the Federal District in the background, the banner reads: "Army out of Chiapas!" Photo by author.

Iztacalco, accommodating some 300 families—that has embarked on a novel form of autonomous organizing of self-help housing cooperatives, education, and community issues in solidarity with the EZLN (see FPFVI 2006; Gabriel Juárez-Galeana 2006).

Although beyond the scope of detailed discussion here, it is possible to assess the EZLN's spatialization struggle through *La otra campaña*, including the organization of the *caracoles*, as something that exists between the extremes of "horizontalism," or changing the world through "anti-power" (see Holloway 2002 or Day 2005), and strict "verticalism," or capturing state power as a vehicle of political transformation (see Robinson 2007: 154 or Petras 2008: 477). It would be misleading to characterize the former stress as a "no-power" approach to social change just as much as it would be remiss to underestimate the tangible forms of autonomy based on collective action and organization building (see, respectively, Petras and Veltmeyer 2007 and Holloway 2002). Instead, the processes linked to the *caracoles* and the national program of *La otra campaña* can be seen as both "anti-state" as well as seeking to extend alternative forms of social organization through health and education services, new governance structures, and alternative economy organizing (see Barmeyer 2003: 136; Stahler-Sholk 2008: 124). As the prominent activist-scholar Gustavo Esteva (2009: 51) has noted, the movement for autonomy is not a counterweight to state power but an attempt to render the latter superfluous through "new reformulations of the nature of the state." This stress is reinforced by leading advocates associated with the EZLN indicating that the "high theory" about changing the world without taking power is "too closed around one truth" and ignores the changing Zapatista engagement with alternative social organizational forms.[26] After all, while renouncing revolutionary vanguards, the Zapatistas have also recognized that their "ideas and proposals do not have an eternal horizon."[27]

CONCLUSION: "RATTLING THE LID OF THE CAULDRON OF THE STATE"

In 1910, a hacienda estate owner declared to the Zapatistas of the Mexican Revolution (1910–1920), in the village of Anenecuilco, "If that bunch wants to farm . . . let them farm in a flowerpot, because they are not getting any land" (see Womack 1968: 63). Similarly, the EZLN have struggled to maintain the momentum for their rebellion over land, peasant autonomy through community, health, educational, and alternative development projects and in relation to the San Andrés Accords centered on indigenous rights. However, it would be too pessimistic to accord with Jorge Castañeda, onetime secretary of foreign relations within the Vicente Fox administration, that "despite having enormous international support and the emblematic aspects of a just cause, the movement has gone absolutely nowhere. The Zapatistas have been nowhere, gone nowhere and they are nowhere."[28] After all, as Gramsci (1996: 60–61, Q3§62) forewarned:

> A realistic politics must not concern itself solely with immediate success. . . . It must also create and safeguard those conditions that are necessary for future activity—and one of these is the education of the people. This is the issue. The higher the cultural level and the greater the development of the critical spirit, the more "impartial"—that is, the more historically "objective"—one's position will be.

The conclusions to draw from this chapter, then, center on three dimensions related to the contestation of the modern state and the politics of passive revolution in Mexico.

First, in terms of unpacking a sociology of power, due recognition has to be granted to the intertwined histories of dominant *and* subaltern resistance practices. This entails recognizing the modest expressions of human volition, the vast majority of which might remain anonymous but at the same time demand greater attention in order to understand structured agency. The case of the EZLN under analysis here highlights different dimensions of peasant-based agency and their demands for control over land in Mexico, therefore vitiating claims about the disappearance of the peasantry as a meaningful social class engaged in active forms of resistance. Regardless of whether such agency results in repeated cycles of mass protest/negotiation/agreements/broken promises/mass protest (Petras and Veltmeyer 2002: 64–68), it is clear that the Zapatista rebellion has acted as a catalyst for wider resistance against the neoliberal project in and beyond Mexico. It resonates with Theodor Adorno's (1974a: 151) view that knowledge must proceed less through a consideration of the "fatally rectilinear" succession of victory and defeat and more through a reflection on those dynamics that fall by the wayside, the blind spots that escape the blocked dialectic of revolution-restoration indicative of passive revolution.

Second, the EZLN demonstrates that the existence and reproduction of indigenous identity largely depends on access to land, meaning that there is a class basis to their actions due to the combination of their role as peasant producers and wage laborers. As Gerardo Otero (2004b) has outlined, class grievances and ethnic identity issues are important in the constitution of the peasantry within the EZLN movement, which shapes both their material interests and cultural aspects of identity set against the context of changing social relations of production. Issues of class struggle therefore matter. While the EZLN itself is struggling to retain a presence in leading social movements in Mexico, the wider formation of class struggle through the intersection of labor and social movements continues. The perils of unity, though, still confront movements of the left in Mexico facing the class basis of neoliberalism (Carr 1993). Emblematic here is the continued mobilization of labor unions, such as the Unión Nacional de Trabajadores (UNT) and the Frente Sindical Mexicano (FSM) to contest the neoliberal agenda in Mexico (La Botz 2005); the national mobilizations and protests, since 2009, against labor law reform and the sacking of forty-four thousand workers of the militant Sindicato Mexicano de Electricistas (SME) in relation to the privatization of the state-owned Compañía Luz y Fuerza del Centro (LyFC) alongside the ongoing sell-off of PEMEX;[29] the attempts by the Frente Auténtico del Trabajo (FAT) to challenge the perquisites of state power based on its principles of *auto-gestión* (self-management) and *formación* (consciousness raising) to foster alternative social development programs (Hathaway 2000); or the moves of the FPFVI to sustain its mobilization of a popular urban social movement against the above processes through the Unidad Nacional de Organizaciones Populares de Izquierda Independientes (UNOPII), first formed in 2002. "Today more than ever, the class struggle is inscribed in space" (Lefebvre 1991: 55). According to John Ross, while elements of an anticapitalist force may be evident, the labor movement is the "big gaping hole" in Mexico based on old models; therefore the challenge ahead is to ensure that *La otra campaña* does not simply become a pole of attraction for the most excluded and sectarian leftist tendencies in Mexico.[30] Instead, one can add, it is better to regard the campaign as a process of "'becoming' in a 'concordia discors' [discordant concord] that does not have unity for its point of departure but contains in itself the reasons for a possible unity" (Gramsci 2007: 186, Q7§35).

The third conclusion to draw in terms of antipassive strategies and spaces of resistance relates to the politics of scale. At the heart of the spatial terrain of both hegemony and resistance is a combination of logics that demands due recognition of the different scales that work through transnational, state, and local power matrices (see Hesketh 2010a). One cannot afford to impute a singularly transnational logic to the domains of domination and resistance at the expense of the reterritorialization of space "above" and "below" the construction of the modern state (see Robinson 2008). "Global solidarity activities," as Thomas Olesen (2004: 265) avers, "in fact often originate at the local and national level and revolve around cultural and identity characteristics tied to these spaces." In sum, how the modern state imposes itself as the "stable" center of society and space under conditions of passive revolution is pivotal to the focus of this book. However, it is also crucial to recognize modes of class struggle that are always inscribed in that same space—"rattling the lid of the cauldron of the state" (Lefebvre 1991: 23)—through strategies of resistance that are antipassive revolutionary. The continuum of passive revolution, meaning its relatively "permanent" character as a hallmark of postcolonial state formation caught up in the throes of the uneven and combined development of capitalist modernity, is now contemplated in the conclusion to this book.

NOTES

1. See *Latinamerica Press* (7 September 2005): 12, www.lapress.org; accessed 16 March 2006.

2. It should be made clear that Gramsci's view of the peasantry as a class was not typical of historical materialist theory at the time. Both Lenin (1899/1964) and Kautsky (1899/1988), for example, emphasize the tendency of internal differentiation *among* peasants that developed along class lines rather than holding that the peasantry constitutes a class *distinct* from agrarian capital and wage labor. That this generates tensions within the argument about understanding paths of agrarian change and the dissolution of the peasantry cannot be pursued within the present argument (for contemporary commentaries, see Bernstein 2000: 29–32 and Washbrook 2006).

3. For a more critical analysis of Ruiz, see Krauze (1999: 65–73).

4. But it is worth noting the EZLN communiqué, following the death of Samuel Ruiz, where it is stated that "the thesis at that time (and that is today repeated by idiots of the left at a desk) was that the Diocese had formed the EZLN's bases and leadership cadre," see, Comité Clandestino Revolucionario Indígena-Comandancia General del EZLN, "Communicado sobre la muerte del Obispo don Samuel Ruiz" (26 January 2011), http://enlacezapatista.ezln.org.mx; accessed 7 February 2011.

5. It is therefore important to acknowledge that the identification of the role and function of organic intellectual activity can raise its own controversies, whether that be in relation to a member of the priesthood, or in relation to *mestizos*, supporting indigenous communities, Author's interview with Tom Hansen, Mexico Solidarity Network (MSN), San Cristóbal de las Casas, Chiapas (13 June 2008). Also see the absolutely essential commentary from the EZLN on the social function of intellectuals, opposing the social function of the critical and analytic intellectual against the organic intellectuals of the "neoliberal Prince" under globalization. The latter's social function is to act as the "gravediggers for critical analysis and reflection, jugglers with the millstones of neoliberal theology, prompters for governments who forget the 'script,' commentators of the obvious, cheerleaders for soldiers and police officers, Gnostic judges who hand out labels of 'true' or 'false' at their convenience, theoretical bodyguards for the Prince and announcers of the 'new history,'" see EZLN "Nuestro siguiente programa: ¡Oximoron! La derecha intelectual y el fascismo liberal," [April 2000] in EZLN (2003, vol. 4: 436–37). Also consider the interview with *el Sup* in Castellanos (2008).

6. Although a classic case of *trasformismo* can be witnessed in the way the activism of Adolfo Orive, key founder of Línea Proletaria, was gradually absorbed

within the PRI. In the 1990s, he acted as technical secretary within the Secretaría de Desarrollo Social (SEDESOL) and became the "coordinator of advisers" within the Secretaría de Gobernación (SEGOB), see Womack (1999: 175–76).

7. See *La Jornada* (19 January 1994), reprinted in *¡Zapatistas!* (1994: 68) and Ross (1995: 21, 153).

8. Amnesty International, "Mexico: Torture with Impunity" (London: Amnesty International, AMR 41/04/91) and Amnesty International, "Mexico: The Persistence of Torture and Impunity" (London: Amnesty International, AMR 41/01/93).

9. Report by an Independent Delegation to Mexico, *Chiapas, Before It's Too Late…* (March 1998), 20. This consisted of an eight-person team formed with the help and advice of the aid agencies CAFOD, Trocaire, Save the Children Fund/UK, SCIAF, and the Polden Puckham Charitable Trust that visited Chiapas, 13–23 March 1998. I would like to thank Nikki Craske, who was a member of the delegation, for a copy of the report.

10. Coordinación de Organismos no Gubernamentales por la Paz de Chiapas (CONPAZ), Centro de Derechos Humanos Fray Bartolomé de las Casas, y Convergencia de Organismos Civiles por la Democracia, *Militarisation and Violence in Chiapas* (Servicios Procesados, A.C., 1997).

11. See Report by an Independent Delegation to Mexico, *Chiapas, Before It's Too Late*, 19.

12. *The Guardian* [London], "Sorry for the Inconvenience But This Is a Revolution" (3 January 1994): 18.

13. *The Times* [London], "Doomed Uprising Rips Veil from Mexican 'Miracle,'" (7 January 1994): 9.

14. For a rebuttal see Dunkerley (2000: 20–38) and for a continuation of the debate see Panizza (2005) and Motta (2007).

15. Javier Elorriaga, "An Analysis of Evolving Zapatismo: Deduced from the Four Declarations of the Selva Lacandona," *In Motion Magazine* (6 January 1997), www.inmotionmagazine.com; accessed 30 June 2008.

16. *The Economist* [London], "Back to Square One in Chiapas" (5 May 2001): 32.

17. EZLN, "The Zapatistas Can, and Should, Speak Only about the Indigenous Question?" (29 December 2002), http://palabra.ezln.org.mx; accessed 30 June 2008.

18. Subcomandante Marcos, "The Fourth World War Has Begun," *Le Monde diplomatique* (September 1997), English print edition, www.monde-diplomatique.fr/en; accessed 16 April 2000.

19. Author's interview with Carlos Monsiváis, Mexico City (20 March 1999).

20. *The Economist* [London], "A Fresh Start for Chiapas" (12 August 2000): 53–54.

21. Carlos Monsiváis and Hermann Belinghausen, "Interview with Subcomandante Marcos," *La Jornada* [Mexico City] (8 January 2001), www.ezln.org.mx; accessed 30 January 2001.

22. Author's interview with Tom Hansen, Mexico Solidarity Network (MSN), San Cristóbal de las Casas, Chiapas (13 June 2008).

23. Coordinación General del SERAZLN-ZACH, "Carta del Sistema Educativo Rebelde Autónomo Zapatista de Liberación Nacional-Zona de Los Altos de Chiapas" (15 February 2010); http://enlacezapatista.ezln.org.mx; accessed 7 June 2010.

24. EZLN, "Sixth Declaration of the Lacandón Jungle" (June 2005); http:// enlacezapatista.ezln.org.mx; accessed 14 July 2008.

25. Also see the feature on the regeneration of memory linked to the APPO in *Rebeldía*, no. 59 (2008), which is now also available online at http://revistarebeldia.org.

26. Author's interview with a former member of the National Coordinating Committee of the Frente Zapatista de Liberación Nacional (FZLN), Mexico City (5 July 2008).

27. Subcomandante Marcos, "I shit on all the revolutionary vanguards of this planet," (9 January 2003); http://enlacezapatista.ezln.org.mx; accessed 12 November 2004.

28. Author's interview with Jorge Castañeda, Mexico City (9 and 13 March 1999).

29. See *Mexican Labor News & Analysis*, vol. 15, no. 3 (March 2010), http://www .ueinternational.org/Mexico_info/mlna.php; accessed 1 April 2010.

30. Author's interview with John Ross, Mexico City (8 July 2008).

Chapter Eight

Conclusion

Permanent Passive Revolution?

Following the oil expropriation announced by Lázaro Cárdenas on 18 March 1938, the African American artist Elizabeth Catlett captured the national-popular appeal of the president in a woodcut depicting donations (sewing machines, irons, financial contributions) from Mexican men, women, and children toward the government. As a member of a new generation of print-makers within the Taller de Gráfica Popular (TGP), alongside Arturo García Bustos, Alberto Beltrán, and Marianna Yampolsky (see chapter 1), this print by Catlett was included in a portfolio of works published in 1947 and se-rialized over three months in the newspaper *El Nacional*. In graphic form, Catlett's *Contribución del pueblo en la expropriación petrolera* captures the national *colecta* that was thus called in order to raise something in the region of $350 million to indemnify United States and British oil companies as a result of the expropriation (see figure 8.1). In terms of financing the expro-priation, the Confederación de Trabajadores de México (CTM) proposed a special tax and Cárdenas warned a crowd of two hundred thousand assembled in Mexico City's Zócalo, on 23 March 1938, that "labour will have to bear its share . . . to guarantee the Nation's 'claim to independence'" (as cited in Knight 1992d: 110).

Among other possible interpretations, then, what this composition perhaps conveys best is a further transformation of the Mexican Revolution into a remembrance, a rite, a celebration, and a myth. The woodcut *Contribución del pueblo en la expropriación petrolera* embodies the dissemination and transmission of *la Revolución* to succeeding generations and the attempt to create legitimacy and social cohesion in Mexico. At the same time, it is one further example of how *la Revolución* was transformed and converted into government (*la Revolución hecha gobierno*), in making the modern state and in attempting to unify and stymie Mexico's revolutionary origins (see

237

Figure 8.1. Elizabeth Catlett, *Contribución del pueblo en la expropriación petrolera* [Contribution of the people during the oil expropriation] © Elizabeth Catlett, 1947, woodcut, Design and Artists Copyright Society (DACS), London/VAGA, New York 2010.

Conclusion   239

Benjamin 2000). Therefore, although the oil expropriation was regarded by
Leon Trotsky as one of the "greatest conquests" of the Mexican government,
alongside agrarian reform, it was also recognized as "entirely within the domain of state capitalism" for a country in the throes of uneven and combined
development (Trotsky 1939/1974a: 326). Expropriation was thus the only
effective means through which a relatively weak national bourgeoisie could
safeguard state power against both popular class demands and foreign imperialist interests. "Only lamentable utopians," Trotsky (1939/1974b: 185) wrote
at the time, "can represent the future of Mexico, as well as any other colonial
or semicolonial country, as one of a constant accumulation of reforms and
conquests until complete and definite emancipation has arrived." This amalgam of rupture and continuity, involving "hegemonic activity" but in a situation of minimal hegemony where state power "became merely an aspect of
the function of domination," is emblematic of a passive revolution (Gramsci
1971: 59, Q19§24). It should be no surprise that these contradictions of passive revolution once more find expression in the art (alongside the literature
and architecture) of modern Mexico.

   Through seeking to uncover the historical sociology of modern state formation, this book has contributed to an understanding of uneven and combined
development and the class-driven processes of passive revolution in Mexico.
In the course of the argument that has preceded, this historical sociology of
revolution and state in Mexico has provided a deeper understanding of both
the uneven and combined developmental circumstances constructing modern state formation and a critique of its essentially contested class practices
through the conditions of passive revolution. A passive revolution, it should
be recalled, is a ruptural moment in the history of modern state formation in
which capitalist development is either instituted and/or expanded, resulting
in a blocked dialectic of "revolution-restoration" (see Gramsci 1971: 106–8,
Q15§17). Beyond a fundamental rupture shaping state formation, a passive
revolution can also refer to "the survival and reorganisation of state identity
through which social relations are reproduced in new forms consonant with
capitalist property relations" (Morton 2007a: 68). Both state formation and
state maintenance, therefore, can be major features of passive revolution, especially impinging on postcolonial states encountering the uneven and combined development of capitalism in the periphery. Beyond an initial ruptural
feature of modern state formation, a passive revolution has ongoing effects
that subsequently shape the contingent and structural conditions of uneven
and combined capitalist development. The point, however, is to stress that in
this study the hallmark of passive revolution and the construction and contestation of modern state formation that it exemplifies is an inherent aspect
of capitalist space. This means that the ruptural and restorative aspects of

passive revolution refer to *the passive revolution of capital* (Chatterjee 1986: 46–47); more on this shortly. Rather than as some transhistorical affirmation of intersocietal existence, passive revolution in this book refers to the historically specific transition to and transformations of the social relations of capitalist production (see also Morton 2010b). The major claim, therefore, is that the ruptural conditions of the Mexican Revolution (1910–1920), as well as subsequent transformations in state–civil society relations, can be understood as a condition of passive revolution. Although passive revolution is a counterpart to hegemony (Cox 1983: 167), when it comes to understanding the way in which modern state formation in Mexico fostered violent and coercive dynamics, passive revolution provides a more fruitful approach to breaking with the consensus-based arguments of the "Golden Age" associated with the Pax Priísta. For sure, "hegemonic activity" existed in Mexico but the argument articulated throughout this book has been that this was only a minimal hegemony. To begin with, chapter 2 developed in detail the affinal relation of uneven and combined development and passive revolution that, through the historical experience of the Mexican Revolution, conjoined modern state formation and mass mobilization leading to processes of primitive accumulation and, subsequently, the constitution of capitalist space. The class strategies involved in the latter process were traced in chapter 3 in terms of the rise of the state in capitalist society through import substitution industrialization (ISI) and dominant fractions within the capitalist class. The degree of spatial fixity achieved by capital, for example, across the scales of the state and the urban form, were highlighted in this chapter as crucial in the drive for surplus value in terms of (1) the centralization of capital across the built environment for production purposes; (2) the arbitration and expedition of capital accumulation by state development agencies; and (3) the ability to appropriate from agricultural land via primitive accumulation a surplus, which is the linchpin of modern society as "capital comes dripping from head to foot, from every pore, with blood and dirt" (Marx 1887/1996: 748). The discussion then proceeded in chapter 4 to examine the class-driven struggle to construct a capitalist type of state in light of the world-economy crisis and the rhythm of accumulation experienced throughout the 1970s and 1980s. The restoration of class power through passive revolution and new geographical patterns in the uneven and combined development of capital were assessed in this chapter as features of a neoliberal strategy of capitalist accumulation. Whether or not the capitalist type of state has become consolidated by this logic of accumulation, so that the construction of the modern state in Mexico is now distinguished more by the formal separation of the appearance of the "economic" and the "political," is an open issue that divides not only the organization of the book into two parts but also class struggles in relation to the contemporary contestation of state power.

The second part of the book therefore developed three studies (on the role of intellectuals and the modern state, struggles over democratization, and spaces of resistance) all embedded in the construction and contestation of the revolution and the modern state in Mexico. The epigraph to this book emphasizes, with its reference to that "miserable assassin" Porfirio Díaz—drawn from Mariano Azuela's classic novel of the Mexican Revolution *Los de abajo* (see Azuela 1915/1997: 143)—that the restoration of the *antiguo régimen* was a clear possibility nested within the conditions of revolutionary upheaval. The main thesis put forth in this book, that this amalgam of revolution and restoration proceeded through the subsequent class practices of passive revolution, was also a major feature of chapter 5 and its focus on the role of the intellectual in challenging and conforming to state power. Carlos Fuentes once described *Los de abajo* as a novel that stripped the Mexican Revolution of its "mythic support" because it is possible to argue that

> the epic pattern of this revolution, the Mexican Revolution, may well be translated into a reproduction of the previous despotism because . . . the political, familial, sexual, intellectual and moral matrices of the old order, the colonial, patrimonialist order, have not been radically transformed. (Fuentes 1992c: 138–9)

It was this landscape of the modern Mexican state that Carlos Fuentes contested, in terms of his social function as an intellectual, but in a contradictory fashion. The specific spaces for intellectual production characteristic of modernity in Mexico, albeit generative of critical sensibilities, were greatly shaped by the shadow of the state. It was this absorptive logic that was to define Carlos Fuentes himself as a passive revolutionary performing a function organic to dominant class forces within the state. The process of democratization from above was also exposed in chapter 6 as an element in the class strategy of passive revolution. Within the uneven developmental conditions of regnant neoliberalism and democratic "transitions" in Latin America that inscribe state space, democratization was understood as an aspect of passive revolution abetting new forms of surplus extraction and the expanded reproduction of capital. Contesting the effacement of power relations in the democratization from above, however, have been various dynamics and spaces of resistance, not least the struggle conducted by the Ejército Zapatista de Liberación Nacional (EZLN) against neoliberalism, which have furthered the contestation of revolution and state in Mexico. It was argued here that the EZLN—the "last glow of the Mexican Revolution" (Gilly 1997: 43)— suggests a more diverse and inclusive modernity at the heart of its spatial strategies and antipassive revolution tactics of resistance. This brings us to three pertinent reflections that emerge from the analysis of the book's focus on the historical sociology of revolution and state in Mexico and the form of modernity hewn out of the conditioning situation of uneven and combined development by the passive revolution of capital. These are (1) how best to contemplate the history of Mexico within the continuum of passive revolution, meaning its relatively "permanent" character within historically specific circumstances, as a hallmark of postcolonial state formation; (2) how best to reflect on the possible temporal and spatial occurrence of passive revolutions in world history by providing a methodological steer on the relation of instances of passive revolution in a comparative manner; and (3) how best to reflect on new and future rounds of restructuring of the state in Mexico and Latin America related to the survival of capitalism in the twenty-first century.

BEYOND PERMANENT PASSIVE REVOLUTION

As mentioned in the previous chapter, a critical stance on the thesis of passive revolution has to be established by ensuring that a characterization of its historical and contemporary processes of upheaval avoids a degree of fatalism (see Gramsci 1971: 114, Q15§62). A focus on the dialectical development arising out of the contradictions of existing forces, as demonstrated in the previous chapter, provides some assurance that the implications of passive revolution are "purged of every residue of mechanicism and fatalism" (Gramsci 1971: 107, Q15§17). This is so because "the conception remains a dialectical one—in other words, presupposes, indeed postulates as necessary, a vigorous antithesis which can present intransigently all its potentialities for development" (Gramsci 1971: 114, Q15§62). But to what extent can the concept of passive revolution be stretched across an entire historical period to encompass the formation of modern states? Can the history of Mexico be seen as the history of passive revolution? This type of question was posed by Gramsci on the permanency of passive revolution in asking: "Are we in a period of 'restoration-revolution' to be *permanently consolidated*, to be organised ideologically, to be exalted lyrically?" (Gramsci 1971: 118, Q10I§9, emphasis added). For sure, it is possible to read into such a statement a fundamental transhistorical dynamic. This means the extension of the concept of passive revolution to patterns and regularities across history while positing a fixed and continuing present. Gramsci's own reflections on the Reformation and Renaissance might confirm a flirtation with passive revolution as an essentially unchanging human story. As he noted: "The scattered observations on the differing historical significances of the Protestant Reformation and the Italian Renaissance, of the French Revolution and the Risorgimento (the Reformation is to the Renaissance as the French Revolution is to the Risorgimento) can be collected in a single essay, possibly under the title 'Reformation and Renaissance'"

(Gramsci 1996: 39, Q3§40). Indeed, this analogy may well be suggestive in not only considering the condition of modernity but also in signposting and situating the social transformation and structural changes in capitalism signaling postmodernity (Anderson 1998: 112–13). My argument here, though, is that this act of concept stretching should be resisted (see also Callinicos 2010; Morton 2010b). This is because it can become suspect to a pancapitalist focus on the expansion of the world market and relations of mercantile capitalism, which have been rejected throughout the book due to the failure to delineate the *differentia specifica* of transformations in property relations and thus capitalist production relations. So what does it mean to advance the continuum of passive revolution, meaning its relatively "permanent" character within historically specific circumstances, as a hallmark of postcolonial capitalism and state formation? A central proposition of this book has been that a focus on the continuum of passive revolution reveals pertinent features of modern state formation in a historically specific sense within the twentieth-century transition to and transformation of modern capitalist political space. It has been stated that "uneven development is the systematic geographical expression of the contradictions inherent in the very constitution and structure of capital" and thus unique to capitalism (Smith 1984/2008: 4).[1] Equally, as an affinal concept, the focus on passive revolution in Mexico has revealed specific class strategies and spatial practices that characterize capitalist society and how these have changed with the further development of capitalism. This is what is meant by the passive revolution of capital. Therefore, although uneven development and passive revolution might be treated as universal processes, a historicist mode of thought will emphasize these features of historical sociology as premises of capitalist development.

> The historicist approach to social science does not envisage any general or universally valid laws which can be explained by the development of appropriate generally applicable theories. . . . One cannot therefore speak of "laws" in any generally valid sense transcending historical eras, nor of structures as outside of or prior to history. (Cox 1981/1986: 243–44)

Hence, when Gramsci (1971: 109–9, Q15§11, emphasis added) pronounces on the historical dynamic of passive revolution that "since similar situations almost always arise in every historical development, one should see if it is not possible to draw from this some general principle of political science *and* art," the reference is to the historical structures of capitalist modernity. Arising out of the dialectic of the contradictions of capitalist uneven and combined development, can existing class forces in Mexico blaze a trail beyond the politics of passive revolution? The EZLN have grappled within this struggle.

The Mexico of today finds itself with a structural deformation that cuts across the spectrum of Mexican society, in that it affects all social classes, in economic and political aspects, and includes its geographical urban and rural "organisation" . . . any intent to "reform" or "balance" this deformation is impossible FROM WITHIN THE SYSTEM OF THE PARTY-STATE. There is no "change without rupture." A profound and radical change of all the social relations in today's Mexico is necessary. A REVOLUTION IS NECESSARY, a new revolution. This revolution is possible only from outside the system of the Party-State. (EZLN 2003, vol. 2: 382, original capitalization)

Whether this process of struggle breaks the structural deformation that is passive revolution—the creation of a modern state that produces a bastard offspring (see Gramsci 1971: 90, Q19§28)—and forges a new rupture of revolution is an important issue that remains unresolved.

APPROACHING PASSIVE REVOLUTIONS

If Mexico stands as an instance of passive revolution called forth by capitalist modernity, how then might one approach passive revolutions elsewhere in alternative locales, sites, and situations of state formation without parodying the factors of originality? Could there be something significant about the occurrence and sequencing of initial ruptural features of modern state formation, understood as a passive revolution, within the geopolitical circumstances of uneven and combined development? What importance might then be granted to subsequent passive revolutions in terms of the reorganization of state identity and capitalist reorganization in crisis periods? As well as passive revolutions that might be similar in time and space, how might those passive revolutions that are contemporary to us and thus in the process of becoming be approached? These are questions that should be pursued in more depth than is possible here. However, a few methodological pointers toward approaching passive revolutions with different temporal and spatial characteristics within the historically specific conditions of capitalist production can be sketched. It should be stressed that any endeavor to outline a methodological approach to passive revolutions needs to depart from a consideration of the connections at work in external and separate cases that are then "integrated" through comparative study. There is an ideological function to the specialization of the social sciences within bounded disciplines (e.g., anthropology, sociology, comparative politics, international relations) that separates knowledge so that the dialectical unity of the social world is left unnoticed, leading to a preoccupation with reified entities rather than definite social relations. The social sciences, to paraphrase Eric Wolf (1997: 11), have thus abandoned a holistic perspective and come to resemble the Danaid sisters of classical Greek legend, ever condemned to the endless task of separately carrying water in jars perforated like sieves. As Wolf (1997: 17) goes on to ask: "What, however, if we take cognisance of processes that transcend the separable cases, moving through and beyond them and transforming them as they proceed?" To expand, briefly, by widening the geographical scope of the analysis of passive revolution beyond Latin America, touched on in chapter 1, how can the form of the Italian Risorgimento (1861), the Meiji Restoration (1868–1912), the Mexican Revolution (1910–1920), or modern state formation in Turkey (1919–1923), for example, be incorporated as passive revolutions within the geopolitics of uneven and combined development? There seems something significant here about the time-space patterning of passive revolutions. Rather than constituting instances of passive revolution as isolated and disconnected events in space and time, the challenge is to understand these different social processes as internal to world history (see Burawoy 1989: 770–72). Similarly, what importance can be granted to the temporal and spatial sequencing of *subsequent* passive revolutions in the twentieth century in terms of capitalist reorganization? Again, is there something significant in the occurrence of capitalist restructuring, on one hand, in the form of fascism in Italy (1920s), or Shōwa nationalism in Japan (1930s), and, on the other hand, in the shift from ISI to neoliberalism in Mexico (1980s), or capitalist expansion in Turkey through the rise of the military and then populist policies leading from state-led development to neoliberalism (1980s)? What is common about the peripheral character of capitalist development leading to ruptural conditions of state formation, as well as ongoing forms of capitalist restructuring, that could be approached as passive revolutions? To be a little less equivocal, approaching passive revolutions of various hues can proceed on the basis of Philip McMichael's methodology of *incorporated comparison* (McMichael 1990). First outlined in its methodological relevance to instances of passive revolution elsewhere (see Morton 2010a), this is an interpretive method in historical sociology focusing on interrelated instances of state transition within world-historical processes, where the *particulars* of state formation are realized within the *general* features of capitalist modernity as a self-forming whole. Instances of passive revolution, noted above, might thus be understood as comparable social phenomena or differentiated outcomes of a historically integrated process. Rather than constructing an "external" relationship between "case studies" of passive revolution, "comparison becomes an 'internal' rather than an 'external' (formal) feature of inquiry, relating apparently separate processes (in time and/ or space) as components of a broader, world-historical process" (McMichael 1990: 389). As McMichael persuasively argues, the method of incorporated comparison seeks to develop historical sociology through the dialectical interaction of instances as moments in a self-forming whole (McMichael 1990:

386). This can proceed in two ways: (1) through a cross-time comparison specifying a historical era as composed of temporally differentiated instances of a world-historical process (the multiple form of incorporated comparison), and/or (2) through a cross-space comparison specifying a single conjuncture as combining particular spatially located parts of a global configuration (the single form of incorporated comparison) (see McMichael 2000: 671). As a method of inquiry, my argument is that incorporated comparison is therefore able to conceptualize cross-time instances of passive revolution (moments of state formation across different state forms) posited as part of a self-forming whole (capitalist modernity). Equally, passive revolution can be employed to grasp cross-space comparisons analyzing the multiscalar context of single state formation processes in a specific period capturing national, urban, local, regional, or global scales of uneven development (see Hesketh 2010a). Passive revolution might then turn out to be one approach toward appreciating "genealogies of rebellion": how each revolutionary movement expresses a different but associated space in a genealogy of rebellion (see Gilly 2010: 42–43). In sum, class strategies of passive revolution become the historical path by which the development of capital can occur within spatially linked (peripheral capitalist development) and temporally linked (organic) junctures of uneven and combined development but without resolving or surmounting those very contradictions of capital accumulation. Concurrent with Trotsky's (1929/2004: 131) summary, "the law of uneven development . . . operates not only in the relations of countries to each other, but also in the mutual relationships of the various processes within one and the same country. A reconciliation of the uneven process of economics and politics can be attained only on a world scale." This sentiment similarly lay behind Gramsci's (1971: 117, Q10II§61) deliberation on the role played by "universal concepts with [specific] 'geographical seats'" within the historically specific conditions of capitalism as a mode of production.[2] Michael Burawoy (1998: 27) asserts how Trotsky shows the movement of world history through uneven and combined development. My argument here is that Gramsci also usefully reveals distinct conditions in every passive revolution within the social processes of uneven and combined development. The ambition, then, when approaching passive revolution is to refrain from pouring the concept indiscriminately, like "hotel gravy," over any instance, or dish, that would risk missing the flavor of its own historical peculiarities (Adorno 2000: 29).

THE CONTRADICTIONS OF CONTEMPORARY CAPITALISM

In reflecting on the adaptive capacity of neoliberalism in the current conjuncture in relation to the arguments of uneven development and passive revolution emergent from this book, attention is finally cast toward providing a thumbnail sketch of new and future rounds of capitalist restructuring of the state in Mexico and Latin America. This is not to lose sight of additional pressing developments on the trajectory of state formation in Mexico. Beyond the scope of our discussion here are, for example, the issues swirling around the reproduction of violence and state formation linked to the antidrugs war and the passage of the Mérida Initiative in 2008, entailing at least $1.4 billion in U.S. aid over three years to quell the rise in drug-related violence.[3] From a total of 1,600 murders linked to organized crime in 2005, deaths have risen to 2,200 in 2006, to some 36,000 at this writing, in early 2011.[4] More research is clearly needed to settle important questions about the militarization of the state and the reproduction of violence. Not the least significant here is the U.S. Joint Forces Command positing Mexico as likely for descent into "rapid and sudden collapse"; the fact that there are fifty thousand Mexican troops and federal police actively in the field against the war on drugs; that drug cartel conflict has led to ten thousand troops in Ciudad Juárez alone—"Mexico's murder capital"—and hit cities such as Michoacán and Monterrey; or that state politicians have felt it necessary to deny Mexico's status as a "failed state" (see Cockcroft 2010).[5] Greater consideration of these issues related to state formation awaits further research not least the need to debunk the "failed states" doctrine and its embeddedness in the Cold War annexation of the social sciences (see Bilgin and Morton 2002). For the concluding focus of this book, though, the specific emergence of policy trends claiming to reconstitute an alternative vision to neoliberalism in Latin America through social reform of the state, interventionist forms of governance, democratization, and a focus on growth with equity under the guise of "postneoliberalism" require consideration. This is the case because the policy practices of postneoliberalism, based on the state management of social programs, education, and antipoverty schemes, are shaping not only modernity in the twenty-first century in Latin America but also have a significant undercurrent in Mexico. The trend of postneoliberalism gained prominence, among other developments, within the so-called Alternativa Latinoamericana (Latin American Alternative) to the Washington Consensus, cofounded by Roberto Mangabeira Unger, a Brazilian political scientist, and Jorge Castañeda, well known as the "self-anointed guru of Latin America's 'new left.'"[6] It should therefore be situated, in the terms of such analysis, within the putatively "modern, open-minded, reformist and internationalist" left in Latin America (the "right left") found recently in Chile, Uruguay, or Brazil, rather than the "nationalist, strident and close minded" populism of the left in Latin America (the "wrong left") existing in Venezuela, Cuba, or Bolivia (see Castañeda 2006: 29; Castañeda and Morales 2008). The provenance of postneoliberalism also derives from policy planners within the Comisión Económica para América Latina y el

Caribe (CEPAL) pursuing a grand narrative about how to realize the elusive goals of modernity in Latin America as a viable alternative to neoliberalism (see Conger 1998; Leiva 2008; Macdonald and Ruckert 2009). In 2005, John Durston, of CEPAL's Social Division described the social policies underpinning postneoliberalism as

> an alliance of subaltern communities and organisations with reform minded sectors existing within, on one hand, the state apparatus and, on the other hand, political parties. . . . It emerges when windows of opportunity exist in which the presence of many favourable factors come together: grassroots movements, democratic elections, and the influence of progressive politicians. (as cited in Leiva 2008: 172–73)

Following the initial implementation of stringent neoliberal structural adjustment programs, postneoliberalism entails a mix of social legitimacy and democratization measures based on participatory projects of social service provision. Indicative here would be the antipoverty scheme of Oportunidades (Opportunities) in Mexico that provides conditional cash transfer payments to families in relation to nutrition, health, and educational targets. Linked to earlier poverty alleviation programs discussed throughout this book, notably Programa Nacional de Solidaridad (PRONASOL) and its replacement Programa de Educación, Salud y Alimentación (PROGRESA), Oportunidades was launched in 1997. In that year it covered three hundred thousand families in 6,344 localities across twelve states in Mexico with a budget of $58.8 million and by 2006 had stretched coverage to five million families, representing 24 percent of the country's population, 86,000 localities, and was scaled up to all thirty-one states with a budget of $2.8 billion (Levy 2006: 26, 31). The aim was to subsidize food, hygiene, reproductive health, and consumption in urban and rural poverty-stricken households through cash transfers conditional, among other criteria, on school attendance. In the assessment of Santiago Levy, general director of the Instituto Mexicano del Seguro Social (IMSS) from 2000 to 2005 and responsible for Oportunidades, it was a social welfare reform that was empowering in that "the poor cease to be the subject of political discourse and become instead the subject of their own transformation" (Levy 2006: 150). In context, though, both PROGRESA and its successor Oportunidades reflect a deep-seated social welfare reform of the Mexican state covering not only pensions, health services, childcare, and housing under the rubric of IMSS, for private-sector workers, but also the Instituto de Seguridad y Servicios Sociales de los Trabajadores del Estado (ISSSTE), for public employees.[7] Set against conditions of economic crisis and the NAFTA-driven removal of food subsidies (notably on tortillas and bread), Oportunidades, instead, represents a counterreform consolidating the commodification of social services and benefits. Its role is to demonstrate the state's discursive concern about poverty while rooting reform within the logic of neoliberal capital accumulation (Laurell 2003: 338–44). Despite this, Oportunidades has been "scaled-up" to regional and global levels through the similar Chile Solidario and Bolsa Família programs in Chile and Brazil, respectively.[8] Even Castañeda (2006: 36) has described such schemes "as neoliberal and scantly revolutionary as one can get." Thus, rather than promoting transformation at the point of production, in property relations, the rural and urban sociospatial targeting of such programs aims to anchor poverty and inequality within the functioning of the existing labor process, including the sphere of social reproduction, while increasing consumption and expanding informalized capital-labor relations. Concurrent with Fernando Leiva (2008: xxvi), the result is a sanitized view of Latin American economy and society excised of power relations while aiming to decouple state intervention from the expanded reproduction of capital accumulation and struggles over the distribution of surplus-value. As Castañeda himself has confessed, the supposed traits of postneoliberalism are "only an alternative within the existing framework of globalization rather than purporting to break with it, because you cannot."[9] The emergent debate over postneoliberalism can therefore be regarded as a reformist restoration and resuscitation of neoliberalism (see Peck, Theodore, and Brenner 2009: 103–4). It does not reflect a point of transition to a different pattern of capital accumulation. Although some may conceive of the creation of new spaces of collective resistance through postneoliberalism (Brand and Sekler 2009; Fernandes 2010), it is more fruitful to regard the policy practices of postneoliberalism as a renewal of capitalism, an attempt to attenuate but not resolve its crisis contradictions. In sum, postneoliberalism remains within the framework of passive revolution: it is a strategy undertaken by state classes to maintain the reproduction of the relations of production and the survival of capitalism in the twenty-first century. As Henri Lefebvre (1976: 34) writes, "underneath its pretended and pretentious newness, modernity conceals the tedium of the repetitive, its self-satisfied cud-chewing and regurgitation," which brings the reproduction of changes in capitalism to the fore in all social spheres. Therefore "one may apply to the concept of passive revolution . . . the interpretative criterion of molecular changes which in fact progressively modify the pre-existing composition of forces, and hence become the matrix of new changes" (Gramsci 1971: 109, Q15§11). The postneoliberal era does not mark a fundamental rupture with the conditions of passive revolution in Mexico and its history of modern state formation.

From a regional perspective, what remains open-ended is the extent to which a wider hemispheric antipassive revolution contestation of neoliberalism may further emerge. To that effect the Alianza Bolivariana de los Pueblos de las Américas (ALBA), renamed as such in 2009 and led in its membership by radical left-oriented governments in Venezuela, Bolivia, Ecuador, and Cuba, was created in 2006 envisioning an alternative form of regional integration than that posited by neoliberalism. There is an echo of the resurgence of such radical transformation in Lefebvre's (1991: 386) query: "How could one aim for power without reaching for the places where power resides, without planning to occupy that space and to create a new political morphology?" These left turns have therefore embarked on the production of a counterspace of "alternative territorial forms" (Rénique 2009: 2). Yet the resurgence of leftist governments in Latin America is also embedded within a history of pendular swings between radical populism and incorporation of social movements through state structures, programs, and clientelistic networks (Luna and Filgueria 2009). Could these progressive regimes represent populist versions of passive revolutions? This dilemma has been aptly posed by William Robinson (2008: 340): "How can those who come to power through elections move beyond the constraints of polyarchy and transnationalized capitalist states?" It is radical social movements themselves, then, that should be regarded as the repository of transformative possibilities across Latin America in renewing struggles over, and against, state power. Of course, there is always the danger of such social movements losing out to processes of "statification." Yet, whether in the form of the EZLN's recalcitrance against the state-party system in Mexico; the Comités de Tierra Urbana in Venezuela, radicalizing the path of transformation opened up by Hugo Chávez; the resistance of indigenous movements in Bolivia to the oil and mining developments enacted by Evo Morales; or, in Ecuador, in the form of the Confederación de Nacionalidades Indígenas del Ecuador (CONAIE) in contesting Rafael Correa's exploitation of natural resources and specific mining laws, there is a dynamism that will propel new cycles of class struggle. It is, therefore, to creating new ways out of the historical structure of passive revolution by conceiving and putting into practice anticapitalist social organizations in concrete sites and spaces of struggle that attention should now turn (see Ceceña 2009; Taylor 2009). As the analytical backbone of this book has attested, new rounds of urban and rural resistance contesting state power and the production of space in Mexico and Latin America will therefore be central to the future course of uneven development, state formation, and passive revolution.

NOTES

1. Admittedly Trotsky (1929/2004: 24) asserted that it is "necessary to understand this unevenness correctly, to consider it in its full extent, and also to extend it to the

pre-capitalist past." For some, this licenses a warrant to stretch uneven and combined development as a transhistorical essence, reaching "all the way back into the socio-ecological unevenness characterising the earliest forms of social existence" (Rosenberg 2010: 186; also see Callinicos and Rosenberg 2008). Yet, treated as a universal process, uneven and combined development can be reduced to a triviality telling us very little about capitalism and capitalist restructuring (see Smith 2006: 182). "Far more disturbing," then, "is to find Marxists, despite the historical acuity of their theory, submitting to the same trivialization" (Smith 1984/2008: 3).

2. I was reminded of this point by Chris Hesketh during our excellent and ongoing conversations on state, space, and uneven development.

3. *The Economist* [London], "Just Don't Call It Plan Mexico" (27 December 2007): 65–66.

4. *The Economist* [London], "State of Siege" (18 June 2007): 55–56; BBC News, "Mexico's Drug Related Violence" (19 July 2010), www.bbc.co.uk; accessed 21 July 2010.

5. U.S. Joint Forces Command, "Joint Operating Environment (JOE 2008): Challenges and Implications for the Future Joint Force," www.globalsecurity.org; accessed 21 April 2009; *The Economist* [London], "Taking On the Unholy Family" (25 July 2009): 47–48; *The Economist* [London], "A 'Dying' City Protests" (20 February 2010): 49; BBC News, "Monterrey Caught Up in Mexico's Drug Conflict" (24 June 2010), www.bbc.co.uk; accessed 21 July 2010; and *Financial Times* [London], "Mexico Rebuffs 'Failed State' Claims" (18 January 2009).

6. *The Economist* [London], "A New Breed for Fox" (22 July 2000): 36.

7. The privatization of basic welfare services and the pension system provided by the ISSSTE, whose central office is on the Plaza de la República facing the Monument to the Revolution, has proceeded apace and met strong popular protest, see *La Jornada*, "Aval limitado de la Corte al nuevo sistema de pensiones del ISSSTE" (18 June 2008) and the earlier op-ed tracking of the process, inter alia, by Luis Hernández Navarro, "Ley del ISSSTE: atraco a mano alzada," *La Jornada* (20 March 2007). Again the reader is reminded here of Néstor García Canclini's typology of urban monuments and how, in this case, their presence becomes neutralized or altered due to a disruption in scale, given that the building of ISSSTE overlooks the Monument to the Revolution (see García Canclini 1989: 217–25; García Canclini 1995: 212–22).

8. *The Economist* [London], "Happy Families" (9 February 2008): 54.

9. Author's interview with Jorge Castañeda, Mexico City (9 and 13 March 1999).

References

Abrams, Philip (1977/1988) "Notes on the Difficulty of Studying the State," *Journal of Historical Sociology*, 1(1): 58–89.

Adorno, Theodor W. (1974a) *Minima Moralia: Reflections from Damaged Life*, trans. E. F. N. Jephcott. London: Verso.

———. W. (1974b) "Commitment," *New Left Review* (I), no. 87–88: 75–89.

———. W. (2000) *Introduction to Sociology*. Cambridge: Polity Press.

Agnew, John (1994) "The Territorial Trap: The Geographical Assumptions of International Relations Theory," *Review of International Political Economy*, 1(1): 53–80.

———. (2003) *Geopolitics: Re-Visioning World Politics*, 2d ed. London: Routledge.

Aguayo Quezada, Sergio (2001) "El financiamento extranjero y la transición democrática Mexicana: El caso de Alianza Cívica," http://www.laneta.apc.org/alianza/Conferencia; accessed 11 April 2002.

Aguilar Camín, Héctor (1980) "The Relevant Tradition: Sonoran Leaders in the Revolution," in D. A. Brading (ed.) *Caudillo and Peasant in the Mexican Revolution*. Cambridge: Cambridge University Press.

Aguilar Camín, Héctor and Lorenzo Meyer (1993) *In the Shadow of the Mexican Revolution: Contemporary Mexican History, 1910–1989*, trans. Luis Alberto Fierro. Austin: University of Texas Press.

Amin, Samir (1974) *Accumulation on a World Scale: A Critique of the Theory of Underdevelopment*, vol. 1. New York: Monthly Review Press.

Anderson, Perry (1974) *Lineages of the Absolutist State*. London: Verso.

———. (1983) *In the Tracks of Historical Materialism*. London: Verso.

———. (1998) *The Origins of Postmodernity*. London: Verso.

Appendini, Kirsten Albrechtsen, Daniel Murayama, and Rosa María Domínguez (1972) "Desarrollo desigual en México," *Demografía y economía*, 6(1): 1–39.

Apuleyo Mendoza, Plinio, Carlos Alberto Montaner and Alvaro Vargas Llosa (1996/2000) *Guide to the Perfect Latin American Idiot*, intro. Mario Vargas Llosa, trans. Michaela Lajda Ames. Lanham, MD: Madison Books.

Arditi, Benjamin (2007) "Post-Hegemony: Politics Outside the Usual Post-Marxist Paradigm," *Contemporary Politics*, 13(3): 205–26.

Arizpe, Lourdes (1985) "The State and Uneven Agrarian Development in Mexico," in George Philip (ed.) *Politics in Mexico*. London: Croom Helm.

Aubry, Andrés and Angélica Inda (1998) "Who Are the Paramilitaries in Chiapas?," *NACLA Report on the Americas*, 31(5): 8–10.

Azuela, Alicia (1993) "*El Machete* and *Frente a Frente*: Art Committed to Social Justice in Mexico," *Art Journal*, 52(1): 82–7.

Azuela, Mariano (1915/1997) *Los de abajo*. Madrid: Ediciones Cátedra.

Baer, Werner (1972) "Import Substitution and Industrialisation in Latin America: Experiences and Interpretations," *Latin American Research Review*, 7(1): 95–122.

Bardach, Noah (2008) "Post-Revolutionary Art, Revolutionary Artists: Mexican Political Art Collectives 1921–1960," Ph.D. diss., University of Essex.

Barkin, David (1975) "Mexico's Albatross: The United States Economy," *Latin American Perspectives*, 2(2): 64–80.

———. (1983) "The Internationalisation of Capital and the Spatial Organisation of Agriculture in Mexico," in Frank Moulaert and Patricia Wilson Salinas (eds.) *Regional Analysis and the New International Division of Labour: Applications of a Political Economy Approach*. Dordrecht: Kluwer.

———. (1990) *Distorted Development: Mexico in the World Economy*. Boulder, CO: Westview Press.

Barkin, David and Gustavo Esteva (1982) "Social Conflict and Inflation in Mexico," *Latin American Perspectives*, 9(1): 48–64.

Barmeyer, Niels (2003) "The Guerrilla Movement as a Project: An Assessment of Community Involvement in the EZLN," *Latin American Perspectives*, 30(1): 122–38.

Baronnet, Bruno (2008) "Rebel Youth and Zapatista Autonomous Education," *Latin American Perspectives*, 35(4): 112–24.

Barry, Tom (ed.) (1992) *Mexico: A Country Guide*. Albuquerque, NM: Inter-Hemispheric Education Resource Center.

———. (1995) *Zapata's Revenge: Free Trade and the Farm Crisis*. Boston, MA: South End Press.

Bartra, Roger (1975) "Peasants and Political Power in Mexico: A Theoretical Approach," *Latin American Perspectives*, 2(2): 125–45.

———. (1982) "Capitalism and the Peasantry in Mexico," *Latin American Perspectives*, 9(1): 36–47.

———. (1992) *The Cage of Melancholy: Identity and Metamorphosis in the Mexican Character*, trans. Christopher J. Hall. New Brunswick, NJ: Rutgers University Press.

———. (1993) *Agrarian Structure and Political Power in Mexico*, trans. Stephen K. Ault. Baltimore, MD: Johns Hopkins University Press.

Bartra, Roger and Gerardo Otero (1987) "Agrarian Crisis and Social Differentiation in Mexico," *Journal of Peasant Studies*, 14(3): 334–62.

Baxandall, Lee (1962) "An Interview with Carlos Fuentes" [10 August 1962, Mexico City], *Studies on the Left*, 3(1): 48–56.

Beasley-Murray, Jon (2003) "On Posthegemony," *Bulletin of Latin American Research*, 22(1): 117–25.

———. (2010) *Posthegemony: Political Theory and Latin America*. Minneapolis: University of Minnesota Press.

Beasley-Murray, Jon and Alberto Moreiras (1999) "After Hegemony: Culture and the State in Latin America," *Journal of Latin American Cultural Studies*, 8(1): 17–20.

Benjamin, Thomas (1985) "The Leviathan on the Zócalo: Recent Historiography of the Post-Revolutionary Mexican State," *Latin American Research Review*, 20(3): 195–217.

———. (1996) *A Rich Land, A Poor People: Politics and Society in Modern Chiapas*, with a foreword by Lorenzo Meyer. Albuquerque: University of New Mexico Press.

———. (2000) *La Revolución: Mexico's Great Revolution as Memory, Myth and History*. Austin: University of Texas Press.

Benjamin, Walter (1940/1970) "Theses on the Philosophy of History," in Walter Benjamin, *Illuminations*, trans. Harry Zohn. London: Jonathan Cape Ltd.

Bennett, Douglas and Kenneth Sharpe (1982) "The State as Banker and Entrepreneur: The Last Resort Character of the Mexican State's Economic Intervention, 1917–1970," in Sylvia Ann Hewlett and Richard S. Weinert (eds.) *Brazil and Mexico: Patterns in Late Development*. Philadelphia: Institute for the Study of Human Issues.

Berman, Marshall (1982) *All That Is Solid Melts Into Air: The Experience of Modernity*. London: Verso.

Berins Collier, Ruth (1992) *The Contradictory Alliance: State-Labour Relations and Regime Change in Mexico*. Berkeley: University of Berkeley Press.

Bernstein, Henry (2000) "'The Peasantry' in Global Capitalism: Who, Where and Why?" in Leo Panitch and Colin Leys (eds.) *The Socialist Register: Working Classes, Global Realities*. London: Merlin Press.

———. (2002) "Land Reform: Taking a Long(er) View," *Journal of Agrarian Change*, 2(4): 433–63.

Bieler, Andreas and Adam David Morton (2003) "Globalisation, the State and Class Struggle: A 'Critical Economy' Engagement with Open Marxism," *British Journal of Politics and International Relations*, 5(4): 467–99.

———. (2008) "The Deficits of Discourse in IPE: Turning Base Metal into Gold?," *International Studies Quarterly*, 52(1): 103–28.

Bieler, Andreas, Werner Bonefeld, Peter Burnham and Adam David Morton (2006) *Global Restructuring, State, Capital and Labour: Contesting Neo-Gramscian Perspectives*. London: Palgrave.

Bilgin, Pinar and Adam David Morton (2002) "Historicising Representations of 'Failed States': Beyond the Cold War Annexation of the Social Sciences?," *Third World Quarterly*, 23(1): 55–80.

Binford, Leigh (2004) "A Hegemony-Influenced Analysis of Posthegemony." Paper presented at the XXV International Congress of the Latin American Studies Association (LASA), Las Vegas (7–9 October).

Blair, Calvin (1964) "Nacional Financiera: Entrepreneurship in a Mixed Economy," in Raymond Vernon (ed.) *Public Policy and Private Enterprise in Mexico*. Cambridge, MA: Harvard University Press.

Blaut, J. M. (1993) *The Colonizer's Model of the World: Geographical Diffusionism and Eurocentric History*. New York: Guilford.

———. (1999) "Marxism and Eurocentric Diffusionism," in Ronald M. Chilcote (ed.) *The Political Economy of Imperialism: Critical Appraisals*. Dordrecht: Kluwer Academic Publishers, 127–39.

Bobrow-Strain, Aaron (2007) *Intimate Enemies: Landowners, Power and Violence in Chiapas*. Durham, NC: Duke University Press.

Boelhower, William Q. (1981) "Antonio Gramsci's Sociology of Literature," *Contemporary Literature*, 22(4): 574–99.

Boldy, Steven (1987) "Carlos Fuentes," in John King (ed.) *Modern Latin American Fiction: A Survey*. London: Faber and Faber.

Bonfil Batalla, Guillermo (1996) *México Profundo: Reclaiming a Civilisation*, trans. Philip A. Dennis. Austin: University of Texas Press.

Borges, Jorge Luis (1960/2000) *Collected Fictions*, trans. Andrew Hurley. London: Penguin.

Brand, Uli and Nicola Sekler (guest eds.) (2009) "Postneoliberalism—A Beginning Debate," *Development Dialogue*, 51(January).

Branford, Sue and Jan Rocha (2002) *Cutting the Wire: The Story of Landless Movement in Brazil*. London: Latin America Bureau.

Brass, Tom (2002) "Latin American Peasants: New Paradigms for Old?," *Journal of Peasant Studies*, 29(3/4): 1–40.

———. (2005) "Neoliberalism and the Rise of (Peasant) Nations within the Nation: Chiapas in Comparative and Theoretical Perspective," *Journal of Peasant Studies*, 32(3/4): 651–91.

Braunmühl, Claudia (1978) "On the Analysis of the Bourgeois Nation State and the World Market Context: An Attempt to Develop a Methodological and Theoretical Approach," in John Holloway and Sol Picciotto (eds.) *State and Capital: A Marxist Debate*. London: Edward Arnold.

Brenner, Neil (1997) "State Territorial Restructuring and the Production of Spatial Scale: Urban and Regional Planning in the Federal Republic of Germany, 1960–1990," *Political Geography*, 16(4): 273–306.

———. (1998) "Between Fixity and Motion: Accumulation, Territorial Organisation and the Historical Geography of Spatial Scales," *Environment and Planning D: Society and Space*, 16(1): 459–81.

Brenner, Robert (1977) "The Origins of Capitalist Development: A Critique of Neo-Smithian Marxism," *New Left Review* (I), no. 104: 25–92.

———. (1985a) "Agrarian Class Structure and Economic Development in Pre-Industrial Europe," in T. H. Aston and C. H. E. Philpin (eds.) *The Brenner Debate: Agrarian Class Structure and Economic Development in Pre-Industrial Europe*. Cambridge: Cambridge University Press, 10–63.

———. (1985b) "The Agrarian Roots of European Capitalism," T. H. Aston and C. H. E. Philpin (eds.) *The Brenner Debate: Agrarian Class Structure and Economic Development in Pre-Industrial Europe*. Cambridge: Cambridge University Press, 213–327.

————. (1989) "Bourgeois Revolution and Transition to Capitalism," in A. L. Beier, David Cannadine and James M. Rosenheim (eds.) *The First Modern Society: Essays in English History in Honour of Lawrence Stone*. Cambridge: Cambridge University Press, 271–304.

Brewster, Claire (2005) *Responding to Crisis in Contemporary Mexico: The Political Writings of Paz, Fuentes, Monsiváis and Poniatowska*. Tucson: University of Arizona Press.

Bruff, Ian (2010) "European Varieties of Capitalism and the International," *European Journal of International Relations*, 16(4): 615–38.

Bruhn, Kathleen (1997) *Taking on Goliath: The Emergence of a New Left Party and the Struggle for Democracy in Mexico*. University Park: Pennsylvania State University Press.

————. (1999) "Antonio Gramsci and the *Palabra Verdadera*: The Political Discourse of Mexico's Guerrilla Forces," *Journal of InterAmerican Studies and World Affairs*, 41(2): 29–55.

Brushwood, John S. (1966) *Mexico in Its Novel: A Nation's Search for Identity*. Austin: University of Texas Press.

————. (1992) "A Comparative View of Mexican Fiction in the Seventies," in Raymond Leslie Williams (ed.) *The Novel in the Americas*. Niwot: University of Colorado Press.

Bruton, Henry J. (1998) "A Reconsideration of Import Substitution," *Journal of Economic Literature*, 36(2): 903–36.

Buci-Glucksmann, Christine (1979) "State, Transition and Passive Revolution," in Chantal Mouffe (ed.) *Gramsci and Marxist Theory*. London: Routledge.

————. (1980) *Gramsci and the State*, trans. David Fernbach. London: Lawrence and Wishart.

Burawoy, Michael (1989) "Two Methods in Search of Science: Skocpol versus Trotsky," *Theory and Society*, 18(6): 759–805.

————. (1998) "The Extended Case Method," *Sociological Theory*, 16(1): 4–33.

Burgos, R. (2002) "The Gramscian Intervention in the Theoretical and Political Production of the Latin American Left," *Latin American Perspectives*, 29(1): 9–37.

Burnham, Peter (2000) "Globalisation, Depoliticisation and 'Modern' Economic Management," in Werner Bonefeld and Kosmas Psychopedis (eds.) *The Politics of Change: Globalisation, Ideology and Critique*. London: Palgrave.

Buttigieg, Joseph A. (1982–1983) "The Exemplary Worldliness of Antonio Gramsci's Literary Criticism," *Boundary 2*, 11(1–2): 21–39.

C. de Grammont, Hubert (2003) "The Agricultural Sector and Rural Development in Mexico: Consequences of Economic Globalisation," in Kevin J. Middlebrook and Eduardo Zepeda (eds.) *Confronting Development: Assessing Mexico's Economic and Social Policy Challenges*. Stanford: Stanford University Press.

Calhoun, Craig (2003) "Why Historical Sociology?," in Gerard Delanty and Engin F. Isin (eds.) *Handbook of Historical Sociology*. London: Sage.

Callinicos, Alex (1982) "Trotsky's Theory of Permanent Revolution and Its Relevance to the Third World Today," *International Socialism* (Second Series), 16: 98–112.

———. (1989) "Bourgeois Revolutions and Historical Materialism," *International Socialism* (Second Series), 43: 113–71.

———. (2010) "The Limits of Passive Revolution," *Capital & Class*, 34(3): 491–507.

Callinicos, Alex and Justin Rosenberg (2008) "Uneven and Combined Development: The Social-Relational Substratum of 'the International'? An Exchange of Letters," *Cambridge Review of International Affairs*, 21(1): 77–112.

Cammack, Paul (1989) "Review Article: Bringing the State Back In?," *British Journal of Political Science*, 19(2): 261–90.

———. (1997) *Capitalism and Democracy in the Third World: The Doctrine for Political Development*. London: Leicester University Press.

———. (2002) "Attacking the Poor," *New Left Review* (II), no. 13: 125–34.

Camp, Roderic Ai (1985) *Intellectuals and the State in Twentieth-Century Mexico*. Austin: University of Texas Press.

Cancian, Frank and Peter Brown (1994) "Who Is Rebelling in Chiapas?," *Cultural Survival Quarterly*, 18(1): 22–25.

Cárdenas, Enrique (2000) "The Process of Accelerated Industrialisation in Mexico, 1919–1982," in Enrique Cárdenas, José Antonio Ocampo and Rosemary Thorp (eds.) *An Economic History of Twentieth-Century Latin America*, vol. 3: *Industrialisation and the State in Latin America: The Postwar Years*. London: Palgrave.

Carothers, Thomas (1991) *In the Name of Democracy: US Policy toward Latin America in the Reagan Years*. Berkeley: University of California Press.

———. (1994) "The NED at 10," *Foreign Policy*, no. 95 (Summer): 123–38.

———. (1999) *Aiding Democracy Abroad: The Learning Curve*. Washington DC: Carnegie Endowment for International Peace.

———. (2001) "The Resurgence of United States Political Development Assistance to Latin America in the 1980s," in Laurence Whitehead (ed.) *The International Dimensions of Democratisation: Europe and the Americas*, expanded edition. Oxford: Oxford University Press.

———. (2002) "The End of the Transition Paradigm," *Journal of Democracy*, 13(1): 5–21.

Carr, Barry (1983) "Marxism and Anarchism in the Formation of the Mexican Communist Party, 1910–19," *Hispanic American Historical Review*, 63(2): 277–305.

———. (1985) *Mexican Communism, 1968–1983: Eurocommunism in the Americas?* San Diego, CA: Center for US-Mexican Studies.

———. (1991) "Labour and the Political Left in Mexico," in Kevin J. Middlebrook (ed.) *Unions, Workers and the State in Mexico*. San Diego, CA: Center for US-Mexican Studies.

———. (1993) "Mexico: The Perils of Unity and the Challenge of Modernisation," in Barry Carr and Steve Ellner (eds.) *The Latin American Left: From the Fall of Allende to Perestroika*. Boulder, CO: Westview Press.

Carranza, Luis E. (2010) *Architecture as Revolution: Episodes in the History of Modern Mexico*, foreword Jorge Francisco Liernur. Austin: University of Texas Press.

Castañeda, Jorge G. (1994) *Utopia Unarmed: The Latin American Left After the Cold War*. New York: Vintage.

———. (1995) *The Mexican Shock: It's Meaning for the US*. New York: New Press.

———. (2006) "Latin America's Left Turn," *Foreign Affairs*, 85(3): 28–43.

Castañeda, Jorge G. and Marco A. Morales (eds.) (2008) *Leftovers: Tales of the Latin American Left*. London: Routledge.

Castellanos, Laura (2008) *Corte de Caja: entrevista al Subcomandante Marcos*. México, DF: Naucalpan.

Casullo, Nicolás (2007) *Las cuestiones*. Buenos Aires: Fondo de Cultura Económica.

———. (2009) "Memory and Revolution," *Journal of Latin American Cultural Studies*, 18(2/3): 107–24.

Ceceña, Ana Esther (2009) "Postneoliberalism and Its Bifurcations," *Development Dialogue*, 51(January): 33–43.

Centeno, Miguel Ángel (1994) *Democracy Within Reason: Technocratic Revolution in Mexico*. University Park: Pennsylvania State University Press.

Centeno, Miguel Ángel and Sylvia Maxfield (1992) "The Marriage of Finance and Order: Changes in the Mexican Political Elite," *Journal of Latin American Studies*, 24(1): 57–85.

Charnock, Greig (2006) "Improving the Mechanisms of Global Governance? The Ideational Impact of the World Bank on National Reform Agendas in Mexico," *New Political Economy*, 11(1): 73–98.

Chatterjee, Partha (1986) *Nationalist Thought and the Postcolonial World*. London: Zed Books.

———. (1993) *The Nation and Its Fragments: Colonial and Postcolonial Histories*. Princeton: Princeton University Press.

Chevalier, François (1967) "The Ejido and Political Stability in Mexico," in Claudio Veliz (ed.) *The Politics of Conformity in Latin America*. Oxford: Oxford University Press.

Chilcote, Ronald (2000) *Theories of Comparative Political Economy*. Boulder, CO: Westview Press.

———. (ed.) (2003) *Development in Theory and Practice*. Lanham, MD: Rowman & Littlefield.

Clark D'Lugo, Carol (1997) *The Fragmented Novel in Mexico: The Politics of Form*. Austin: University of Texas Press.

Clarke, Colin (1996) "Opposition to PRI 'Hegemony' in Oaxaca," in Rob Aitken, Nikki Craske, Gareth A. Jones and David E. Stansfield (eds.) *Dismantling the Mexican State?* London: Macmillan.

Cliff, Tony (1963/1999) "Deflected Permanent Revolution," in Tony Cliff, *Trotskyism after Trotsky: The Origins of the International Socialists*. London: Bookmarks.

Clifton, Judith (2000) *The Politics of Telecommunications in Mexico: Privatisation and State-Labour Relations, 1982–1995*. London: Macmillan.

Coates, David (2000) *Models of Capitalism: Growth and Stagnation in the Modern Era*. Cambridge: Polity Press.

Cockcroft, James D. (1974) "Mexico," in Ronald H. Chilcote and Joel C. Edelstein (eds.) *Latin America: The Struggle with Dependency and Beyond*. New York: Wiley & Sons.

———. (1983) *Mexico: Class Formation, Capital Accumulation and the State*. New York: Monthly Review Press.

———. (1998) *Mexico's Hope: An Encounter with Politics and History*. New York: Monthly Review Press.

———. (2010) *Mexico's Revolution, Then and Now*. New York: Monthly Review Press.

Cockcroft, James, D. et al. (eds.) (1972) *Dependence and Development: Latin America's Political Economy*. New York: Anchor Books.

Collier, David (1995) "Trajectory of a Concept: 'Corporatism' in the Study of Latin American Politics," in Peter H. Smith (ed.) *Latin America in Comparative Perspective: New Approaches to Methods and Analyses*. Boulder, CO: Westview Press.

Collier, George A. (1987) "Peasant Politics and the Mexican State: Indigenous Compliance in Highland Chiapas," *Mexican Studies/Estudios Mexicanos*, 3(1): 71–98.

———. (1994a) "The Rebellion in Chiapas and the Legacy of Energy Development," *Mexican Studies/Estudios Mexicanos*, 10(2): 371–82.

———. (1994b) "Reforms of Mexico's Agrarian Code: Impact on the Peasantry," *Research in Economic Anthropology*, 15: 105–27.

———. (1994c) "Roots of the Rebellion," *Cultural Survival Quarterly*, 18(1): 14–18.

———. (1994d) "The New Politics of Exclusion: Antecedents to the Rebellion in Mexico," *Dialectical Anthropology*, 19(1): 1–44.

Collier, George A., Daniel C. Mountjoy, and Ronald B. Nigh (1994) "Peasant Agriculture and Global Change: A Maya Response to Energy Development in Southeastern Mexico," *BioScience*, 44(6): 398–407.

Collier, George A. with Elizabeth L. Quaratiello (1994) *basta! Land and the Zapatista Rebellion in Chiapas*, foreword by Peter Rossett. Oakland, CA: Institute for Food and Development Policy.

Collier, Ruth Berins (1992) *The Contradictory Alliance: State-Labor Relations and Regime Change in Mexico*. Berkeley: University of California Press.

Combined Mexican Working Party (1953) *The Economic Development of Mexico*. Baltimore: Johns Hopkins University Press.

Comisión Económica para América Latina/Nacional Financiera (1971) *La política industrial en el desarrollo económico de México*. México, DF: NAFINSA.

Comninel, George C. (1987) *Rethinking the French Revolution: Marxism and the Revisionist Challenge*. London: Verso.

Conger, Lucy (1998) "A Fourth Way? The Latin American Alternative to Neoliberalism," *Current History*, 97(22): 380–84.

Cook, Maria Lorena (1995) "Mexican State-Labour Relations and the Political Implications of Free Trade," *Latin American Perspectives*, 22(1): 77–94.

Cook, Maria Lorena, Kevin J. Middlebrook and Juan Molinar Horcasitas (1994) "The Politics of Economic Restructuring in Mexico: Actors, Sequencing, and Coalition Change," in Maria Lorena Cook, Kevin J. Middlebrook and Juan Molinar Horcasitas (eds.) *The Politics of Economic Restructuring: State-Society Relations and Regime Change in Mexico*. San Diego, CA: Center for US-Mexican Studies.

Cooper-Clark, Diana (1986) "An Interview with Carlos Fuentes," in Diana Cooper-Clark (ed.) *Interviews with Contemporary Novelists*. London: Macmillan.

Córdova, Arnaldo (1973) *La ideología de la Revolución Mexicana: La formación del nuevo régimen*. México, DF: Ediciones Era.

———. (1974) *La política de masas del cardenismo*. México, DF: Ediciones Era.

————. (1978) *La formación del poder popular en México.* México, DF: Ediciones Era.

Cornelius, Wayne A. (1973) "Nation-Building, Participation and Distribution: The Politics of Social Reform under Cárdenas," in Gabriel A. Almond, Scott C. Flanagan, and Robert J. Mundt (eds.) *Crisis, Choice and Change: Historical Studies of Political Development.* Boston: Little, Brown and Company.

————. (1985) "The Political Economy of Mexico Under de la Madrid: Austerity, Routinised Crisis and Nascent Recovery," *Mexican Studies/Estudios Mexicanos*, 1(1): 83–123.

————. (1995) "Designing Social Policy for Mexico's Liberalised Economy: From Social Services and Infrastructure to Job Creation," in Riordan Roett (ed.) *The Challenge of Institutional Reform in Mexico.* Boulder, CO: Lynne Rienner.

————. (1996) *Mexican Politics in Transition: The Breakdown of a One-Party Dominant Regime.* San Diego, CA: Center for US-Mexican Studies.

————. (1999) "Subnational Politics and Democratisation: Tensions between Centre and Periphery in the Mexican Political System," in Wayne A. Cornelius, Todd A. Eisenstadt and Jane Hindley (eds.) *Subnational Politics and Democratisation in Mexico.* San Diego, CA: Center for US-Mexican Studies.

Cornelius, Wayne A., Anne L. Craig, and Jonathan Fox (1994) "Mexico's National Solidarity Program: An Overview," in Wayne A. Cornelius, Anne L. Craig and Jonathan Fox (eds.) *Transforming State-Society Relations in Mexico: The National Solidarity Strategy.* San Diego, CA: Center for US-Mexican Studies.

Cornelius, Wayne A., Todd A. Eisenstadt, and Jane Hindley (eds.) (1999) *Subnational Politics and Democratisation in Mexico.* San Diego, CA: Center for US-Mexican Studies.

Cornelius, Wayne A., Judith Gentleman, and Peter H. Smith (eds.) (1989) *Mexico's Alternative Political Futures.* San Diego, CA: Center for US-Mexican Studies.

Cox, Robert W. (1981/1986) "Social Forces, States and World Orders: Beyond International Relations Theory," in Robert O. Keohane (ed.) *Neorealism and Its Critics.* New York: Columbia University Press.

————. (1982) "Production and Hegemony: Toward a Political Economy of World Order," in Harold K. Jacobson and Dusan Sidjanski (eds.) *The Emerging International Economic Order: Dynamic Processes, Constraints and Opportunities.* London: Sage.

————. (1983) "Gramsci, Hegemony and International Relations: An Essay in Method," *Millennium: Journal of International Studies*, 12(2): 162–75.

————. (1987) *Production, Power and World Order: Social Forces in the Making of History.* New York: Columbia University Press.

Craske, Nikki (1994) *Corporatism Revisited: Salinas and the Reform of the Popular Sector.* London: Institute of Latin American Studies.

Craske, Nikki and Victor Bulmer-Thomas (eds.) (1994) *Mexico and the North American Free Trade Agreement: Who Will Benefit?* London: Macmillan.

Cypher, James M. (1990) *State and Capital in Mexico: Development Policy Since 1940.* Boulder, CO: Westview Press.

———. (2009) "Latin America and Globalisation, Reconsidered," *NACLA Report on the Americas*, 42(2): 46–48.

Cypher, James M. and Raúl Delgado Wise (2010) *Mexico's Economic Dilemma: The Developmental Failure of Neoliberalism*. Lanham, MD: Rowman & Littlefield.

Dahl, Robert A. (1954) *A Preface to Democratic Theory*. Chicago: University of Chicago Press.

———. (1971) *Polyarchy: Participation and Opposition*. New Haven: Yale University Press.

Davidson, Alastair (1977) "The Literary Criticism of Antonio Gramsci: An Introduction," in Stephen Knight and Michael Wilding (eds.) *The Radical Reader*. Sydney: Wild and Woolley.

Dávila Flores, Alejandro (2008) "Los clusters industriales del noreste de México, 1993–2003," *Región y Sociedad*, 20(41): 57–89.

Davis, Diane E. (1993) "The Dialectic of Autonomy: State, Class and Economic Crisis in Mexico," *Latin American Perspectives*, 20(3): 46–75.

———. (1994) *Urban Leviathan: Mexico City in the Twentieth Century*. Philadelphia: Temple University Press.

———. (2009) "From the Reforma-Peralvillo to the Torre Bicentenario: the Clash of 'History' and 'Progress' in the Urban Development of Modern Mexico City," in Linda A. Newson and John P. King (eds.) *Mexico City through History and Culture*, British Academy Occasional Paper, no.13. Oxford: Oxford University Press.

Day, Richard J. F. (2005) *Gramsci Is Dead: Anarchist Currents in the Newest Social Movements*. London: Pluto Press.

De Janvry, Alain (1981) *The Agrarian Question and Reformism in Latin America*. Baltimore: Johns Hopkins University Press.

De Janvry, Alain and Lynn Ground (1978) "Types and Consequences of Land Reform in Latin America," *Latin American Perspectives*, 5(4): 90–112.

De Janvry, Alain, Gustavo Gordillo and Elisabeth Sadoulet (1997) *Mexico's Second Agrarian Reform: Household and Community Responses, 1990–1994*. San Diego, CA: Center for US-Mexican Studies.

Desmarais, Annette Aurélie (2007) *La Vía Campesina: Globalisation and the Power of Peasants*. London: Pluto Press.

Dewalt, Billie R. and Martha W. Ress with Arthur D. Murphy (1994) *The End of Agrarian Reform in Mexico: Past Lessons and Future Prospects*. San Diego, CA: Center for US-Mexican Studies.

Diamond, Larry (2002) "Winning the New Cold War on Terrorism: The Democratic-Governance Imperative," *Institute for Global Democracy*, Policy Paper No. 1.

Diamond, Larry, Juan J. Linz, and Seymour Martin Lipset (1989) (eds.) *Democracy in Developing Countries*, 4 vols. Boulder, CO: Lynne Rienner.

Doezema, Herman P. (1972–1973) "An Interview with Carlos Fuentes" [7 February 1972, Mexico City], *Modern Fiction Studies*, 18(4): 491–503.

Dombroski, Robert S. (1982–1983) "Antonio Gramsci and the Politics of Literature: A Critical Introduction," *Italian Quarterly*, 25(1–2): 41–55.

———. (1986) "On Gramsci's Theatre Criticism," *Boundary 2*, 14(3): 91–117.

Dresser, Denise (1991) *Neopopulist Solutions to Neoliberal Problems: Mexico's National Solidarity Program*. San Diego, CA: Center for US-Mexican Studies.

———. (1994) "Bringing the Poor Back In: National Solidarity as a Strategy of Regime Legitimation," in Wayne A. Cornelius, Anne L. Craig and Jonathan Fox (eds.) *Transforming State-Society Relations in Mexico: The National Solidarity Strategy*. San Diego, CA: Center for US-Mexican Studies.

———. (1996a) "Mexico: The Decline of Dominant-Party Rule," in Jorge I. Domínguez and Abraham F. Lowenthal (eds.) *Constructing Democratic Governance: Mexico, Central America and the Caribbean in the 1990s*. Baltimore: Johns Hopkins University Press.

———. (1996b) "Treading Lightly Without a Stick: International Actors and the Promotion of Democracy in Mexico," in Tom Farer (ed.) *Beyond Sovereignty: Collectively Defending Democracy in the Americas*. Baltimore: Johns Hopkins University Press.

———. (2008) "Mexico: Dysfunctional Democracy," in Jorge I. Domínguez and Michael Shifter (eds.) *Constructing Democratic Governance in Latin America*. Baltimore: Johns Hopkins University Press.

Dussel Peters, Enrique (2000) *Polarizing Mexico: The Impact of Liberalisation Strategy*. Boulder, CO: Lynne Rienner.

Dunkerley, James (2000) *Warriors and Scribes: Essays in the History and Politics of Latin America*. London: Verso.

Eagleton, Terry (1976/2006) *Criticism and Ideology: A Study in Marxist Literary Theory*, new edition. London: Verso.

Earle, Duncan (1994) "Indigenous Identity at the Margin: Zapatismo and Nationalism," *Cultural Survival Quarterly*, 18(1): 26–30.

Eber, Christine and Christine Kovic (eds.) (2003) *Women of Chiapas: Making History in Times of Struggle and Hope*. London: Routledge.

Eder, Rita (1989) "The Icons of Power and Popular Art," in Helen Escobedo (ed.) *Mexican Monuments: Strange Encounters*. New York: Abbeville.

Ejército Zapatista de Liberación Nacional (EZLN) (2003) *Documentos y comunicados*, 5 vols. México, DF: Ediciones Era.

El Kilombo Intergaláctico (2007) *Beyond Resistance Everything: An Interview with Subcomandante Marcos*. Durham, NC: Paperboat Press.

Erol, Ertan (2010) "Review of *Passive Revolution: Absorbing the Islamic Challenge to Capitalism* by Cihan Tuğal," *Capital & Class*, 34(3): 537–40.

Escobar, Arturo (1995) *Encountering Development: The Making and Unmaking of the Third World*. Princeton: Princeton University Press.

Esteva, Gustavo (2003) "The Meaning and Scope of the Struggle for Autonomy," in Jan Rus, Rosalva Aída Hernández Castillo and Shannan L. Mattiace (eds.) *Mayan Lives, Mayan Utopias: The Indigenous Peoples of Chiapas and the Zapatista Rebellion*. Lanham, MD: Rowman & Littlefield.

———. (2007) "Oaxaca: The Path of Radical Democracy," *Socialism and Democracy*, 21(2): 74–96.

———. (2009) "Another Perspective, Another Democracy," *Socialism and Democracy*, 23(3): 46–60.

Evans, Peter B., Dietrich Rueschemeyer, and Theda Skocpol (eds.) (1985) *Bringing the State Back In*. Cambridge: Cambridge University Press.

Faris, Wendy B. (1983) *Carlos Fuentes*. New York: Frederick Ungar.

——. (1988) "Desire and Power, Love and Revolution: Carlos Fuentes and Milan Kundera," *The Review of Contemporary Fiction*, 8(2): 273–84.

——. (1995) "Scheherazade's Children: Magical Realism and Postmodern Fiction," in Lois Parkinson Zamora and Wendy B. Faris (eds.) *Magical Realism: Theory, History, Community*. Durham, NC: Duke University Press.

Femia, Joseph V. (1981) *Gramsci's Political Thought: Hegemony, Consciousness and the Revolutionary Process*. Oxford: Clarendon Press.

Fernandes, Sujatha (2010) "Revolutionary Praxis in a Post-neoliberal Era," *Interventions*, 12(1): 88–99.

Fernández, Raúl and José F. Ocampo (1974) "The Latin American Revolution: A Theory of Imperialism, Not Dependence," *Latin American Perspectives*, 1(1): 30–61.

Fiddian, Robin (1990) "Carlos Fuentes: *La muerte de Artemio Cruz*," in Philip Swanson (ed.) *Landmarks in Modern Latin American Fiction*. London: Routledge.

Fitzgerald, E. V. K. (1977) "On State and Accumulation in Latin America," in E. V. K. Fitzgerald, E. Floto and A. D. Lehmann (eds.) *The State and Economic Development in Latin America*. Cambridge: Centre of Latin American Studies.

——. (1978) "The State and Capital Accumulation in Mexico," *Journal of Latin American Studies*, 10(2): 263–82.

——. (1984) "Restructuring through the Depression: The State and Capital Accumulation in Mexico, 1925–1940," in Rosemary Thorpe (ed.) *An Economic History of Twentieth-Century Latin America*, vol. 2: *Latin America in the 1930s: The Role of the Periphery in World Crisis*. London: Macmillan.

——. (1985) "The Financial Constraint on Relative Autonomy: The State and Capital Accumulation in Mexico, 1940–1982," in Christian Anglade and Carlos Fortin (eds.) *The State and Capital Accumulation in Latin America*, vol. 1: *Brazil, Chile, Mexico*. London: Macmillan.

Foran, John (2005) *Taking Power: On the Origins of Third World Revolutions*. Cambridge: Cambridge University Press.

Foster-Carter, Aidan (1977) "The Modes of Production Controversy," *New Left Review* (I), No. 107: 47–77.

Foweraker, Joe (1993) *Popular Mobilisation in Mexico: The Teachers' Movement, 1977–1987*. Cambridge: Cambridge University Press.

——. (1995) *Theorising Social Movements*. London: Pluto Press.

Foweraker, Joe, Todd Landman and Neil Harvey (2003) *Governing Latin America*. Cambridge: Polity Press.

Fox, Jonathan (1993) *The Politics of Food in Mexico: State Power and Social Mobilisation*. Ithaca: Cornell University Press.

——. (1994) "The Difficult Transition from Clientelism to Citizenship: Lessons from Mexico," *World Politics*, 46(2): 151–84.

——. (2004) "Assessing Binational Civil Society Coalitions: Lessons from the Mexico-U.S. Experience," in Kevin J. Middlebrook (ed.) *Dilemmas of Political Change in Mexico*. London: Institute of Latin American Studies.

Frank, Andre Gunder (1969a) *Latin America: Underdevelopment or Revolution*. New York: Monthly Review Press.

——. (1969b) *Capitalism and Underdevelopment in Latin America*. New York: Monthly Review Press.

——. (1979) *Mexican Agriculture, 1521–1630: Transformation of the Mode of Production*. Cambridge: Cambridge University Press.

Frente Popular Francisco Villa Independiente (FPFVI) (2006) "Por la Unidad del Pueblo en la Lucha por su Liberación" (November); http://www.unopii.org; accessed 19 July 2008.

Fuentes, Carlos (1958/1971) *Where the Air Is Clear*, trans. Sam Hileman. New York: Farrar, Straus and Giroux.

——. (1959/1968) *The Good Conscience*, trans. Sam Hileman. New York: Farrar, Straus and Giroux: New York.

——. (1962/1991) *The Death of Artemio Cruz*, trans. Alfred MacAdam. New York: Farrar, Straus and Giroux.

——. (1963) "The Argument of Latin America: Words for the North Americans," in Carlos Fuentes et al., *Whither Latin America?* New York: Monthly Review Press.

——. (1967/1972) *Holy Place*, trans. Suzanne Jill Levine, in *Triple Cross*. New York: E. P. Dutton and Co.

——. (1969a) *La nueva novela hispanoamericana*. México, DF: Joaquín Mortiz.

——. (1969b) *El mundo de José Luis Cuevas*, trans. Consuelo de Aerenlund. New York: Tudor.

——. (1969c) "Viva Zapata," Review of *Zapata and the Mexican Revolution*, by John Womack, *New York Review of Books* (13 March): 5–12.

——. (1971) *Tiempo mexicano*. México, DF: Joaquín Mortiz.

——. (1973) "Mexico and Its Demons," Review of *The Other Mexico: Critique of the Pyramid*, by Octavio Paz, *New York Review of Books* (20 September): 16–21.

——. (1978/1979) *The Hydra Head*, trans. Margaret Sayers Peden. New York: Farrar, Straus and Giroux.

——. (1980/1981) *Burnt Water*, trans. Margaret Sayers Peden. New York: Farrar, Straus and Giroux.

——. (1980/1982) *Distant Relations*, trans. Margaret Sayers Peden. New York: Farrar, Straus and Giroux.

——. (1984/2001) *Latin America: At War with the Past*, CBC Massey Lectures 1984. Toronto: House of Anansi Press.

——. (1985/1986) *The Old Gringo*, trans. Margaret Sayers Peden. New York: Farrar, Straus and Giroux.

——. (1987/1990) *Christopher Unborn*, trans. Alfred MacAdam. London: Picador.

——. (1988) "History out of Chaos," Review of *Revolutionary Mexico: The Coming and Process of the Mexican Revolution*, by John Mason Hart, *New York Times Book Review* (13 March): 12–13.

——. (1990/1992) *The Campaign*, trans. Alfred MacAdam. London: Picador.

——. (1992a) "Latin America and the Universality of the Novel," in Raymond Leslie Williams (ed.) *The Novel in the Americas*. Boulder: University of Colorado Press.

———. (1992b) *The Buried Mirror: Reflections on Spain and the New World*. London: André Deutsch.

———. (1992c) "The Barefoot Iliad," in Mariano Azuela, *The Underdogs*, trans. Frederick H. Fornoff. Pittsburgh: University of Pittsburgh Press.

———. (1994/1995) *Diana: The Goddess Who Hunts Alone*, trans. Alfred MacAdam. London: Bloomsbury.

———. (1994/1997) *A New Time for Mexico*, trans. Marina Gutman Castañeda. London: Bloomsbury.

———. (1995/1998) *The Crystal Frontier: A Novel in Nine Stories*. London: Bloomsbury.

———. (1998) "The Storyteller," in Carlos Fuentes and Julio Ortego (eds.) *The Picador Book of Latin American Stories*. London: Picador.

———. (1999/2000) *The Years with Laura Díaz*, trans. Alfred MacAdam. New York: Farrar, Straus and Giroux.

———. (2000) *Instinto de Inez*. México, DF: Alfaguara.

———. (2002/2006) *The Eagle's Throne*, trans. Kristina Cordero. London: Bloomsbury.

———. (2008) *La voluntad y la fortuna*. México, DF: Alfaguara.

———. (2009) *Adán en Edén*. México, DF: Alfaguara.

Gabriel Juárez-Galeana, Luis (2006) "Collaborative Public Open Space in Self-Help Housing: Minas-Polvorilla, Mexico City," in Roger Zetter and Georgia Butina Watson (eds.) *Designing Sustainable Cities in the Developing World*. Aldershot: Ashgate.

Gall, Olivia (1998) "Racism, Interethnic War and Peace in Chiapas," *Peace and Change*, 23(4): 531–44.

García Canclini, Néstor (1988) "Culture and Power: The State of Research," *Media, Culture and Society*, 10(4): 467–97.

———. (1989) "Monuments, Billboards and Graffiti," in Helen Escobedo (ed.) *Mexican Monuments: Strange Encounters*. New York: Abbeville.

———. (1995) *Hybrid Cultures: Strategies for Entering and Leaving Modernity*, trans. Christopher L. Chiappari and Silvia L. López. Minneapolis: University of Minnesota Press.

García de León, Antonio (1994/2003) "Prólogo," to Ejército Zapatista de Liberación Nacional (EZLN) *Documentos y comunicados*, 5 vols. México, DF: Ediciones Era.

———. (1995) "Chiapas and the Mexican Crisis," *NACLA Report on the Americas*, 29(1): 10–13.

———. (2005) "From Revolution to Transition: The Chiapas Rebellion and the Path to Democracy in Mexico," *Journal of Peasant Studies*, 32(3/4): 508–27.

Garza, Gustavo (1999) "Global Economy, Metropolitan Dynamics and Urban Policies in Mexico," *Cities*, 16(3): 149–70.

———. (2003) "The Dialectics of Urban and Regional Disparities in Mexico," in Kevin J. Middlebrook and Eduardo Zepeda (eds.) *Confronting Development: Assessing Mexico's Economic and Social Policy Challenges*. Stanford: Stanford University Press.

———. (2006) "Technological Innovation and the Expansion of Mexico City, 1870–1920," *Journal of Latin American Geography*, 5(2): 109–26.

Gendzier, Irene L. (1998) "Play It Again Sam: The Practice and Apology of Development," in Christopher Simpson (ed.) *Universities and Empire: Money and Politics in the Social Sciences During the Cold War*. New York: New Press.

Geras, Norman (1986) *Literature of Revolution: Essays on Marxism*. London: Verso.

Gibler, John (2009) *Mexico Unconquered: Chronicles of Power and Revolt*, foreword Gloria Muñoz Ramírez. San Francisco: City Lights Books.

Gilbreth, Chris and Gerardo Otero (2001) "Democratisation in Mexico: The Zapatista Uprising and Civil Society," *Latin American Perspectives*, 28(4): 7–29.

Gill, Stephen (2008) *Power and Resistance in the New World Order*, second edition. London: Palgrave.

Gills, Barry K., Joel Rocamora and Richard Wilson (eds.) (1993) *Low Intensity Democracy: Political Power in the New World Order*. London: Pluto Press.

Gilly, Adolfo (1971/2007) *La revolución interrumpida*, segunda edición. México, DF: Ediciones Era.

———. (1979) "La guerra de clases en la revolución mexicana (Revolución permanente y auto-organización de las masas)," in Adolfo Gilly et al., *Interpretaciones de la revolución mexicana*. México, DF: Editorial Nueva Imagen.

———. (1994) *El cardenismo, una utopía mexicana*. México, DF: Aguilar, León y Cal Editores.

———. (1997) *Chiapas: la razón ardiente. Ensayo sobre la rebelión del mundo encantado*. México, DF: Ediciones Era.

———. (2005) *The Mexican Revolution*, trans. Patrick Camiller. New York: New Press.

———. (2006) *Historia a contrapelo: Una constelación*. México, DF: Ediciones Era.

———. (2010) "'What Exists Cannot Be True,'" *New Left Review* (II), no. 64: 29–45.

Giordano, Al (2006) "Mexico's Presidential Swindle," *New Left Review* (II), no. 41: 5–27.

Gledhill, John (1996) "The State, the Countryside . . . and Capitalism," in Rob Aitken, Nikki Craske, Gather A. Jones and David E. Stansfield (eds.) *Dismantling the Mexican State?* London: Macmillan.

Gollinger, Eva (2007) *The Chávez Code: Cracking US Intervention in Venezuela*. London: Pluto Press.

González, Alfonso (1989) "Krauze's Carlos Fuentes: Toward the Creation of a Myth," *The International Fiction Review*, 16(2): 98–102.

Gonzalez, Michael (1974) "*Cambio de piel* or The Myth of Literature," Occasional Paper 10. Glasgow University: Institute of Latin American Studies.

González Casanova, Pablo (1968) "Mexico: The Dynamics of an Agrarian and 'Semicapitalist' Revolution," in James Petras and Maurice Zeitlin (eds.) *Latin America: Reform or Revolution?* New York: Fawcett Publications.

———. (1970) *Democracy in Mexico*, trans. Danielle Salti. Oxford: Oxford University Press.

Görg, Christoph and Joachim Hirsch (1998) "Is International Democracy Possible?," *Review of International Political Economy*, 5(4): 585–615.

Gott, Richard (2006) "Venezuela's Murdoch," *New Left Review* (II), no. 39: 149–58.

Gramsci, Antonio (1971) *Selections from the Prison Notebooks*, ed. and trans. Quintin Hoare and Geoffrey Nowell-Smith. London: Lawrence and Wishart.

———. (1918/1975) "Republic and Proletariat in France," *Il Grido del Popolo* [20 April] in Antonio Gramsci, *History, Philosophy and Culture in the Young Gramsci*, ed. Pedro Cavalcanti and Paul Piccone. St. Louis, MO: Telos Press.

———. (1977) *Selections from Political Writings, 1910–1920*, intro. Quintin Hoare, trans. John Matthews. London: Lawrence and Wishart.

———. (1978) *Selections from Political Writings, 1921–1926*, ed. and trans. Q. Hoare. London: Lawrence and Wishart.

———. (1985) *Selections from Cultural Writings*, ed. David Forgacs and Geoffrey Nowell-Smith, trans. William Boelhower. London: Lawrence and Wishart.

———. (1992) *Prison Notebooks*, vol. 1, ed. Joseph A, Buttigieg, trans. Antonio Callari. New York: Columbia University Press.

———. (1994a) *Letters from Prison*, vol. 1, ed. and intro. Frank Rosengarten, trans. Raymond Rosenthal. New York: Columbia University Press.

———. (1994b) *Letters from Prison*, vol. 2, ed. Frank Rosengarten, trans. Raymond Rosenthal. New York: Columbia University Press.

———. (1994c) *Pre-Prison Writings*, ed. Richard Bellamy, trans. Virginia Cox. Cambridge: Cambridge University Press.

———. (1995) *Further Selections from the Prison Notebooks*, ed. and trans. Derek Boothman. London: Lawrence and Wishart.

———. (1996) *Prison Notebooks*, vol. 2, ed. and trans. Joseph A. Buttigieg. New York: Columbia University Press.

———. (2007) *Prison Notebooks*, vol. 3, ed. and trans. Joseph A. Buttigieg. New York: Columbia University Press.

Grayson, George W. (2007) *Mexican Messiah: Andrés Manuel López Obrador*. University Park: Pennsylvania State University Press.

Green, Marcus (2002) "Gramsci Cannot Speak: Presentations and Interpretations of Gramsci's Concept of the Subaltern," *Rethinking Marxism*, 14(3): 1–24.

Greene, Graham (1939/2006) *The Lawless Roads*. London: Penguin Books.

Grugel, Jean (2002) *Democratisation: A Critical Introduction*. London: Palgrave.

———. (2003) "Democratisation Studies Globalisation: The Coming of Age of a Paradigm," *British Journal of Politics and International Relations*, 5(2): 258–83.

Haber, Stephen (1997) "The Worst of Both Worlds: The New Cultural History of Mexico," *Mexican Studies/Estudios Mexicanos*, 13(2): 363–83.

———. (1999) "Anything Goes: Mexico's 'New' Cultural History," *Hispanic American Historical Review*, 79(2): 309–30.

Halliday, Fred (1999) *Revolution and World Politics: The Rise and Fall of the Sixth Great Power*. London: Macmillan.

Hamilton, Nora (1981) "State Autonomy and Dependent Capitalism in Latin America," *British Journal of Sociology*, 32(3): 305–29.

———. (1982a) "The State and the National Bourgeoisie in Postrevolutionary Mexico: 1920–1940," *Latin American Perspectives*, 9(4): 31–54.

———. (1982b) *The Limits of State Autonomy: Post-Revolutionary Mexico*. Princeton: Princeton University Press.

———. (1984) "State-Class Alliances and Conflicts: Issues and Actors in the Mexican Economic Crisis," *Latin American Perspectives*, 11(4): 6–32.

Hansen, Roger D. (1974) *The Politics of Mexican Development*. Baltimore: Johns Hopkins University Press.

Harris, Richard L. (1978) "Marxism and the Agrarian Question in Latin America," *Latin American Perspectives*, 5(4): 2–26.

Harris, Richard L. and David Barkin (1982) "The Political Economy of Mexico in the Eighties," *Latin American Perspectives*, 9(1): 2–19.

Harss, Luis and Barbara Dohmann (1967) "Carlos Fuentes, or the New Heresy," in Luis Harss and Barbara Dohmann (eds.) *Into the Mainstream: Conversations with Latin American Writers*. New York: Harper and Row.

Hart, John M. (1987) *Revolutionary Process: The Coming and Process of the Mexican Revolution*. Berkeley: University of California Press.

———. (2002) *Empire and Revolution: The Americans in Mexico since the Civil War*. Berkeley: University of California Press.

Harvey, David (1982/2006) *The Limits to Capital*, new edition. London: Verso.

———. (1985/2001) "The Geopolitics of Capitalism," in David Harvey, *Spaces of Capital: Towards a Critical Geography*. Edinburgh: Edinburgh University Press.

———. (1996) *Justice, Nature and the Geography of Difference*. Oxford: Blackwell Publishing.

———. (2003a) *The New Imperialism*. Oxford: Oxford University Press.

———. (2003b) *Paris, Capital of Modernity*. London: Routledge.

Harvey, Neil (1988) "Personal Networks and Strategic Choices in the Formation of an Independent Peasant Organisation: The OCEZ of Chiapas, Mexico," *Bulletin of Latin American Research*, 7(2): 299–312.

———. (1990) *The New Agrarian Movement in Mexico, 1979–1990*. London: Institute of Latin American Studies.

———. (1995) "Rebellion in Chiapas: Rural Reforms and Popular Struggle," *Third World Quarterly*, 16(1): 39–73.

———. (1996) "Rural Reforms and the Zapatista Rebellion: Chiapas, 1988–1995," in Gerardo Otero (ed.) *Neoliberalism Revisited: Economic Restructuring and Mexico's Political Future*. Boulder, CO: Westview Press.

———. (1998) *The Chiapas Rebellion: The Struggle for Land and Democracy*. Durham, NC: Duke University Press.

———. (2000) "The Zapatistas, Radical Democratic Citizenship and Women's Struggle," *Social Politics*, 5(2): 158–87.

Hathaway, Dale (2000) *Allies Across the Border: Mexico's "Authentic Labor Front" and Global Solidarity*. Cambridge, MA: South End Press.

Hellman, Judith Adler (1983) *Mexico in Crisis*, second edition. New York: Holmes & Meier.

———. (1994) "Mexican Popular Movements, Clientelism and the Process of Democratisation," *Latin American Perspectives*, 21(2): 124–42.

———. (1995) "The Riddle of New Social Movements: Who They Are and What They Do," in Sandor Halebsky and Richard L. Harris (eds.) *Capital, Power and Inequality in Latin America*. Boulder, CO: Westview Press.

———. (1999) "Real and Virtual Chiapas: Magic Realism and the Left," in Leo Panitch and Colin Leys (eds.) *The Socialist Register: Necessary and Unnecessary Utopias*. London: Merlin Press.

———. (2008) *The World of Mexican Migrants: The Rock and the Hard Place*. New York: New Press.

Helmuth, Chalene (1997) *The Postmodern Fuentes*. Cranbury: Associated University Press.

Henfrey, Colin (1981) "Dependency, Modes of Production and the Class Analysis of Latin America," *Latin American Perspectives*, 8(3–4): 17–54.

Heredia, Blanca (1996) "State-Business Relations in Contemporary Mexico," in Mónica Serrano and Victor Bulmer-Thomas (eds.) *Rebuilding the State: Mexico After Salinas*. London: Institute of Latin American Studies.

Hernández Castillo, Rosalva Aída (1995) "Reinventing Tradition," *Cultural Survival Quarterly*, 19(1): 24–25.

Hernández Delgado, José (1959) "Nacional Financiera, S.A. Symbolises Mexico's Industrialisation," in Adolfo López Mateos, *The Economic Development of Mexico During a Quarter of a Century (1934–1959)*. México, DF: Nacional Financiera.

Hernández Navarro, Luis (1998) "The Escalation of the War in Chiapas," *NACLA Report on the Americas*, 31(5): 7–10.

———. (2004) "The Global Zapatista Movement," America Program, Silver City. NM: Interhemispheric Resource Centre.

Hesketh, Chris (2010a) "Spaces of Capital/Spaces of Resistance: Mexico and the Global Political Economy, Ph.D. diss., University of Nottingham.

———. (2010b) "From Passive Revolution to Silent Revolution: Class Forces and the Production of State, Space and Scale in Modern Mexico," *Capital & Class*, 34(3): 383–407.

Hewitt de Alcántara, Cynthia (1984) *Anthropological Perspectives on Rural Mexico*. London: Routledge.

———. (1994) "Introduction: Economic Restructuring and Rural Subsistence in Mexico," in Cynthia Hewitt de Alcántara (ed.) *Economic Restructuring and Rural Subsistence in Mexico: Corn and the Crisis of the 1980s*. San Diego, CA: Center for US-Mexican Studies.

Higgins, Nicholas (2004) *Understanding the Chiapas Rebellion: Modernist Visions and the Invisible Indian*. Austin: University of Texas Press.

Hobsbawm, Eric (1975) *The Age of Capital, 1848–1875*. London: Weidenfeld & Nicolson.

———. (1983) "Mass-Producing Traditions: Europe, 1870–1914," in Eric Hobsbawm and Terence Ranger (eds.) *The Invention of Tradition*. Cambridge: Cambridge University Press.

———. (1987) *The Age of Empire, 1875–1914*. London: Weidenfeld & Nicolson.

———. (1994) *Age of Extremes: The Short Twentieth Century, 1914–1991*. London: Penguin.

———. (1999) "Peasants and Politics" [1973] in Eric Hobsbawm, *Uncommon People: Resistance, Rebellion and Jazz*. London: Abacus.

Hodges, Donald C. and Ross Gandy (1979) *Mexico 1910–1976: Reform or Revolution?* London: Zed Books.

———. (1983) *Mexico 1910–1982: Reform or Revolution?* London: Zed Books.

———. (2002a) *Mexico, the End of the Revolution*. Westport, CT: Praeger.

——. (2002b) *Mexico Under Siege: Popular Resistance to Presidential Despotism.* London: Zed Books.

Holloway, John (2002) *Change the World Without Taking Power: The Meaning of Revolution Today.* London: Pluto Press.

Holloway, John and Sol Picciotto (1977) "Capital, Crisis and the State," *Capital & Class*, no. 2: 76–101.

Huber, Evelyn (1995) "Assessments of State Strength," in Peter H. Smith (ed.) *Latin America in Comparative Perspective: New Approaches to Methods and Analyses.* Boulder, CO: Westview Press.

Huntington, Samuel P. (1968) *Political Order in Changing Societies.* New Haven: Yale University Press.

——. (1991) *The Third Wave: Democratisation in the Late Twentieth Century.* Norman: University of Oklahoma Press.

——. (1991–1992) "How Countries Democratise," *Political Science Quarterly*, 106(4): 579–616.

Jameson, Fredric (1971) *Marxism and Form: Twentieth-Century Dialectical Theories of Literature.* Princeton: Princeton University Press.

Janes, Regina (1979) "'No More Interviews': A Conversation with Carlos Fuentes," *Salmagundi*, 43: 87–95.

Jessop, Bob (1990) *State Theory: Putting the Capitalist State in its Place.* Cambridge: Polity Press.

——. (2002) *The Future of the Capitalist State.* Cambridge: Polity Press.

——. (2006) "Gramsci as a Spatial Theorist," in Andreas Bieler and Adam David Morton (eds.) *Images of Gramsci: Connections and Contentions in Political Theory and International Relations.* London: Routledge.

——. (2008) "Dialogue of the Deaf: Some Reflections on the Poulantzas-Miliband Debate," in Paul Wetherly, Clyde W. Barrow and Peter Burnham (eds.) *Class, Power and the State in Capitalist Society: Essays on Ralph Miliband.* London: Palgrave.

Johns, Michael (1997) *The City of Mexico in the Age of Díaz.* Austin: University of Texas Press.

Joseph, Gilbert M. and Daniel Nugent (eds.) (1994) *Everyday Forms of State Formation: Revolution and the Negotiation of Rule in Modern Mexico.* Durham, NC: Duke University Press.

Joseph, Gilbert M., Anne Rubenstein, and Eric Zolov (eds.) (2001) *Fragments of a Golden Age: The Politics of Culture in Mexico since 1940.* Durham, NC: Duke University Press.

Kampwirth, Karen (1998) "Peace Talks, But No Peace," *NACLA Report on the Americas*, 31(5): 15–19.

Katz, Friedrich (1981) *The Secret War in Mexico: Europe, the United States and the Mexican Revolution.* Princeton: Princeton University Press.

Kautsky, Karl (1899/1988) *The Agrarian Question*, trans. Pete Burgess, intro. Hamza Alavi and Teodor Shanin. 2 vols. London: Zwan Publications.

Kay, Cristóbal (2000) "Latin America's Agrarian Transformation: Peasantisation and Proletarianisation," in Deborah Bryceson, Cristóbal Kay and Jos Mooij (eds.)

Disappearing Peasantries? Rural Labour in Africa, Asia and Latin America. Bourton-on-Dunsmore: Intermediate Technology Development Group Publications.

Kearney, Michael (1996) *Reconceptualising the Peasantry: Anthropology in Global Perspective*. Boulder, CO: Westview Press.

Kerr, Lucille (1980) "The Paradox of Power and Mystery: Carlos Fuentes' *Terra Nostra*," *Publications of the Modern Language Association of America* (PMLA), 95(1): 91–102.

Kiely, Ray (2005) "Capitalist Expansion and the Imperialism-Globalisation Debate: Contemporary Marxist Explanations," *Journal of International Relations and Development*, 8(1): 27–57.

King, John (1987) "An Interview with Carlos Fuentes [November 1986, Cambridge]," in John King (ed.) *Modern Latin American Fiction: A Survey*. London: Faber and Faber.

Knei-Paz, Baruch (1978) *The Social and Political Thought of Leon Trotsky*. Oxford: Oxford University Press.

Knight, Alan (1984) "The Working Class and the Mexican Revolution, c.1900–1920," *Journal of Latin American Studies*, 16(1): 51–79.

———. (1985) "The Mexican Revolution: Bourgeois? Nationalist? Or Just a 'Great Rebellion,'" *Bulletin of Latin American Research*, 4(2): 1–37.

———. (1986a) *The Mexican Revolution*, vol. 1: *Porfirians, Liberals and Peasants*. Cambridge: Cambridge University Press.

———. (1986b) *The Mexican Revolution*, vol. 2: *Counter-revolution and Reconstruction*. Cambridge: Cambridge University Press.

———. (1987) *US-Mexican Relations: An Interpretation*. San Diego, CA: Centre for US-Mexican Studies.

———. (1990a) "Social Revolution: A Latin American Perspective," *Bulletin of Latin American Research*, 9(2): 175–202.

———. (1990b) "Revolutionary Project, Recalcitrant People: Mexico, 1910–1940," in Jaime O. Rodríguez O. (ed.) *The Revolutionary Process in Mexico: Essays on Political and Social Change, 1880–1940*. Los Angeles: University of California Los Angeles Latin American Centre.

———. (1991a) "Land and Society in Revolutionary Mexico: The Destruction of the Great Haciendas," *Mexican Studies/Estudios Mexicanos*, 7(1): 73–104.

———. (1991b) "The Rise and Fall of Cardenismo, c.1930–c.1946," in Leslie Bethell (ed.) *Mexico Since Independence*. Cambridge: Cambridge University Press.

———. (1992a) "Revisionism and Revolution: Mexico Compared to England and France," *Past and Present*, 134: 159–99.

———. (1992b) "The Peculiarities of Mexican History: Mexico Compared to Latin America, 1821–1992," *Journal of Latin American Studies*, 24: Quincentenary Supplement: 99–144.

———. (1992c) "Mexico's Elite Settlement: Conjuncture and Consequences," in John Higley and Richard Gunther (eds.) *Elites and Democratic Consolidation in Latin America and Southern Europe*. Cambridge: Cambridge University Press.

———. (1992d) "The Politics of the Expropriation," in Jonathan C. Brown and Alan Knight (eds.) *The Mexican Petroleum Industry in the Twentieth Century*. Austin: University of Texas Press.

———. (1993) "State Power and Political Stability in Mexico," in Neil Harvey (ed.) *Mexico: Dilemmas of Transition*. London: Institute for Latin American Studies.

———. (1994a) "Popular Culture and the Revolutionary State in Mexico, 1910–1940," *Hispanic American Historical Review*, 74(3): 393–444.

———. (1994b) "Cardenismo: Juggernaut or Jalopy?," *Journal of Latin American Studies*, 26(1): 73–107.

———. (1994c) "Weapons and Arches in the Mexican Revolutionary Landscape," in Gilbert M. Joseph and Daniel Nugent (eds.) *Everyday Forms of State Formation: Revolution and the Negotiation of Rule in Modern Mexico*. Durham, NC: Duke University Press.

———. (1999) "Political Violence in Post-Revolutionary Mexico," in Kees Koonings and Dirk Kruijt (eds.) *Societies of Fear: The Legacy of Civil War, Violence and Terror in Latin America*. London: Zed Books.

———. (2001) "The Modern Mexican State: Theory and Practice," in Miguel Angel Centeno and Fernando López-Alves (eds.) *The Other Mirror: Grand Theory Through the Lens of Latin America*. Princeton: Princeton University Press, 177–218.

———. (2002a) *Mexico, From the Beginning to the Spanish Conquest*, vol. I. Cambridge: Cambridge University Press.

———. (2002b) *Mexico, The Colonial Era,* vol. II. Cambridge: Cambridge University Press.

———. (2002c) "Subalterns, Signifiers and Statistics: Perspectives on Mexican Historiography," *Latin American Research Review*, 37(2): 136–58.

———. (2006) "Patterns and Prescriptions in Mexican Historiography," *Bulletin of Latin American Research*, 25(3): 340–66.

———. (2007) "Mexico's Three Fin de Siècle Crises," in Elisa Servín, Leticia Reina and John Tutino (eds.) *Cycles of Conflict, Centuries of Change: Crisis, Reform and Revolution in Mexico*. Durham, NC: Duke University Press.

Kovic, Christine (2003) "The Struggle for Liberation and Reconciliation in Chiapas, Mexico," *Latin American Perspectives*, 30(3): 58–79.

Krauze, Enrique (1988) "The Guerrilla Dandy," *New Republic*, (27 June): 28–38.

———. (1999) "Chiapas: The Indians' Prophet," *New York Review of Books*, 46(20): 65–73.

La Botz, Dan (1988) *The Crisis of Mexican Labor*. Westport, CT: Praeger.

———. (1995) *Democracy in Mexico: Peasant Rebellion and Political Reform*. Boston, MA: South End Press.

———. (2005) "Mexico's Labor Movement," *Monthly Review*, 57(2): 62–72.

Le Bot, Yvon (1997) *El sueño zapatista*. México, DF: Plaza y Janés.

Lacher, Hannes (1999) "Embedded Liberalism, Disembedded Markets: Reconceptualising the Pax Americana," *New Political Economy*, 4(3): 343–60.

———. (2002) "Making Sense of the International System: The Promises and Pitfalls of Contemporary Marxist Theories of International Relations," in Mark Rupert and Hazel Smith (eds.) *Historical Materialism and Globalisation*. London: Routledge.

———. (2003) "Putting the Capitalist State in Its Place: The Critique of State-Centrism and Its Limits," *Review of International Studies*, 29(4): 521–41.

———. (2006) *Beyond Globalisation: Capitalism, Territoriality and the International Relations of Modernity*. London: Routledge.

Laclau, Ernesto (1971/1977) "Feudalism and Capitalism in Latin America" in Ernesto Laclau, *Politics and Ideology in Marxist Theory: Capitalism-Fascism-Populism.* London: Verso, 15–50.

Latin American Subaltern Studies Group (1993) "Founding Statement," *Boundary 2,* 20(3): 110–21.

Laurell, Asa Cristina (2003) "The Transformation of Social Policy in Mexico," in Kevin J. Middlebrook and Eduardo Zepeda (eds.) *Confronting Development: Assessing Mexico's Economic and Social Policy Challenges.* Stanford: Stanford University Press.

Leal, Juan Felipe (1974) *La burguesía y el estado mexicano.* México, DF: Ediciones El Caballito.

———. (1986) "The Mexican State, 1915–1973: A Historical Interpretation," in Nora Hamilton and Timothy F. Harding (eds.) *Modern Mexico: State, Economy, and Social Conflict.* London: Sage.

Lefebvre, Henri (1976) *The Survival of Capitalism: Reproduction of the Relations of Production,* trans. Frank Bryant. London: Allison & Busby.

———. (1978/2009) "Space and the State," in Henri Lefebvre, *State, Space, World: Selected Essays,* ed. Neil Brenner and Stuart Elden, trans. Gerald Moore, Neil Brenner and Stuart Elden. Minneapolis: University of Minnesota Press.

———. (1991) *The Production of Space,* trans. Donald Nicholson-Smith. Oxford: Blackwell Publishing.

———. (2008) *Critique of Everyday Life,* 3 vols. trans. John Moore. London: Verso.

Leiva, Fernando Ignacio (2008) *Latin American Neostructuralism: The Contradictions of Post-Neoliberal Development.* Minneapolis: University of Minnesota Press.

Lenin, Vladimir I. (1899/1964) "The Development of Capitalism in Russia," in V. I. Lenin, *Collected Works,* vol. 3. London: Lawrence and Wishart.

———. (1907/1962) "The Agrarian Programme of Social-Democracy in the First Russian Revolution, 1905–1907," in V. I. Lenin, *Collected Works,* vol. 13. London: Lawrence and Wishart.

———. (1916/1964) *Imperialism, The Highest Stage of Capitalism: A Popular Outline,* in V. I. Lenin, *Collected Works,* vol. 12. London: Lawrence and Wishart.

Levy, Daniel C. and Kathleen Bruhn with Emilio Zebadúa (2001) *Mexico: The Struggle for Democratic Development.* Berkeley: University of California Press.

Levy, Santiago (2006) *Progress Against Poverty: Sustaining Mexico's Progresa-Oportunidades Program.* Washington DC: Brookings Institution Press.

Leyva Solano, Xochitl (1998) "The New Zapatista Movement: Political Levels, Actors and Political Discourse in Contemporary Mexico," in Valentina Napolitano and Xochitl Leyva Solano (eds.) *Encuentros Antropológicos: Power, Identity and Mobility in Mexican Society.* London: Institute of Latin American Studies.

Linz, Juan and Alfred Stepan (1996) *Problems of Democratic Transition and Consolidation.* Baltimore: Johns Hopkins University Press.

Lipietz, Alain (1982) "Towards a Global Fordism?," *New Left Review* (I), no. 132: 33–47.

———. (1984) "How Monetarism has Choked Third World Industrialisation," *New Left Review* (I), no. 145: 71–87.

———. (1987) *Mirages and Miracles: The Crises of Global Fordism*, trans. David Macey. London: Verso.

Lomnitz, Claudio (1992) *Exits from the Labyrinth: Culture and Ideology in the Mexican National Space*. Berkeley: University of California Press.

———. (2001) *Deep Mexico, Silent Mexico: An Anthropology of Nationalism*. Minneapolis: University of Minnesota Press.

Long, Ryan (2008) *Fictions of Totality: The Mexican Novel, 1968 and the National-Popular State*. West Lafayette, IN: Purdue University Press.

López Mateos, Adolfo (1959) *The Economic Development of Mexico During a Quarter of a Century (1934–1959)*. México, DF: Nacional Financiera.

Lorenzano, Luis (1998) "Zapatismo: Recomposition of Labour, Radical Democracy and Revolutionary Project," in John Holloway and Eloína Peláez (eds.) *Zapatista! Reinventing Revolution in Mexico*. London: Pluto Press.

Löwy, Michael (1975) "Is There a Law of Arrested and Un-combined Development?," *Latin American Perspectives*, 2(4): 118–20.

———. (1981) *The Politics of Combined and Uneven Development: The Theory of Permanent Revolution*. London: Verso.

Luna, Matilda (1995) "Entrepreneurial Interests and Political Action in Mexico: Facing the Demands of Economic Modernisation," in Riordan Roett (ed.) *The Challenge of Institutional Reform in Mexico*. Boulder, CO: Lynne Rienner.

Luna, Juan Pablo and Fernando Filgueria (2009) "The Left Turn as Multiple Paradigmatic Crises," *Third World Quarterly*, 30(2): 371–95.

MacAdam, Alfred and Charles Ruas (1981) "An Interview with Carlos Fuentes [December 1980, Princeton]," *Paris Review*, 82: 140–75.

Macciocchi, Maria-Antonietta (1975) *Gramsci y la revolución occidente*, trans. José Sazbón. México, DF: Siglo XXI.

Macdonald, Laura and Arne Ruckert (eds.) (2009) *Post-Neoliberalism in the Americas*. London: Palgrave.

MacEoin, Gary (1996) *The People's Church: Bishop Samuel Ruiz of Mexico and Why He Matters*. New York: Crossroad.

Mackinlay, Horacio and Gerardo Otero (2004) "State Corporatism and Peasant Organisations: Towards New Institutional Arrangements," in Gerardo Otero (ed.) *Mexico in Transition: Neoliberal Globalism, the State and Civil Society*. London: Zed Books.

Mallon, Florencia E. (1995) *Peasant and Nation: The Making of Postcolonial Mexico and Peru*. Berkeley: University of California Press.

———. (1999) "Time on the Wheel: Cycles of Revisionism and the 'New Cultural History,'" *Hispanic American Historical Review*, 79(2): 331–51.

Malloy, James M. (1977) "Authoritarianism and Corporatism in Latin America: The Modal Pattern," in James M. Malloy (ed.) *Authoritarianism and Corporatism in Latin America*. Pittsburgh: University of Pittsburgh Press.

Mandel, Ernest (1975) *Late Capitalism*, trans. Joris De Bres. London: Verso.

Manuel Durán, Victor (1994) *A Marxist Reading of Fuentes, Vargas Llosa and Puig*. Lanham, MD: University Press of America.

Manzoni, Alessandro (1997) *The Betrothed* and *History of the Column of Infamy*, ed. David Forgacs and Matthew Reynolds. London: J. M. Dent.

Marcuse, Herbert (1965/1968) "Industrialisation and Capitalism in the Work of Max Weber," in Herbert Marcuse, *Negations*, trans. Jeremy J. Shapiro. London: Allen Lane.

———. (1978) *The Aesthetic Dimension: Toward a Critique of Marxist Aesthetics*. Boston: Beacon Press.

Markiewicz, Dana (1993) *The Mexican Revolution and the Limits of Agrarian Reform, 1915–1946*. Boulder, CO: Lynne Rienner.

Marnham, Patrick (1998) *Dreaming With His Eyes Open: A Life of Diego Rivera*. London: Bloomsbury.

Martin, Gerald (1989) *Journeys Through the Labyrinth: Latin American Fiction in the Twentieth Century*. London: Verso.

Martin, Patricia (2007) "Mexico's Neoliberal Transition: Authoritarian Shadows in an Era of Neoliberalism," in Helga Leitner, Jamie Peck and Eric S. Sheppard (eds.) *Contesting Neoliberalism: Urban Frontiers*. New York: Guilford Press.

Marx, Karl (1843/1975) "Contribution to the Critique of Hegel's Philosophy of Law," in Karl Marx and Friedrich Engels, *Collected Works*, vol. 3. London: Lawrence and Wishart.

———. (1852/1979) *The Eighteenth Brumaire of Louis Bonaparte*, in Karl Marx and Friedrich Engels, *Collected Works*, vol. 11. London: Lawrence and Wishart.

———. (1857–1858/1973) *Grundrisse*, trans. Martin Nicolaus. London: Penguin.

———. (1857–1861/1986) *Outlines of the Critique of Political Economy*, in Karl Marx and Friedrich Engels, *Collected Works*, vol. 28. London: Lawrence and Wishart.

———. (1887/1996) *Capital*, vol. I, in Karl Marx and Friedrich Engels, *Collected Works*, vol. 35. London: Lawrence and Wishart.

———. (1894/1998) *Capital*, vol. III, in Karl Marx and Friedrich Engels, *Collected Works*, vol. 37. London: Lawrence and Wishart.

Marx, Karl and Friedrich Engels (1848/1976) *Manifesto of the Communist Party*, in Karl Marx and Friedrich Engels, *Collected Works*, vol. 6. London: Lawrence and Wishart.

Massey, Doreen (1995) S*patial Divisions of Labour: Social Relations and the Geography of Production*, 2nd edition. London: Palgrave.

———. (2005) *For Space*. London: Sage Publications.

Maxfield, Sylvia (1993) "The Politics of Mexican Financial Policy," in Stephan Haggard, Chung H. Lee and Sylvia Maxfield (eds.) *The Politics of Finance in Developing Countries*. Ithaca: Cornell University Press.

Mazza, Jacqueline (2001) *Don't Disturb the Neighbors: The United States and Democracy in Mexico, 1980–1995*. London: Routledge.

McCaughan, Edward J. (1993) "Mexico's Long Crisis: Toward New Regimes of Accumulation and Domination," *Latin American Perspectives*, 20(3): 6–31.

McClean, Alison (2009) "Committed to Print: Print Making and Politics in Mexico and Beyond, 1934–1960," in Dawn Ádes and Alison McClean (eds.) *Revolution on Paper: Mexican Prints, 1910–1960*. London: British Museum.

McKay, Ian (2009) "'O dark dark dark. They all go into the dark': The Many Deaths of Antonio Gramsci—Review of *Gramsci Is Dead: Anarchist Currents in the Newest Social Movements* by Richard Day," *Capital & Class*, 34(3): 131–40.

McMichael, Philip (1990) "Incorporated Comparison within a World-Historical Perspective: An Alternative Comparative Method," *American Sociological Review*, 55(3): 385–97.

———. (2000) "World-Systems Analysis, Globalisation and Incorporated Comparison," *Journal of World Systems Research*, VI(3): 668–90.

———. (2001) "Revisiting the Question of the Transnational State: A Comment on William Robinson's 'Social Theory of Globalisation,'" *Theory and Society*, 30(2): 201–9.

Medeiros, Carlos Aguiar de (2009) "Asset-Stripping the State: Political Economy of Privatisation in Latin America," *New Left Review* (II), no. 55: 109–32.

Mendoza-Berrueto, Eliseo (1968) "Regional Implications of Mexico's Economic Growth," *Weltwirtschaftliches Archiv* [Review of World Economics], 101: 87–121.

Meyer, Jean (1976) *The Cristero Rebellion: The Mexican People Between Church and State, 1926–1929*, trans. Richard Southern. Cambridge: Cambridge University Press.

———. (1991) "Revolution and Reconstruction in the 1920s," in Leslie Bethell (ed.) *Mexico Since Independence*. Cambridge: Cambridge University Press.

Meyer, Lorenzo (1977) "Historical Roots of the Authoritarian Regime," in José Luis Reyna and Richard S. Weinert (eds.) *Authoritarianism in Mexico*. Philadelphia: Institute for the Study of Human Issues.

Meyer, Michael C. and William L. Sherman (1987) *The Course of Mexican History*, third edition. Oxford: Oxford University Press.

Michaels, Albert L. (1970) "The Crisis of Cardenismo," *Journal of Latin American Studies*, 2(1): 51–79.

Middlebrook, Kevin J. (1986) "Political Liberalisation in an Authoritarian Regime: The Case of Mexico," in Guillermo O'Donnell, Philippe C. Schmitter and Laurence Whitehead (eds.) *Transitions From Authoritarian Rule: Latin America*, vol. 2. Baltimore: Johns Hopkins University Press.

———. (1995) *The Paradox of Revolution: Labour, the State and Authoritarianism in Mexico*. Baltimore: Johns Hopkins University Press.

———. (ed.) (2004a) *Dilemmas of Political Change in Mexico*. London: Institute of Latin American Studies.

———. (2004b) "Mexico's Democratic Transitions: Dynamics and Prospects," in Kevin J. Middlebrook (ed.) *Dilemmas of Political Change in Mexico*. London: Institute of Latin American Studies.

Middlebrook, Kevin J. and Eduardo Zepeda (eds.) (2003) *Confronting Development: Assessing Mexico's Economic and Social Policy Challenges*. Stanford: Stanford University Press.

Migdal, Joel S. (1988) *Strong Societies and Weak States: State-Society Relations and State Capabilities in the Third World*. Princeton: Princeton University Press.

———. (2001) *State in Society: Studying How States and Societies Transform and Constitute One Another*. Cambridge: Cambridge University Press.

Mijares Bracho, Carlos G. (1997) "The Architecture of Carlos Obregón Santacilia: A Work for Its Time and Context," in Edward R. Buran (ed.) *Modernity and the Architecture of Mexico*. Austin: University of Texas Press.

Miller, Nicola (1999) *In the Shadow of the State: Intellectuals and the Quest for National Identity in Twentieth-Century Spanish America*. London: Verso.

Millin, Sarah Gertrude (1933) *Rhodes*. London: Chatto & Windus.

Minns, John (2006) *The Politics of Developmentalism: The Midas States of Mexico, South Korea and Taiwan*. London: Palgrave.

Monsiváis, Carlos (1975) "Clasismo y Novela en México," *Latin American Perspectives*, 11(2): 164–79.

———. (1989) "On Civic Monuments and their Spectators," in Helen Escobedo (ed.) *Mexican Monuments: Strange Encounters*. New York: Abbeville.

———. (1990) "From '68 to Cardenismo: Toward a Chronicle of Social Movements," *Journal of International Affairs*, 43(2): 385–93.

———. (1997) *Mexican Postcards*, trans. and intro. John Kraniauskas. London: Verso.

Mora, Manuel Aguila (1979) "Estado y revolución en el proceso mexicano," in Adolfo Gilly et al., *Interpretaciones de la revolución mexicana*. México, DF: Editorial Nueva Imagen.

———. (1982) *El Bonapartismo Mexicano*. México, DF: Juan Pablos Editor.

Morton, Adam David (2005) "The Age of Absolutism: Capitalism, the Modern States-System and International Relations," *Review of International Studies*, 31(3): 495–517.

———. (2007a) *Unravelling Gramsci: Hegemony and Passive Revolution in the Global Political Economy*. London: Pluto Press.

———. (2007b) "Waiting for Gramsci: State Formation, Passive Revolution and the International," *Millennium: Journal of International Studies*, 35(3): 597–621.

———. (2007c) "Disputing the Geopolitics of the States-System and Global Capitalism," *Cambridge Review of International Affairs*, 20(4): 597–615.

———. (2010a) "Reflections on Uneven Development: Mexican Revolution, Primitive Accumulation, Passive Revolution," *Latin American Perspectives*, 37(1): 7–34.

———. (2010b) "The Continuum of Passive Revolution," *Capital & Class*, 34(3): 315–42.

Motta, Sara (2007) "Utopias Re-imagined: A Reply to Panizza," *Political Studies*, 54(4): 898–905.

———. (2008) "The Chilean Socialist Party (PSCh): Constructing Consent and Disarticulating Dissent to Neo-liberal Hegemony in Chile," *British Journal of Politics and International Relations*, 10(2): 303–27.

Moyo, Sam and Paris Yeros (2005) "The Resurgence of Rural Movements under Neoliberalism," in Sam Moyo and Paris Yeros (eds.) *Reclaiming the Land: The Resurgence of Rural Movements in Africa, Asia and Latin America*. London: Zed Books.

Munck, Ronaldo (1979) "State and Capital in Dependent Social Formations: The Brazilian Case," *Capital & Class*, 8: 34–53.

———. (1989) *Latin America: The Transition to Democracy*. London: Zed Books.

———. (1993) "After the Transition: Democratic Disenchantment in Latin America," *European Review of Latin American and Caribbean Studies*, no. 55 (December): 7–45.

———. (2003) *Contemporary Latin America*. London: Palgrave.

Murray, Robin (1971) "The Internationalisation of Capital and the Nation State," *New Left Review* (I), no. 67: 84–109.

Nacional Financiera (1978) *La economía mexicana en cifras*. México, DF: NAFIN.

Nadal, Alejandro (1998a) "Terror in Chiapas," *The Bulletin of the Atomic Scientists*, 54(2): 18–25.

———. (1998b) "Political Cleansing in Chiapas," *The Bulletin of the Atomic Scientists*, 54(3): 20–22.

Nash, June (1995) "The Reassertion of Indigenous Identity: Mayan Responses to State Intervention in Chiapas," *Latin American Research Review*, 30(3): 7–41.

Nash, June and Christine Kovic (1996) "The Reconstitution of Hegemony: The Free Trade Act and the Transformation of Rural Mexico," in James H. Mittelman (ed.) *Globalisation: Critical Reflections*. Boulder, CO: Lynne Rienner.

Nations, James D. (1994) "The Ecology of the Zapatista Revolt," *Cultural Survival Quarterly*, 18(1): 31–33.

Navarrete R., Alfredo (1967) "The Financing of Economic Development," in Tom E. Davis (ed.) *Mexico's Recent Economic Growth*. Austin, TX: Institute of Latin American Studies.

———. (1968) "Mexico's Balance of Payments and External Financing," *Weltwirtschaftliches Archiv* [Review of World Economics], 101: 70–84.

Noelle Merles, Louise (1997) "The Architecture and Urbanism of Mario Pani: Creativity and Compromise," in Edward R. Buran (ed.) *Modernity and the Architecture of Mexico*. Austin: University of Texas Press.

Novack, George (1972) *Understanding History: Marxist Essays*. New York: Pathfinder Press.

———. (1976) "The Law of Uneven and Combined Development and Latin America," *Latin American Perspectives*, 3(2): 100–106.

Nugent, Daniel (ed.) (1998) *Rural Revolt in Mexico: U.S. Intervention and the Domain of Subaltern Politics*. Durham, NC: Duke University Press.

O'Donnell, Guillermo (1973) *Modernisation and Bureaucratic Authoritarianism: Studies in South American Politics*. Berkeley: Institute of International Studies.

———. (1978) "Reflections on the Patterns of Change in the Bureaucratic-Authoritarian State," *Latin American Research Review*, 13(1): 3–38.

O'Donnell, Guillermo and Philippe C. Schmitter (1986) *Transitions from Authoritarian Rule: Tentative Conclusions about Uncertain Democracies*, vol. 4. Baltimore: Johns Hopkins University Press.

O'Donnell, Guillermo, Philippe C. Schmitter, and Laurence Whitehead (eds.) (1986) *Transitions from Authoritarian Rule: Prospects for Democracy*, 4 vols. Baltimore: Johns Hopkins University Press.

O'Malley, Ilene V. (1986) *The Myth of the Revolution: Hero Cults and the Institutionalisation of the Mexican State, 1920–1940*. Westport, CT: Greenwood Press.

O'Toole, Gavin (2003) "A New Nationalism for a New Era: The Political Ideology of Mexican Neoliberalism," *Bulletin of Latin American Research*, 22(3): 269–90.

Olesen, Thomas (2004) "Globalising the Zapatistas: from Third World solidarity to global solidarity?," *Third World Quarterly*, 25(1): 255–67.

———. (2005) *International Zapatismo: The Construction of Solidarity in the Age of Globalisation*. London: Zed Books.

Olsen, Patrice Elizabeth (2008) *Artifacts of Revolution: Architecture, Society and Politics in Mexico City, 1920–1940*. Lanham, MD: Rowman & Littlefield.

Ortega, Julio (1988) "*Christopher Unborn*: Rage and Laughter," *The Review of Contemporary Fiction*, 8(2): 285–92.

Otero, Gerardo (1996) "Mexico's Economic and Political Futures," in Gerardo Otero (ed.) *Neoliberalism Revisited: Economic Restructuring and Mexico's Political Futures*. Boulder, CO: Westview Press.

———. (1999) *Farewell to the Peasantry? Political Class Formation in Rural Mexico*. Boulder, CO: Westview Press.

———. (2004a) "Global Economy, Local Politics: Indigenous Struggles, Civil Society and Democracy," *Canadian Journal of Political Science*, 37(2): 325–46.

———. (2004b) "Contesting Neoliberal Globalism from Below: The EZLN, Indian Rights, and Citizenship," in Gerardo Otero (ed.) *Mexico in Transition: Neoliberal Globalism, the State and Civil Society*. London: Zed Books.

Oxhorn, Philip D. (1998) "Is the Century of Corporatism Over? Neoliberalism and the Rise of Neopluralism," in Philip D. Oxhorn and Graciela Ducatenzeiler (eds.) *What Kind of Democracy? What Kind of Market?: Latin America in the Age of Neoliberalism*. University Park: Pennsylvania State University Press.

Oxhorn, Philip D. and Graciela Ducatenzeiler (1998) "Economic Reform and Democratisation in Latin America," in Philip D. Oxhorn and Graciela Ducatenzeiler (eds.) *What Kind of Democracy? What Kind of Market?: Latin America in the Age of Neoliberalism*. University Park: Pennsylvania State University Press.

Padilla, Tanalís (2008) *Rural Resistance in the Land of Zapata: The Jaramillista Movement and the Myth of the Pax Priísta*. Durham, NC: Duke University Press.

Paine, Thomas (1791/1985) *Rights of Man*, intro. Eric Foner. London: Penguin.

Panitch, Leo (1994) "Globalisation and the State," in Leo Panitch and Ralph Miliband (eds.) *The Socialist Register: Between Globalism and Nationalism*. London: Merlin Press.

Panizza, Francisco (2005) "Unarmed Utopia Revisited: The Resurgence of Left-of-Centre Politics in Latin America," *Political Studies*, 53(4): 716–34.

Pansters, Wil (1999) "The Transition Under Fire: Rethinking Contemporary Mexican Politics," in Kees Koonings and Dirk Krujit (eds.) *Societies of Fear: The Legacy of Civil War and Terror in Latin America*. London: Zed Books.

Paz, Octavio (1950/1990) *The Labyrinth of Solitude: Life and Thought in Mexico*, trans. Lysander Kemp. London: Penguin Books.

———. (1967/1983) "Mask and Transparency," in Octavio Paz, *Alternating Current*, trans. Helen R. Lane. New York: Seaver Books.

———. (1979/1990) "The Philanthropic Ogre," in Octavio Paz, *The Labyrinth of Solitude*, trans. Lysander Kemp. London: Penguin Books.

Peck, Jamie, Nik Theodore, and Neil Brenner (2009) "Post-neoliberalism and Its Malcontents," *Antipode*, 41(S1): 94–116.

Perelman, Michael (2007) "Primitive Accumulation from Feudalism to Neoliberalism," *Capitalism Nature Socialism*, 18(2): 44–61.

Petras, James (2008) "Social Movements and Alliance-Building in Latin America," *Journal of Peasant Studies*, 35(3): 476–528.

Petras, James and Henry Veltmeyer (2002) "The Peasantry and the State in Latin America: A Troubled Past, an Uncertain Future," *Journal of Peasant Studies*, 29(3/4): 41–82.

———. (2007) "The "Development State" in Latin America: Whose Development, Whose State?," *Journal of Peasant Studies*, 34(3): 371–407.

Philip, George (2003) *Democracy in Latin America: Surviving Conflict and Crisis?* Cambridge: Polity Press.

Piester, Kerianne (1997) "Targeting the Poor: The Politics of Social Policy Reforms in Mexico," in Douglas A. Chalmers, Carlos M. Vilas, Katherine Hite, Scott B. Martin, Kerianne Piester and Monica Segarra (eds.) *The New Politics of Inequality in Latin America: Rethinking Participation and Representation.* Oxford: Oxford University Press.

Pitarch, Pedro (2004) "The Zapatistas and the Art of Ventriloquism," *Journal of Human Rights*, 3(3): 291–312.

Poniatowska, Elena (1971/1975) *Massacre in Mexico*, trans. Helen R. Lane. New York: Viking Press.

Portelli, Hugues (1973) *Gramsci y el bloque histórico*, trans. Maria Braun. México, DF: Siglo XXI.

Portes, Alejandro and Kelly Hoffman (2003) "Latin American Class Structures: Their Composition and Change during the Neoliberal Era," *Latin American Research Review*, 38(1): 41–82.

Poulantzas, Nicos (1973) *Political Power and Social Classes*, trans. Timothy O'Hagan. London: New Left Books.

———. (1975) *Classes in Contemporary Capitalism*, trans. David Fernbach. London: New Left Books.

———. (1978) *State, Power, Socialism*, trans. Patrick Camiller. London: Verso.

Powell, Kathy (1996) "Neoliberalism and Nationalism," in Rob Aitken, Nikki Craske, Gather A. Jones and David E. Stansfield (eds.) *Dismantling the Mexican State?* London: Macmillan.

Przeworski, Adam (1991) *Democracy and the Market: Political and Economic Reforms in Eastern Europe and Latin America.* Cambridge: Cambridge University Press.

Radice, Hugo (2008) "The Developmental State under Global Neoliberalism," *Third World Quarterly*, 29(6): 1153–74.

Ramírez, Miguel D. (1986a) *Development Banking in Mexico: The Case of the Nacional Financiera, S.A.* Westport, CT: Praeger.

———. (1986b) "Mexico's Development Experience 1950–1985: Lessons and Future Prospects," *Journal of Interamerican Studies and World Affairs*, 28(2): 39–65.

———. (1989) *Mexico's Economic Crisis: Its Origins and Consequences.* Westport, CT: Praeger.

————. (1994) "Privatisation and the Role of the State in Post-ISI Mexico," in Werner Baer and Melissa H. Birch (eds.) *Privatisation in Latin America: New Roles for the Public and Private Sectors.* Westport, CT: Praeger.

Rankin, Monica A. (2009) *¡México, la patria! Propaganda and Production During World War II.* Lincoln: University of Nebraska Press.

Reeve, Richard M. (1982) "The Making of *La región más transparente*: 1949–1974," in Robert Brody and Charles Rossman (eds.) *Carlos Fuentes: A Critical View.* Austin: University of Texas Press.

Rénique, Gerardo (2007) "Subaltern Political Formation and the Struggle for Autonomy in Oaxaca," *Socialism and Democracy*, 21(2): 62–73.

————. (2009) "Latin America: The New Neoliberalism and Popular Mobilisation," *Socialism and Democracy*, 23(3): 1–26.

Reyna, José Luis (1977) "Redefining the Authoritarian Regime," in José Luis Reyna and Richard S. Weinert (eds.) *Authoritarianism in Mexico.* Philadelphia: Institute for the Study of Human Issues.

Riley, Dylan J. and Manali Desai (2007) "The Passive Revolutionary Route to the Modern World: Italy and India in Comparative Perspective," *Comparative Studies in Society and History*, 49(4): 815–47.

Rivera Ríos, Miguel Ángel (1986) *Crisis y Reorganización del Capitalismo Mexicano, 1960–1985.* México: Ediciones Era.

Robinson, William I. (1996) *Promoting Polyarchy: Globalisation, US Intervention and Hegemony.* Cambridge: Cambridge University Press.

————. (2000) "Promoting Capitalist Polyarchy: The Case of Latin America," in Michael Cox, G. John Ikenberry and Takashi Inoguchi (eds.) *American Democracy Promotion: Impulses, Strategies and Impacts.* Oxford: Oxford University Press.

————. (2001a) "Transnational Processes, Development Studies and Changing Social Hierarchies in the World System: A Central American Case Study," *Third World Quarterly*, 22(4): 529–63.

————. (2001b) "Social Theory and Globalisation: The Rise of a Transnational State," *Theory and Society*, 30(2): 157–200.

————. (2003) *Transnational Conflicts: Central America, Social Change and Globalisation.* London: Verso.

————. (2004a) *A Theory of Global Capitalism: Production, Class and State in a Transnational World.* Baltimore: Johns Hopkins University Press.

————. (2004b) "Global Crisis and Latin America," *Bulletin of Latin American Research*, 23(2): 135–53.

————. (2006a) "Gramsci and Globalisation: From Nation-State to Transnational Hegemony," in Andreas Bieler and Adam David Morton (eds.) *Images of Gramsci: Connections and Contentions in Political Theory and International Relations.* London: Routledge.

————. (2006b) "Promoting Polyarchy in Latin America: The Oxymoron of 'Market Democracy,'" in Eric Hershberg and Fred Rosen (eds.) *Latin America After Neoliberalism: Turning the Tide in the 21st Century.* New York: New Press.

——. (2007) "Transformative Possibilities in Latin America," in Leo Panitch and Colin Leys (eds.) *The Socialist Register: Global Flashpoints—Reactions to Imperialism and Neoliberalism*. London: Merlin Press.

——. (2008) *Latin America and Global Capitalism: A Critical Globalisation Perspective*. Baltimore: Johns Hopkins University Press.

Rodríguez, Victoria E. and Peter M. Ward (1996) "The New PRI: Recasting Its Identity," in Rob Aitken, Nikki Craske, Gareth A. Jones and David E. Stansfield (eds.) *Dismantling the Mexican State?* London: Macmillan.

Rodríguez Araujo, Octavio (1979) *La reforma política y los partidos en México*. México, DF: Siglo XXI.

Romagnolo, David J. (1975) "The So-Called 'Law' of Uneven and Combined Development," *Latin American Perspectives*, 1(2): 7–31.

Roman, Richard and Edur Velasco Arregui (1997) "Zapatismo and the Workers Movement in Mexico at the End of the Twentieth Century," *Monthly Review*, 49(3): 98–116.

Romano, James V. (1989) "Authorial Identity and National Disintegration in Latin America," *Ideologies & Literature*, 4(1): 167–98.

Roseberry, William (1994) "Hegemony and the Language of Contention," in Gilbert M. Joseph and Daniel Nugent (eds.) *Everyday Forms of State Formation: Revolution and the Negotiation of Rule in Modern Mexico*. Durham, NC: Duke University Press.

Rosen, Fred and Jo-Marie Burt (1997) "16 Activists Reflect on the Current Political Moment: Bishop Samuel Ruiz García," *NACLA: Report on the Americas*, 31(1): 38–43.

Rosenberg, Justin (1994) *The Empire of Civil Society: A Critique of the Realist Theory of International Relations*. London: Verso.

——. (2006) "Why Is There No International Historical Sociology?," *European Journal of International Relations*, 12(3): 307–40.

——. (2010) "Basic Problems in the Theory of Uneven and Combined Development. Part II: Unevenness and Political Multiplicity," *Cambridge Review of International Affairs*, 23(1): 165–89.

Ross, John (1995) *Rebellion from the Roots: Indian Uprising in Chiapas*. Monroe, MN: Common Courage Press.

——. (2006) *¡Zapatistas! Making Another World Possible: Chronicles of Resistance, 2000–2006*. New York: Nation Books.

——. (2009) *El Monstruo: Dread and Redemption in Mexico City*. New York: Nation Books.

Rovira, Guiomar (2000) *Women of Maize: Indigenous Women and the Zapatista Rebellion*, trans. Anna Keene. London: Latin America Bureau.

Rubin, Jeffrey W. (1990) "Popular Mobilisation and the Myth of State Corporatism," in Joe Foweraker and Ann L. Craig (eds.) *Popular Movements and Political Change in Mexico*. Boulder, CO: Lynne Rienner.

——. (1997) *Decentering the Regime: Ethnicity, Radicalism and Democracy in Juchitán, Mexico*. Durham, NC: Duke University Press.

Ruccio, David F. (2010) *Development and Globalisation: A Marxian Class Analysis.* London: Routledge.

Rus, Jan (1994) "The 'Comunidad Revolucionario Institucional': The Subversion of Native Government in Highland Chiapas, 1936–1968," in Gilbert Joseph and Daniel Nugent (eds.) *Everyday Forms of State Formation: Revolution and the Negotiation of Rule in Modern Mexico.* Durham, NC: Duke University Press.

———. (1995) "Local Adaptation to Global Change: The Reordering of Native Society in Highland Chiapas, Mexico, 1974–1994," *European Review of Latin American and Caribbean Studies*, 58: 71–89.

———. (2004) "Rereading Tzotzil Ethnography: Recent Scholarship from Chiapas, Mexico," in John M. Watanabe and Edward F. Fischer (eds.) *Pluralising Ethnography: Comparison and Representation in Maya Cultures, Histories and Identities.* Oxford: James Currey.

Rus, Jan, Rosalva Aída Hernández Castillo and Shannan L. Mattiace (eds.) (2003) *Mayan Lives, Mayan Utopias: The Indigenous Peoples of Chiapas and the Zapatista Rebellion.* Lanham, MD: Rowman & Littlefield.

Saad-Filho, Alfredo (2005) "The Political Economy of Neoliberalism in Latin America," in Alfredo Saad-Filho and Deborah Johnston (eds.) *Neoliberalism: A Critical Reader.* London: Pluto Press.

Said, Edward W. (1990) "Figures, Configurations, Transfigurations," *Race & Class*, 32(1): 1–16.

Salinas de Gortari, C. (2002) *México: The Policy and Politics of Modernisation*, trans. Peter Hearn and Patricia Rosas. Barcelona: Plaza & Janés Editores.

Santos, Boaventura de Sousa and Leonardo Avritzer (2007) "Opening up the Canon of Democracy," in Boaventura de Sousa Santos (ed.) *Democratising Democracy: Beyond the Liberal Democratic Canon.* London: Verso.

Sartre, Jean-Paul (1948/2001) *What Is Literature?* trans. Bernard Frechtman. London: Routledge.

Sassoon, Anne Showstack (1980) "Gramsci: A New Concept of Politics and the Expansion of Democracy," in Alan Hunt (ed.) *Marxism and Democracy.* London: Lawrence and Wishart.

———. (1987) *Gramsci's Politics*, second edition. Minneapolis: University of Minnesota Press.

Saunders, Frances Stonor (1999) *Who Paid the Piper? The CIA and the Cultural Cold War.* London: Granta Books.

Schedler, Andreas (2005) "From Electoral Authoritarianism to Democratic Consolidation," in Russell Crandall, Guadalupe Paz and Riordan Roett (eds.) *Mexico's Democracy at Work: Political and Economic Dynamics.* Boulder, CO: Lynne Rienner.

Schmitter, Philippe C. (1979) "Still the Century of Corporatism?," in Philippe C. Schmitter and Gerhard Lehmbruch (eds.) *Trends Towards Corporatist Intermediation.* London: Sage.

Schumpeter, Joseph A. (1942/1975) *Capitalism, Socialism and Democracy*, third edition. New York: Harper & Row.

Scott, James C. (1994) "Foreword," in Gilbert M. Joseph and Daniel Nugent (eds.) *Everyday Forms of State Formation: Revolution and the Negotiation of Rule in Modern Mexico*. Durham, NC: Duke University Press.

Semo, Enrique (1978) *Historia mexicana: economía y lucha de clases*. México, DF: Ediciones Era.

———. (1979) "Reflexiones sobre la revolución mexicana," in Adolfo Gilly et al. (eds.) *Interpretaciones de la revolución mexicana*. México, DF: Editorial Nueva Imagen.

———. (1993) *The History of Capitalism in Mexico*, trans. Lidia Lozano. Austin: University of Texas Press.

———. (1997/2003) "Revoluciones pasivas en México," in Programa de Sociología Academia de Estudios Culturales, *Antología de Cultura y Sociedad Mexicana*. Chihuahua: Universidad Autónoma de Ciudad Juárez.

Serrano, Mónica (1994) "The End of Hegemonic Rule? Political Parties and the Transformation of the Mexican Party System," in Neil Harvey and Mónica Serrano (eds.) *Party Politics in 'An Uncommon Democracy': Political Parties and Elections in Mexico*. London: Institute of Latin American Studies.

———. (1997) "Civil Violence in Chiapas: The Origins and the Causes of the Revolt," in Mónica Serrano (ed.) *Mexico: Assessing Neoliberal Reform*. London: Institute of Latin American Studies.

Shifter, Michael (2008) "Emerging Trends and Determining Factors in Democratic Governance," in Jorge I. Domínguez and Michael Shifter (eds.) *Constructing Democratic Governance in Latin America*, third edition. Baltimore: Johns Hopkins University Press.

Short, Nicola (2007) *The International Politics of Post-conflict Reconstruction in Guatemala*. London: Palgrave.

Sklair, Leslie (1993) *Assembling for Development: The Maquila Industry in Mexico and the United States*, expanded edition. San Diego, CA: Center for US-Mexican Studies.

———. (2001) *The Transnational Capitalist Class*. Oxford: Blackwell Publishing.

Skocpol, Theda (1979) *States and Social Revolutions: A Comparative Analysis of France, Russia and China*. Cambridge: Cambridge University Press.

Slater, David (2004) *Geopolitics and the Post-Colonial: Rethinking North-South Relations*. Oxford: Blackwell Publishing.

Slaughter, Cliff (1980) *Marxism, Ideology and Literature*. London: Macmillan.

Smith, Benjamin T. (2009) *Pistoleros and Popular Movements: The Politics of State Formation in Postrevolutionary Oaxaca*. Lincoln, NE: University of Nebraska Press.

Smith, Hazel (2000) "Why is There no International Democratic Theory?," in Hazel Smith (ed.) *Democracy and International Relations: Critical Theory/Problematic Practices*. London: Macmillan.

Smith, Neil (1984/2008) *Uneven Development: Nature, Capital and the Production of Space*, third edition. Athens: University of Georgia Press.

———. (2006) "The Geography of Uneven Development," in Bill Dunn and Hugo Radice (eds.) *100 Years of Permanent Revolution: Results and Prospects*. London: Pluto Press.

Soederberg, Susanne (2001) "From Neoliberalism to Social Liberalism: Situating the National Solidarity Program within Mexico's Passive Revolutions," *Latin American Perspectives*, 28(3): 102–23.

Soja, Edward (1989) *Postmodern Geographies: The Reassertion of Space in Critical Social Theory*. London: Verso.

Stahler-Sholk, Richard (1998) "The Lessons of Acteal," *NACLA Report on the Americas*, 31(5): 11–14.

———. (2008) "Resisting Neoliberal Homogenisation: The Zapatista Autonomy Movement," in Richard Stahler-Sholk, Harry E. Vanden and Glen David Kuecker (eds.) *Latin America Social Movements in the Twenty-First Century: Resistance, Power and Democracy*. Lanham, MD: Rowman & Littlefield.

Standish, Peter (ed.) (1986) *Aura*. University of Durham: Modern Language Series.

Steenland, Kyle (1975) "Notes on Feudalism and Capitalism in Chile and Latin America," *Latin American Perspectives*, 2(1): 49–58.

Stephen, Lynn (1995) "The Zapatista Army of National Liberation and the National Democratic Convention," *Latin American Perspectives*, 22(4): 88–99.

———. (1997) "Election Day in Chiapas: A Low-intensity War," *NACLA Report on the Americas*, 31(2): 10–11.

———. (2002) *¡Zapata Lives! Histories and Cultural Politics in Southern Mexico*. Berkeley: University of California Press.

Stern, Steve J. (1988) "Feudalism, Capitalism and the World-System in the Perspective of Latin America and the Caribbean," *American Historical Review*, 93(4): 829–72.

Taller de Gráfica Popular (1937/1989) "Declaration of Principles of the Taller de Gráfica Popular" in Dawn Ádes (ed.) *Art in Latin America: The Modern Era, 1820–1980*. London: South Bank Centre.

Tardanico, Richard (1981) "Perspectives on Revolutionary Mexico: The Regimes of Obregón and Calles," in Richard Rubinson (ed.) *Dynamics of World Development*. London: Sage.

———. (1982) "State, Dependency, and Nationalism: Revolutionary Mexico, 1924–1928," *Comparative Studies in Society and History*, 24(3): 400–423.

Taylor, Marcus (2009) "The Contradictions and Transformations of Neoliberalism in Latin America: From Structural Adjustment to 'Empowering the Poor,'" in Laura Macdonald and Arne Rickert (eds.) *Post-Neoliberalism in the Americas*. London: Palgrave.

Teichman, Judith A. (1996) "Mexico: Economic Reform and Political Change," *Latin American Research Review*, 31(2): 252–62.

Tello Díaz, Carlos (1995) *La rebelión de las Cañadas*. México, DF: Aguilar, León y Cal Editores.

Teschke, Benno (2003) *The Myth of 1648: Class, Geopolitics and the Making of Modern International Relations*. London: Verso.

Thomas, Peter (2007) "Gramsci and the Intellectuals: Modern Prince versus Passive Revolution," in David Bates (ed.) *Marxism, Intellectuals and Politics*. London: Palgrave.

———. (2009) *The Gramscian Moment: Philosophy, Hegemony and Marxism.* Leiden: Brill.

Thompson, E. P. (1978) "Eighteenth Century English Society: Class Struggle Without Class?," *Social History*, 3(2): 133–65.

Tittler, Jonathan (1980) "An Interview with Carlos Fuentes' [Fall, 1979, Cornell], *Diacritics*, 10(3): 46–56.

Trotsky, Leon (1919/2004) "Results and Prospects," in Leon Trotsky, *The Permanent Revolution and Results and Prospects.* London: Wellred Books.

———. (1922–1923/2005) *Literature and Revolution*, trans. Rose Strunsky, ed. William Keach. Chicago: Haymarket Books.

———. (1924/1970) "Class and Art," in Leon Trotsky, *Art and Revolution: Writings on Literature, Politics and Culture.* New York: Pathfinder Press.

———. (1929/2004) "The Permanent Revolution," in Leon Trotsky, *The Permanent Revolution and Results and Prospects.* London: Wellred Books.

———. (1934/1971) "Bonapartism and Fascism" [15 July], in Leon Trotsky, *The Struggle Against Fascism in Germany.* New York: Pathfinder Press.

———. (1936/1980) *The History of the Russian Revolution*, 3 vols. New York: Pathfinder Press.

———. (1937/1972) *The Revolution Betrayed: What Is the Soviet Union and Where Is It Going?* New York: Pathfinder Press.

———. (1938/1979) "Latin American Problems: A Transcript" [4 November], in Leon Trotsky, *Writings of Leon Trotsky, Supplement: 1934–1940.* New York: Pathfinder Press.

———. (1939/1974a) "Nationalised Industry and Workers' Management" [12 May], in Leon Trotsky, *Writings of Leon Trotsky, 1938–1939*, second edition. New York: Pathfinder Press.

———. (1939/1974b) "Ignorance Is Not a Revolutionary Instrument" [30 January], in Leon Trotsky, *Writings of Leon Trotsky, 1938–1939*, second edition. New York: Pathfinder Press.

———. (1940/1990) "Trade Unions in the Epoch of Imperialist Decay" [August], in Leon Trotsky, *Trade Unions in the Epoch of Imperialist Decay.* New York: Pathfinder Press.

Tuğal, Cihan (2009) *Passive Revolution: Absorbing the Islamic Challenge to Capitalism.* Stanford: Stanford University Press.

Tutino, John (1986) *From Insurrection to Revolution in Mexico: Social Bases of Agrarian Violence, 1750–1940.* Princeton: Princeton University Press.

Ugalde, Franciso Valdés (1994) "From Bank Nationalisation to State Reform: Business and the New Mexican Order," in Maria Lorena Cook, Kevin J. Middlebrook and Juan Molinar Horcasitas (eds.) *The Politics of Economic Restructuring: State-Society Relations and Regime Change in Mexico.* San Diego, CA: Center for US-Mexican Studies.

———. (1996) "The Private Sector and Political Regime Change in Mexico," in Gerardo Otero (ed.) *Neoliberalism Revisited: Economic Restructuring and Mexico's Political Future* Boulder, CO: Westview Press.

Unger, Mark (2002) *Elusive Reform: Democracy and the Rule of Law in Latin America*. Boulder, CO: Lynne Rienner.

Urquidi, Víctor L. (1994) "The Outlook for Mexican Economic Development in the 1990s," in Maria Lorena Cook, Kevin J. Middlebrook and Juan Molinar Horcasitas (eds.) *The Politics of Economic Restructuring: State-Society Relations and Regime Change in Mexico*. San Diego, CA: Center for US-Mexican Studies.

Vacca, Giuseppe (1982) "Intellectuals and the Marxist Theory of the State," in Anne Showstack Sassoon (ed.), *Approaches to Gramsci*. London: Writers and Readers.

Van Delden, Martin (1998) *Carlos Fuentes, Mexico and Modernity*. Liverpool: Liverpool University Press.

Van der Haar, Gemma (2005) "Land Reform, the State and the Zapatista Uprising in Chiapas," *Journal of Peasant Studies*, 32(3/4): 484–507.

Van der Pijl, Kees (2006a) *Global Rivalries from the Cold War to Iraq*. London: Pluto Press.

———. (2006b) "A Lockean Europe?," *New Left Review* (II), no. 37: 9–37.

Vaughan, Mary Kay (1997) *Cultural Politics in Revolution: Teachers, Peasants and Schools in Mexico, 1930–1940*. Tucson: University of Arizona Press.

———. (1999) "Cultural Approaches to Peasant Politics in the Mexican Revolution," *Hispanic American Historical Review*, 79(2): 269–305.

Veltmeyer, Henry (1997) "New Social Movements in Latin America: The Dynamics of Class and Identity," *Journal of Peasant Studies*, 25(1): 139–69.

———. (2000) "The Dynamics of Social Change and Mexico's EZLN," *Latin American Perspectives*, 27(5): 88–110.

Veltmeyer, Henry, James Petras and Steve Vieux (1997) *Neoliberalism and Class Conflict in Latin America: A Comparative Perspective on the Political Economy of Structural Adjustment*. London: Macmillan.

Villareal, René (1977) "The Policy of Import-Substituting Industrialisation, 1929–1975," in José Luis Reyna and Richard S. Weinert (eds.) *Authoritarianism in Mexico*. Philadelphia: Institute for the Study of Human Issues.

Vilas, Carlos M. (1996) "Are There Left Alternatives? A Discussion from Latin America," in Leo Panitch (ed.) *The Socialist Register: Are There Alternatives?* London: Merlin Press.

Villafuerte Solís, Daniel (2005) "Rural Chiapas Ten Years after the Armed Uprising: An Economic Overview," *Journal of Peasant Studies*, 32(3/4): 461–83.

Wald, Alan (1995) "Literature and Revolution: Leon Trotsky's Contributions to Marxist Cultural Theory and Literary Criticism," in Hillel Ticktin and Michael Cox (eds.) *The Ideas of Leon Trotsky*. London: Porcupine Press.

Wallerstein, Immanuel (1974) *The Modern World-System I: Capitalist Agriculture and the Origins of the European World-Economy in the Sixteenth Century*. London: Academic Press.

———. (1979) *The Capitalist World-Economy*. Cambridge: Cambridge University Press.

Ward, Peter M. (1990) *Mexico City: The Production and Reproduction of an Urban Environment*. London: Belhaven Press.

Washbrook, Sarah (2006) *Rural Chiapas Ten Years after the Zapatista Uprising*. London: Routledge.

Weinberg, Bill (2000) *Homage to Chiapas: The New Indigenous Struggles in Mexico*. London: Verso.

Weiss, Jason (1991) "An Interview with Carlos Fuentes" [December 1981, Paris], in Jason Weiss (ed.) *Writers at Risk: Interviews in Paris with Uncommon Writers*. Iowa City: University of Iowa Press.

Whitehead, Laurence (1980) "Mexico From Bust to Boom: A Political Evaluation of the 1976–1979 Stabilisation Program," *World Development*, 8(11): 843–64.

———. (1989) "Political Change and Economic Stabilisation: The 'Economic Solidarity Pact,'" in W. A. Cornelius, J. Gentleman and P. H. Smith (eds.) *Mexico's Alternative Political Futures*. San Diego, CA: Center for US-Mexican Studies.

———. (1991) "Mexico's Economic Prospects: Implications for State-Labour Relations," in Kevin J. Middlebrook (ed.) *Unions, Workers and the State in Mexico*. San Diego, CA: Center for US-Mexican Studies.

———. (1994) "Prospects for a 'Transition' from Authoritarian Rule in Mexico," in Maria Lorena Cook, Kevin J. Middlebrook and Juan Molinar Horcasitas (eds.) *The Politics of Economic Restructuring: State-Society Relations and Regime Change in Mexico*. San Diego, CA: Center for US-Mexican Studies.

———. (ed.) (2001) *The International Dimensions of Democratisation: Europe and the Americas*, expanded edition. Oxford: Oxford University Press.

———. (2002) *Democratisation: Theory and Experience*. Oxford: Oxford University Press.

———. (2008) "The Fading Regional Consensus on Democratic Convergence," in Jorge I. Domínguez and Michael Shifter (eds.) *Constructing Democratic Governance in Latin America*. Baltimore: Johns Hopkins University Press.

Williams, Raymond (1977) *Marxism and Literature*. Oxford: Oxford University Press.

Williams, Raymond Leslie (1996) *The Writings of Carlos Fuentes*. Austin: University of Texas Press.

———. (1998) *The Modern Latin American Novel*. New York: Twayne.

Williamson, John (1993) "Democracy and the 'Washington Consensus,'" *World Development*, 21(8): 1329–36.

Wilson, Jason (1989) "In Defence of the Cosmopolitan," *Third World Quarterly*, 11(1): 167–88.

Wing, George Gordon (1982) "Some Remarks on the Literary Criticism of Carlos Fuentes," in Robert Brody and Charles Rossman (eds.) *Carlos Fuentes: A Critical View*. Austin: University of Texas Press.

Wolf, Eric (1997) *Europe and the People Without History*. Berkeley: University of California Press.

Wolfreys, Jim (2007) "Twilight Revolution: François Furet and the Manufacturing of Consensus," in Mike Haynes and Jim Wolfreys (eds.) *History and Revolution: Refuting Revisionism*. London: Verso, 50–70.

Womack, John JNR. (1978) "The Mexican Economy During the Revolution, 1910–1920: Historiography and Analysis," *Marxist Perspectives*, 1(4): 80–123.

———. (1968) *Zapata and the Mexican Revolution*. New York: Random House.

———. (1999) *Rebellion in Chiapas: An Historical Reader*. New York: New Press.

Wood, Ellen Meiksins (1991) *The Pristine Culture of Capitalism: An Historical Essay on Old Regimes and Modern States*. London: Verso.

———. (1995) *Democracy Against Capitalism: Renewing Historical Materialism*. Cambridge: Cambridge University Press.

———. (2002) *The Origin of Capitalism*. London: Verso.

World Bank (1975) "Appraisal of Integrated Rural Development Project (PIDER I)," Loan 1110-ME [16 April], Report No. 660a-ME.

World Bank (1986) "Project Completion Report, Integrated Rural Development Project (PIDER II)," Loan 1462-ME [30 June], Report No. 6333.

World Bank (1990) "Project Completion Report: Integrated Rural Development Project (PIDER III)," Loan 2043-ME [11 December], Report No. 9175.

¡*Zapatistas!* (1994) *Documents of the New Mexican Revolution*. New York: Autonomedia.

Zermeño, Sergio (1997) "State, Society and Dependent Neoliberalism in Mexico: The Case of the Chiapas Uprising," in William C. Smith and Roberto Patrocinio Korzeniewicz (eds.) *Politics, Social Change and Economic Restructuring in Latin America*. Miami, FL: North-South Center Press.

Index

Adorno, Theodor, 231
agrarian reform, 18, 44, 47–48, 54–57,
  74–76, 83–86, 96n7, 206–7, 211–17
Aguayo Quezada, Sergio, 180, 18
Alemán, Miguel, 57, 76, 145, 148
Alianza Cívica, 179–82, 184–85, 189,
  196n8
Asamblea Popular de los Pueblos de
  Oaxaca (APPO), 229, 235n25
Ávila Camacho, Manuel, 57, 76, 80,
  148

Bartra, Roger, 83, 163n14
Benjamin, Walter, 204
Bonapartism, 97n10
bourgeois revolution, 19, 34, 37, 46–47,
  52, 150
Brenner, Robert: social property
  relations, 24
Burawoy, Michael, 246

Calderón, Felipe, 29n16, 190, 194
Calles, Plutarco Elías, 46, 49–50,
  52–55, 90, 146
Cámara Nacional de la Industria de
  Transformación (CANACINTRA),
  80, 91, 118
Canclini, Néstor García, xiii, 49, 97n9,
  251n7

capitalism/ist, 4, 7–8, 10–12, 16–19,
  22–27, 33–37, 39–40, 43, 46–47,
  56–57, 60, 63–65, 67, 71, 73–75,
  79, 81, 93–95, 99–112, 117, 120,
  123,125, 127–28, 135, 144, 146, 150,
  158, 161, 166–68, 171–74, 192–95,
  200–201, 205, 239, 242–43, 246,
  249; colonial, 40, 48; dependent,
  6, 58, 258, 205, 206; expansion of,
  3, 23, 35–36, 41, 51, 65, 135, 167;
  merchant capitalism, 23, 243; origins
  of, 24, 33, 40–41; state capitalism,
  48, 56, 60–61, 75, 89, 239
Cárdenas, Cuauhtémoc, 96n9, 165, 178
Cárdenas, Lázaro, 1–2, 22, 35, 44,
  53–59, 75, 84, 90, 96n7, 145–46,
  148, 150, 165, 178, 205, 237
Cardenismo, 2, 35, 54–59, 219
Carranza, Venustiano, 45, 49
Castañeda, Jorge, 217, 230, 247
Catlett, Elizabeth, 1, 237, 238
civil society, 124, 137, 149, 152, 157,
  170–71, 177, 182, 188–89, 192, 214,
  217–19, 222; Marx on, 175; liberal
  understanding of, 171–73; and the
  state, 123, 129, 136, 143, 160–61,
  175, 191, 204, 211, 240
class: identity, 200, 208, 222, 231;
  intellectuals and, 161; power, 25–26,

About the Author

Adam David Morton is associate professor of political economy and co-director as well as fellow of the Centre for the Study of Social and Global Justice (CSSGJ) in the School of Politics and International Relations at the University of Nottingham. His research interests include state theory, the political economy of development, historical sociology, and Marxism in their relevance to the study of modern Mexico. He is the author of *Unravelling Gramsci: Hegemony and Passive Revolution in the Global Political Economy* (2007) and coeditor (with Andreas Bieler) of *Images of Gramsci: Connections and Contentions in Political Theory and International Relations* (2006). He has also published articles in various prominent journals, including *Bulletin of Latin American Research*, *Latin American Perspectives*, *New Political Economy*, *Review of International Political Economy*, *Third World Quarterly*, and *The Journal of Peasant Studies*. Recently, he edited a major special issue of the journal *Capital & Class*, entitled "Approaching Passive Revolutions," which is a definitive statement on the contribution of passive revolution to debates in and beyond historical sociology.

About the Book

This groundbreaking study develops a new approach to understanding the formation of the postrevolutionary state in Mexico. In a shift away from dominant interpretations, Adam Morton considers the construction of the revolution and the modern Mexican state through a fresh analysis of the Mexican Revolution, the era of import substitution industrialization, and neoliberalism. Throughout, the author makes interdisciplinary links among geography, political economy, postcolonialism, and Latin American studies in order to provide a new framework for analyzing the development of state power in Mexico. He also explores key processes in the contestation of the modern state, specifically through studies of the role of intellectuals, democratization and democratic transition, and spaces of resistance. As Morton argues, all of these themes can only be fully understood through the lens of uneven development in Latin America.

Centrally, the book shows how the history of modern state formation and uneven development in Mexico is best understood as a form of passive revolution, referring to the ongoing class strategies that have shaped relations between state and civil society. As such, Morton makes an important interdisciplinary contribution to debates on state formation relevant to Mexican studies, postcolonial and development studies, historical sociology, and international political economy by revitalizing the debate on the uneven and combined character of development in Mexico and throughout Latin America. In so doing, he convincingly contends that uneven development can once again become a tool for radical political economy analysis in and beyond the region.